ACADEMIC WRITING

ACADEMIC WRITING

Writing and Reading in the Disciplines

third edition

Janet Giltrow

broadview press

National Library of Canada Cataloguing in Publication Data

Giltrow, Janet Lesley
    Academic writing : writing and reading in the disciplines

3rd ed.
Includes index.
ISBN 1-55111-395-3

1. Report writing. 2. English language—rhetoric. 3. Exposition (Rhetoric)
I. Title

PE1408.G54 2001   808'.042   C2001-930163-4

Broadview Press Ltd. is an independent, international publishing house, incorporated in 1985

North America
Post Office Box 1243, Peterborough, Ontario, Canada K9J 7H5
3576 California Road, Orchard Park, NY 14127
Tel: (705) 743-8990; Fax: (705) 743-8353;
e-mail: customerservice@broadviewpress.com

United Kingdom
Thomas Lyster, Ltd.,
Units 3 & 4a, Ormskirk Industrial Park, Burscough Rd, Ormskirk,
Lancashire L39 2YW Tel: (1695) 575112; Fax: (1695) 570120;
E-Mail: books@tlyster.co.uk

Australia
St. Clair Press, P.O. Box 287, Rozelle, NSW 2039
Tel: (02) 818-1942; Fax: (02) 418-1923

www.broadviewpress.com

Broadview Press gratefully acknowledges the financial support of the Book Publishing Industry Development Program, Ministry of Canadian Heritage, Government of Canada.

Typesetting and assembly: True to Type Inc., Mississauga, Canada.
PRINTED IN CANADA

Contents

Preface

This book develops from a strong claim: namely, that style is meaningful. A textbook may not be the best place to advance a strong claim, so, to make this claim less conspicuous, I could downgrade it by describing it as in keeping with established views. I could point out that few authors of composition textbooks deny the importance of style, and most offer advice on words and sentences. And I could point out that many researchers, especially those working in English for Special Purposes, have analysed style in the scholarly genres. In turn, these inquiries could be seen as developing the long-standing sociolinguistic idea of "register," the condition which indexes language for use in definable social settings.

Both the textbook tradition and the research tradition could absorb the claim that style is meaningful, and thus make it less outstanding. But I prefer that this claim about style remain conspicuous. I prefer that it not be absorbed into customary ideas about the decorum or efficiency of writing smoothly, or even into the more exacting observation of the distribution of linguistic features across social groups and social roles. I prefer that the meaningfulness of style be taken seriously, and not be allowed to slip into peripheral vision, where it becomes only a marker of appropriateness, or a factor in readability.

Writing teachers may intuit the meaningfulness of style when they read a certain kind of student essay. This is the essay that is coherent by generalized measures — an identifiable introduction and conclusion govern a discussion that would seem logical to a sensible person. It is "correct" by most measures of Standard English. It demonstrates that the author has done the assigned reading, listened to lectures, and worked studiously. Yet, despite these virtues, it fails to speak to an academic audience, or enter into the discourse of the discipline. Its way of speaking locates it out of earshot of scholarly interests.

Often it is hard to respond helpfully to such an essay. Pressed, some might refer its failure to address academic interests to a lack of "original" thinking, or to another condition equally resistant to overt correction: some might observe "surface" shortcoming — maybe something like a naïve plainness, or an undue bloom on sentences. But I would argue that there is no "surface" to writing, and that the stylistic qualities which tax our capacity to name them are more than skin-deep. And, moreover, I would suggest that the "originality" academic readers value *depends on style* — on the typical ways of speaking that produce certain kinds of knowledge of the world. A writer involved in the char-

acteristic wordings of a discipline is involved in its practices and perspectives and its procedures for interpreting the world. A discipline's
typical wordings embody its representation of the world, what Kenneth
Burke (1966) called "tribal [idiom]," this idiom being in a sense a set of
tacit instructions for understanding the world and making statements
about it. Style constitutes a position in the world, and shared methods
for thinking about it. Without access to scholarly ways of speaking, student writers cannot occupy scholarly positions, or use scholarly methods for producing statements, or speak to academic interests.

A strong stand on the matter of style can be supported by deliberately broad definitions of style. Such definitions would include global
conditions of coherence and connectedness — how elements of a text
make themselves available for the reader's construction of meaning.
They would include conditions of assertion and presupposition — how
texts deliver some propositions explicitly but leave others assumed
rather than asserted, and how these patterns configure a discourse community's ground of shared knowledge. The analyses offered in this book
not only respect these larger conditions as features of style but also
observe their effect on areas more traditionally regarded as the domain
of style: the character of phrases and sentences. The distinctive grammar
of scholarly writing provides the footings for larger schemes.

Broad definitions of style are useful, but can still beg the question.
After all, if style is everything, it must be important. So this book's
approach to academic writing offsets the enlargement of style to universal (and thus tautological) proportions by insisting that style is both
a representation of and a guide to practice. Borrowing Carolyn Miller's
(1984) motto "genre as social action," and grafting onto it Carol
Berkenkotter and Thomas Huckin's (1992) characterization of genre as
"socio-cognitive," I would suggest that *style* is "socio-cognitive action."
The social and cognitive agency of style is often invisible to us, and the
very efficacy of style as an instigator lurks in its tacitness, its low profile
in our consciousness, and its tendency to naturalize itself. But we can
coax it out for inspection by taking one relatively noticeable example
of style representing and guiding practice: parenthetical citations. These
expressions distinguish scholarly writing, displaying a scholarly stance.
They represent a scholarly practice: the way researchers systematically
consult other research, and estimate its relevance and proximity to their
work, these activities being stylized as a summoning of voices to sub-
stantiate, by accord or contrast, the individual speaker's utterance.
Through the semiotics of style, parenthetical expressions represent the
research community's routines of association. At the same time, these
typical wordings not only represent but also *guide* practice. They instruct
a writer in the research genres to read other writers, and to read them

in a particular way, so as to be able to construct gist compactly and dialectically. Parenthetical citations — a feature of style — constitute for the writer a position in the world, one contingent on other positions.

Other stylistic features — nominalization, for example, or expressions of indeterminacy — also constitute a position, and instructions for thinking about the world. These are among features I take to be *salient* to research writing: that is, they are the genre's distinguishing insignia, the linguistic-pragmatic features which make it recognizable, and which particularly define its service to the equally recognizable research and knowledge-making situations of academic life, guiding people to the kinds of thinking that are productive in those situations.

One might ask whether students can acquire scholarly know-how simply by mastering scholarly wording. Common sense could suggest that students would acquire only a surface glibness, an empty compliance with form. But the strong claim about the meaningfulness of style suggests, first, that there are no "surfaces" to language, and, second, that language is constitutive of experience. The social and cognitive behaviours which attend the production of scholarly utterance are scholarly behaviours.

Moreover, this book doesn't simply prescribe the wordings characteristic of scholarly writing. Rather, it convenes a colloquy of voices from the academic disciplines, speaking in their characteristically scholarly ways, and assuming characteristically scholarly attitudes. It presents these voices to students, asking them to listen for the accents of the research genres, to interpret them as functional tokens of academic culture, and to adopt in their own writing those features which can represent their position as apprentice workers in knowledge-making settings. This book also asks them, in the process of developing an ear for the characteristic sounds of scholarly voices and developing their own positions as writers, to learn some things about how language constructs our experience of the world. Teachers in English departments may shy away from such direct attention to language. They may want to avoid the stigma associated with the teaching of "grammar" — a pedagogical focus with a bad reputation — or they may object to such direct attention to language as too technical, or too difficult. But both objections would be hard to sustain in the long run. First, the discourse on language — or the discourse on discourse — transformed the intellectual climate of the end of the twentieth century, and it seems unreasonable to exclude the study of university writing from this transformation. And, second, other areas of study do not exempt students from learning complex or "technical" principles on the grounds of difficulty, and these disciplines survive and flourish despite the demands they make on students. Moreover, the linguistic-pragmatic principles which inform this book's analysis of research writing provide a basis for approaching the social and political implications of the research genres and their salient features: if style is meaningful, we should ask *what it means*, and if style is social action, we should ask *what it does*. We should ask by what principles a way of speaking organizes knowledge of the world, and organizes systems of association, solidarity, and advantage.

In its analysis of scholarly ways of speaking, this book locates style in new conceptualizations of genre which emphasize the reciprocity between, on the one hand, social context and its typical occasions and, on the other hand, the discursive practices which serve and maintain these recurring occasions. So it benefits from the work of a community of researchers who have developed powerful new ideas about genre: Carolyn Miller (1984), John Swales (1990), Carol Berkenkotter and Thomas Huckin (1992), Aviva Freedman (1993), Aviva Freedman and Peter Medway (1994), Richard Coe (1987, 1994). Exemplifying the best results of scholarly exchange, the discourse on genre has proceeded richly, and productively, and I am grateful for the contact I have had with these people and their ideas.

With others I have had only the remote contact of a respectful reader. M.A.K. Halliday and J.R. Martin's (1993) research into the language of science — research also mindful of reconceptualizations of genre — provided a boost for my analysis of the relation between abstraction and the kind of coherence peculiar to research writing; Greg Myers's (1989) analysis of "politeness" in science writing confirms my analysis of the pragmatics of indeterminacy; and in general my approach to the linguistic-pragmatics of the research genres is indebted to a company of theorists whose work offers instruments for measuring the subtle service of words and sentences to the maintenance of positions, attitudes, and relations in the social order. Members of this company include Ellen Prince (1981), Herbert Clark (1992) and Herbert Clark and Catherine Marshall (1981), Dan Sperber and Deirdre Wilson (1986), M.A.K. Halliday (1985), Georgia Green (1989), F.R. Palmer (1990), Eve Sweetser (1990), Wallace Chafe (1986), Gennaro Chierchia and Sally McConnel-Ginet (1990). Readers of this book will also catch a glimpse of influence from celebrated thinkers whose reasonings have helped me postulate the character of the social order and its manifestations in both language and language learning: Michel Foucault, Mikhail Bakhtin, Pierre Bourdieu, Anthony Giddens.

In the third edition, the focus stays on **genre**. For some of us, new-rhetorical genre theory has become such an old hat (while for others it may be *chapeau nouveau*) that we forget that we are wearing it, or why we put it on in the first place. So here I remind myself and my readers of genre theory's most practical claim for the study of writing: that the scholarly genres (and other genres) should be studied in their own terms. These terms are themselves full of interest, as indications of **ways of life**. But it is not just in redeeming these terms for our admiration and scrutiny that genre theory has important effects. When we instate these terms as our reference, we also overrule other terms to which academic writing has traditionally been referred. Some of these terms come from the public discourse on language. These seize student writing as material on which to practise unexamined assumptions about "good" writing, or the state of being "literate" or "logical." Or they commandeer instances of professional scholarly writing on which to practise untested views about "clarity" or folk allegations about "jargon." The terms which come from the public discourse on language emit petty stylistic prohibitions on the one hand and paralysing generalities on the other. They produce an authority at once ineffective and domineering: people continue to write and speak in a variety of ways, and continue to cower in the presence of these prescriptions.

Some other terms which traditionally accompany the study of writing are more local to educational discourses and institutions. Terms like "self-expression" and the student's "own voice" seem to be uncalled for, but they nevertheless volunteer for many occasions. How did they get in on the game? Ian Hunter's *Culture and Government* (1988) suggested to me the genealogy of these terms: artefacts of systems for administering populations, they derived from educational techniques for the cultivation of the "self." An administratively designed unit, this "self" is conjured in the classroom, projected and assessed by the teacher's (schooled) imagination of the child's being. In a never-to-be-completed process of disclosing the original person, the student remains childlike, attending the teacher's signal that "self" has been rendered or apprehended. Although Hunter focusses more on literary reception than on literate production (the child discloses herself in her response to literary text[1]), his analyses helped me begin to understand not only the service and persistence of "self-expression" and "own voice" but also the repetitiveness of writing instruction. Every year from Grade Eight (or Seven, or Six) till first-year university (or beyond), students unify their paragraphs and vary their sentences. What for? Seemingly to produce a "voice" or express a "self" to be adjudicated by the teacher. While in their other university courses, students venture into the complications of the scholarly disciplines, in composition class they remain in a perpetual childhood. I hope that the genre-theoretical approach of this book helps to rescue them from their captivity by mapping a route to their participation *as writers* in the grown-up, professional activities of research communities.

Reading the research genres in their own terms, the second edition offered means of analysing these genres' characteristic markers of **position** and **subjectivity** (real-world, available identities, alternative to the "self" of the classroom world); the second edition and this one recognize modality, reporting expressions, and the "discursive *I*" as stylistic saliences of the research genres, signifying **position**. In this edition I have also touched on wordings of **attitude** and **imperative** — expressions which appear to be sensitive to discipline-specific ethos and moral orientation. I have also gathered summary, definition, and comparison under the higher-level term **citation** — on the one hand, to get at the distinctive play and protocol of scholarly conversation and, on the other hand, to regard the finesse and subtlety with which all users of language, in many (or all?) genres reiterate and re-accent the words of others. I hope that, by regarding the poetics of both everyday and specialist citation, writers will sense that it is a practice far more complex and socially involving than merely seeking "back-up" for one's own "opinions." And in this edition I have included transcripts of academic readers responding to student writing — real-time performances by readers-at-work, making meaning from what they read. I hope these sections of the book will provide alternatives not only to the traditional terms of marking commentary but also to the notion that **convention** — in the sense of empty formality or petrified mannerliness — is responsible for the features of successful writing.

Studying the research genres in their own terms, we recognize their situational motivations, restore them to the contexts in which they function, and redeem them from suspicion. We can acknowledge but also answer those critiques of scholarly writing which deplore its inscrutability and single out, for example and scoffing, the heavy nominalizations of the language of research. Addressed in their own terms, the research genres can justify this stylistic distinction, and others. In context, the features of scholarly writing are functional.

But contexts are not airtight. They breathe, and share atmospheres with other occasions for speaking and reasoning. While a genre-theoretical approach positions us to witness stylistic features as motivated by research situations, it can also tend to indemnify discourse practices as worlds-unto-themselves — to be addressed in their own terms and no others. The second edition and this one offer the case of ethnography as one opportunity to interrogate the research genres, interrupt their apparent self-sufficiency, and ask about the class interests and political intentions they speak to, or feel at home with. Preparing this edition, and concerned that writers be encouraged to reflect seriously on the problematics of knowledge and authority, I have added ideas from Bruno Latour (2000) on research subjects "talking back" to the researchers who make statements about them, and from Romy Clark and Roz Ivanic (Clark and Ivanic 1997, Ivanic 1997) on the relations between the authority of scholarly style and the positions of non-traditional students. And, tracking the construction and uses of *expertise*, I have summarized Dara Culhane's account (1998) of the land-claims suit brought by the Gitksan and Wet'suwe'ten against the governments of Canada and British Columbia: an episode in legal history where research statements were **cited** — and re-accented and refracted in ways that show undeniably that the research genres are *not* worlds-unto-themselves. On the contrary, they are in contact with other sectors and other interests, and their authority is up for grabs at every instance of citation. In the meantime, other genre theorists (Russell 1997, for example) have been saying as much — saying that, while we need to understand genres in their own terms, we can't stop there.

Many questions that arrived in preparing this edition continue to pester my attention and understanding. I still want to know, for example, how the scholarly disciplines produce and reproduce middle-class (and usually urban?) identities, and the epistemological consequences of this. (We might refer to Bourdieu's *Distinction* [1984].) I want to know about the connections between the "back talk" which Latour recommends and "common sense" — the plain-speaking folk knowledge which pooh-poohs the fancy claims of specialists. Typically, these discourses are far apart politically, yet both oppose the authority of research language. I want to know more about the **deontic modality** — the moral suggestiveness — of the discourses of the disciplines: their indications of what actions should be taken, their assumptions about what is good and bad, the desires nesting in the underbrush of "Discussion" sections. (We might refer to work like Knorr-Cetina's [1999] on the "epistemic cultures" of high-energy physics and molecular biology.) And I plan to think more about "readability" — a condition or concern I may have dismissed too readily in the second edition. Now I'm thinking that complaints about "jargon" and lack of "readability" mark places of disturbance and contest where we (all) get beaten about the head with the fact that language is the site not only of affinity but also of estrangement.

These questions (and more) are still on the table. So I have to ask: what kind of book is this? If it has so many questions and so few answers, does it belong to the textbook genre? Does it introduce newcomers to a discipline, as other university textbooks do? It *is* a textbook in that it asks students to shed some commonsense notions and adopt some specialist ones. But it may not be clear what discipline students are being introduced to. Traditionally, the discourse on student writing has belonged to no one. Serving a "how-to" function, it has been a long-term house guest, or hired hand, in English departments, but, because no particular discipline has owned or been responsible for its epistemology, it has been wide open to suggestions and inferences from the public domain — including suspicions and anxieties about research discourse itself. So, in introducing students to a research location, this book takes them to English studies as practised within earshot of and in proximity to scholars who from many points of departure — from rhetoric and composition, linguistics, cultural studies, discourse analysis, education — approach writing and, especially, writing in the disciplines. It involves students in this aspect of English studies as *inquiry* — questions and conversations amongst those who are putting together a picture of research discourse. And by involving students in research activity the book fulfills its "how-to" function. Like the apprentice tailors in Vai and Gola, who are described by Lave and Wenger (1991), and who begin their participation in a way of life by attaching buttons and sewing hems, performing authentic tasks logical to production of the whole suit, students who begin with summary and arrange for scholarly speakers to come to the pages of their own writing are performing authentic tasks. They are producing scholarly knowledge, and participating in the scholarly way of life, in a disciplinary context which at the same time recognizes them as newcomers and conceptualizes their positions.

This dimension of *Academic Writing* — as a potential setting for students' participation in scholarly life — has had an actual, working counterpart in the Centre for Research in Academic Writing at Simon Fraser University, where students and teachers — not only graduate students but undergraduates as well; not only regular faculty but those who worked with us temporarily as well — inquired together into scholarly discourse, and into language and culture. So resourceful and imaginative were members of this consortium of scholars that we got used to hearing exciting findings and compelling questions from any position — from Ph.D. and M.A. students working on their theses and papers, from sessional faculty contracted for research, from third-year students in a seminar on writing and response in the research genres, from undergraduate and graduate teaching assistants working one-on-one with writers, from students in our own first- and second-year classes. The Centre was defined by their critical habits: their questions about the methods they were learning; the models of language which theorized our practice; and the social, political, and intellectual intentions of their own projects. I was the most fortunate of scholars: a member of a community of inquiry with a life of its own.

Much of what appears in this book is owing to a remarkable and spirited group of students: Kathryn Alexander, Ruth Derksen, Daniel Dunford, Sharon Josephson, Shurli Makmillen, Heather Millar, Jackie Rea, Tania Teslenko, Nadeane Trowse, Bonnie Waterstone, Yaying Zhang. And to faculty who joined us in the mid-1990s and whose professionalism as teachers and thinkers have been a model for me: Marlene Sawatsky and Wendy Strachan. And to long-time colleagues: Rick Coe, who in his especially astute ways knew how to remind me of the bigger picture; Michele Valiquette, who has been a scholarly companion from the start of this venture, when we were afraid of nothing and willing to try anything. Presiding over these happy times were two administrators courageous enough to give the go-ahead, and untie the study of writing from its institutional service to the management of student populations: as Dean of Arts, Evan Alderson provided stable, respectable funding for a project which defied long-standing expectations about what writing teachers do; as Chair of English, Kathy Mezei was a brilliant advocate, visionary and unselfish in her intelligence of opportunities. And Heather Skibeneckyj, as Coordinator of the Centre, not only made the vision work day-to-day but also live up to its promise and principle. It was a Golden Age.

Golden Ages do, however, have an expiry date, and even Happy Valleys are open to freak storms. Some of us have moved on. I am again fortunate to be amongst inspiring colleagues, at the University of British Columbia, where Glenn Deer, with exquisite good will, puts rhetorical study in meaningful political context; Judy Segal takes rhetorical study to interdisciplinary frontiers; Laurel Brinton and Lilita Rodman carry on immaculate scholarship on style; and Sherrill Grace, as Head of English, offers brave and generous hospitality to new ideas.

Adjacent to these institutional neighbourhoods are other friendly circles of encouragement. Don LePan has earned wide admiration as an adventurous Canadian publisher, and my own projects owe a great deal to his confident spirit. In thinking about the largest cultural settings for writing, I refer again and again to Susan Miller's work — and to her companionable intellect. And close to home, very close, Maegen M. Giltrow has been a Fabulous Research Assistant.

Note

1 See also Heather Murray (1996) for a parallel analysis of the classroom techniques of *close reading*.

References

Berkenkotter, Carol, and Thomas Huckin. 1992. "Rethinking genre from a sociocognitive perspective." Paper presented at Colloquium on Rethinking Genre. Ottawa.

Bourdieu, Pierre. 1984. *Distinction: A Social Critique of the Judgement of Taste*. Trans. R. Nice. Cambridge, MA: Harvard UP.

Burke, Kenneth. 1966. *Language as Symbolic Action: Essays on Life, Literature, and Method*. Berkeley: U of California P.

Cameron, Deborah. 1990. "Demythologizing sociolinguistics: Why language does not reflect society." In *Ideologies of Language*, ed. John E. Joseph and Talbot J. Taylor. London: Routledge.

Chafe, Wallace. 1986. "Evidentiality in English conversation and academic writing." In *Evidentiality: The Linguistic Encoding of Epistemology*, ed. Wallace Chafe and Johanna Nichols. Norwood, NJ: Ablex.

Chierchia, Gennaro, and Sally McConnel-Ginet. 1990. *Meaning and Grammar: An Introduction to Semantics*. Cambridge, MA: MIT Press.

Clark, Herbert H. 1992. *Arenas of Language Use*. Chicago: U of Chicago P.

Clark, Herbert H., and Catherine R. Marshall. 1981. "Definite reference and mutual knowledge." In *Linguistic Structure and Discourse Setting*, ed. A.K. Joshi, B. Webber, and I. Sag. Cambridge: Cambridge UP.

Coe, Richard. 1987. "An Apology for form; or, who took the form out of the process." *College English* 49(1): 13-28.

——. 1994. "Teaching genre as process." In *Learning and Teaching Genre*, ed. Aviva Freedman and Peter Medway. Portsmouth, NH: Boynton/Cook, Heinemann.

Freedman, Aviva. 1993. "Show and tell? The role of explicit teaching in the learning of new genres." *Research in the Teaching of English* 27(3): 222-51.

Freedman, Aviva, and Peter Medway. 1994. "Introduction." In *Learning and Teaching Genre*, ed. Aviva Freedman and Peter Medway. Portsmouth, NH: Boynton/Cook, Heinemann.

Green, Georgia M. 1989. *Pragmatics and Natural Language Understanding*. Hillsdale, NJ: Erlbaum.

Halliday, M.A.K. 1985. *An Introduction to Functional Grammar*. London: Edward Arnold.

Halliday, M.A.K., and J.R. Martin. 1993. *Writing Science: Literacy and Discursive Power*. Pittsburgh: U of Pittsburgh P.

Hunter, Ian. 1988. *Culture and Government: The Emergence of Literary Education*. Houndmills, Hampshire: Macmillan.

Knorr-Cetina, Karin. 1999. *Epistemic Cultures: How the Sciences Make Knowledge*. Cambridge, MA: Harvard UP.

Lave, Jean, and Etienne Wenger. 1991. *Situated Learning: Legitimate Peripheral Participation*. Cambridge: Cambridge UP.

Miller, Carolyn. 1984. "Genre as social action." *Quarterly Journal of Speech* 70(2): 151-67.

Murray, Heather. 1996. *Working in English: History, Institution, Resources*. Toronto: U of Toronto P.

Myers, Greg. 1989. "The pragmatics of politeness in scientific articles." *Applied Linguistics* 10: 1-35.

Palmer, F.R. 1990. *Modality and the English Modals*. London: Longman.

Prince, Ellen F. 1981. "Toward a taxonomy of given-new information." In *Radical Pragmatics*, ed. Peter Cole. New York: Academic Press.

Russell, David. 1997. "Rethinking genre in school and society." *Written Communication* 14(4): 504-54.

Sperber, Dan, and Deirdre Wilson. 1986. *Relevance: Communication and Cognition.* Cambridge, MA: Harvard UP.

Swales, John. 1990. *Genre Analysis: English in Academic and Research Settings.* Cambridge: Cambridge UP.

Sweetser, Eve E. 1990. *From Etymology to Pragmatics: Metaphorical and Cultural Aspects of Semantic Structure.* Cambridge: Cambridge UP.

Introducing genre

1.1 Hearing voices

PASSAGE 1
Vokey and Read (1992) further extend their findings by applying
a regression analysis to the general familiarity and memorability
components to predict recognition discrimination, criterion, and
hit and false alarm rates. They reason that if the effect of typicality on recognition is a function of both general familiarity and
memorability, each of these should be a significant predictor of
recognition performance. To do this, they derived a regression
equation composed of differential additive weightings of the general familiarity and memorability components to predict discrimination performance. In fact, they found that both familiarity and
memorability were significant predictors of discrimination performance, but not of criterion.[1]

PASSAGE 2
TALENTED, successful, good looking male, 30's, seeks attractive,
intelligent, petite female, who knows authentic gems are rare.
Toronto area. Box 000.

PASSAGE 3
My husband and I spent a recent vacation driving along the spec-
tacular California coast. One morning we stopped at Big Sky

Cafe in San Luis Obispo for breakfast. Their menu includes a hash with delicious "glazed" eggs. What's the secret to the eggs?

Eileen Gilbert
Casper, Wyoming

PASSAGE 4

Eugenics theory powerfully influenced late nineteenth- and early twentieth-century U.S. policies concerning the groups then known as "the dependent, defective, and delinquent classes" (Henderson 1901, U.S. Department of the Interior 1883). In essence, eugenicists held that the "fit" should be encouraged to reproduce ("positive" eugenics) and the "unfit" prevented from doing so ("negative" eugenics). Historians generally agree that between 1900 and 1920 this doctrine formed the basis for a full-fledged social movement with research centers, propaganda vehicles, and strong middle-class support (Haller 1963, Kevles 1985, Ludmerer 1972, Pickens 1968). Less commonly acknowledged is the fact that eugenics theory affected public policy for decades before becoming the social movement's foundation and that eugenic ideas long outlived the movement itself, in ways that a new generation of historians is just starting to explore (Dann 1991, Noll 1990, Reilly 1991). Even today, eugenics arguments occasionally make their way into debates about such matters as population growth and crime control (e.g., Wattenberg 1987, Wilson 1989; for a recent analysis see Duster 1990).[2]

PASSAGE 5

PANORAMIC VIEW! Super 2 yr old 1 bedroom apartment in prime South Slopes, features 180 degree Gulf Island view, 9' ceilings, in-suite laundry, 6 appliances, fantastic kitchen with oak cabinets, track lighting, balcony off living room & bedroom, gas f/p & more. Comes with 2 parking places. Unit located at 0000 Station Hill Court. Call now, priced to sell $147,900. Barry Wilson, Viewtime Realty.

PASSAGE 6

PROVIDED that the Mortgagor, when not in default hereunder, shall have the privilege of prepaying, at any time and without notice or bonus, the whole or any part of the Principal Amount. Where any such additional payment is made the Payment Dates of all remaining monthly instalments, if any, of the Principal Amount and interest thereon shall thereupon be advanced so that the Mortgagor shall pay the Amount of Each Periodic Payment in each and every month commencing with the month immediately following the month in which the additional principal is repaid and continuing until all the monies secured by this Mortgage shall have been fully paid.

These passages are all English. But what they have in common as English may be less important than the grounds on which they differ. Issuing from decidedly different moments in North American life, they voice different situations. No one could say which of these passages is "best," or which is proper English or which is not. But one can estimate the efficiency of each voice — each style of expression — in serving the situation from which it arises.

1.2 Hearing genres

The passages above not only serve the situations in which they arise, they also embody them, representing certain recognizable occasions. So, when we hear these different voices, we also "hear" the setting in which they operate. The sounds of these passages signify typical moments which culture has produced: occasions of mating or marketplace, social distinction, or professional publication. In each case, situation has imprinted English. It has pressed into the general shape of the language features which mark it for use in particular contexts. The imprint makes language characteristic: something we recognize as typical.

> **Exercise**
> Name the types of writing exemplified in Passages 1-6 in
> Section 1.1. Try to name the cultural situation which each serves.

To do the exercise above, you have to call on your knowledge of North American culture. Perhaps Passage 3 escaped you: your life experience may not have included contact with the situation which has produced a type of writing which we could call "request for recipe" and which appears in cooking magazines. Or, if you are not from North America, you may be surprised by the boastfulness of the author of Passage 2, and by his search for a person of a certain size. Hearing and speaking, reading and writing, we enact our experience of the world as that experience has been shaped by culture.

As the diversity of the six passages shows, language is sensitive to situation. In recent years, this sensitivity has been captured and studied in new conceptualizations of genre. This book takes advantage of new reasoning about genre.

Before sketching the new genre theories, let us glance at the old ones. Chances are, if you have heard the term "genre" before, you heard it in connection with literary studies. Genre was, for instance, a way of saying that poems, novels, and plays are different: they are different **genres**. So the notion of genre helped English departments keep courses separate, and made their curriculum orderly. For these purposes, genre was a docile concept, tending towards traditional ideas.

But then, as intellectual trends at the end of the twentieth century moved scholars in new directions, genre was wakened from its long service to the study of forms and categories. These trends encouraged people to take account of the social and political **contexts** of knowledge, and to calculate the degree to which the quality of statements about the world depended on who — in the world — was making the statement. Alert to new opportunities, genre offered itself as a way of thinking about the context-dependency of language.

While old ideas of genre had slipped into regarding only **form**, the new ideas insisted that it was not form alone that constituted genre, but form and situation:

$$\text{form} + \text{situation} = \text{genre}$$

The new conceptualizations of genre gave researchers a way of talking about these similarities not as rules but as signs of common ground amongst communities of readers and writers: shared attitudes, practices, positions in the world, habits of being. Forms of speaking are connected to social contexts where people *do* things — like selling a house, or finding a mate. Different routines of social behaviour — habits of acting in the world — create different genres of speech and writing.

In this light, consider the thank-you note as a genre. People who know this genre not only know how to compose the note — what to mention, how much to say, how to begin, how to conclude, what kind of writing materials to use — but also *when* to do all this: soon after receipt of a certain type of gift from a person in a certain relation to the recipient. (So, in all probability, you would not send a thank-you note to your spouse for the gift of a laptop computer or to the local garage for the gift of a calendar or a window scraper. And if you delay sending a thank-you note where one is called for, you will feel — consciously or unconsciously — that you are failing to comply with the genre's norms, no matter how perfectly you compose the note itself.) The thank-you note genre is made up of not only a characteristic type of written expression but also of the situation in which it occurs. It is a way of acting in the world. People with know-how in this genre understand not only its form but also its situation. We could even say that, at some deep, unconscious level, these people also share an understanding of the role of the genre in larger social or cultural situations — systems of relationship amongst kin and friends, symbolized by the exchange of commodities and expressions of recognition.

Once wakened from its long servitude to the project of keeping poems and novels separate, genre no longer saw literary studies as its only, or even its best, place of work. It went abroad, and applied itself to many kinds of writing: auditors' reports, news accounts of violent crime, case reports in publications in veterinary medicine, architects' proposals, primary school show-and-tell sessions, and — most important to our interests — academic writing. At all these sites, genre was an avenue to investigating similarities in documents occurring in similar situations.

The new conceptualizations of genre gave researchers a way of talking about these similarities not as rules but as signs of common ground amongst communities of readers and writers: shared attitudes, practices, positions in the world, habits of being. So the style of Passage 5 comes about not because somebody followed rules, but because it embodies a widely recognized situation — property transaction in a market economy — through its typical, list-like naming of qualities which the users of this genre recognize as valued and translatable into dollars. Views are good, so is newness, and so is a particular type of finishing on kitchen cabinets. The document assumes in readers a knowledge of local practices of transportation, and of laundering clothes. It assumes that readers will not interpret "6 appliances" as a sign of overcrowding in a small apartment, and that readers don't need to be told what these appliances are, or what they do. It also assumes in readers a knowledge of the customary practice of finding and disposing of a dwelling — contacting a broker specializing in this kind of transaction. Note that such knowledge is not universal but **cultural**. In another culture, where people inherit their homes from their parents, or share them with co-workers, such a genre would not exist at all. Or some culture, somewhere, might value a home not for its appliances or parking spaces but for its human history: while in our culture we exchange homes with strangers, in some other place, dwellings might be identified with their residents. Then the genre accompanying property transactions might develop techniques for describing the dwelling's current occupant in appealing or prestigious terms. In either case, the genre suits the situation.

Perhaps, a hundred years from now, scholars will examine personal ads or requests for recipes or mortgage documents to piece together vanished systems of association amongst people. Or they will look at the genres which report research in cognitive psychology or social history to understand the systems of relationship and production which held academic communities together at the end of the twentieth century and the beginning of the next one.

1.3 What is an essay, Alex?

Genre theory predicts that diversity of expression will reflect the complexities of social life. Because people interact for a lot of different purposes, they write and speak in a lot of different ways. And, as the world changes, so too will ways of writing and speaking change.

Writing *instruction*, however, has tended to focus on one type of writing: the schoolroom essay. Different kinds of assignments may produce slightly different versions of the essay — the "argument" essay, for example, or the "expository" essay — but, generally, when students arrive at college or university, they are experienced in producing a form of writing which serves schoolroom situations. Along with this experience, they absorb — from teachers, from handbooks, from public sentiments — ideas about writing. It should be "clear" and "concise," for example; it should not be "vague" or "wordy." Writing should also be "logical" and "well organized."

But then, at university, students encounter writing that would not be "clear" to most people, and writing that most people would not call "concise." And what seems to be "logical" in one discipline is not thought to be "logical" in another discipline. "Organization" in history is not "organization" in psychology, and neither resembles "organization" in an "argument" essay learned in composition class. After long experience in the schoolroom essay, and long contact with maxims about good writing, university students face many examples of expression which contradict the schoolroom tradition.

Genre theory tells us that the schoolroom essay — in its style — serves its situation. (Inspecting the situation, we might look for connections between the kinds of features prized in student essays and the larger function of the schoolroom itself. We might consider the schoolroom's role in socializing youth, in controlling the time of young people, in accrediting some and discrediting others, in scheduling some for further education — in well-paid occupations that structure and regulate social life — and scheduling others for poorly paid or low-prestige occupations.) Since the essay is a persistent genre, it must be doing an adequate job of serving and maintaining and defining schoolroom situations.

But the schoolroom situation and the university-classroom situation are different. Accordingly, the kind of writing that suits the schoolroom tends not to suit the university classroom. That is, they represent two different genres of scholarly writing.

The most important distinction between school situations and university situations is that the latter are located in research institutions. While students may see themselves as learners rather than researchers, they nevertheless do their learning under the direction of people who are trained as researchers and who read and write research publications. The knowledge students acquire is the kind of knowledge that comes from the techniques of inquiry developed by the various academic disciplines. We could go so far as to say that the very wording of the facts and concepts students must absorb derives from research practice: the routines, habits, and values which motivate scholars to do the work they do. This wording represents research communities' beliefs and their members' shared techniques for interpreting the world. At the same time, such wording is also the medium in which students must work.

If university students are not writing schoolroom essays, what are they writing? What wordings will represent the student's position in the university situation? While it would be too much to say that students should write research articles, it is not too much to say that their writing shares features of the research genres. The style of the information they encounter in their university courses is shaped by the research situations which produced it. So, as students work with a particular type of research information, the style of that research genre becomes the most appropriate wording for them to adopt. And while the wording of research writing shares some features with the schoolroom essay — both are, after all, English — the differences are perhaps more meaningful than the similarities. (Equally, as you may already have found out, the styles of the different disciplines share many features, but the differences can be meaningful, and can have consequences.)

This book puts student writers in touch with the wording of the research genres. It shows student writers what the salient features of scholarly expression are — features which distinguish the scholarly genres and which we recognize as typical of academic situations. At the same time, it encourages informed perspectives on scholarly styles and situations. As sites for shared understandings, and shared means of interpreting the world, genres can seem like worlds unto themselves — self-justifying, "natural," immemorial. But the research genres (like any others) are not in fact worlds unto themselves, but involved in all the social and political complexities of their times.

Exercise

The styles of expression in Passages 1 to 6 differ in many respects. In the chapters which follow, you will acquire means of identifying and using salient features of 1 and 4 — the two passages from research genres. But you might begin to develop your awareness of style here by inspecting and comparing all six samples. First, and most broadly, what distinguishes 1 and 4 from the others? Second, and more narrowly, can you distinguish between the style of 1 and 4? (Passage 4 is the first paragraph of the article's introduction; Passage 1 is the sixth paragraph of the article's introduction.) In approaching these tasks, you might take into account these features:

- ways the writers are represented in the text (most obviously, do they mention themselves?);
- words — their commonness (would they show up in, for example, conversation between neighbours?), their recurrence (to what degree do these writers repeat the same words?); and sentences — their length, completeness;
- capitals, parentheses, names, numbers.

How would you describe the relation between writer and reader in each of these passages?

From what you know (or can guess) about the ways of life which surrounded each of these samples, estimate how each of the writers learned to write this way (on the job? in class? on a weekend seminar?).

As far as I know, each of these passages was written by a different person. But say this were not the case. Which passages could have been written by the same people? What are your reasons for thinking so?

Notes

1 Alice J. O'Toole, Kenneth A. Deffenbacher, Dominique Valentin and Hervé Abdi. 1994. "Structural aspects of face recognition and the other-race effect." *Memory and Cognition* 22(2): 209.

2 Nicole H. Rafter. 1992. "Claims-making and socio-cultural context in the first U.S. eugenics campaign." *Social Problems* 39(1): 17.

Citation, summary, and authority

In this chapter we head for **summary** — an important feature of the research genres.

Summary may not seem, at first, an attractive destination. Or a serious one. With its schoolroom role as a check to see if you've done assigned reading, or its role in exams in seeing if you understand what you read ("List the three main points the author makes. Write in complete sentences."), summary can appear to be dead-end, or servile. I can tell you that summary is important to scholarly writers — researchers and professors — but that still might not redeem it. You might still be reluctant, suspecting that summary is make-work for students. If I show you some examples of summary in published scholarship, summary might still look like a peripheral formality rather than a central activity of scholarly life.

So, to put summary in the context of research itself, we are going to begin by examining manifestations of **citation** — as a way of understanding summary as part of the scholarly community of practice: shared ways of doing things amongst those who make knowledge.

2.1 Citation

Here is a way of writing which somebody unaccustomed to scholarly writing might find peculiar:

PASSAGE 1
Initial skepticism over the impact of neighborhood conditions and neighborhood contexts on the behavior of adolescents and

young adults (Jencks and Mayer 1990) has spurred considerable research purportedly documenting such effects (Aneshensel and Sucoff 1996; Billy, Brewster, and Grady 1994; Corcoran et al. 1992; Duncan 1994; Duncan, Connel, and Klebanov 1997; Elliott et al. 1996; Entwisle, Alexander, and Olson 1994; cf. Evans, Oates, and Schwab 1992). Grounded primarily in Wilson's (1987) prominent treatise on *The Truly Disadvantaged*, several recent studies have examined the impact of neighborhood disadvantage on family-related events, including the timing of first sexual activity (Billy et al. 1994; Brewster 1994; Brewster, Billy, and Grady 1993), first marriage (Hoffman, Duncan, and Mincy 1991; Massey and Shibuya 1995), and nonmarital and/or teenage childbearing (Billy and Moore 1992; Brooks-Bunn et al. 1993; Crane 1991).

Scott J. South and Kyle D. Crowder 1999 "Neighborhood effects on family formation: Concentrated poverty and beyond." *American Sociological Review* 64, 113-32, 113-14.

But it's not so peculiar. Other people write this way, too:

PASSAGE 2

Increasing concern over the possibility of global climate change has heightened interest in the factors that affect clouds in climatically pivotal areas such as the Arctic (e.g., Goody 1980; Abelson 1989; Ackerman *et al.* 1986). Changes in either the areal coveral or radiative properties of arctic layer clouds could modify the arctic climate and ice pack and potentially affect global climate (e.g., Schlesinger 1986; Walsh and Crane 1992; Curry *et al.* 1996).

Information on the structures of arctic clouds is relatively scant. Most previous microstructural measurements for summer were obtained in June 1980 during the Arctic Stratus Experiment (ASE) (e.g., Tsay and Jayaweera 1984; Herman and Curry 1984; Curry and Ebert 1992) when stratocumulus clouds were widespread (Warren *et al.* 1988). Cloud measurements in the Arctic at other times of the year by Witte (1968) and Jayaweera and Ohtake (1973) suggest that cloud structures are fairly simple and homogeneous over large areas, with cloud liquid-water content (LWC) generally increasing above cloud base.

Peter V. Hobbs and Arthur L. Rangno 1998 "Microstructures of low and middle-level clouds over the Beaufort Sea." *Quarterly Journal of the Royal Meteorological Society* 124, 2035-2071, 2035.

PASSAGE 3

There have been several well-conducted efforts to understand childhood disorders of emotion in terms of distinct and meaningful components (e.g., Fox and Houston, 1983; Ollendick and Yule, 1990; Papy, Costello, Hedl, and Spielberger, 1975). In particular, several investigators have found considerable overlap between the constructs of anxiety and depression (e.g., Lonigan, Carey, and Finch, 1994; Norvell, Brophy, and Finch, 1985; Tannenbaum, Forehand, and McCombs-Thomas, 1992; Wolfe et al., 1987) and have suggested a higher order construct of negative affect (Watson and Clark, 1984). Although the evidence for this relation is compelling, the latent structure of childhood negative emotions is only beginning to be conceptualized in detail (e.g., Joiner, Catanzaro, and Laurent, 1996).

Bruce F. Chorpita, Anne Marie Albano, and David H. Barlow 1998 "The structure of negative emotions in a clinical sample of children and adolescents." *Journal of Abnormal Psychology* 107, 1, 74–85, 74.

These topics are all familiar: neighbourhoods, weather, sad feelings. But they are being talked about in rather unfamiliar ways. Besides somewhat rare wordings (e.g., "childhood disorders of emotion," "radiative properties"), there are some conspicuous formal features — long parenthetical interruptions to the sentences, with only names and years in them. Why do South and Crowder write "the timing of first sexual activity **(Billy et al. 1994; Brewster 1994; Brewster, Billy, and Grady 1993)**, first marriage **(Hoffman, Duncan, and Mincy 1991; Massey and Shibuya 1995)**, and nonmarital and/or teenage childbearing **(Billy and Moore 1992; Brooks-Bunn et al. 1993; Crane 1991)**"? What kind of writing is that?

These parenthetical patches are a condensed, concentrated way of telling us that somebody other than the present writer has said something: they signal **citation**.

Other writers in different research disciplines, or perhaps in different sub-specialties, cite in less apparently peculiar ways. They unpack the clumps of names and dates, show us that these statements have been uttered by other speakers, and even permit us to hear their actual words. In Passage 4, an historian is beginning a discussion of what others have said about moods of uncertainty at the turn of the previous century (people feeling insecure, alienated). I have emphasized the reporting expressions which attribute statements about those moods to writers other than the present one.

PASSAGE 4

Most of the literature on European and North American intellectual history at the turn of the century emphasizes the problematic and disorienting effects of **(as Everdell puts it)**, "the impossibility of knowing even the simplest things that the nineteenth century took for granted."[1] In fact, **the characterization of** the period from 1890 to 1914 as an era of pessimism, alienation, and anxiety has become a cliché of intellectual history. In German political thought, **Fritz Stern describes** a mood of "cultural despair";[2] for the social sciences, **writes Lawrence Scaff**, "the central problem appears to be the same in every case: a sense that unified experience lies beyond the grasp of the modern self and that malaise and self-conscious guilt have become inextricably entwined with culture."[3] **Eugen Weber remarks** that, in France at the turn of the century, "the discrepancy between material progress and spiritual dejection reminded me of my own era."[4] In Britain, **the literary critic Terry Eagleton refers to** a "cataclysmic crisis of Victorian rationality."[5]

Notes
1   William R. Everdell, *The First Moderns: Profiles in the Origins of Twentieth-Century Thought* (Chicago, 1997), 10–11.
2   Fritz Stern, *The Politics of Cultural Despair: A Study in the Rise of the Germanic Ideology* (1961; rpt. edn., New York, 1965).
3   Lawrence A. Scaff, *Fleeing the Iron Cage: Culture, Politics, and Modernity in the Thought of Max Weber* (Berkeley, Calif., 1989), 80.
4   Eugen Weber, *France: Fin de Siècle* (Cambridge, Mass., 1986), 3. For other examples, see […].
5   Terry Eagleton, "The Flight to the Real," in *Cultural Politics at the Fin de Siècle*, Sally Ledger and Scott McCracken, eds. (Cambridge, 1995), 13.

Ann Taylor Allen 1999 "Feminism, social science, and the meanings of modernity: The debate on the origin of the family in Europe and the United States, 1860–1914." *The American Historical Review* 104, 4, 1085–1113, 1085–86.

The attributing of a statement to another speaker, **citation** produces one of the distinctive sounds (and looks) of scholarly writing. The distinctiveness of this way of writing could lead to one or two views of scholarly writing which, while not necessarily unfounded, may be slightly misleading. The first is that repeating the words or ideas of others is peculiar to scholarly expression. Another is that these citations are a shortcut to "authority," and that scholarly writing is a platform for those who have a knack for repeating the words of others. We discuss each of these views below.

2.1.1 "Citation is peculiar to scholarly writing"

So commonly do people in everyday conversation repeat the sayings of others that specialists in language studies investigate this speech habit. For example, Wallace Chafe (1994) devotes much attention to the "distal" properties of citation — how speakers' representations of others' words involve consciousness of contexts distant from the setting of the conversation; Patricia Mayes's study of citation in spoken English finds that "at least half of the direct quotations are not authentic renditions, and many are the invention of the speaker" (1990:358); Greg Myers (1999) proposes methods for classifying the many functions of citation, showing that the speech technique of representing the words of others involves complex purposes and, on the listener's part, subtle interpretive schemes. These are all studies of citation in commonplace settings: people telling about their experiences and feelings, explaining themselves or passing on information about others.

And, if we consult our own experience, we too can readily tune into citation in our daily encounters:

(a) So this guy comes over and says is that your car and I'm like yeah and he goes you gonna leave it there and I'm like — *what???*

(b) Barb in Protection calls me and says the C-7 isn't done and I say you've had it on your desk for a week oh she says

(c) So they say the urban coyotes are getting pretty bad

(d) The weatherman says showers in the morning but then clearing

(e) I suspect, from what I glean from the papers, news and so on that what has happened that people have been let out and they've been put in circumstances in the community where they're not capable of looking after themselves.

> Cited in Keith Tuffin and Jo Danks 1999 "Community care and mental disorder: An analysis of discursive resources." *British Journal of Social Psychology* 38, 289–302, 297.

Sometimes we even report thirdhand. Here a speaker, telling a dog-bites–man story, says what her mother said she said, and what her mother said someone else said (notice how the daughter quotes the mother directly, but the stranger's words are swallowed by descriptions of his attitude, e.g., "this man was going absolutely mad"):

(f) [My mother] took — she's got these two Dobermans who are really unruly but very sweet. She took them for a walk on the beach one day, and this was at the height of the Rottweiler scare, and this jogger's running along the beach at Liverpool, and Sophie, her dog that she can't control, decided to run along after the jogger and bit him on the bottom. And this man was going absolutely mad, and my mother started off by being nice to him and saying, "I'm terribly sorry; she's only a pup and she was just being playful," and so on, and he got worse, so the more she tried to placate him, the more he decided he was gonna go to the police station and create a scene about it. So she said, "Let me have a look", and she strode over to him and pulled his <LAUGHS> pulled his tracksuit bottoms down, and said, "Don't be so bloody stupid, man, there's nothing wrong with you, you're perfectly all right". At which point he was so embarrassed he just jogged away.

Cited in Jennifer Coates 1996 *Women Talk: Conversation between Women Friends* Cambridge, MA: Blackwell,100-01.

Why is citation so common in everyday conversation? Possibly because much of what we know about the world we learn only from what others have said, and because conveying this knowledge as coming from a particular source gives us a chance to take a position in relation to other people's positions in the world. For example, the speakers in (a) and (b) take an oppositional stance vis-à-vis the other speakers they cite, and cite their own speech to confirm this position. Mentioning coyotes, the conversationalist in (c) cites a consensus he has detected in news reports of the day; the speaker in (d) uses citation to show the source of his prediction about the weather. (I think it is rare, in Western culture, to hear a weather prediction without at least an implicit citation of weather professionals, e.g., "it's supposed to rain then clear up.") The speaker in (e) identifies her source generally ("the papers, news"). In (f), the story about the jogger and the dog, the storyteller manages the speech of others in such a way as to lead us to sympathize with the dog owner rather than with the man who was bitten.

Sometimes writers in non-academic genres — in (g), a writer of a letter to the editor of a small-town newspaper — use citation to typify what they take to be a general message from other sources (in this case, sources with which the writer strongly disagrees) by putting words in others' mouths:

(g) Disincentives are everywhere for drivers ...."take transit so we can clog our arteries with fuel-hogging buses." I don't like it, and there is nothing I can do about it.

Letter to the editor, *Tri-City News* 26 April 2000

In (h), the speaker is one of a group of British "working-class men" who are on probation after having been convicted of money-related crimes (447). Like the speaker in (g), he puts words in others' mouths:

(h) They can rip off millions and pay nothing, then someone gets caught, twenty, thirty pounds DSS an' "they're a criminal scum-bag"

Sara Willott and Chris Griffin 1999 "Building your own lifeboat: Working-class male offenders talk about economic class." *British Journal of Social Psychology* 38, 445-60, 451.

Notice that the speaker is *not* stating that small-time thieves are criminal scum-bags. He is stating that *others* (Big Interests) say that small-time thieves are criminal scum-bags, and he aligns himself in opposition to these others: his citation distinguishes his interests from the interests of those he perceives as embezzling and pillaging on a large scale. On the other hand, the next speakers (from the same group) self-cite not to oppose others but to establish solidarity amongst themselves:

(i) Mark: always said, right, you don't take from somebody who's just as bad off as you. I'd rather take from somebody who could *afford* to lose.
Andy: What you say, "you don't take off your own kind."
Mark: Exactly
Steve: Your own doorstep.
Andy: Yup, your own doorstep ...

(Willott and Griffin 1999:456)

Sometimes in everyday conversation, we simply repeat what we have heard, sewing it with invisible stitches into our utterances. Someone who has himself conducted no studies of climate change and has not visited South Asia could say —

(j) There are droughts in South Asia ... global warming

— and his listeners could infer that he read this somewhere, or heard it on television.

Other times, a view of our own gets a boost from citing a source people consider authoritative.

> (k) He was black and blue from head to toe, the doctor says it was a miracle he survived.

Or writers approach their general audience with a "saying" handed down through nearly mythic channels from an ancestral speaker:

> (l) Voltaire is said to have been fond of remarking that doctors pour drugs of which they know little, to cure diseases of which they know less, into human beings of whom they know nothing.
>
> Emily Laber 2000 "Designer drugs: Tailoring medicines to fit the patient." *The Sciences* July-August, 8-9, 8.

Much of our performances as speakers is citation — repeating what others have said, attributing statements to those with authority, or those with whom we disagree: naming some of our sources ("Barb," "my mother"), typifying others ("the doctor," "the weatherman"), leaving some anonymous ("they say"), or leaving some cited claims unattributed. Some citation is verbatim; some is paraphrase; some is invented.

Seeking recognition and sympathy for our position, or spreading the news or playing our part in rumour and hearsay, we repeat what others have said.

Exercise

(1) Without offending anyone's privacy, listen to discussions which you overhear or in which you participate: listen for, and record, two or three instances of citation in everyday conversation. How does this speaker (who might be you) attribute his or her cited statement to a source? Is the source named ("Barb," "Prince Charles"), typified ("the Registrar's Office," "the vet"), anonymous ("I heard ...," "they")? What role did the citation play in the conversation?

(2) Citation not only plays a part in many conversational situations, it also has a major function in news genres, in Western cultures especially. To get a sense of its characteristic operation in constructing public information, inspect the passage below. Identify those statements which are citations. Which are

paraphrase? Which are verbatim? Which cited speakers are fully identified? Which are typified or anonymous? What would the passage sound like if we removed the expressions which attribute statements to others? For example, removing reporting expressions from the first sentence —

> A second jury has found Saskatchewan farmer Robert Latimer guilty of murder in what he called the mercy killing of his disabled daughter, Tracy.

— we would get:

> Saskatchewan farmer Robert Latimer is guilty of murder in the mercy killing of his disabled daughter, Tracy.

Speculate on the function of citation in the news genres generally — and in this article in particular.

BATTLEFORD, Saskatchewan — A second jury has found Saskatchewan farmer Robert Latimer guilty of murder in what he called the mercy killing of his disabled daughter, Tracy. [★ ★ ★] As the verdict was delivered last night, Mr. Latimer's wife, Laura, leaped from her chair in the courtroom, ran to the jurors' rail and cried, "No! No! No! No!" Mr. Latimer left the prisoner's box to console his wife before the stunned, silent spectators. The judge, Mr. Justice G.E. Noble, said he was obliged to sentence Mr. Latimer to life imprisonment. [★ ★ ★] Mr. Latimer first told police that Tracy died in her bed. Later, however, he confessed that he gassed the child in the cab of his truck on the family farm near Wilkie on Oct. 24, 1993. He told police he did so to relieve her pain and said that caring for her had become increasingly difficult.

The court heard that Tracy loved music, could smile, laugh and move her hands, relate to her friends and siblings and was in no immediate mortal danger from the debilitating effects of cerebral palsy. [★ ★ ★ (16 sentences)] Asked outside the court last week why he had first told police his daughter died in bed, Mr. Latimer paused 10 seconds and replied, "Why?" He paused another 10 seconds and said: "I think you just have to appreciate the situation and what was going on. There was a lot of stuff going on. I said she passed away in her sleep. She just went to sleep. At that time, I didn't feel like a long-winded whole bunch of business with 14 police officers that day. Tracy had passed away that day and I wanted to deal with it in a more normal way." During the ... trial, the jurors heard that Mr. Latimer was a kind, loving father and devoted family man who did not trust doctors and was at the end of his rope at the prospect of his daughter's continued suffering. [* * *]

"New jury convicts Latimer of murder," *The Globe and Mail*, 5 Nov. 1997

2.1.2 "Scholarly writers repeat others to sound impressive and authoritative"

In the last section we saw that citation is a feature of everyday conversation; it is therefore not peculiar to scholarly writing. It is nevertheless *conspicuous* in this kind of writing. It is a salient feature: it sticks up or stands out; it makes the research genres recognizable from a distance. Citation is a feature which these genres don't seem to be able to do without. So conspicuous is it that it can be caricatured, or parodied —

> Summer is warmer than winter (Blink 1971; Buzzy 1978 [1976]; Bingo 1980; Buffy and Blooper 1982; Binky et al. 1986; Beastie 1992 [1989]).

— although not everyone would find this much of a joke.

Are these citations for the sole purpose of making the writer sound authoritative — learned and important?

Let's look again at the passage with which the chapter began, starting with the first sentence:

> Initial skepticism over the impact of neighborhood conditions and neighborhood contexts on the behavior of adolescents and young adults (Jencks and Mayer 1990) has spurred considerable research purportedly documenting such effects (Aneshensel and Sucoff 1996; Billy, Brewster, and Grady 1994; Corcoran et al. 1992; Duncan 1994; Duncan, Connel, and Klebanov 1997; Elliott et al. 1996; Entwisle, Alexander, and Olson 1994; cf. Evans, Oates, and Schwab 1992).

Notice that South and Crowder don't claim that neighbourhoods have good or bad effects or no effects on the young people who live in them. Instead they report that someone (Jencks and Meyer) has said that neighbourhoods may not have much effect on young people, and that some sceptical researchers (the remaining citations) reacted and set out to test this possibility. Are South and Crowder sceptical themselves? No, they attribute the scepticism to these other researchers. But then the adverb "purportedly" suggests that they do not necessarily occupy the same position as those whose work has challenged that scepticism.

In the next sentence, South and Crowder interpret the eight clusters of speakers (appearing at the end of the sentence) as having been influenced by yet another speaker — the author of what they call a "prominent treatise":

> Grounded primarily in Wilson's (1987) prominent treatise on *The Truly Disadvantaged,* several recent studies have examined the impact of neighborhood disadvantage on family-related events, including the timing of first sexual activity (Billy et al. 1994; Brewster 1994; Brewster, Billy, and Grady 1993), first marriage (Hoffman, Duncan, and Mincy 1991; Massey and Shibuya 1995), and nonmarital and/or teenage childbearing (Billy and Moore 1992; Brooks-Bunn et al. 1993; Crane 1991).

So, have South and Crowder got "authority" by citing others? So far, they have told a story of others speaking, and taken a reserved position, neither disputing nor accepting others' statements. In fact, rather than imparting an authoritative status, the citations seem to cultivate a stance of uncertainty, which is elaborated as the discussion continues:

> While a general consensus appears to be emerging that, net of individual and family attributes, at least some neighborhood characteristics significantly influence these and other life-course events, thus far these studies have generated inconsistent findings regarding the existence, strength, and functional form of neighborhood effects on marriage and nonmarital childbearing.

South and Crowder don't say that neighbourhoods *do in fact* influence young people's "family-related" behaviour, but that, from a certain position (theirs), you can see that researchers might be beginning to agree that some aspects of neighbourhoods *can* have some effect. But now they do make a claim of their own — and it turns out to be not about neighbourhoods, but about the **state of knowledge** about neighbourhoods. What they claim is that findings are "inconsistent": taken together, these studies do not provide a clear answer to questions about the influence of neighbourhoods on young people growing up in them. They continue with more assertions of their own:

> More important, several key elements in Wilson's theory relating neighborhood socioeconomic disadvantage to family formation patterns have been treated only cursorily, if at all. And virtually all prior studies of neighborhood effects on marriage and childbearing suffer from one or more methodological deficiencies that limit their contribution to our knowledge in this area.

What is South and Crowder's position on this topic? Neither embracing nor disputing any of the studies they refer to, South and Crowder assemble the findings of a group of speakers and, taking these findings together, estimate the state of knowledge on a topic: in this case they find a **deficit** in the current state of knowledge. Moreover, at the same time they position their own voice amongst these other voices — they *identify with* this deficit: "**our** knowledge in this area" (emphasis added). Collectively, all these speakers, including the present authors, own the knowledge (such as it is).

Someone looking for answers to questions about "good" neighbourhoods and "bad" ones, desirable behaviour and undesirable, might be disappointed. Experts seem to be less sure of these things than non-experts.

Exercise
Inspecting Passages 2 and 3 from the beginning of the chapter, describe the state of knowledge about arctic clouds, and about children's negative emotions.

Examining Passage 4, we find, in the first sentence, that Allen does not say that it is impossible to know "even the simplest things," but that people *now say* that (other) people *thought* this way at the end of the nineteenth century and beginning of the twentieth. She goes on to bring other speakers to the page who seem to agree that, at that time, people felt that way. While she arranges for these voices to converse with one another, and come to an agreement, she positions herself at some distance from these views, referring to them as "a cliché of intellectual history." Although in this passage Allen does not explicitly identify a deficit in our understanding of this period of Western thought, we can anticipate that she will show that, despite this apparent agreement amongst experts, something has been missed. (She will show us what it is.)

Do scholarly writers acquire authority by citing? Few (if any) of the citations we've looked at here "back up" the writer who refers to others, or who repeats the words of others. Moreover, the citations can add up to uncertainty rather than authority.

We will find cases, though, where scholarly writers do position themselves beside an important figure and share his or her prestige. It would be wrong to say that scholarly writers don't acquire some status — and a right to speak — by citing others. By convening fellow scholars, and arranging for conversation amongst them, the writer gets to

- take a position in relation to the other voices;
- identify himself or herself as a member of a group collectively;
- construct knowledge;
- take a turn in the conversation.

In the research genres, citation represents and enables certain actions: listening to the statements of others; identifying the position from which the statement comes; evaluating established knowledge and paying attention to the possibility that it may be incomplete, contradictory, or even wrong; watching for opportunities to improve the state of knowledge.

Exercise
(1) In this passage, I have identified those expressions which attribute a statement to another speaker.

> Within the context of the tecato subculture, **previous researchers have linked** machismo almost exclusively to hypermasculine aspects of drug use and aggression. Thus **Bullington (1977:108, 115) regards** machismo as both an adaptive, efficacious attitude in navigating through prison experience and an underlying variable related to the expression of criminal behavior. Likewise **Casavantes (1976), in his study of "el tecato" [the male Mexican heroin addict], emphasizes** the hypermasculine aspects of this model. **He notes that** "… machismo in its exaggerated form [includes] fighting, drinking, performing daring deeds, seducing women, asserting independence from women, and … bragging about escapades" (Casavantes, 1976:149).
>
> Gilbert A. Quintero and Antonio L. Estrada 1998 "Cultural models of masculinity and drug use: 'Machismo,' heroin, and street survival on the U.S.-Mexican border." *Contemporary Drug Problems* 25, 147-65.

What happens when I remove those expressions?

> Within the context of the tecato subculture, machismo is connected with hypermasculine aspects of drug use and aggression. Machismo is both an adaptive, efficacious attitude in navigating through prison experience and an underlying variable related to the expression of criminal behavior. Machismo in its exaggerated form includes fighting, drinking, performing daring deeds, seducing women, asserting independence from women, and bragging about escapades.

(2) Identify the reporting expressions in this passage, and re-write the passage removing these reporting expressions.

> The problem of teenage parenthood, acknowledged to be a significant social problem in the United States since the late 1960s, has been the subject of much study (Alan Guttmacher Institute, 1985; Chilman, 1980; Furstenberg, Lincoln, and Menken, 1981; Lancaster and Hamburg, 1986; Hayes, 1987). Efforts to understand its causes have generally focused on the issue of individual choice regarding the decision to engage in sexual behavior (Chilman, 1978; Pete and DeSantis, 1990) and to use contraceptive devices (Finkel and Finkel, 1975; Goldsmith, Gabrielson, 1972). The association of teenage motherhood with dropping out of school prematurely (Gray and Ramsey, 1986; Roosa, 1986), not being employed (Trussell, 1976), and becoming dependent on government subsidies (Klerman, 1986; Moore, 1978) is well-documented. In general, consideration of how schools and educational policies contribute to the high rate of teenage motherhood has been limited to how dropping out affects the likelihood of a girl becoming pregnant, how pregnancy affects the probability of dropping out, and the relationship between education aspirations and pregnancy rates (Moore, Simms, and Betsey, 1986).
>
> Helen Rauch-Elnekave 1994 "Teenage motherhood: Its relationship to undetected learning problems." *Adolescence* 29, 113, 91-103, 91-92.

2.2 Summary

At the beginning of the chapter we mentioned that we needed to examine citation in order to understand summary. This is because we can look at each of the cited statements in our passages as tiny **summaries**. In one sentence, South and Crowder present the gist of one report (that type of neighbourhood may not affect young people's behaviour) as well as the gist of what eight others have said (that neighbourhoods do affect behaviour).

> Initial skepticism over the impact of neighborhood conditions and neighborhood contexts on the behavior of adolescents and young adults (Jencks and Mayer 1990) has spurred considerable research purportedly documenting such effects (Aneshensel and Sucoff 1996; Billy, Brewster, and Grady 1994; Corcoran et al. 1992; Duncan 1994; Duncan, Connel, and Klebanov 1997; Elliott et al. 1996; Entwisle, Alexander, and Olson 1994; cf. Evans, Oates, and Schwab 1992).

Likewise, in one sentence, Allen repeats the words of two other writers. Each repetition represents an aspect of the cited work which is relevant to the current discussion:

> In German political thought, Fritz Stern describes a mood of "cultural despair"; for the social sciences, writes Lawrence Scaff, "the central problem appears to be the same in every case: a sense that unified experience lies beyond the grasp of the modern self and that malaise and self-conscious guilt have become inextricably entwined with culture."

Sometimes the summaries are tiny (one sentence), like those we've just seen above; sometimes they're much longer. South and Crowder go on to summarize more extensively (two paragraphs) the "prominent treatise" by Wilson. (I have emphasized the expressions which attribute, characterize, and evaluate the statements about neighbourhoods.)

> **Perhaps the most prominent and influential theoretical explanation** of how neighborhoods influence the life course of young adults **comes from Wilson (1987; 1996)**. To some extent, **Wilson's thesis subsumes** the main causal mechanisms linking disadvantaged neighborhoods to undesirable behavioral outcomes **described by Jencks and Mayer**

(1990:115). These include the *epidemic* (or contagion) *model,* which emphasizes the role of peer influence, the *collective socialization perspective,* which emphasizes the positive impact of successful adult role models (and **which is Wilson's main focus**), and the *institutional model,* which focuses on how adults from outside the community, such as teachers and police officers, affect the behavior of children and young adults. **The thrust of all these models — and Wilson's argument —** is that the presence of disadvantaged neighbors (or the relative absence of advantaged neighbors) increases the likelihood that young persons will engage in nonnormative or otherwise undesirable behaviors, such as dropping out of school, committing crimes, eschewing marriage, and bearing children out of wedlock.

For Wilson (1987:56-60), the most important mechanism linking neighborhood economic disadvantage to deleterious outcomes is the absence of middle- and working-class families in ghetto neighborhoods. When such families are present they provide a "social buffer" that deflects the impact of high unemployment and poverty among the "truly disadvantaged." Their absence, in contrast, isolates poor families, thereby exacerbating problematic behavior and social dislocation. **As Wilson (1987) argues**, "the very presence of these families [...] provides mainstream role models that help keep alive the perception that education is meaningful, that steady employment is a viable alternative to welfare, and that family stability is the norm, not the exception" **(p. 56)**. The importance of conventional role models for promoting "mainstream" familial behavior — including marrying and bearing children only within marriage — **is echoed and reinforced by ethnographic observations of inner-city communities (Anderson 1990)**.

Without summary, these writers would not be able to join the scholarly conversation. With summary, they arrange to take their turn — and go on, in this article, to report and discuss their inquiries into the influence of concentrated poverty on "nonmarital fertility" (finding that effects of increasing disadvantage are observed among white women but not among black women, and finding that white women in increasingly disadvantaged neighbourhoods tend to marry *earlier* than otherwise — "[c]ontrary to expectation").

Summary
South and Crowder are not the only sociologists to summarize Wilson. Looking at this other summary of Wilson, this time by Quillian, will prepare you to appreciate (a) how important summary of even well-known works is to scholarly discussion (South and Crowder may read Quillian, and Quillian may read South and Crowder), and (b) how each summary is a *new* version for *new* purposes and emphases.

> William Wilson's book *The Truly Disadvantaged* (1987) first
> pointed out that, starting in the 1970s, areas of concentrated
> urban poverty increasingly took on a different character than
> they had earlier in the century. Like the ethnic ghettos that
> have long interested urban sociologists, dwellers in modern
> poor urban neighborhoods are almost all members of minori-
> ty races or ethnicities. Unlike older ethnic ghettos, however,
> Wilson argues that the minority-populated urban neighbor-
> hoods of the 1970s and 1980s contained an especially high
> concentration on poor families. He hypothesizes that one
> cause of this trend is that middle-class blacks in the 1970s and
> 1980s increasingly relocated to predominately white suburbs,
> leaving behind neighborhoods composed largely of poor or
> new poor families.
>
> Lincoln Quillian 1999 "Migration patterns and the growth of high-poverty
> neighborhoods, 1970-1990." *American Journal of Sociology* 105, 1, 1-37, 1.

Summary isn't just for researchers and professors; it also provides students with an invitation to the scholarly conversation. While you may not be ready to cite 18 sources in two sentences, as South and Crowder do at the beginning of their article, you can compose the kinds of summaries we see above, bringing to the page the voices you read. This section is devoted to developing your skills as a summariz-er of scholarly material, and becoming involved in the kinds of activ-ities which are enabled by and represented in the research genres. I offer here two related methods for approaching summary: the first notes for **gist** as you read; the second explores the original as an arrangement of **levels** — levels of generality and detail, of abstract and concrete reference.

2.2.1 Noting for gist

In this method, we write as we read, noting what we predict should be remembered in preparation for writing. To demonstrate, I have made notes alongside a scholarly passage in preparation for summarizing. The notes answer this question: if I were reading this with the intention of going on to write, what would I estimate as important from each paragraph? Avoiding full sentences and straight copying, the notes capture the "gist" — the point or basis — of each section in a form that is temporary, pliable, ready for other uses.

Social practices, norms, and institutions are designed to meet heterosexual systems' need to produce sex/gender dimorphism — masculine males and feminine females — so that desire can then be heterosexualized. Gendered behavioral norms, gendered rites of passage, a sexual division of labor, and the like, produce differently gendered persons out of differently sexed persons. Prohibitions against gender crossing (e.g., against cross-dressing, effeminacy in men, mannishness in women) also help sustain the dimorphism necessary to heterosexualize desire.

heterosexual systems: social norms → the masc. & fem. genders

Children and especially adolescents are carefully prepared for heterosexual interaction. They are given heterosexual sex education, advice for attracting the opposite sex, norms of heterosexual behavior, and appropriate social occasions (such as dances or dating rituals) for enacting desire. Adult heterosexuality is further sustained through erotica and pornography, heterosexualized humor, heterosexualized dress, romance novels, and so on.

children: social customs → preparation for heterosexuality

adults: gendered attitudes, clothes → sustain heterosexual desire

Heterosexual societies take it for granted that men and women will bond in an intimate relationship ultimately founding a family. As a result, social conventions, economic arrangements,

expected, socially, legally, econ.: men & women in intimate couple, for family and the legal structure treat the hetero-sexual couple as a single, singularly important, social unit. The couple is represented linguistically (boyfriend-girlfriend, husband-wife) and is treated socially as a single unit (e.g., in joint invitations or in receiving joint gifts). It is legally licensed and legally supported through such entitlements as communal property, joint custody or adoption of children, and the power to give proxy consent within the couple. The couple is also recognized in the occupational structure via such provisions as spousal healthcare benefits and restrictions on nepotism. Multiple practices and insti-tutions help heterosexual individuals to couple and create families and support the continuation of those couples and couple-based families. These include dating services, match-makers, intro-ductions to eligible partners, premarital counseling, marriage counseling, mar-riage and divorce law, adoption services, reproductive technologies, family rates, family health care benefits, tax deduc-tions for married couples and so on.

social, linguistic conven-tion: M/F couple

law: M/F couple

economic & institution-al structures: M/F couple

The sum total of all the social, eco-nomic, and legal arrangements that sup-port the sexual and relational coupling of men with women constitutes hetero-sexual privilege. And it is privilege of a peculiar sort. Heterosexuals do not sim-ply claim *greater* socio-political-legal standing than nonheterosexuals. They claim as natural and normal an arrange-ment where *only* heterosexuals have socio-political-legal standing. Lesbians and gay men are not recognized as social beings because they cannot enter into the most basic social unit, the male-female couple. Within heterosex-ual systems the only social arrange-

all this ("multiple") → privilege for hetero-sexual couple seems normal, natural

the privilege makes non-heterosexuals unrecognizable…

ments that apply to nonheterosexuals are eliminative by nature. The coercive force of the criminal law, institutionalized discrimination, "therapeutic" treatment, and individual prejudice and violence is marshalled against the existence of lesbians and gay men. At best, lesbians and gay men have negative social reality. Lesbians are not-women engaged in nonsex with nonrelationships that may constitute a nonfamily.

...except as something to be "fixed"

only negative social standing for nonheterosexuals

Cheshire Calhoun 1994 "Separating lesbian theory from feminist theory." *Ethics* 104, 558-82, 579-80.

Reading for gist, we produce a set of wordings which partly depend on the original wordings but are also partly free of the original, too. These wordings prepare for a new version of what has been said by someone else, incorporating ties to the first speaker but also putting a new accent on those words.

2.2.2 Recording levels

We could write a summary from these gists alone. But, doing so, we might be missing an opportunity to get a better picture of the original, or leaving to chance some of our recollection of that original when we write the summary.

You might notice that our gist notes eliminate details — "cross-dressing," for example, "dances," "romance novels," "family rates." In our everyday conversational "summarizing," we also eliminate details. For example, we'd probably say —

  A. How was your cruise?
  B. Excellent, very well organized, good food and tours at each port.

— instead of —

  A. How was your cruise?
  B. On the third night I had a delicious salmon terrine with juniper berries, followed by a peach sorbet garnished with a sprig of mint. Binky had the .... In Copenhagen we went on a bus to

Tivoli, there were two buses, we got on the second one, the buses were waiting when we went ashore … and then …

— although some people tend towards the detail technique, and may encounter social disapproval as a result. If we don't eliminate details, the summary would be too long, and risk not being a summary at all (imagine if the traveller told every detail — then the answer to the question might be as long as the cruise itself!). Yet, still, some details seem to be important, since they give specific examples of more abstract ideas.

Abstraction
Cutting across the high levels of generality are planes of abstraction. "Prohibition" is an abstraction — an abstract reference. Mention of the stop sign at the bottom of my lane, prohibiting me from rolling down the lane and directly out into the road, is a concrete reference. I can touch the sign, and locate it in the physical world, the way I cannot "touch" *prohibition*, although I experience the abstract phenomenon *prohibition* each time I encounter the stop sign. (On the plane of *generality*, the stop sign would be a "detail," or "specific.")

At a *general level*, the first paragraph is about something like *the heterosexualization of desire* through *sex/gender dimorphism* — what *is* that? At a less general level, we encounter "prohibitions against gender crossing" … and "gender crossing" would be … *what*? At a still less general and more specific level, we get the answer, finding prohibitions "against cross-dressing" as an example. Now we have a grasp on "sex-gender dimorphism" (probably).

The second paragraph begins at a high level, too — "Children and especially adolescents are carefully prepared for heterosexual interaction" — and then *goes down* to the level of specifics: dating, dances, and so on.

We could diagram the levels — the organization of generality and detail — as in figure 2.1.

What might we learn from this pattern? *As readers*, if we find the beginning claims of a scholarly paragraph difficult (what *is* "dimorphism"?!), we might be patient, and wait to see if these high-level claims are demonstrated with examples or instances that might link the claim to our concrete experience; *as writers*, we might anticipate that our readers will look for these lower levels, so they can get a firmer grasp of what we're talking about.

Fig. 2.1

heterosexualization of desire

social practices, norms, institutions which produce sex/gender dimorphism

prohibitions

[against] cross-dressing, etc.

preparation of children & adolescents

sex educ, advice, social occasions

dances, dating

sustaining of heterosexuality in adults

erotica, porn, clothes, romance novels, jokes

expectation of man/woman bonding in intimate relationship to produce family

social conventions, economic, legal structures

[social:] "husband-wife," joint gifts & invitations
[economic]: spousal health benefits, etc.
[legal]: adoption, joint custody

law, institutions, practices against gay & lesbian

discrimination, therapy, violence

The chart above is a portrait of reasoning in a scholarly passage — a snapshot, maybe, in that it takes elements out of the real-time of reading. Restored to time, put in a video instead of a snapshot, the passage would reconfigure as a series of descents from high levels to lower ones, and then ascents again, as below.

hetero-sexualized desire

sex/gender dimorphism

prohibitions

[against] cross-dressing, etc.

children heterosexualized

sex ed, social occasions

dances, dating

adults' heterosexuality sustained

erotica, jokes, novels, etc.

Taking the clusters of gist produced by reading-and-noting Calhoun's passage, and keeping an eye on the structure of generality and detail, I can write a one-sentence summary of these four paragraphs.

> To explain the means by which heterosexual society produces heterosexuality as "natural," and produces "negative social reality" for lesbians and gay men, Calhoun (1994) catalogues the social practices (e.g., dating, sex education, erotica) which construct sex/gender dimorphism, and the social conventions (e.g., joint gifts and invitations to husband-and-wife) and legal and economic structures (e.g., adoption procedures, spousal health benefits) which produce the "single unit" of intimately bonded man and woman.

As well as representing content, the summary:

- **attributes these statements** as originating with another writer ("Calhoun (1994)");
- **characterizes the action** of the original ("To explain" how society has come to view heterosexuality as natural); and
- **describes the development** of the discussion (it "catalogues" examples).

Calhoun's persuasiveness (to me) depends at least partly on the way she summons so many examples of the practices and norms which heterosexualize desire: the summary preserves this quality of the original. Similarly, when South and Crowder summarize Wilson, they also recover some details from the original:

> These include the *epidemic* (or contagion) *model*, which emphasizes the role of peer influence, the *collective socialization perspective*, which emphasizes the positive impact of successful adult role models (and which is Wilson's main focus), and the *institutional model*, which focuses on how adults from outside the community, **such as teachers and police officers**, affect the behavior of children and young adults.

While noting-for-gist is a means of recording compactly — or "remembering" — a spread of details which might otherwise escape your recollection, you might also think of it as a "forgetting": once the high-level gist is transferred to the summary, it "forgets" the details which accompanied it. By re-introducing a telling detail or two, as

South and Crowder do above, you can help generalities "remember" their origins, and show them to your reader.

With each of these moves — identifying the speaker-who-is-not-me, characterizing the action of the original, describing its development — I **take a position** in relation to the original.

I might develop this position by saying what larger phenomenon this one is part of; for example:

> Calhoun's discussion reminds us that what we view as "natural" can often be traced not to nature but to social custom. She takes a social constructionist view of ...

I could also develop the position by estimating the commonness or uncommonness of the claims made by the original; for example, by saying —

> Summoning arguments established by feminist reasoning, Calhoun ...

— I locate Calhoun in current, and fairly common, claims about the social construction of gender.

I have also secured a position for myself and made this my own version by not sticking to the order of the original. By beginning with points from the last paragraph — heterosexuality produced as "natural," "negative social" reality for gays and lesbians — I take my reader to this element of the original first, thereby thematizing this aspect of Calhoun's discussion. This is not to say that it is more correct to do so, only that for *my* intentions — perhaps an emphasis on the naturalizing effects of social norms — this order is good. With *other* intentions, or another perspective on the topic, I might have started at another point — for example:

> Calhoun (1994) describes legal and institutional discrimination against gays and lesbians (adoption and custody laws, for example, spousal benefits in the workplace), but also brings to light the array of social habits which extend such discrimination: we learn what is "natural" and expected — and what is "unnatural" — not only from laws and policy but also from everyday practice — routines of socializing like dating and dances among adolescents, for instance, and, among adults, social invitations to the man-woman couple.

Other summaries might arrange for still other emphases by selecting another point at which to begin, and another order to follow.

While there are no rules for recording and manipulating these "gists," it can be a good idea to arrange them on a single page —

Fig. 2.2

	heterosexual systems: social norms → the masc. & fem. genders	expected, social, legal, econ.: men & women in intimate couple, for family	
children: social customs → preparation for heterosexuality	social, linguistic convention: M/F couple	law: M/F couple	only negative social reality for non-heterosexuals
adults: genres, attitudes, clothes → sustain heterosexual desire	economic & institutional structures: M/F couple all this ("multiple") privilege for heterosexual couple which seems normal, natural		privilege → non-hetero couples unrecognizable, except to be "fixed"

— so you can see them all at once. That way, you can escape the order of the original, and design your own. And by arranging gists in a non-linear way, you can induce them to make new connections with one another. By making new connections amongst claims, you offer new perspectives on the original. That is, *even if* the reader of the summary had already read the original, the summarized version is *new*: it is reconfigured for the present purposes. Your arrangement of the materials of the original is an expression of your position *vis-à-vis* the original, and, however familiar readers are with the original, the summary will be new to them. We might reckon, for example, that many of South and Crowder's readers — people who consult the *American Sociological Review* — have read or at least know about Wilson's "prominent" book, *The Truly Disadvantaged*. That condition does not make the summary redundant. The summary secures common ground with readers, inviting them to take, for the time being, the writer's perspective on the cited author.

Exercise

Here is a passage from an article reporting an anthropological study of "RVers." RVers are people who spend much of their year in recreational vehicles: motorhomes, truck-campers, trailers. In the fieldwork reported below, researchers found, amongst RVers, sub-categories: "boondockers," who park their "rigs," usually for free and unofficially, on (US) federal lands; and "private-park RVers," who stay in organized, commercial facilities.

Use the reading-and-noting technique to capture the passage's gists, and the mapping technique to survey its range from generality to detail. Write a two- or three-sentence summary of the passage.

In one sense shared territory does not create community for RVers who treasure their mobility and their ability to turn on the key and be gone if they don't like their neighbours. In another sense it does. As Davis observes, "People cluster together for protection, contact, organization, group integration, and for the purpose of exploitation of a particular region and the community is the smallest territorial group that can embrace all aspects of social life" (Davis 1949:312). As we have said, RVers choose different sorts of places to cluster and they define themselves and are defined by others by where they park. These definitions reinforce the sense of community among RVers who cluster together, but also emphasize differences that alienate RVers from each other. We look first at the way in which their choice of place separates RVers and then turn to a discussion of how space unites them through common values, interests and experience.

When RVers select a place to park their rigs they are also making a choice about lifestyle and about identity. Some choose private resort parks where their personal space is limited but where they feel safe and comfortable. They seek the protection of walls and guards; they enjoy the luxury of water and sewer hookups, electricity and cable TV; their space is organized into streets and blocks where each RV has its own "pad";[5] and leisure activities are organized by professionals who encourage and promote contact among park residents. Many private resort parks have strictly enforced rules about how a rig may be parked, where dogs may be walked, the conditions under which residents may have guests, and for how long and under what circumstances children and grand-children may visit. Many of the people who choose this lifestyle see themselves holding standards of affluence, respectability and orderliness and they particularly appreciate the fact that the other park residents are similar to themselves in age, social standing, consumption level and interests. In thinking about private parks one is reminded of the distinction made by Bellah et al. between "lifestyle enclaves" and communities. Lifestyle, they point out, "brings together those who are socially, economically, or culturally similar, and one of its chief aims is the enjoyment of being with those who 'share one's lifestyle'" (Bellah et al. 1985:72). In their terms, groups such as retirement "communities," organized around a common lifestyle, are "lifestyle enclaves," not communities. A community is inclusive and focusses on the interdependence of private and public life while recognizing and tolerating the differences of those within it. In contrast, "lifestyle is fundamentally segmental and celebrates the narcissism of similarity. It usually explicitly involves a contrast with others who 'do not share one's lifestyle'" (Bellah et al. 1985: 72). Resort park residents make a sharp distinction between their standard of living and lifestyle and that of boondockers. Our non-boondocking informants advised us that, as part of our research, we should go to one of the boondocking areas. "You should spend one night there, just to see it, but you won't want to stay longer," one couple said about Slab City. Another marvelled that boondockers "sit out there on the desert, happy as clams," adding, "but I couldn't do it."

Boondockers agree that they are unlike the folks who live in resort parks and many of them treasure the difference. They are not a homogeneous lot, for people from all social classes, level of education and degrees of affluence can be found boondocking. They opt for economy and simplicity, the absence of rules and organization and unlimited external space. They particularly want to avoid the crowding — what one person calls sites "like cemetery plots" and another referred to as being "crammed in like sardines" — that they see as characteristic of private parks. Boondockers often used the term "freedom" to describe their way of life and many of them said that resort park residents had simply exchanged the restriction and crowding of urban life for an RV version of the same thing.

Boondockers are regarded by others (and sometimes they regard each other) with considerable ambivalence. On the one hand, the lives of boondockers epitomize the values on which America was founded: they are independent of rules and regulations, they live simply with a minimum of luxury and expense, they embody the qualities of individualism and ingenuity and they co-operate on their own terms for mutual security and to share resources. On the other hand, they are marginal to North American society. Many of them have no fixed address — not even a mail box in an RV park. Many, particularly those who are flea marketers, participate in an underground economy that avoids regulations and taxes — a fact that is not lost on officials of nearby towns. Most instructive and, we think, representative of the attitude of civic officials toward boondocking flea marketers, is a letter cited by Errington that expresses the resentment of a small-town businessman towards transient vendors (1990:642). He bitterly resents the fact that they pay no taxes and little rent and face none of the risks and costs endured by town retailers. "Let's tax 'em," he says. "Let's set up a licensing procedure that will discourage the money hounds" (Errington 1990:642).

Note
5   A pad is a private space that includes the place where the RV is parked and an area round it that is usually only a few feet wide.

Dorothy Ayers Counts and David R. Counts 1992 "'They're my family now': The creation of community among RVers." *Anthropologica* 34, 153–82, 168–70.

2.2.3 Coordinates of the summarizer's position

We have identified several ways in which summarizers take a position in relation to the writer whose ideas they are representing. They use reporting expressions ("Calhoun (1994) describes"; "Wilson argues"), which can also contribute to a characterization of the action of the original — as a description, or an argument, in these examples. Or the original might be characterized as an analysis, or some observations, or a commentary on something, or a review of research on something, or an explanation. Summary can also mention what kind of study produces the knowledge: field research, for example, or statistical analysis, or experimental or theoretical inquiry. Summarizers can also take a position by pointing to larger issues not mentioned in the original but whose wider applications the original suggests.

Along these lines, summarizers can also estimate the generalizability or limits of the statements in the original. For example, Calhoun reports a wide range of social practices which discriminate against gays and lesbians: could this kind of analysis be generalized and applied to other marginalized groups? At the same time, those social practices all derive from Western — and possibly mainly North American — cultures: a summarizer might mention this limitation to Calhoun's discussion, and suggest questions which arise as a result.

Exercise

Write a two- to three-sentence summary for each of the five passages below. Practise the reading-and-noting technique, producing gists whose order you can arrange or re-arrange according to the perspective you want to offer your reader. To get a feel for the structure of each passage, attempt a rough sketch of its levels: pick out the lowest level of detail, and the higher levels of generality.

> If you are writing in a classroom situation, it might be worthwhile to allot the passages: some members of the class doing Passage 1, others doing Passage 2, and so on. That way, you can test your summary both on readers who do know the original and on readers who don't know the original, or, at least, don't know it as well as you do. For techniques on arranging for readers to give writers feedback on their writing, see Chapter Four.

(a) In "Two Kinds of Judgement," Milroy and Milroy are reviewing some ideas that would be familiar to language specialists, but managing these ideas to develop an analysis of "authority" in language. You will see that their analysis is arranged around a couple of contrasts. One is the conflict between what people *think* "grammar" is and what it *actually* is. The other is the distinction between writing and speech.

popular belief vs. actual case

speech vs. writing

The "lowest," most detailed levels of the passage are the example words and sentences, e.g., ★ The house white. (In the linguistic disciplines, "★" indicates that what follows is ungrammatical.)

Two Kinds of Judgement

Grammar and speech

Grammar, in the popular view (and this is based on the standard ideology), is believed to consist of a number of "rules" that are imposed on usage from the outside, for example by some authority on correctness. These rules are largely a set of prohibitions against particular expressions (such as *different to*) that are recurrent and persistent. The grammar of a language or dialect is actually something much more wide-ranging than this. It is a complex and abstract system inherent in the language and not imposed by overt prescription. All native speakers have implicit knowledge of the grammar of English: it is this knowledge that enables speakers to use and understand their language. Amongst other things, this knowledge enables the speaker to judge what sentences are possible in the language. For instance, native speakers intuitively know that Set 1 (below) consists of grammatical sequences and that Set 2 consists of ungrammatical sequences.

Set 1	*Set 2*
The white house	★The house white
John was hit by Jack	★Was hit by Jack John
Charlie died	★Died Charlie

These Set 1 sequences are grammatical, not because the order or choice of words is necessarily the best or the most "logical", but because the rules of English grammar require these sequences. In other languages, the conventions may be different. French, for example, requires *the house white* ("la maison blanche"), and Gaelic requires *died Charlie* ("bhàsaich Tearlach").

The most general grammatical rules of a language, or dialect of a language, are learnt by the native speaker in infancy and childhood without explicit instruction; they are rules of speech. It is a fallacy to believe that most of language is learnt at school: children are taught *reading* and *writing* at school. The basic grammar of the spoken language has already been acquired by the time they go to school, i.e. children "know" the main conventions and rules, even if their performance is imperfect in some details (e.g. the use of "goed" for *went* or "buyed" for *bought*). What they implicitly know about grammar at the age of five is infinitely greater than what they do not know. We now turn to some aspects of spoken usage and consider the relevance of prescriptive norms to those usages.

The differences between spoken and written grammar arise largely from the different properties and functions of the two channels. As speech is adapted to social use, certain kinds of sentence-structure are more common in speech than in writing, for example utterances that *point* to something in the environment and which therefore have a structure that we can broadly call "topicalised": "That's me in the photograph"; "This is the boy who stole the apples". Another type of sentence that is more common in speech than in writing is the *elliptical* sentence. In reply to a question "Where is the squirrel?", a speaker might answer: *In the tree*, deleting the noun-phrase and verb: *The squirrel is* …. He can do this because the topic has already been specified. Traditionally, however, utterances like *In the tree* have been labelled incomplete sentences and have even been said to be "wrong". The reason for this, of course, is the traditional emphasis on writing and neglect of speech; as writing is not so much assisted by immediate situational context, it is necessary to be more specific in writing than in speech.

James Milroy and Lesley Milroy 1991 (1985) *Authority in Language: Investigating Language Prescription and Standardisation* 2nd ed. London: Routledge, 71-73.

(b) In "Sickness as a resource," Mary Douglas demonstrates an "anthropological approach" to the study of cultural difference in the medical disciplines. From the evidence of this passage we might say that an anthropological approach would not focus on testing different practices for their success in "curing" sick people (and such tests in themselves might be regarded as culture-specific — what counts as a cure for one group may not count as a cure for another group). Instead, the anthropological approach would focus on *social norms* and *community*.

social norms	community
norms for being sick	therapeutic community

At the lowest levels, you will find a congregation of types, including "the sick Londoner," "the African patient," "friends [asking] if the doctor has been called in yet." At the end of the first paragraph, you will find a fairly high-level statement which does not descend directly to particulars: Douglas refers to situations where there may be "political pressures not to convert to the other side" — not to go over to alternative medical practices, whether those be "exotic" or "traditional." Can you think of examples of what such situations might be? (An exercise in Chapter Three revisits this question.)

In the first sentence, Douglas mentions "complementary medicine": from a Western point of view, complementary medicine might include acupuncture, herbal therapies, and homeopathic healing.

Sickness as a resource

[...] the sick Londoner who is choosing complementary medicine [is] equivalent to the African villager who is confronted by the reverse option. The choice is not between science or mumbo-jumbo, but choosing the traditional versus the exotic system, and in effect it means choosing between therapeutic communities. The African patient faced with the choice between the Christian missionary doctor with an exotic pharmacopoeia and the traditional diviner with his familiar repertoire is under the same sort of pressures as a Westerner choosing between traditional and exotic medicine. For minor ailments he can pick and choose separate remedial items without incurring censure, but if it is his own life or the life of his child that is at risk, his therapeutic community will take a strong line. He may have friends on either side of the divide, or choosing may involve him in a complete switch of loyalties. It is rather like religious conversion: if there is a strong political alignment dividing the two therapies, there will be political pressure not to convert to the other side. That is a good beginning for the anthropological approach.

The next step is to follow the monitoring that is going on in any community. Wherever there is illness, warnings are being issued, and informal penalties being threatened. Talcott Parsons founded medical sociology when he identified and named the "sick role." When a person defines himself as sick, he can escape censure for doing his work badly, being late, being bad-tempered, and so on, but the community which indulges the sick role also exacts a price: the sick person is excused his remiss behaviour on condition of accepting the role, eating the gruel or whatever is classified as invalid food, taking the medicine, and keeping to the sick room, out of other people's way.

Having adopted the sick role, a person cannot play his or her normally influential part. The patient is reproved for trying to go on working; if the patient complains of pain, the answer is that complaining is aggravating the condition and a more severely restricted diet may have to be prescribed; every complaint is met with potential criticism so that the patient ends by lying back and accepting the way others have defined the sick role. Dragging around looking tired, his friends ask if the doctor has been called in yet, and if so, they want to know who, and are free with advice as to who can be trusted. It is a matter of pride for them if their favourite doctor is called, and a threat of withdrawn sympathy if it is one they disapprove. These friends interacting with the patient, listening to symptoms and offering advice, form what the anthropologist John Janzen (1978) calls the "therapeutic community."

At the early stages of illness, there is some choice: either behave as if you are well or admit to being sick and bear the consequences. If the illness worsens and the invalid refuses the advice of friends and family, it is going to be difficult to ask for the neighbourly services or the loans of money on which lying in bed depends. The rival merits of traditional and alternative medicines are put to the test, not according to the patient's recovery but according to the negotiating of the sick role. The outcome will depend on the therapeutic community. For the sick person, the power of the medical theory counts for less than issues of loyalty and mutual dependability, unless he or she is completely isolated.

The background assumption is that any society imposes normative standards on its members. That is what being in society involves. Living in a community means accepting its standards, which means either playing the roles that are approved, or negotiating the acceptability of new ones, or suffering from public disapproval. The option for spirituality is a form of negotiation. But of course communities differ in the amount of control they exert: some are quite lax and standardization is weak; others exert ferocious control. In this perspective it would be interesting to know whether the persons who have chosen alternative therapy have also chosen a therapeutic community to support them with friendship and counsel.

Mary Douglas 1996 "The choice between gross and spiritual: Some medical preferences." In *Thought Styles* London: Sage, 33-35.

(c) Most of us don't know much about how our cars or our computers — or our kidneys for that matter — work: for repair, or advice on maintenance, we ask experts. In "Trust and Expertise," an excerpt from *The Consequences of Modernity*, Anthony Giddens' opening question asks how we acquire confidence in others' expertise. In the second paragraph of his reply, you will find a conflict — a "but" situation clearly marked by "However, at the same time" introducing a description of "typically ambivalent" attitudes.

trust	BUT	scepticism
education		ignorance
science		mad scientist

Trust and Expertise

[W]hy *do* most people trust in practices and social mechanisms about which their own technical knowledge is slight or nonexistent? The query can be answered in various ways. We know enough about the reluctance with which, in the early phase of modern social development, populations adapted to new social practices — such as the introduction of professionalised forms of medicine — to recognise the importance of socialisation in relation to such trust. The influence of the "hidden curriculum" in processes of formal education is probably decisive here. What is conveyed to the child in the teaching of science is not just the content of technical findings but, more important for general social attitudes, an aura of respect for technical knowledge of all kinds. In most modern educational systems, the teaching of science always starts from "first principles," knowledge regarded as more or less indubitable. Only if someone stays with science training for some while is she or he likely to be introduced to contentious issues or to become fully aware of the potential fallibility of all claims to knowledge in science.

Science has thus long maintained an image of reliable knowledge which spills over into an attitude of respect for most forms of technical specialism. However, at the same time, lay attitudes to science and to technical knowledge generally are typically ambivalent. This is an ambivalence that lies at the core of all trust relations, whether it be trust in abstract systems or in individuals. For trust is only demanded where there is ignorance — either of the knowledge claims of technical experts or of the thoughts and intentions of intimates upon whom a person relies. Yet ignorance always provides grounds for scepticism or at least caution. Popular representations of science and technical expertise typically bracket respect with attitudes of hostility or fear, as in the stereotypes of the "boffin," a humourless technician with little understanding of ordinary people, or the mad scientist. Professions whose claim to specialist knowledge is seen mainly as a closed shop, having an insider's terminology seemingly invented to baffle the layperson — like lawyers or sociologists — are likely to be seen with a particularly jaundiced eye.

Anthony Giddens 1990 *The Consequences of Modernity* Stanford UP, 88-90.

(d) At the lowest level in this excerpt from James Clifford's book about "people going places" (1997:2) — about people's place being the product not only of their location but also of their journeys and others' journeys — we find the example of Matthew Henson and Robert Peary, and their trip to the North Pole. At the highest level, we find the abstractions *racism* and *class* — but you may also be able to construct other high-level terms in which to understand the episodes Clifford refers to.

Traveling cultures

What about all the travel that largely avoids the hotel, or motel, circuits? The travel encounters of someone moving from rural Guatemala or Mexico across the United States border are of a quite different order; and a West African can get to a Paris *banlieu* without ever staying in a hotel. What are the settings that could realistically configure the cultural relations of these "travelers"? As I abandon the bourgeois hotel setting for travel encounters, sites of intercultural knowledge,

I struggle, never quite successfully, to free the related term "travel" from a history of European, literary, male, bourgeois, scientific, heroic, recreational meanings and practices (Wolff, 1993).

Victorian travelers, men and women, were usually accompanied by servants, many of whom were people of color. These individuals have never achieved the status of "travelers." Their experiences, the cross-cultural links they made, their different access to the societies visited — such encounters seldom find serious representation in the literature of travel. Racism certainly has a great deal to do with this. For in the dominant discourses of travel, a nonwhite person cannot figure as a heroic explorer, aesthetic interpreter, or scientific authority. A good example is provided by the long struggle to bring Matthew Henson, the black American explorer who reached the North Pole with Robert Peary, equally into the story of this famous feat of discovery — as it was constructed by Peary, a host of historians, newspaper writers, statesmen, bureaucrats, and interested institutions such as *National Geographic* magazine (Counter, 1988). And this is still to say nothing of the Eskimo travelers who made the trip possible![11] A host of servants, helpers, companions, guides, and bearers have been excluded from the role of proper travelers because of their race and class, and because theirs seemed to be a dependent status in relation to the supposed independence of the individualist, bourgeois voyager. The independence was, in varying degrees, a myth. As Europeans moved through unfamiliar places, their relative comfort and safety were ensured by a well-developed infrastructure of guides, assistants, suppliers, translators, and carriers (Fabian, 1986).

Note
11 Lisa Bloom (1993) has written insightfully on Peary, Henson, Eskimos, and the various efforts by *National Geographic* to retell a deeply contested story of discovery.

James Clifford 1997 *Routes: Travel and Translation in the Late Twentieth Century* Cambridge, MA: Harvard UP, 33-34.

(e) The following passage occurs in an article which states that we need to understand managers "as social agents in a particular time and place" and to understand "what aspects of their social being might tend systematically to produce inappropriate corporate strategies as, for example, an inability to change when change is necessary" (Shoenberger 1994:434). In other sections of the article, Schoenberger refers to General Motors, Xerox, and Lockheed as examples of firms which resisted change even as they had in hand evidence not only of the necessity for change but also of the types of changes that would ensure their survival. The passage excerpted here touches, at its highest levels, notions of *power* (and, possibly, *entitlement*) and "social capital." Social capital, in turn, descends through "educational capital" and "cultural capital" to much more specific levels of reference: the "MBA from Harvard," the "opera," the "symphony orchestra."

Managers

In this section I will try to relate the "objective" source of managers' power with some propositions about what the sense of power entails and how it shapes identity. This part of the argument draws heavily on Bourdieu's analysis of the divergent sources of social capital, how and to what ends they are mobilized, and how they are defended (Bourdieu, 1977; 1984).

One of the interesting things about the social power of high-level managers is that it derives from a variety of seemingly disconnected materials, historical, geographical, and cultural sources. This very diversity creates a kind of tacit coherence and self-reinforcement, as the manager's experience in different spheres of his life tends to yield the same message. Further, it tends to naturalize the experience and the sense of power: the manager knows that he has it and feels that this is right without having to explain it, to himself or anyone else ("it comes with the territory").

The material sources of a manager's power include class and position, income and wealth. Technically, what makes someone a capitalist is ownership of capital which is used to accumulate more capital. What makes a capitalist a socially powerful agent is *control* over capital and the ability to mobilize the power of money (see Harvey, 1985). Whether or not they own significant portions of their firm, top managers are, in a sense, honorary capitalists: they have the authority to allocate capital via their investment decisions (for a different view of the class status of managers, see Wright, 1985).

Though they may not be immune from later sanctions, they have the authority to risk the existence of the firm even if they do not own it, a power summed up in the widely used phrase "to bet the company."

High-level managers also, needless to say, generally have high incomes and are relatively wealthy. The titles attached to their corporate and civic positions, moreover, mark them as powerful agents in the perceptions of others — including other powerful people. The reflection of their status in the eyes of others, particularly as this implies a shared yet unspoken sense of recognition with others of their type, feeds back upon and reinforces the sense of power derived from purely material sources.

Differential access to educational capital (a university education or, better, graduate degrees in business, finance, or technical disciplines, especially from the "right" schools) provides another kind of support that can function in various ways. In some cases, it is the educational capital itself that is mobilized to gain access to economic capital in the first place (as when an MBA from Harvard University provides entrée to a managerial position despite the inexperience or humble origins of the person in question). Academic credentials also provide a tacit guarantee of the general suitability of a person for a managerial career — that is, a career as a socially powerful actor — that goes beyond the specific competences formally attested to be the degree itself. That is to say, although the Harvard MBA only formally guarantees that the holder is well versed in the latest management techniques, the aura of the degree confers a broader social acceptability and a tacit marker of the social power of the individual (see Bourdieu, 1984).

Following Bourdieu, we may also expect that economic and educational capital can be mobilized to reinforce one's control of cultural capital expressed in forms (taste, judgment) and mechanisms (collecting, patronage) of cultural consumption and in a particular relationship to cultural production (for example, personal and corporate philanthropy). In turn, privileged access to cultural capital provides another form of validation of the sense of social power derived from economic and educational capital. We can see this fusion of different forms of social capital at work in the participation by corporate leaders (and/or their spouses) in support of their cultural institutions (museums, the opera, the symphony orchestra, etc.), often in their headquarters' cities. The point, however, is not about the control of cultural production but rather the way in which different forms of social capital reinforce each other and provide a coherent substrate to the sense of social power.

One presumably does not need to amass large quantities of statistical data to claim that most high-level managers in the USA are white males (but see *Fortune* 1990; 1992). They are also typically American, and rose to their positions in the postwar period of global US economic and military dominance. Race, gender, geography, and historical moment also combine to foster a generalized sense of power.

Here it can also be seen how the position of top managers differs from that of, say, other white American males in being reinforced on all fronts. The white male blue-collar worker may feel himself empowered within family or among his peers. He may feel himself entitled to look down upon women, minorities, or immigrants or upon the Japanese or Germans who, after all, lost the war. But this sense of power is more likely to be contradicted, hence qualified, in other settings, as when he applies for a loan at the bank, for example, or writes to his senator and receives a form letter in response, or when he enters the workplace.

E. Shoenberger 1994 "Corporate strategy and corporate strategists: Power, identity, and knowledge within the firm." *Environment and Planning* 26, 3, 433–51, 443–44.

2.3 Reporting reporting

Since scholarly writers so often cite the words of others, summarizers of scholarly writing can find themselves citing others' citations — reporting reporting. In one of the passages for summary above, Counts and Counts include in their observations on RVers' notions of "place" other scholars' ideas:

In thinking about private parks one is reminded of the distinction made by Bellah et al. between "lifestyle enclaves" and communities. Lifestyle, they point out, "brings together those who are socially, economically, or culturally similar, and one of its chief aims is the enjoyment of being with those who 'share one's lifestyle'" (Bellah et al. 1985:72). In their terms, groups such as retirement "communities," organized around a common lifestyle, are "lifestyle enclaves," not communities. A community is inclusive and focusses on the interdependence of private and public life while recognizing and tolerating the differences of those within it. In contrast, "lifestyle is fundamentally segmental and celebrates the narcissism of similarity. It usually explicitly involves a contrast with others who 'do not share one's lifestyle'" (Bellah et al. 1985:72).

Writing about the experience of undocumented immigrants in the southwestern US, and analysing that experience for evidence of "community," Leo R. Chavez also cites another's ideas:

> Suffice it to say that despite all the work that has been carried out on communities, the question still remains: What underlies a sense of community? Anderson (1983) examined this question and suggested that communities are "imagined." Members of modern nations cannot possibly know all their fellow-members, and yet "in the minds of each lives the image of their communion[....] It is imagined as a *community* because, regardless of the actual inequality and exploitation that may prevail in each, the nation is always conceived as a deep, horizontal comradeship" (Anderson 1983:15-16). In this view, members of a community internalize an image of the community not as a group of anomic individuals but as interconnected members who share equally in their fundamental membership in the community.
>
> Leo R. Chavez 1994 "The power of the imagined community: The settlement of undocumented Mexicans and Central Americans in the United States." *American Anthropologist* 96, 1, 52-73, 54.

If I were to summarize these passages, I would account for these writers' own summarizing activity:

> Investigating the nomadic experience of North American RVers for signs of community formation, Counts and Counts (1994) refer to Bellah et al.'s distinction between "lifestyle enclave" — groups based on the "narcissism of similarity" (Bellah et al. cited in Counts and Counts [p. 169]) and community — groups which include and tolerate difference.

In his study of the settlement patterns of undocumented immigrants in the US southwest, Chavez (1994) cites Anderson's notion of community as "imagined": a subjective sensation of being connected with others, despite inequality and the absence of face-to-face contact, an "image of [...] communion with others" (Anderson cited in Chavez [p. 54]).

This sort of "double reporting" defines my own position. I am not saying that groups based on similarity are only enclaves and not communities, or that people imagine communities. Nor am I saying that Counts and Counts say that groups based on similarity are only enclaves, or that Chavez says people imagine communities. What I *am* saying is that Counts and Counts say that Bellah et al. say that groups based on similarity are only enclaves, and Chavez says that Anderson says that people imagine communities.

Part of my contribution to the scholarly conversation is my work in tracing the statement. I follow its footprints. In the summarized version, "imagined community" starts with Anderson, then steps over to Chavez, and then steps again — onto my page. My summary records this journey: the idea's point of departure, its use in another location, its arrival in my writing, trailing behind it mementos of its journey.

In the cases above, the writers I am summarizing are citing other scholars. But sometimes, in some kinds of scholarly writing, the cited voice belongs not to a scholar but to a research subject: someone who has been interviewed, or whose voice has been otherwise captured for study. In this next passage, researchers have studied racist and anti-racist attitudes in an inner-city neighbourhood in Rotterdam.

The existence of discrimination is not denied by the participants who hold more racist views. Dutch people 'haven't always been angels themselves, that's for sure, because they've completely discriminated against people', and 'foreigners are certainly discriminated against, if only because their skin's a different colour' (participants 'K' and 'L' respectively). Several times during the discussions, however, it is pointed out that it is not so much ethnic minorities who are discriminated against, but Dutch local residents (K: 'I feel now like I'm discriminated against instead of them'). Community and social workers, housing corporations, schools, and also municipality officials were accused of favouring ethnic minorities and of only standing up for minority groups. It was held, for instance, that Dutch children would receive less attention in schools and might even be left behind.

Maykel Verkuyten, Wiebe de Jong, and Kees Masson 1994 "Similarities in anti-racist and racist discourse: Dutch local residents talking about ethnic minorities." *New Community* 20, 2, 253-67, 257.

Whereas Chavez appears to agree with Anderson's notion of "imagined community" — or at least to take a position very near Anderson's — and Counts and Counts at least entertain the possibility that what Bellah et al. say is useful and insightful, the writers of the passage above probably do not agree with some of what they cite from their research subjects. But, in a way, whether they agree or disagree is not the point. They are not arguing for or against the idea that ethnic minorities are favoured by official policy, and their study provides no evidence to support either position. Instead, Verkuyten et al. cite the words of others as indications of social phenomena. If I summarize the passage above as —

> In their research into attitudes towards ethnic minorities in an inner-city neighbourhood in Rotterdam, Verkuyten et al. (1994) discovered not only a generally shared acknowledgement of racism but also a perception of a kind of reverse discrimination: some informants expressed the view that ethnic minorities were favoured by official policy and institutional practice.

— I am not saying that racism exists or that ethnic minorities are officially favoured; nor am I saying Verkuyten et al. say that racism exists or that ethnic minorities are favoured. Rather I am saying that Verkuyten et al. say that *some people say* that racism exists and that minorities are favoured. If I were to summarize the passage as —

> Verkuyten et al. report that, in the inner-city neighbourhood of Rotterdam which they studied, ethnic minorities were favoured by official policy and institutional practice.

— I would be misrepresenting the original.

We could say that when Counts and Counts cite Bellah et al., and when Chavez cites Anderson, they are citing fellow experts, and joining them in conversation. And when Verkuyten et al. cite "K," they are reporting the words of a person who is non-specialist, not involved in the research conversation. But these categories **expert** and **non-expert** are not airtight, and the boundary between them can be politically contested nowadays. In Chapter Six, we will see interesting examples of innovation and incursion around the expert/non-expert border. In the meantime, below is an example where experts — "scientific circles" — and non-experts are cited, both groups providing examples of attitudes toward creole languages. (When different language groups come into contact with one another regularly — in, for example, situations of trade, and especially in colonial situations — a **pidgin** often develops: a language shared by these groups so they can communicate with one another on matters of trade, labour, transport. When a pidgin becomes the native tongue of some people — that is, it is the language they learn as children, in the family, at play and on the street corner — then the pidgin has become a **creole**.)

Today, even in scientific circles, a persistent stigma is attached to creole languages.[1] Because their formative period was relatively recent, the 17th and 18th centuries, they are often seen as not yet fully formed complex languages. The descriptions of creole languages in some linguistic circles are similar to the attitudes of many creole speakers toward their languages. These languages are described as "reduced," simple, and easy to learn; lacking in abstract terms, they are inadequate for scientific, philosophical, and logical operations. For most of their histories, creole languages have not been considered adequate for government, schooling or Western religious services.

The effect of pseudoscientific arguments or preconceived emotional ideas are evident in the negative attitudes lay persons generally hold toward creole languages and their speakers, and are revealed by the many pejorative terms used by both native and non-native speakers alike. Folk terminologies describe the French lexicon creoles as "broken French," "patois," "dialects," or "jargons," and many assume that creole languages are "diminished," "reduced," "deformed," "impoverished," "vitiated," "bastard" forms of the European standard languages that contributed to their birth.[2] Many educated and middle-class Haitians, members of the petite-bourgeoisie, as well as Haitian élites, view kreyòl [creole] as a simplified form of French at best. Many claim it is not a real language at all, but a mixture of languages without a grammar. The different varieties of kreyòl are viewed by Haitians of these social categories with a great deal of ambivalence. *Kreyòl rèk* [rough creole] and *gwo kreyòl* [vulgar creole] are often associated with pejorative connotations regarding the sounds (harsh, not harmonious, guttural, deformed), the grammatical features (debased, corrupted, elementary, lacking complexity), the social origin of speakers (rural, lower class), and defects usually attributed to the speakers themselves (coarse, clumsy, stupid, illiterate, uneducated). On the positive side, the same varieties have been associated with national identity, authenticity, independence, sincerity, and trustworthiness. Much of this is connected to romantic notions abut rural people — rough, coarse, but also authentic, real.

Notes

1 Diamond's (1991) article in *Natural History* titled "Reinventions of Human Language: Children Forced to Reevolve Grammar Thereby Reveal Our Brain's Blueprint for Language" includes the following:

> Between human languages and the vocalizations of any animal lies a seemingly unbridgeable gulf [....] One approach to bridging this gulf is to ask whether some people, deprived of the opportunity to hear any of our fully evolved modern languages, ever spontaneously invented a primitive language [....] Children placed in a situation comparable to that of the wolf-boy [...] hearing adults around them speaking a grossly simplified and variable form of language somewhat similar to what children themselves usually speak around the age of two [...] proceeded unconsciously to evolve their own language, far advanced over vervet communication but simpler than *normal* languages. These new languages were the ones commonly known as creoles. [p. 23, emphasis added]

2 August Brun, a French scholar writing in the early part of the 20th century, claimed that "une langue est un dialecte qui a réussi. Un patois est une langue qui s'est dégradée" (quoted in Pressoir 1958:27). (A language is a dialect that has been successful. A patois is a language that has deteriorated.) Such a view is still held by some educated Haitians today.

Bambi B. Shieffelin and Rachelle Charlier Doucet 1994 "The 'real' Haitian creole: ideology, metalinguistics, and orthographic choice" *American Ethnologist* 21, 1, 176-200, 181-82.

An account of what people say can be analysed for levels, with the lowest levels (in my analysis below) being named speakers quoted directly. (Notice that only the specialist speakers, in this passage, are specifically identified. What do you make of that?) In the analysis I've added a higher level than appears in the original, naming the larger phenomenon to which this situation belongs. (Higher still could be *social distinction, ranking*.)

[social judgements of speech]
stigmatization of creole languages

professional or scholarly stigmatization of creoles	lay stigmatization of creoles French creoles
in linguistic circles: only recent, therefore simple, easy; lacking abstractions for gov't, schooling... Diamond says "..."; Brun is said to have said "..."	among élite, middle-class, petite bourgeois Haitians: pejorative descriptions of sounds, grammar and origins of speakers "broken," "impoverished"
	BUT romantic notions re. rural people and national authenticity

I've also used the analysis to diagram a *conflict*, a *complication* or *ambivalence* the passage presents: the co-occurrence of negative and positive attitudes toward Haitian Creole.

My summary assigns statements to this company of speakers:

> Shieffelin and Doucet's (1994) survey of attitudes toward creoles reminds us of the persistent social habit of evaluating and ranking speech and speakers. In their descriptions of creoles, even linguists have tended to stigmatize these languages, referring to them as incomplete, and insufficient for use in government or schooling. Lay people also stigmatize creoles, characterizing these languages as illegitimate, "deformed," "impoverished": middle-class Haitians, for example, according to Shieffelin and Doucet, judge the sounds of Haitian Creole and the origins of its speakers pejoratively, yet, at the same time, celebrate an ideal notion of the rural classes.

Think of what the summary would be like without reporting expressions — something like "Haitian Creole is a reduced, simple language unfit for use in government or education; its sounds are coarse..." This would be a radical misrepresentation of the original.

Exercise
The following passage comes from a report of a study carried out in Aotearoa/New Zealand to explore people's attitudes toward community care and mental disorder: how do people feel about the "others" who might be housed in their neighbourhood in facilities accommodating those with "mental" or psychological afflictions? Write a two- or three-sentence summary of this

excerpt, making sure you preserve elements of the context in which original comments were uttered: under what circumstances did people say these things?

> Participants' talk about disorders was notable for the enormous variability in what was claimed to be "common" among people with disorders. This is demonstrated in the following extracts where severity varies considerably.

(6) Bev: I think simply because they may happen to have a mental disorder does not preclude them from doing a job, holding down a job.

Here disorders are constituted as a matter of inconvenience, with possession not being sufficient to avoid the world of work. The casting of disorder as excuse has the effect of minimalizing the seriousness of having a disorder, which contrasts strongly with other occasioned constructions where issues of dependence or dangerousness were highlighted. In the above, "simply because" works to minimize the potentially debilitating impact of a disorder, thereby supporting her general point of self-sufficiency.

(7) Val: ... BUT supervision comes into it. It does (.) there's got to be back-ups, people are going to be frightened if they know there's a bunch of people there and the fact is they don't know which one is going to (.) you know, go berserk. It's not always the case, but this is what goes in people's minds (.) and they don't want police cars going in there every five minutes or something or other.

Here, particular constructions of "disorder" are deployed to support an argument about the importance of supervision. Val draws on a construction of disorder as violent rage with the associations of dangerousness invoked by the notion of people going "berserk". In claiming 'this is what goes [on] in people's minds,' she purports knowledge of "others'" views. In appearing to represent these views she fails to claim them as her own. What this does is to distance Val from such fears because they are attributed to others and not herself. Another function served by this consensual claim is to legitimate these fears by making them generalized. This works to strengthen her argument for supervision. An additional function is

> served by generalizing these fears: it deflects from her the charge of prejudice, as she makes no claim regarding the validity of such fears.
>
> (Tuffin and Danks 1999: 296-97)

While the distinction between experts and non-experts is pretty clear when social psychologists ask people for their views of community care, it's not so clear in the next passage, which comes from an article analysing the historical circumstances of "open admissions" in the US in the 1970s, when large numbers of "non-traditional" students entered university: members of minority and marginalized groups joined members of the groups which had traditionally comprised university populations. Here Lu cites Geoffrey Wagner (Professor of English at City College [New York]) and author of *The End of Education*. Wagner is one of the "gatekeepers" whose reaction to open admissions Lu analyses.

> To Wagner, open admissions students are the inhabitants of the "world" outside the sort of scholarly "community" which he claims existed at Oxford and City College. They are dunces (43), misfits (129), hostile mental children (247), and the most sluggish of animals (163). He describes a group of Panamanian "girls" taking a Basic Writing course as "abusive, stupid, and hostile" (128). […] Wagner predicts "the end of education" because of the "*arrival* in urban academe of *large*, indeed *overwhelming, numbers* of *hostile* mental children" (247; emphasis mine).
>
> Min-Zhan Lu 1992 "Conflict and struggle: The enemies or preconditions of basic writing?" *College English* December, 891-913, 893-94.

Notice the scholarly technique for indicating added emphasis: "(emphasis mine)." Sometimes you will see "(emphasis added)" or "(italics added)."

Originally, Wagner might have considered himself an "expert," but Lu's citation seems to have the effect of transforming his words into indications of social attitudes, or earmarks of a political phenomenon. Just as

Counts and Counts do not enter into scholarly conversation with the RVers whom they cite, and Verkuyten et al. do not enter into scholarly conversation with the Rotterdam residents whom they cite, Lu also captures Wagner as a social type rather than a fellow scholar. Similarly, the linguists cited by Shieffelin and Doucet become examples of social attitudes toward creole rather than collaborators in a scholarly project. Possibly, when a scholarly community's outlook on certain issues (such as marginalized languages, or the education of marginalized groups) is changing radically, authoritative speakers can come in for some rough handling. In this passage, for example, Lu cites isolated patches ("dunces (43), misfits (129)"); commandeers verbatim wordings ("'girls,'" "'abusive, stupid, and hostile'") to exemplify the original; adds emphasis by using italics where none appear in the original — in all, forcefully *re-accents* the original.

Let's take one more look at this process of contexualizing reported statements. The next passage comes from an elderly woman's memoir (recorded as oral history) of her childhood experiences, 60 years before in a Catholic boarding school for aboriginal children in Canada.

> … oh my was I ever homesick. You know home wasn't much, in fact the nuns didn't call it home, they called it our *camp*. And that used to hurt me. It still does when I think about it. When we'd talk about going home, they'd say, "You're not going home you're going back to your camp." That was their impression of the reserve. Well in a way they were right because the homes we had in those days were made out of great big log houses.
>
> Mary Englund 1981 "An Indian remember." In *Now You Are My Brother*, ed. Margaret Whitehead Victoria, BC: Provincial Archives, 59.

An accurate summary would *not* be:

The children's homes were only camps.

At the very least, quotation marks would show that the writer is *not* vouching for this word:

The children's homes were only "camps."

More explicitly, the word can be attributed to its original speakers:

The nuns at the school referred to the children's homes as "camps."

But still we are missing aspects of context, which we can retrieve by adding another layer of citation —

> Mary Englund remembers that the nuns at the school referred to the children's homes as "camps."

— and another layer of context:

> Sixty years later, Mary Englund remembers that the nuns at the school referred to the children's homes as "camps."

Now the citation process includes a record of the survival of that word "camp" — enduring a lifetime in Englund's recollection, uttered once more on the occasion of the oral historian's research.

2.4 Extreme landscapes

It is unlikely that, in everyday scholarly tasks, writers would formally analyse the levels of what they were reading. But a little practice in mapping levels can give you a feel for the landscape of scholarly writing: its high altitudes of generality and its deep valleys of detail. And before we put this technique away, we can use it one more time to explore different kinds of summarizing situations and get a picture of the different challenges that these situations present.

2.4.1 High country

Some passages (and even whole articles and books) maintain a high level of mentions. This passage, for example, presents no details, no specifics — only high-level generality and abstraction:

> According to commemorative rhetoric, the past makes the present. Commemoration is a way of claiming that the past has something to offer the present, be it a warning or a model. In times of rampant change, the past provides a necessary point of reference for identity and action (Shils 1981). In contrast, the literature on social memory often emphasizes the importance of contextual factors in shaping commemorative practices and symbolism (Olick and Robbins 1998). Images of the past are malleable. Traditions are "invented" and memories are altered for instrumental reasons in the present (Hobsbawm and Ranger 1983). Social

memories are subject to, and are products of, production conflict and purposeful memory entrepreneurship (Wagner-Pacifici and Schwartz 1991). Producers, moreover, cannot control the ways in which images of the past are perceived (Savage 1994). Scholars therefore look at how people use memory to create identities and at how dominant narratives suppress alternative ones, and view the past as a terrain on which competing groups struggle for position (Bodnar 1992; Foucault 1977). These accounts emphasize that commemoration is explainable in terms of its contemporary circumstances: the present, from this perspective, makes the past.

Jeffrey K. Olick 1999 "Genre memories and memory genres: A dialogical analysis of May 8, 1945, commemorations in the Federal Republic of Germany." *American Sociological Review* 64, 381-402, 381.

Analysing this passage for levels of generality, I get something like this:

commemorative rhetoric	study of social memory
the past as message for the present	past as invention of the present
warnings, models	identity needs struggle for dominance

Lower levels are empty — and if, in summarizing this passage, I wanted to put my reader in closer touch with these ideas, I would have to come up with my own specifics. Because I'm not entirely sure what "commemorative rhetoric" is, I feel there are some hazards here, but I will try this:

Describing scholarly approaches to study of public commemorations of the past — monuments, ceremonies, speeches, anthems — Olick (1999) points to contrasting conceptualizations. One school of thought, "commemorative rhetoric," analyses commemoration — of, for example, a war or a social movement — as a message from the past for the present: an example to avoid or follow. Theories of social memory, on the other hand, analyse commemoration as a story about the past invented in the present to advance some present interests over others. Memorials of the Vietnam War, for example, might be seen as promoting ideas which benefit some groups rather than others thirty years after the war has ended. In Canada, accounts of the "birth" of national health care in the 1960s are repeated 40 years later: applying Olick's distinction, we can speculate that commemorative rhetoricians would analyse them as a "warning or a model" (381); sociologists of public memory would analyse them as strategies in the current struggle to control the culture and economy of health care.

It's hard work summarizing a passage that is composed at a very high level of abstraction. And risky — I'm not sure if my examples are right. But, by looking for specifics in my own experience, I measure my understanding of the passage, and also offer readers handholds as they make their way across these high-level ideas. (I notice, though, that my summary is nearly as long as the original. This may be a tendency of summary that attempts to represent a voice tuned to the higher "levels.")

Exercise

Here again is Leo R. Chavez summarizing the ideas of a much-cited theory of nation and national community. The summary stays at high levels. Can you think of specifics which would illustrate these ideas, and build a lower level?

What underlies a sense of community? Anderson (1983) examined this question and suggested that communities are "imagined." Members of modern nations cannot possibly know all their fellow-members, and yet "in the minds of each lives the image of their communion [....] It is imagined as a *community* because, regardless of the actual inequality and exploitation that may prevail in each, the nation is always conceived as a deep, horizontal comradeship" (Anderson 1983:15-16). In this view, members of a community internalize an image of the community not as a group of anomic individuals but as interconnected members who share equally in their fundamental membership in the community. The internalizations of the image and a sense of connectedness to the community is as important as actual physical presence in the community.

(Chavez 1994: 54)

2.4.2 Low country

Analysing the next passage, we find that mentions tend to be much lower than those we met in reading about "commemorative rhetoric" and "imagined community."

Brian

Brian is 14; his behaviour at school troubles staff and other students; he has become aggressive at home and at school; he sniffs glue. He is referred to a counselling clinic, and a schedule is arranged for him.

Brian is escorted each day to and from school either by family or by social services personnel. At school he is given "jobs" in the classroom during breaks. Two evenings weekly he is taken to a voluntary youth club run by some police officers in their spare time, and at weekends he joins a church youth centre for young-sters like himself, for outings and organized games. Once a week he also goes to an intermediate treatment centre, and one morn-ing weekly he attends the clinic for group counselling and activ-ities like painting and building models.

Adapted from Denis O'Connor 1987 "Glue sniffers with special needs." *British Journal of Education* 14, 3, 94-97.

The levels of this passage are roughly as follows:

troublesome,   arrangements
aggressive behaviour

sniffs glue   escorted; "jobs" in breaks; youth-club visits;
                       outings and games; counselling; painting ...

If I were to summarize this passage, I might find it hard to get free of the details or to make the summary any shorter than the original. Encountering a low, "flat" passage like this, I need to construct the higher levels myself — find the words which condense the details. That is, I need to interpret the details as *meaning* something. So, on top of the low foundation, I might propose the high-level abstractions *deviance* and *surveillance*. Then I would have **interpreted** these details as **meaning** "deviance" and "surveillance." And I might construct an even higher level: *social control*.

                        social control
        deviance   surveillance

troublesome, aggressive behaviour   arrangements
        sniffs glue   escorted; "jobs" in breaks; youth-club
                                 visits; outings and games; counselling,
                                          painting ...

Maybe *deviance* is a rather negative interpretation of Brian's behaviour. Someone else might take a more positive view, and might interpret

Brian's behaviour as *resistance*, to school and family impositions, for example. Or *surveillance* might fail to capture someone else's idea of the arrangements for Brian as *good* for him. That person might interpret the details as evidence of *therapy*, and *healing*. Or his troublesomeness might be interpreted as *dysfunction*. Each of these high-level abstractions is an interpretation of the details, and the summary which uses them will express the writer's point of view. One person might summarize the passage this way:

> The case of Brian, reported in O'Connor (1987), illustrates institutional practices of therapeutic surveillance. The 14-year-old's deviant behaviour is identified, and then managed through a series of monitoring activities, mechanisms of social control executed at the level of daily life.

Another person might summarize the passage as illustrating means of attending humanely to dysfunction and incorporating the troubled boy into supportive social networks. As interpretations, such high-level abstractions show the summarizer's position: his or her perspective on the material summarized.

Exercise

(1) In "Interview with Mae" below, a report from sociological research on attitudes toward crime, we come across expressions which lead us to the abstraction FEAR:

> She lives ... **afraid** of "home invasion."

> In the local paper she ... reads the court cases, finding here the accounts of "home invasions" which she **fears** so much.

Both "afraid" and "fears" lead easily to the abstract noun *fear*. But there is more to this passage than just *fear*. Other details or aspects of Mae's life can also be interpreted through high-level abstractions. For example, *isolation* might interpret "lives alone" and "does not go out much." Then a reading of the passage would involve reasoning about the connection between *fear* and *isolation*. And you will see that the account presents other circumstances, too, which call on us to reason beyond *fear* and *isolation*.

Find abstract words to construct higher levels of meaning in this passage. In a two- or three-sentence summary, report Mae's situation, using the abstract terms you have come up with. (It's possible that not all the terms you propose will come into play in your summary.)

Interview with Mae

Mae is 68 years old, Australian-born of British ancestry; she lives alone in a small country town in New South Wales. She lives in her home behind multiply-deadlocked front and back doors and windows, afraid of "home invasion." The only time Mae has had to contact the police was when a neighbour threw a firework on her roof. Mae is not poor — living in her own home in retirement — and is reasonably fit and well. Eighteen months ago, her husband died of natural causes. Since then, Mae has stopped watching any crime series on television — even series she had watched comfortably with her husband before he died. Indeed, the same shows seem to have changed for her since then: "That's the trouble, they're getting too much like what's happening out on the streets … like what you read in the paper."

While she avoids all crime on television because "You see these things happening and I think you imagine that it's going to happen to you," Mae has taken to reading the local and national newspapers far more since her husband died. Her knowledge of crime comes almost entirely from this media source, since she does not go out much and has never experienced a criminal incident. It is in these newspapers that Mae has "become far more aware of the drug problem now." In the local paper she scrupulously reads the court cases, finding here the accounts of "home invasions" which she fears so much. Her reading of the paper tells her that nine out of ten cases are "about drugs"; and Mae is thus quite able to construct a causal narrative of crime, where youth unemployment leads to drug-taking and thus to "home invasions." As a result, she has "only recently" begun worrying about her grandchildren and drugs. This is also something she "sees so much of on TV, where people are dying from taking drugs. Peer pressure and all those sorts of things. It doesn't matter how good a child is — they can be turned around, can't they?"

Adapted from Deborah Lupton and John Tulloch 1999 "Theorizing fear of crime: Beyond the rational/irrational oppositions." *British Journal of Sociology* 50, 3, 507-23, 516-17.

(2) "Making lead," below, seems to present parallel routes: one follows production processes; another follows the effects on workers; another tracks the categories of workers in each job. A summary could offer the abstractions which represent the details clustered along each of these routes, and could also suggest the relationships between them. Write a two- to three-sentence summary which offers high-level abstractions to interpret lower-level details: *risk*, for example, or *ethnic segregation*. ("Plumbism" is chronic lead poisoning.)

Making lead

The process of making "pure" lead paint that "white-leaders" [a paint-industry lobby group in early 20th-century U.S.] demanded began cleanly enough, as workmen hauled hundred-pound ingots, or "pigs," of dull, bluish-gray metallic lead to the smelter to be recast in the shape of large thin belt buckles. The largely unskilled laborers whose only contact with lead was in its metallic state were likely to contract the milder or chronic forms of plumbism; smelter workers faced considerably higher risk.[22]

Now began the process of corroding "blue" metallic lead buckles with acid, in the presence of carbon dioxide. Most plants in the United States corroded lead by the "Dutch Process" developed in the seventeenth century. Loading the "blue" beds was considered less hazardous than most processes in the paint factory: here one could find native-born Americans at work.[23] In many European paint factories, women, banned by law from the most hazardous jobs, were permitted by law and by custom to build blue stacks. In the United States, custom — not law — forbade their employment in any lead-using departments.[24] The "setting crew" stacked the lead "buckles" inside ceramic pots containing a few ounces of dilute acetic acid, usually vinegar [...]. Then they filled the stack-house room with layer upon layer of spent tanbark, buckle-filled pots, and boards until the "stack" nearly touched the ceiling. After six to fourteen hours, the chemical reaction was complete, transmuting the "blue bed" into a "white bed." The pots now overflowed with the frothy ceruse. The white lead encrusting the buckles often grew so thick as to crack the vessels.[25]

Disassembling the white beds began the riskiest phase of lead production, and was largely carried out by men who, if they spoke at all while they worked, did so in Polish, Czech or Italian. In the worst factories, workers dumped the ceramic pots onto separating tables where they hand-scraped and pounded the flaky lead carbonate from what remained of the buckles. The more modern plants often employed mechanical separators, although the workers who fed these machines still stood in clouds of toxic dust with no protection beyond the bandanna they might wear if the day were not too hot.[26] After the "stripping" and drying processes, laborers dumped the fine powder into wooden casks for shipment.[27]

The Pullman Palace Car Company purchased hundreds of these casks to make paints for their train carriages. In Pullman's paint department, unskilled workers pried off the barrel lid, scooped some of the powder into buckets and blended linseed oil, pigments, and turpentine. Experienced painters then brushed thin coats of the oily suspension to the cars' exteriors. Meanwhile, inside the train cars — within a cloud of turpentine vapors and dust — unskilled painters spread the paint on the ceilings and in the car's tiny dressing rooms. Skilled painters almost never undertook the most hazardous work in the shop — "rubbing down," or sanding each coat in preparation for the next in a series of thin coats. The plant's medical department, which, according to factory investigator Alice Hamilton, "consisted of one old doctor who had been a surgeon in the Civil War," frequently sent lead-poisoned workers to the Cook County Hospital, sometimes within the first month of their employment.[28]

Notes

22 This description draws upon case studies reported by Edward E. Pratt, *Occupational Diseases: A Preliminary Report on Lead Poisoning in the City of New York, with an Appendix on Arsenical Poisoning* (Albany, N.Y., 1912), 454–55 and 478–80.

23 In the plants Pratt investigated, the same workers who built the "blue" beds also stripped the white beds, *Occupational Diseases*, 451. Excellent descriptions of the stack process appear in Gordon Thayer, "The Lead Menace," *Everybody's Magazine*, 1 Mar. 1913.

24 In 1919, Alice Hamilton declared that because of the exclusion of women from most hazardous lead manufacturing jobs, "lead poisoning in women is still a rarity in the Untied States," Hamilton, "Lead Poisoning in American Industry," *The Journal of Industrial Hygiene* 1 (May 1919): 8–22. The 1910 Census of

Manufacturers reported that of 13,618 paint factory employees, only 1,946 were women. Three fifths (1197) of these women worked in the front office. On the factory floor, the most hazardous jobs were highly sex-segregated: only 4 percent were women. Judging by the nearly total exclusion of women from work in American lead smelting and fabrication factories, their numbers in lead paint plants were probably lower than the aggregate data. The great exception to the rule among lead-using industries was the pottery industry; on this subject see Marc Stern, *The Pottery Industry of Trenton: A Skilled Trade in Transition, 1850-1919* (New Brunswick, NJ, 1994).

25 Harrison Brothers and Company, "The Chemistry of Paints" (1890), 10.

26 Pratt, *Occupational Diseases*, 397.

27 Pratt reported the cases of two young Russian Poles at work in the packing rooms who contracted serious lead colic only months after starting work. Pratt, *Occupational Diseases*, 489; 450.

28 For conditions in the Pullman plant, see Alice Hamilton, "What One Stockholder Did," *The Survey* 28 (June 1912): 387-89; and in Hamilton, *Exploring the Dangerous Trades*, 145-48 and 156-69.

Christopher Warren 1999 "Toxic purity: The progressive era origins of America's lead paint poisoning epidemic." *Business History Review* 73, 705-35, 714-16.

2.5 Narrative: a special case for summary

Narratives are organized chronologically: things, people, places are mentioned according to the order in which events occurred. The mentions tell a story.

Scholarly writers meet narratives in many sectors of the disciplines, but they are probably most likely to encounter them in history and literary studies.

When we look at narrative from a summarizer's point of view, we find conditions something like those we have just been investigating in Section 2.4.2. Most mentions are at a low level: particular people and things, particular actions. Consider, for example, the narrative passage on the next page. It is the beginning of the well-known fairy tale "Little Thumb," and can be analyzed for these mentions:

man and wife	7 children, ages 7-10,			a decision
	puny youngest	blaming of youngest, who is silent	no food	"...to lose them in the wood tomorrow"

And we could write a summary from this analysis:

> Having seven sons between the ages of seven and ten, and no food, a man and wife decide to abandon their offspring in the forest. The youngest child is puny, and gets unfairly blamed for everything.

However, such an analysis might raise questions as to the significance of these events and conditions — the connections between blame and abandonment, for example. And some aspects of the story which are evident in the original — the father's ambivalent sentiments, the smallest boy's intelligent silence — are lost in condensation. Telling details vanish. By using the techniques suggested in Section 2.4.2, we can write a more conceptual summary which preserves the effect of these details. We can build the higher levels ourselves by reading for abstractions which interpret the lower-level details.

There was once upon a time a man and his wife, fagot-makers by trade, who had seven children, all boys. The eldest was but ten years old and the youngest only seven.

many children, close in age → ***fertility***
8 males → ***masculine dominance?***
poor → ***poverty***
needy children → ***dependency***

They were very poor, and their seven children incommoded them greatly, because not one of them was able to earn his bread. That which gave them yet more uneasiness was that the youngest was of a very puny constitution, and scarce ever spoke a word, which made them take that for stupidity which was a sign of good sense. He was very little, and when born no bigger than one's thumb, which made him be called Little Thumb.

very small → ***diminutiveness***

LT says quiet → ***reticence***

people are wrong about him → ***misjudgement***

The poor child bore the blame of whatsoever was done amiss in that house, and, guilty or not, was always in the wrong; he was, notwithstanding, more cunning and had far greater share of wisdom than all his brothers put together; and if he spake little he heard and thought the more.

always blamed → ***injustice***

wiser, alert → ***intelligence, attentiveness***

There happened now to come a very bad year, and the famine was so great that these poor people resolved to rid themselves of their children. One evening, when they were all in bed and the fagot-maker was sitting with his wife at the fire, he said to her, with all his heart ready to burst with grief:

they get even poorer →
hardship, scarcity

decide to get rid of children

father is sad → sentiment, love

"Thou seest plainly that we are not able to keep our children, and I cannot face to see them starve to death before my face; I am resolved to lose them in the wood tomorrow, which will be very easily done; for while they are tying up fagots, we may run away and leave them without their taking any notice."

but he plans to leave them → trickery, conspiracy, ambivalence

"Ah!" cried the wife, "and cans't thou thyself have the heart to take thy children out along with thee on purpose to lose them?"

mother loves the boys, protests → love, sentiment, conflict

In vain did her husband represent to her their extreme poverty: she would not consent to it; she was indeed poor, but she was their mother. However having considered what a grief it would be to her to see them perish with hunger, she at last consented, and went to bed all in tears.

mother resists, father persuades → dispute, conflict, persuasion

mother agrees but weeps → grief, regret

Little Thumb heard every word that had been spoken; for observing, as he lay in his bed, that they were talking very busily, he got up softly and hid himself under his father's stool that he might hear what they said without being seen.

LT notices the talk → attentiveness

hides & listens → concealment, cunning

Charles Perrault 1969 "Little Thumb." In *The Blue Fairy Book* ed. Andrew Lang New York: Airmont, 266-67.

This reading for abstraction provides materials for a more conceptual, interpretive summary:

In a situation of great **scarcity**, Little Thumb's parents resolve to abandon their seven hungry sons in the forest. But **scarcity** and

abandonment are complicated by **injustice** in the family — Little Thumb is unfairly blamed for everything — and by **misjudgement** — he is reckoned as dull, when in fact his **intelligence** of the world is sharper than others': he overhears the parents' **conspiracy**. This is a story not only of **hardship** and **scarcity** but also of **concealments** lurking in **abandonment**, hidden **virtue**, and secret **intentions**.

Other summarizers might come up with different abstractions to interpret the story's details, and still others might have different focuses, for example, *fertility* — the abundance of children amidst this scarcity, or *grief* and *ambivalence* — the complexity of the father's sentiments, or *masculine dominance* — the mother is outnumbered by males, and the father overcomes the mother's objections. (If you know the rest of the story, you may remember that Little Thumb and his brothers come to an ogre's house in the forest. The ogre's wife is genuinely concerned for the little boys, while her husband plans to eat them. But Little Thumb outsmarts everybody.)

In literature courses, students are often warned not to retell the story; their papers may be penalized for what their readers call "plot summary." But professional scholars often summarize plot. Here, a literary scholar, publishing in a major journal in the field, summarizes the plot of a novel his readers may or may not know about, although the opening phrase — "**A** novel by **a** Maori writer from New Zealand" — suggests that he estimates that many of his readers do not know about this book:

> A novel by a Maori writer from New Zealand, Witi Ihimaera's *Tangi*, shows how a strategic refusal to accommodate the reader can stand at the very core of a work's meaning.
>
> The story of a young man's coming to terms with the death of his father, *Tangi* revolves around the Maori extended funeral service that gives the book its title. Tama has left the small Maori community in which he was born, gone to the "big city" (Wellington), and found a *pakeha* (white) girlfriend, but by the end of the novel he has decided to come home to take care of the family farm. Though the point is not spelled out, this return, a return to the Maori values represented by Tama's father, entails leaving his *pakeha* girlfriend and, in a larger sense, the *pakeha* world that he has entered in Wellington.
>
> The novel thus is about arrivals and departures and the greetings and partings that accompany them.
>
> Reed Way Dasenbrock 1987 "Intelligibility and meaningfulness in multicultural literature in English." *PMLA* 102, 10-19, 16.

What makes "plot summary" like this acceptable? Its generalizing, interpretive abstractions seem to be the features which distinguish it from the kind of "plot summary" that literature teachers object to. For example, Dasenbrock begins with "strategic refusal to accommodate the reader." This interpretive abstraction brings the story within the range of the research question Dasenbrock is asking: how to understand misunderstanding; how to understand "multicultural literature" without resorting to either the idea that "good" literature is "universal" and should be comprehensible to everybody (we are all the same) or the idea that authentic literature will be understandable only to the particular, local culture which produces it (we are all different).

Exercise

(1) Can you find the other abstractions (or generalities) which interpret the novel Dasenbrock is summarizing? In the passage below, can you find the abstractions which interpret the story another literary scholar, Sidonie Smith, is summarizing?

Apparently conforming to audience expectations that famous people who write their autobiographies will track their rise from obscurity to prominence, [Zora Neale] Hurston begins her narrative in historical origins. In the ethnographic opening, the narrator recalls a frontier culture, locating her story in the history of the Eatonville folk from whence she has come. She chronicles family history, the courtship of her parents, and the subsequent marriage of alternative cultural voices represented by mother and father. The narrative of childhood follows, a pastoral idyll full of fantasy and magic, language and love, increasingly punctuated by the child's developing sense of inner homelessness and fate. Homelessness emerges as the controlling metaphor with the death of the adolescent girl's mother and her subsequent search for economic security and educational opportunities.

Sidonie Smith 1993 *Subjectivity, Identity and the Body: Women's Autobiographical Practices in the Twentieth Century* Bloomington: Indiana UP, 106.

(2) It's not only literary study which turns to summary of narratives. Here is a passage from an article which reports folk story and history in South India, studying these discourses to develop a better understanding of how Christian and Hindu populations

co-exist relatively peacefully in that part of the world, and finding in them an idea of the two religions as "siblings" — "described alternately as contrary and cooperative" (Dempsey 1998).

Find the abstractions which interpret detail in Dempsey's account of folk story and folk history in South India. Identify the details these abstractions interpret.

Independence and Cooperation Between Deity and Devotee

As intimated by these last few stories, the well-being of the community itself (in terms of its members' physical health and ability to perform rituals) may rely significantly upon positive interdynamics between sacred siblings. Rather than simply portraying saints or deities as tending only to their respective religious communities, local stories often associate the sibling duo's relationship with the well-being of all concerned — Christians and Hindus alike. These sibling stories, which portray the well-being of the larger community as being dependent upon peaceful saint-deity relations, express most vividly the connection between the sacred and earthly realms. A Syrian Catholic man in his fifties provided an example of this genre of sacred sibling stories through a tale of Manarkad Mary and Kannaki engaged in yet another sisterly spat:

> These two females are generally on good terms. One day, however, when there was a procession for one of the figures, the two did not look at each other. One of them, I think it was the *devi*, became offended because she was not acknowledged by the other. Following this, there was an epidemic of chicken pox. The temple oracle (*veliccappatu*) cast his divining shells (*kavati*) and found out the reason, which was that the *devi* was offended by the other. Because the people were affected by the quarrel, the two sisters needed to come to a reconciliation and thus today they are friends again.

A Syrian Catholic priest outside Ernakulam relates a similar situation in which broken relations between sacred siblings — this time in Kannur — result in calamity. According to Fr. Anthony, a Hindu tradition enacted during St. Sebastian's annual church procession involves the opening of the main temple doors so that his sister Kali can greet her brother as he passes by her domain. Four to five years ago, village members of the R.S.S., a "fundamentalist" Hindu political party, decided that this local tradition of Hindu-Christian relations had gone far enough. As a tangible symbol of their position, they convinced temple officials to keep Kali's doors closed during St. Sebastian's annual jaunt. Following that year's procession, a number of misfortunes occurred in the Hindu community. As a result community members reasoned, with support from the *pujari* (ritual specialist) at Kali's temple, that the goddess was angry for being kept from her customary viewing of her brother and was therefore seeking revenge by causing trouble. Convinced that interreligious exchange between sacred figures was more to their benefit than exclusivity, the temple resumed its yearly practice of opening its doors to the passing Christians and their saint.[12]

Note

12 As implied by sacred sibling stories, relations between Hindu and Christian communities are not always perfectly harmonious. Religiously motivated political groups in Kerala such as the R.S.S., the Muslim League, and the Congress Party occasionally become forces for interreligious division. Nonetheless, full-blown violence is currently a rarity — something for which many Keralites express great pride.

Corinne G. Dempsey 1998 "Rivalry, reliance, and resemblance: Siblings as metaphor for Hindu-Christian relations in Kerala State." *Asian Folklore Studies* 57, 51-70, 58-59.

(3) Using the reading-and-noting techniques introduced earlier in this chapter, including note-taking for abstraction, write three- to four-sentence summaries of the four narrative fragments below.

(a) "The Goose-Girl" passage is the beginning of a tale from the Brothers Grimm.

The Goose-Girl

Once upon a time an old queen, whose husband had been dead for many years, had a beautiful daughter. When she grew up she was betrothed to a prince who lived a great way off. Now, when the time grew near for her to be married and to depart into a foreign kingdom, her old mother gave her much costly baggage, and many ornaments, gold and silver, trinkets and knickknacks, and, in fact, everything that belonged to a royal trousseau, for she loved her daughter very dearly. She gave her a waiting-maid also, who was to ride with her and hand her over to the bridegroom, and she provided each of them with a horse for the journey. Now the Princess's horse was called Falada, and could speak.

When the hour for departure drew near the old mother went to her bedroom, and taking a small knife she cut her fingers until they bled; then she held a white rag under them, and letting three drops of blood fall into it, she gave it to her daughter, and said: "Dear child, take great care of this rag: it may be of use to you on the journey."

So they took a sad farewell of each other, and the Princess stuck the rag in front of her dress, mounted her horse, and set forth on the journey to her bridegroom's kingdom. After they had ridden for about an hour the princess began to feel very thirsty, and said to her waiting-maid: "Pray get down and fetch me some water in my golden cup out of yonder stream: I would like a drink." "If you're thirsty," said the maid, "dismount yourself, and lie down by the water and drink; I don't mean to be your servant any longer." The Princess was so thirsty that she got down, bent over the stream, and drank, for she wasn't allowed to drink out of the golden goblet. As she drank she murmured: "Oh! heaven, what am I to do?" and the three drops of blood replied:

> "If your mother only knew,
> Her heart would surely break in two."

But the Princess was meek, and said nothing about her maid's rude behaviour, and quietly mounted her horse again. They rode on their way for several miles, but the day was hot, and the sun's rays smote fiercely on them, so that the Princess was soon overcome by thirst again. And as they passed a brook she called once more to her waiting-maid: "Pray get down and give me a drink from my golden cup," for she had long ago forgotten her maid's rude words. But the waiting-maid replied, more haughtily even than before: "If you want a drink, you can dismount and get it: I don't mean to be your servant." Then the Princess was compelled by her thirst to get down, and bending over the flowing water she said: "Oh! heaven, what am I to do?" and the three drops of blood replied:

"If your mother only knew,
Her heart would surely break in two."

Grimm Brothers 1969 "The Goose-Girl." In *The Blue Fairy Book* ed. Andrew
Lang New York: Airmont, 266-67.

(b) The next passage, "School," is from the memoir of Mary
Englund, a transcribed oral history collected in 1980, late in
Englund's life (we encountered another passage from her memoir in
Section 2.3). Englund is answering an historian's questions about her
experience in a residential school in the second decade of the twentieth century. As Englund reports at the beginning of this memoir,
children of school age were gathered from First Nations villages and
settlements by priests, and transported to boarding schools.

School

So anyway this one big girl — she'd been there quite a while
— she took me over to this other building. Way at the back
of the convent was another big building where they did all
the washing and you did your bath and there were square
wooden tubs. You heat the water and you filled it and that's
where you had to have your bath. You didn't go to bed —
when you first got there — without your bath. Every girl
that came in had to be taken to the laundry and put through
the wash. And then you had to take all your clothes off and
leave them there and then they gave you other clothes to put
on. Sort of a uniform. They were white blouses, they buttoned at the back and there was a sort of jumper with frills
around the sleeves and buttoned at the back — 'course I
couldn't button them so I had to have somebody help me —
and underwears and long black stockings and underwears
down to the ankles and then the black stockings over it. Oh
my! It didn't please me. I very seldom had these long big
longjohns on — I would call them now long underwear —
and then these big black stockings on, because at home we
never wore any of those things. We had little panties on down
to the knees with little frills around and I couldn't figure out
these long things and then these stockings over. And then we
had to have garters to hold them up. Then black shoes with
little high-top laces … the only shoes I had were boys' lecky
boots and I thought, "Oh boy I was dressed up." Because we

at home hardly ever wore any shoes. We wore moccasins and we ran all summer bare-footed. I really was uncomfortable. But they were handy when it came cold.

But oh my was I ever homesick. You know home wasn't much, in fact the nuns didn't call it home, they called it our *camp*. And that used to hurt me. It still does when I think about it. When we'd talk about going home, they'd say, "You're not going home, you're going back to your camp." That was their impression of the reserve. Well in a way they were right because the homes we had in those days were made out of great big log houses. And the house we got into didn't even have a floor in it. It was just dirt floor. Then we used to have to every so often go out and chop boughs and put them on the floor just to keep the dust down, until mother was able to get some lumber and put the floor down. You know we were raised in a hard way, so going to school and going in the convent it was very unusual.

This one girl she was very good to me. Apparently she had come from the same reserve but I don't ever remember her. So anyway she was awfully good with me. She helped me in the morning to dress. We were given a basin and a towel, toothpowder and toothbrush and comb. That was ours. We had little squares in the washroom and the washroom was quite a length and all window in front so the Sister could look in from the dormitory. And this great big galvanized trough with the cold water, cold taps, and in there were the basins. You filled up your basin then you went over to the counter — no hot water, all cold water — then you had to scrub your teeth in the sink, then you had to wash your basin and put it underneath the counter. You had to fold up your towel and take it with you and put it at the head of your bed. And there was squares for your comb and your tooth-brush and tooth-powder. So that was our gadgets.

An older girl saw to it that you were dressed. Then of course it took us time to put on these long black stockings and high boots, and laces. And your hair had to be braided at the back and put up in a knob. You couldn't have one little hair hanging on your face. It had to be smoothed back. So she used to help me comb my hair. She'd wet my hair and comb it and braid it here and braid it there, then she'd braid it at the back and roll it up and pin it up. That was the way we were supposed to have our hair. At home we got up, washed our face and we didn't think of combing our hair; we just took it and tied it up and that was it.

We lived a simple life you know and then to go in to one of these places where we didn't know that we didn't have to talk. That was another big thing. Everything was *silent*. You lived by the bell. The bell rang you shut up. Not another word. And here we'd keep on talking, us that were new, and we had to be shushed and shaken and what-not. Then we had to go in lines you see, one behind the other and go upstairs. No matter where you went you were in line. You never moved until the bell rang. There was a little bell always, no matter where you went. Or one of those desk push-bells.

(Englund 1981:58-60)

(c) "New Broom Sweeps Clean" is excerpted from an article reporting the period of US business history when domestic tire manufacturers lost their market dominance, a period which concluded in four of the five major US tire firms being owned by foreign interests.

New Broom Sweeps Clean

Three months after joining the company, John Nevin announced that he would close five of the seventeen North American tire plants, which were then operating at 50 percent of capacity, cut inventories from 16.7 million tires in 1979 to 9.7 million in 1981, and slash the number of different tires produced from 7,300 to 2,600.[95] In addition to restructuring Firestone's North American Tire operations, Nevin also terminated or sold several overseas tire subsidiaries and non-tire businesses. These actions resulted in a sharp reduction in revenues, and 24,000 workers (22 percent in 1979) leaving the payroll. Although some considered Nevin's actions "brutal," one tire-industry analyst concluded that "Nevin did exactly what the board had hired him to do … rescue the company from the brink of financial disaster."[96]

The operational and financial results of Nevin's actions were dramatic. After these steps, Firestone's remaining tire facilities ran at 91 percent of capacity, North American operating profit increased from a $31 million loss in 1979 to a profit of $85 million in 1981, and debt was pared to 29 percent of book equity in 1981 from its peak of 70 percent the previous year.[97] Firestone's average annual return to shareholders in Nevin's first two years was 41 percent, easily outperforming both the rest of the tire industry at 32 percent and the S&P index return of 14 percent. A consultant to Firestone observed "that Nevin did more in five weeks than had been done in the previous fifty years."[98]

What Nevin needed to do was pretty obvious, and one advisor noted that "you could almost outline the restructuring on a piece of paper ... that company had overcapacity and it was pretty simple to figure out which plants were worst."[99] The specific steps Nevin took in restructuring Firestone, however, provide insights into the sources of inertia. When Nevin arrived at Firestone, he found the incumbent management team "a bunch of clones" who all viewed the world in the same way, an observation that he shared with a reporter from a national business magazine.[100] Nevin quickly proceeded to hire outside managers who brought a fresh perspective to the tire business, and by 1983 only five of the twenty-five corporate officers remained from 1979.[101] The influx of outside managers rankled many Firestone veterans, who resented having to "humiliate themselves and take advice from these young Harvard Business School people who think they know everything."[102] Nevin, in contrast, believed that some of the outsiders were not aggressive enough. He replaced Firestone's CFO three times in as many years, leading the wife of one Firestone executive to quip "John, I hope you're not planning to make this an annual event."[103] Nevin also raised the number of outsiders on Firestone's board from 4 of 10 when he joined, to 7 of 12 two years later.[104]

To drive necessary plant closure, Nevin bypassed the traditional channels within Firestone in gathering data, and instead engaged an outside consulting firm to gather market information. He personally met with Firestone's top 100 managers, over 100 sales people, all three automotive companies and over 200 dealers and store managers in his first four months on the job.[105] To analyze the data and evaluate alternatives, Nevin relied on a team of six hand picked executives whom he forbade to discuss their work with anyone else in the company.[106] Although previous investment and disinvestment proposals had always gone through the Executive Committee before moving on to the board, Nevin took his initial restructuring proposal directly to the board without consulting anyone but Riley, whom he informed of his recommendations the night before the March 1980 board meeting.[107] "We were shocked," recalls board member Lee Brodeur. "He made one big move and bango we closed five plants."[108] In the months that followed his initial restructuring proposal, Nevin repeatedly bypassed the Executive Committee and brought recommendations to close or sell operations directly to the board.[109]

After initially circumventing Firestone's bottom-up investment process, Nevin later dismantled it altogether. In his first board meeting as CEO, Nevin stripped the Executive Committee of responsibility for "new plants, major expansions, acquisitions, new business ventures, and major capital expenditures." He also mandated that the six-member committee include three outside directors, although it had historically consisted solely of insiders. Nevin also dissolved the Appropriations Committee of line managers that screened capital requests at the behest of the Executive Committee.[110] Six months later Nevin assumed the Chair of the Executive Committee, and decreased its membership to himself, one other inside manager, and three outside board members, thereby seizing what little influence the Executive Committee still had.[111]

Nevin also took steps to dissolve historical relationships with customers and employees. Private brand customers had grown accustomed to Firestone bearing the costs of short production runs, warehousing, and carrying large inventories and were shocked when Nevin stated that Firestone would only sell tires with a 15 percent return on investment, and proceeded to slash the least profitable 60 percent of the private brand business.[112] While sharply curtailing the private brand business, the new CEO maintained relationships with automakers, primarily to maintain the company's attractiveness as an acquisition for a foreign tire maker trying to enter the U.S. market.[113]

Firestone's relationships with employees were shattered through repeated layoffs and management's new policy of pitting one plant against another to ensure their survival.[114] While sympathetic to veteran managers' concern for their employees, Nevin also realized that this loyalty had driven Firestone to the brink of bankruptcy, and wanted to replace the implicit contract of loyalty in exchange for lifetime employment with a new deal that emphasized pay for performance. "Philosophically," Nevin later recalled, "I believe very strongly that executives should get rewarded in some direct relation to shareholder value."[115] Nevin fundamentally restructured Firestone's incentive structure to reflect this change in values. Nevin granted stock options extensively at all levels of the organization, and instituted performance-based bonuses for top executives which could reach 25 to 50 percent of their base pay if the company and their divisions met or exceeded budget.[116]

Nevin also took a series of actions that had tremendous symbolic impact in signaling the break with Firestone's traditional values. He kept his distance from the Akron tire elite, maintaining his house in Chicago and renting a small apartment in Akron, well outside the five block radius where most top tire executives lived.[117] He later moved corporate headquarters to Chicago, in part to distance the company's top executives from its Akron past.[118] In what was perhaps the most symbolic break from the past, however, Nevin sold off the Firestone Country Club in 1981, ending a decades old tradition, and inspiring a flurry of hostile press in Akron.[119]

Notes
95 Nevin, "The Bridgestone/Firestone Story," 114–132.
96 Zachary Schiller and Marc Frons, "John Nevin Rescued Firestone," *Business Week*, 11 May 1987, 96.
97 Ibid.
98 Managing Director of Management Consulting Firm, interview with author, tape recording, Boston, Mass., 19 Sept. 1994. This consultant, who consented to an interview under the condition of anonymity, had worked closely with John Nevin.
99 Ibid.
100 Nevin interview; Brodeur interview.
101 Robert W. Ackerman, "Firestone, Inc.," Harvard Business School, Case 9-388-127 (1988): 13.
102 Brodeur interview.
103 Nevin interview.
104 *Proxy Statements* (1979–1982).
105 *Transcript of John Nevin's Remarks to the Annual Stockholder's Meeting* (9 Feb. 1980).
106 Nevin interview.
107 Ibid.
108 Brodeur interview.
109 *Minutes of the Board of Directors' Meetings* (16 Sept. 1980, 21 Oct. 1980, 17 Mar. 1981, 16 June 1981).

110 *Minutes of the Board of Directors' Meeting* (19 Aug. 1980).
111 *Minutes of the Board of Directors' Meeting* (28 Feb. 1981).
112 Reese interview.
113 Nevin interview.
114 Ibid. See also "Surviving Shakedown:Three Firestone Plants Pro-
      vide Contrasts in Survival," *Akron Beacon Journal*, 21 Jan. 1980.
115 Nevin interview.
116 For general discussion of traditional and revised management
      incentives see Nevin, Brodeur and Gilbert interviews.
117 Nevin interview; Love and Giffels, *The Wheels of Fortune*, 261.
118 Nevin interview.
119 Love and Giffels, *The Wheels of Fortune*, 261.

Donald N. Sull 1999 "The dynamics of standing still: Firestone Tire & Rubber and the radial revolution." *Business History Review* 73, 430-464, 449-53.

(d) Providing historical context for a study of medical practice
(and malpractice) in a coastal British Columbian village,
passage (d), "Alert Bay," intersects with both (b) and (c) above.
It tells about the colonial period leading up to the era of residential schools which Englund remembers; it also reports a period of
international commerce: "foreign" and "domestic" interests coming into contact, as they did in the period which saw changes in
the US tire industry.

Alert Bay
The first recorded European contact with the Kwak-
waka'wakw was the arrival of Captain George Vancouver in
1792, who described his visit to a village at the mouth of the
Nimpkish River, located directly across Johnstone Strait from
Alert Bay [....]

The Kwakwaka'wakw became actively involved in the fur
trade during the first half of the nineteenth century and in
1849, the Hudson's Bay Company established Fort Rupert in
the central Kwakwaka'wakw area. To the Kwakwaka'wakw,
the new opportunities for trade and the increasing availability
of European manufactured goods provided an opportunity
for the elaboration of the central institution of aboriginal
society: the potlatch. Potlatches became more frequent and
access to, and the ability to accumulate, large amounts of
European goods became a determining factor in achieving
rank. During the fur trade era, such an elaboration of the
potlatch did not directly conflict with the objectives of the

Europeans, who were clearly interested in trade rather than settlement. Ships' logs and journals kept by traders testify to the fact that Native peoples on the Northwest Coast exercised significant control over the trade by such means as withholding furs to drive up prices, placing "advance orders" for specific trade goods, and refusing to trade unless satisfied with the goods being offered in exchange.

The latter half of the nineteenth century brought with it the collapse of the European and Asian fur markets and, consequently, the decline of the fur trade. This corresponded to the advent of the Gold Rush and the beginning of intensive and permanent European settlement on the B.C. coast. These years mark the period during which basic colonial structures that continue to shape the relationship between Euro-Canadians and Native peoples came into being. On the [British Columbian] coast, as elsewhere, the decimation of the aboriginal population by epidemic diseases brought by Europeans played a major role in establishing the foundations of this relationship. Indigenous people found themselves rapidly becoming minorities in their own lands, and while a certain degree of economic independence could be maintained by continuing to live off the land, social demoralization, sickness, and dependence on European medical care to cure European diseases began to take their toll.

As early as 1787 epidemics of smallpox, influenza and measles had been recorded among the native populations of B.C. However, with more and more Indians traveling to trading forts and camping around new cities like Victoria, these contagious diseases, against which the Indians had neither natural immunity nor effective medicine, began to threaten their very existence. [In 1862, a white man with small pox arrived in Victoria from San Francisco. The disease reached the Native camps around the city, killing many people. The survivors returned to their coastal communities, taking the disease with them. The only medical aid available was provided by missionaries.] [...] The first census of the Kwak-waka'wakw was conducted by John Work around 1835 and he estimated the total population to be around 10,700. Fifty years later, in 1885, this figure had dropped by approximately 72 percent, to around 3000.

Dara Culhane Speck 1987 *An Error in Judgement: The Politics of Medical Care in an Indian/White Community* Vancouver, B.C.: Talonbooks, 70-72.

Works Cited

Bakhtin, Mikhail. 1981. *The Dialogic Imagination*, ed. M. Holquist, trans. C. Emerson and M. Holquist. Austin: U of Texas P.

Chafe, Wallace. 1994. *Discourse, Consciousness, and Time*. Chicago: U of Chicago P.

Coates, Jennifer. 1996. *Women Talk: Conversation between Women Friends* Cambridge, MA: Blackwell.

Mayes, Patricia. 1990. "Quotation in spoken English" *Studies in Language* 14(1): 325-63.

Myers, Greg. 1999. "Functions of reported speech in group discussions" *Applied Linguistics* 20(5): 376-401.

3

Arrangements for readers, arrangements for speakers

The previous chapter found writers taking a position in relation to other speakers, and this chapter continues to explore writers' opportunities to take a position.

However, it is not only the writers who occupy positions in the research community: readers themselves also occupy positions in it — sometimes near the writer, sometimes further away. Sections on **definition** and **apposition** describe means of negotiating the space between writer and reader. Furthermore, cited speakers also occupy various positions — in relation to one another, and to the reader. Sections on **arrangements for speakers** describe means of bringing several voices together to speak to one another, and to the reader.

3.1 Definitions and appositions

In Chapter Two, we found that sometimes — mainly in narrative — we have to make interpretive abstractions to build higher levels from some fairly concrete, lower-level foundations.

Most passages you summarize, however, will already be built up to higher levels, and will present you with ready-made abstractions (which is not to say that you cannot then build a little higher still, or cantilever the higher levels with your own interpretive abstractions). Since these abstractions in themselves condense and interpret lower-level specifics, you will probably transfer them from the original to your summary.

Summarizing this passage (which follows from a passage we looked at in Chapter Two) —

> Since it is imagined, a sense of community is not limited to a specific geographic locale (Gupta and Ferguson 1992). Immigrants are said to live in "binational communities" (Baca and Bryan 1980), "extended communities" (Whiteford 1979), "transnational communities" in "hyperspace" (Rouse 1991), and "transnational families" (Chavez 1992). These concepts highlight the connections migrants maintain with life in their home communities; living dislocated on the other side of a political border does not necessarily mean withdrawing from community or membership.
> (Chavez 1994:54)

— I keep the abstraction *transnational communities*:

> Chavez's work (1994) on undocumented immigrants offers new perspectives on transnational communities.

But now I might consider that my readers may not all be familiar with Chavez's work, or familiar enough with the term "transnational communities" to be exactly sure of what I mean to say that Chavez has said. So I'm going to *define* the term, using a grammatical structure called an **appositive**:

> Chavez's work (1994) on undocumented immigrants offers new perspectives on transnational communities: communities, that is, whose members leave their homes and settle in another country but nevertheless maintain important connections with those original homes.

In effect, I say "transnational communities" *again* — in other words. By doing so, I recognize the position of my readers, and their possible unfamiliarity with or uncertainty about the term. I recognize the term as somewhat specialized, and limited in its distribution — at least for the time being — to certain research genres. I also demonstrate a respect for the complexity of the term: its capacity to capture cumulative reasoning of people researching issues in human migration. At the same time, by using my own words, I am developing my position on the concept — my emphasis, my version.

Definitions bring important terms into focus. For readers who need some clarification, definition sharpens the picture; it helps me to address readers unfamiliar with Chavez, or with the particular research tradition in which he works.

But definition is by no means only for the purpose of informing the uninformed. For readers already familiar with the term, definition confirms common ground: I hope they will identify with the spirit of my definition. In this case, definition has the goal of corroborating and engaging what the informed reader already knows, involving this established knowledge in developing a discussion. So, for example, when a colleague and I investigated academic readers' responses to student writing (Giltrow and Valiquette 1994), one of our subjects, a criminologist, stopped at a student's use of the term "probation," and said it should be defined. At first this surprised us: surely a criminologist would know what "probation" meant. After all, we *non*-criminologists know what it means: we read the papers and watch TV news and crime shows; we hear about probation. But, reflecting, we realized that this was a situation where the reader wanted the term displayed and inspected — for its components of surveillance and institutional measures of improvement and normalization. Displayed, these components would also have spoken to the overall research question of the essay, which inquired into policies regarding young offenders and historical definitions of deviance and correction.

Appositives

More on appositives in Chapter Five, but for now, we can say that an appositive creates a structure with equivalent material on each side of it, for example:

They left a mess: empty soft-drink cans, styrofoam cups, fast-food wrappers.

     a mess   empty soft-drink cans, Styrofoam cups, fast-food wrappers

Exercise: Complete these sentences with appositives – that is, by saying the underlined term again, in other words.

Sample: Despite their nomadic lifestyle, RVers studied by Counts and Counts (1994), exhibit territoriality: an identification with the spaces they temporarily occupy.

Little Thumb experiences injustice:

Referring to social practices such as dating, sex education, and provision of spousal benefits, Calhoun (1994) describes their outcome as the heterosexualization of desire:

Mary Englund's memoir of life in a residential school suggests a regime of surveillance:

As instruments of definition, appositives can help the writer to develop a position by narrowing the application of an abstraction. In this passage —

> Academic knowledge is now generally recognized to be a social accomplishment, the outcome of a cultural activity shaped by ideology and constituted by agreement between a writer and a potentially sceptical discourse community.
>
> Ken Hyland 1999 "Academic attribution: Citation and the construction of disciplinary knowledge." *Applied Linguistics* 20, 3, 341-67, 341.

— "social accomplishment" could mean a lot of things. What does it mean for knowledge to be *social*? What is it about knowledge that makes it an *accomplishment*? Using an appositive, the writer specifies what "social" will mean in this case, and also unpacks terms hidden in "social accomplishment": *cultural activity, ideology, community*. Appositives are a relatively unobtrusive way of activating an abstraction or specialized term. While a more extensive definition might inappropriately suggest that the reader is ignorant, the appositive quickly enriches established understandings or improves uncertain ones. By doubling a mention, appositives intensify the atmosphere around an abstraction.

We have been looking at definitions introduced by colon or comma, but other structures can also open a sentence for an appositive definition. Parentheses can do this, and so can "or." Explanatory footnotes can elaborate a term. Or nearly synonymous terms can accumulate to confirm the sense in which a term in being used. The next passage shows some of these techniques. Here, an historian reports his study of the controversy in the 1920s surrounding the unsolved murder of a young Scottish nanny working for a well-to-do family on the west coast of Canada, a case in which the racist press and political figures accused the family's Asian butler. Kerwin interprets these events through a series of accumulating abstractions, which I have emphasized in bold.

> **Contemporary knowledge (or "discourses") about racial biology**, the effects of race-mixing, and the ability of two races to live within the same nation limited the vocabulary of the major players in this story, setting the ground rules for the debate. **Scientific knowledge of the day**, which concluded that miscegenation between Europeans and Asians was biologically disastrous, was **common sense** to people like Victor Odlum and Mary Ellen Smith. **Dominant understandings of British Columbia's history**, constructed through various narratives,

further shaped interpretations of the Janet Smith case and the **"problem" of miscegenation**.

Scott Kerwin 1999 "The Janet Smith Bill of 1924 and the language of race and nation in British Columbia." *BC Studies* 121, 83-114, 104.

Notice that Kerwin places the more specialist abstraction "discourses" in parentheses, to elaborate on "contemporary knowledge." Doubling the two terms like this both (1) improves our sense of what "discourses" are, reminding us that a discourse is a form of knowledge and that it carries the signs of its historical period, and (2) attaches "contemporary knowledge ... about racial biology" to other research that inquires into the themes and preoccupations of public discussion — into "discourses," that is. (I have just made my own appositive definition of "discourses" here.) The doubling also selects the sense in which the term "discourses" is being used in this passage.

Like summary, definition has a classroom history as a form of expression called for by teachers to see if students have committed something to memory.

Bhatia (1993:7-8), referring to the work of John Swales, describes a focus on definition in research writing as "misleading": closer analysis, he says, reveals that, in science writing at least, definition belongs to the genres of the textbook (students are told what a term means) and examinations (students repeat what they have been told). The research genres of science, he says, do not rely on definition. It's possible that Bhatia's observation develops from different social settings and motivations for definition: in textbooks and examinations, definitions clearly construct first the reader of the textbook as uninformed and then the exam-writer of the definition as only recently informed and now just barely informed. (Or this observation may develop from the somewhat different roles definitions play in the humanities on the one hand and the sciences on the other hand, and the social sciences between these two hands — a circumstance which we will begin to inquire into below.) For, in fact, definitions do occur in scientific research articles. Here the technical term and its acronym — "traditional ecological knowledge (TEK)" — *follow* the non-specialist abstractions "expertise of local hunters" and "local expertise."

> Beluga whales (*Delphinapterus leucas*) are circumpolar in distribution and are hunted by indigenous peoples throughout the Arctic (Kleinberg et al., 1964). While some previous biological research on belugas has used the expertise of local hunters to plan the research and to add to data gathered from scientific observations (e.g., Frost and Lowry, 1990), a practice which continues through

the work of the Alaska Beluga Whale Committee (Adams et al., 1993), little has been done to document systematically such local expertise, also known as traditional ecological knowledge (TEK). The primary purpose of this research was to capture TEK data in order to (1) describe beluga ecology as seen by indigenous hunters and elders and (2) identify specific contributions such data can make to scientific understanding of beluga ecology.

Henry Huntington and the Communities of Buckland, Elim, Koyuk, Point Lay, and Shaktoolik 1999 "Traditional knowledge of the ecology of beluga whales (*Delphinapterus leucas*) in the Eastern Chukchi and Northern Bering Seas, Alaska." *Arctic* 52, 1, 49-61, 69.

Exercise

This passage introduces an article on methods of decision-making in the management of fisheries: ways of deciding, for example, when and for how long to permit fishing, what size of catch to allow, and how to control ecological factors affecting fish habitat. It acknowledges the competing interests and contexts in which such decisions are made: while marine biologists count fish stocks, proponents of ecological concerns advocate certain measures, and those whose livelihoods depend on catching fish may advocate other measures. The authors of this article recommend "fisheries management science" as an approach to this situation, and focus on *risk* as a term of this "science." In a two- or three-sentence summary of this passage, include a definition of *risk*. What does *risk* mean in this context? (And why is it an important concept in this context?)

> Recent and spectacular resource crises have brought pressure on fisheries management agencies to change the way they do business. Shortcomings of current fisheries management systems include the inability to account for the inherent uncertainty of fisheries systems, and the inability to meet a multiplicity of fisheries objectives such as socio-economic and operational management considerations in decision-making (Hannesson, 1996). Future management must focus on management of integrated fisheries, rather than solely on fish populations (Larkin, 1988). This integrated emphasis will require a change in approach and development of modified methodologies to allow evaluation of options against a suite of diverse management objectives including conservation,

economics, and social and operational considerations within a stochastically varying system. This requires conceptual change towards analysis of fisheries management decisions characterized by an integration of traditional biological science methods with operational management considerations and a scientific approach to decision-making. In previous papers we coined the term "fisheries management science" to describe this approach (Stephenson and Lane, 1995).

Making decisions in fisheries management, as with all practical management decision problems, involves what in common parlance is termed "risk". Specifically, the outcomes of decisions depend on occurrences beyond our control that may have undesirable consequences. Since most decision problems cannot be avoided, it is incumbent on decision makers to deal with all potential consequences of proposed actions — undesirable and otherwise — and to include their possibilities of occurrence in developing and evaluating decision alternatives. The extent to which decision alternatives must be considered, and undesirable outcomes may occur, provide a measure of the riskiness of the decision problem. The absence of this notion of "risk analysis" in decision-making is a major weakness in fisheries management systems.

From the decision analysis literature, it is generally accepted that "risk analysis" is comprised of two components: (i) risk assessment and (ii) risk management (Balson *et al.*, 1992). Risk assessment is the process that evaluates possible outcomes or consequences and estimates their likelihood of occurrence as a function of a decision taken and the probabilistic realization of the uncontrollable state dynamics of the system. Hilborn *et al.* (1993), for example, describe the results of this risk analysis component through a simple two-dimensional decision table model. Risk management is a process whereby decision makers use information from risk assessment to compare and evaluate decision alternatives.

D.E. Lane and R.L. Stephenson 1998 "A framework for risk analysis in fisheries decision-making." *ICES Journal of Marine Science* 55, 1-13, 1-2.

3.1.1 Sustained definitions

Definition can be as short as a gesture — a brief delay in the discussion as an abstraction is glossed and readers make contact with its complexity.

But definition can also command more sustained attention. The researcher writing in a marine-science journal, above, takes some time to dwell on the phenomenon of *risk*. In the next passage, an economist leads up to a definition of *revolution*. The definition presents this event not in the usual political or historical terms but in new, economic or market ones: entrepreneurship, clients, employees, property transfer.

> The potential revolutionary leader is an entrepreneur who recruits, deploys, and compensates insurgents. The potential revolutionary leader maximizes the expected wealth of his clientele, which is an alternative set of property owners and/or an alternative parasitic ruling class. A revolution in this theory is an attempt to depose the incumbent ruler and his clientele in favor of the revolutionary leader and his clientele. In other words, a revolution attempts either to establish new property rights, or to enthrone a new ruling class, or both.
>
> Herschel I Grossman 1999 "Kleptocracy and revolutions." *Oxford Economic Papers* 51, 267-83, 268.

It is quite challenging and (to me) unusual to think about revolution in this way instead of in terms of oppression and liberation, or disorder and violence. Happily, Grossman doesn't rest with just one statement of the definition. He **doubles the definition**, and says it again — "[i]n other words."

Exercise

Using an appositive, write a one-sentence definition of *revolution* — "According to Grossman (1999) ...."

In the next passage, a philosopher conducts one stage of his inquiry into ways to understand debate over gun control.

> Most defenders of private gun ownership claim we do have a moral right [to bear arms] — as well as a constitutional one — and this right is not an ordinary right but a fundamental one [....]

If they are correct, they would have the justificatory upper hand. Were this a fundamental right, it would not be enough to show that society would benefit from controlling access to guns.[1] The arguments for gun control would have to be overwhelming. Yet there is also a hefty cost in claiming that this is a fundamental right: the evidence for the right must meet especially rigorous standards.

What makes a right fundamental? A fundamental right is a non-derivative right protecting a *fundamental* interest. Not every interest we individually cherish is fundamental. Since most interests are prized by someone, such a notion of "fundamental interest" would be anemic, serving no special justificatory role. Fundamental interests are special; they are integrally related to a person's chance of living a good life, *whatever her particular interests, desires, and beliefs happen to be.* For example, living in a society that protects speech creates an environment within which each of us can pursue our particular interests, goals, needs, and development, whatever our interests happen to be. Is the purported right to bear arms like this paradigmatic fundamental right?

Note

1 Todd C. Hughes and Lester H. Hunt, "The Liberal Basis of the Right to Bear Arms," *Public Affairs Quarterly* (in press).

Hugh LaFollette 2000 "Gun control." *Ethics* 110, 263-81, 264.

Here the definition advances the inquiry. Rather than activate readers' established knowledge of the abstraction *fundamental right* or improve or clarify their understanding of the term, LaFollette stipulates the exact conditions that must be met for a right to be "fundamental." This contribution advances the inquiry by bringing the focus of the discussion to a particularly elusive and potentially controversial abstraction.

Exercise

Write a two- or three-sentence definition of *fundamental right*: "In LaFollette's discussion (2000) of the elements of debate over gun control, a **fundamental right** is…." You may want to include in your definition what is *not* a *fundamental right*. You might also try to come up with an example of a fundamental right other than the one LaFollette uses (freedom of speech). And you might find that his definition still leaves some things unclear, or uncertain. If so, you can include this uncertainty in your definition: "It is unclear from this part of LaFollette's discussion whether…."

The following passage also uses definition to advance the inquiry. In a discussion of savings and proposals for taxation reform, an economist presents the "mainstream" definition of *savings* and its operation in measuring rates of saving in the US economy, and then offers an alternative definition of *savings*. His alternative definition paves the way for revised perspectives on tax-inducements to saving.

> In the early 1970s [the personal saving rate in the US] averaged more than 8 percent, while it had fallen to near 5 percent by the mid-1980s, or a decline of more than one-third from its initial value. By 1994, according to government statistics, the rate had fallen further, to just under 4 percent, although it bounced back to nearly 5 percent in 1995 (with roughly $250 billion in saving, and disposable income nearing $5 trillion).
>
> However, it is important to clarify just what the term saving means in this context. Saving is being computed as the amount remaining from disposable income after subtracting consumption, interest payments made by individuals, and money paid to recipients abroad (as when a worker in the United States sends part of his or her income to family members living in other countries). Typically, the latter category is minuscule (totaling 0.2 percent of disposable income in 1995), while interest payments are more significant (usually amounting to more than half of total computed personal saving).
>
> It turns out, however, that several of the items included in personal consumption expenditures are hardly examples of profligacy. Purchases of durable goods, such as automobiles, furniture, and appliances, are counted as consumption, not saving. Expenditures for education are similarly counted as consumption. In other words, what consumers do to invest in their long-term economic well-being is counted as consumption, rather than saving.
>
> Since saving will increase every time that consumption decreases (assuming a constant level of disposable income — which is both a crucial assumption and an incorrect one), this means that a policy that decreases private expenditures on higher education, for example, would be saving-enhancing. It is worth noting, therefore, that more saving should not automatically be associated with being thrifty or far-sighted in any meaningful sense.
>
> For some reasons, of course, it is perfectly reasonable to define saving in the way that the government's statistics do. The problem is not the statistics, but the uses to which they are put. Nevertheless, the purest definition of saving would be the amount of resources produced in the economy in a given year that are not

consumed today but are put to use in a way that will provide returns to the economy in years to come. (Not coincidentally, this is also the purest definition of investment.) The problem with the definitions of saving commonly used is that they imply that the household sector never makes any purchases that have long-term payoffs. Only private businesses do so.

Neil H Buchanan 1999 "Taxes, saving, and macroeconomics." *Journal of Economic Issues* 33, 1, 59-75, 60-61.

Exercise
In three or four sentences, summarize Buchanan's account of competing definitions of "saving." (You might remember LaFollette's technique of asking a question to stage a definition: "What makes a right fundamental?" Maybe experiment with that technique here.)

Sometimes definition works on **how words are used**, rather than committing the writer (and reader) to a particular use of the term. Here researchers on the processes which turn occurrences into public events analyse how the terms *parade* and *march* are used by both lay people and researchers.

Insiders may accept these forms [of public action] as natural categories of action, while detached observers can observe the ways in which the categories themselves are constructed and evolve over time. The "protest" is one such ritualized form that conveys roughly the same meaning to activists, police, news reporters, the general public, and social scientists alike. This shared meaning has blinded researchers to the constructed nature of "protest" and led them to assume an unproblematic isomorphism between form and content in their definitions of protest events. But, as Tilly (1978) first told us 20 years ago, the forms or repertoires of protest shift across time and space and new forms of protest are often created by adapting nonprotest forms to new purposes. Identical forms may carry very different content. "Parade" and "march" are two names for exactly the same form (McPhail and Wohlstein 1986), and the words can be used interchangeably even though in the United States in the 1990s the popular connotations of *parade* involve entertainment, while the word *march* popularly applies only to message events. Likewise, there are many kinds of rallies, from pep rallies to protest rallies: they share the form of a stationary gathering with speeches containing informational and emotional content, but vary greatly in the "issue" they may address. As protest repertoires evolve, message content is often added to event types created for other purposes. In the United States in the 1990s, ceremonies, musical performances, literature distribution, and amateur street theater are all event types that are typically "apolitical," but all have carried protest content in past times and places and can and do sometimes carry protest content in the 1990s.

At any given time, there are certainly regularities and patterns about the kinds of content conveyed in various forms, but these meanings are always contextual and always evolving. Block parties are generally understood in the United States in this era to be consensual events that convey a sense of sociability and community to residents of a particular area although they do disrupt normal traffic patterns because they require closing a street. However, using a barricade to close a street without permission has been internationally recognized as a protest tactic since the French Revolution. In the context of ongoing student-police battles in the late 1960s, when countercultural residents blocked Madison's Mifflin Street for a block party, the police treated the event as an insurrection, and the ensuing battle between police and residents became a full-scale riot.

Pamela E. Oliver and Daniel J. Myers 1999 "How events enter the public sphere." *American Journal of Sociology* 105, 1, 38-67, 40-41.

Exercise

(1) Write a two- or three-sentence summary of Oliver and Myers' account of the meaning of *march* and *parade*. (What is the significance of this distribution of meanings? What does the discussion of the *block party* add to our understanding of people's ways of naming public events?)

(2) In *Verbal Hygiene* (1995), from which the next passage is excerpted, Deborah Cameron, a linguist, investigates attitudes towards language: people's tendency to associate certain features of speech and writing with decency and orderliness, and other features with slovenliness and defiance. Her analysis of a particular historical expression of such attitudes makes use of an abstraction — *moral panic* — which has been at work in other

disciplines: social theory, criminology, and, as she says, "cultural [history]." In the passage below, she provides a long definition of *moral panic.*

Summarize this passage by note-taking for gist, and then assemble these gists to compose your own definition of *moral panic.* You can elaborate this definition by (1) finding other examples of moral panic, from your experience; (2) explaining why moral panic is an important focus for inquiry; and/or (3) reflecting on the role of the media in producing moral panic.

Appositives

"... attitudes towards language: people's tendency to associate certain features of speech with decency and ..." – this is an appositive. It restricts the possible application of "attitudes towards language" for this case, concentrating on moralizing ones, for the time being, and disallowing ones which might be about bi-lingualism, for example, or tourism in non-English-speaking countries.

Moral Panic

I am going to suggest that the grammar furore [controversy over school curriculum in Britain in the 1980s and early 1990s, accompanied by many claims in the press and from political figures that young people didn't know grammar, and were illiterate] bears more than a passing resemblance to the sort of periodic hysteria cultural historians have labelled "moral panic" (Cohen 1987). Although there are differences as well as similarities, I believe the parallel is an illuminating one if we wish to understand why, in Simon Jenkins's words, "the nation's grammar stir[red] the political juices". Before we consider the grammar debate itself, it is therefore worth looking more generally at the phenomenon of moral panic.

A moral panic can be said to occur when some social phenomenon or problem is suddenly foregrounded in public discourse and discussed in an obsessive, moralistic and alarmist manner, as if it betokened some imminent catastrophe. In the past hundred years in Europe and America we have had outbreaks of this kind centring on prostitution and "white slavery", drugs, the "Jewish problem", juvenile delinquency, venereal disease, immigration, communism, overpopulation, pornography, rock music and pit bull terriers.

These are not claimed as cases of moral panic simply because they inspired public anxiety: some degree of concern about many of them would be perfectly reasonable. But there are times when concern goes far beyond what is reasonable. In the words of the criminologist Jock Young, "moral panic"' describes 'cases where public reaction [is] completely disproportionate to the actual problem faced' (*Guardian*, Letters, 9 July 1994). In a moral panic the scale of the problem is exaggerated, its causes are analysed in simplistic terms, anxiety about it climbs to intolerable levels, and the measures proposed to alleviate it are usually extreme and punitive. Analysts have suggested there are underlying sociological reasons why public concern gets "out of hand" in this way; and that vested interests are often at work encouraging it to do so.

Moral panic works by channelling, at least temporarily, the diffuse anxieties and hostilities that exist in any society towards a single, simple problem, such as "drugs", "Jews" or "communism". The discovery of the "problem" entails the creation of a scapegoat — the junkie, the fifth columnist, the Zionist conspirator. This generic "folk devil" is usually identified with a real social group, whose members then bear the brunt of hostility and blame. Moral panic thus has the potential to lead to such extreme forms of repression as witch-hunts and pogroms, and in some cases may even be orchestrated for that purpose.

Scholars have suggested that moral panic in the form we know it is a product of the modern mass media [....] The most commonplace incident or pedestrian report can be turned into an issue by media attention, whereas without that attention the same incident would go unnoticed and the report would gather dust. Having thus established something as an issue, the media can return to it under the guise of "responding to public concern" — even though that concern is of their own making.

Deborah Cameron 1995 *Verbal Hygiene* London: Routledge, 82-83.

Formal definition, expanded definition

In composing these definitions, you may be helped by techniques which have been derived from classical rhetoric and elaborated since then in composition studies. These techniques focus first on the thing-to-be-defined, using the syntactic structure of a particular kind of sentence to accomplish this focus. Taking the thing-to-be-defined as its subject, the formal sentence definition isolates the entity for scrutiny; the expanded definition relocates the entity or phenomenon in the world. Appendix A describes techniques for composing formal sentence definitions, and for expanding those definitions.

(3) In the passage below, John McGuire, a social historian, is talking about capital punishment, and analysing episodes in the history of capital punishment in Australia. Everyday experience might lead us to expect that he will focus on the debate over whether there should be capital punishment at all, but, actually, his focus is on the staging of the act itself. He refers to Michel Foucault's famous and compelling account (*Discipline and Punish: The Birth of the Prison* 1979 [1975]) of the transformation of public execution — grisly and fatal tortures performed before large audiences of citizens — into the much less public techniques of punishment carried on in modern prisons. But McGuire also says that Foucault's interpretation of the history of state-sponsored punishment is now competing with another interpretation: Norbert Elias's theory of the "civilizing process" (which does not [necessarily] mean the process of things getting better and better).

Summarizing this passage, write a two- or three-sentence definition of *civilizing process*, using techniques of capital punishment as examples of the phenomenon. (To get an angle on this discussion, you might consider that the popular imagination of capital punishment nowadays derives from film and TV representations of execution: death row, the last meal, the condemned person strapped into the electric chair or injected with a lethal substance or collared by the hangman's rope. It's a sequestered event, observed not by throngs but by the few who have credentials to witness it —

chaplain, warden, sometimes a small gallery including reporters, and the family of the convict or victim. Or, at least, that's how popular culture has arranged for *us* to witness this event. So we might have questions to ask about the role of film and television in transforming the spectacle of capital punishment.)

> The decision to conceal the execution ritual from public scrutiny has attracted little scholarly attention from historians of capital punishment in Australia [....] The body of English-speaking work that has been produced on the subject has mainly concentrated upon the end of the spectacle in America and England.[8] Among this work, there is evidence of a trend to de-emphasize what David Garland has described as Foucault's "power perspective",[9] in which the symbolic act of execution is interpreted as having fulfilled a decisive political function in reasserting the power of sovereign over subject until its dramatic replacement in the late eighteenth and early nineteenth centuries by a new disciplinary technology of power — the prison. In its place has emerged a greater attention to the role of cultural factors in determining the movement away from public punishments.[10] Louis Masur's work in particular has emphasized that transforming sensibilities towards violence in American society provided the impetus for the concealment of the offensive and brutalising spectacle of the public execution.[11] The motivation for this culturalist approach has stemmed from the work of the sociologist, Norbert Elias, whose attention to the influence of psychological sensibilities on the process of historical change has inspired scholars in a variety of fields, including the study of punishment.[12] While Elias's work has provoked a number of criticisms,[13] the concept of the "civilizing process" is a useful explanatory tool when applied to the history of capital punishment. In explaining the course of European history from the Middle Ages to the early twentieth century, Elias emphasized the interaction between processes of state formation, on the one hand, and psychological and behavioral transformations in the individual, on the other. As the state gradually began to monopolise the use of physical force and its administrative apparatus became increasingly centralised, there was an accompanying transformation in the individual towards self-restraint or self-discipline — in short, a "civilizing process"

was apparent ("civilizing" being understood here not to refer to a society being civilised in an absolute sense but, rather, to the process by which a society gradually becomes more civilised over time). One must be cautious in applying a theory that was developed to explain a specific historical circumstance to another quite distinct situation, yet it remains to be seen how applicable Elias's theory is to areas other than western Europe. Indeed, for any analysis of the European "civilizing proces" to be complete, the colonial settler states that comprised its margins should be taken into account.

Notes

8 See especially: Randall McGowen, 'Civilizing Punishment: The End of the Public Execution in England', *Journal of British Studies*, vol. 33, no. 3, 1994, pp. 257–82; David D. Cooper, *The Lesson of the Scaffold: The Public Execution Controversy in Victorian England*, Ohio University Press, Athens, Ohio, 1974, and in his article 'Public Executions in Victorian England: A Reform Adrift', in William B. Thesing [....]

9 David Garland, *Punishment and Modern Society: A Study in Social Theory*, Oxford University Press, Oxford, 1990, p. 131.

10 See especially: Masur, *op. cit.*; Pieter Spierenburg, *The Spectacle of Suffering: Executions and the Evolution of Repression: From a Preindustrial Metropolis to the European Experience*, Cambridge University Press, Cambridge, 1984; and Garland, *op. cit.*, especially chaps 9 and 10.

11 Masur, *op. cit.*, especially pp. 103–10.

12 Elias's theoretical contribution is best outlined in *The Civiliz[*] Process*, vol. 1: *The History of Manners* (1939), Blackwell, Oxf[*] 1983 [....]

13 See for example [....]

John McGuire 1998 "Judicial violence and the 'civilizing process': Ra[*] transition from public to private executions in Colonial Australia." *A[*] Historical Studies* 111, 187–209, 188–90.

3.1.2 The social profile of abstractions and their different roles in different disciplines

When we found abstractions to interpret the details of "Little Thumb," the sky was the limit: do you notice that the father's attitude is odd? Let's call that *ambivalence*! Do you notice Little Thumb hiding under the stool? Let's call that circumstance *concealment*!

But it is not quite right to say that the sky is the limit, for some abstractions are more likely than others to participate in the scholarly conversation of the various disciplines. Some are more likely to engage current scholarly concerns and issues, and more likely to enter into exchange with other abstractions which are currently highly valued. For example, amongst the excerpts we have read so far, we have encountered the abstraction *community* at work on a number of research sites. Similarly, reflecting on the positions and representations of "boon-dockers" in Counts and Counts' work, or of the ethnic minorities discussed by subjects of Verkuyten et al.'s research, we might interpret these conditions as related to *marginality*, an abstraction current in many disciplines in the humanities and social sciences. If in reading "Alert Bay" or the passages from Mary Englund's memoirs in Chapter Two you came up with an abstraction like *colonial domination*, you would have begun to participate in discussion which circulates amongst those engaged in post-colonial reasoning. If you'd come up with the abstraction *surveillance* to summarize aspects of Mary Englund's story, you would be joining the talk which has been going on since Foucault's ideas about prisons (see the passage above about executions in Australia) became well known in scholarly circles. Some abstractions enjoy more prestige than others: they attract scholarly interest.

These circumstances of prestige and interest are described by a scholar cited earlier in this chapter. Hyland observes that knowledge in research communities is a "social accomplishment" — the outcome of people listening to one another, addressing one another, being in the same neighbourhood, sharing topics and questions, developing some issues and neglecting others as time goes on, negotiating common understandings and priorities.

Yet, while this kind of exchange is common to all disciplines, the *sociality* of knowledge differs somewhat in different disciplines, and the roles of communal abstractions differ accordingly. Roughly speaking, the differences arrange themselves along the continuum from the so-called hard sciences at one end and the humanities at the other, with the social sciences in between. Later on we will be inquiring further into the differences in the social organization of knowledge in the disciplines. For now, though, we will look at abstractions and their definitions as indications of these differences.

In her detailed and valuable study of writing in the humanities and social sciences, focussing on literary studies, social history, and psychology, Susan Peck MacDonald (1994) observes that abstraction in literary study is much less constrained than it is in psychology. In literary study, interpretations of particulars can compete, and rival one another. Somebody might say, for example, that "Little Thumb" is *not* about *ambiva-*

lence at all; rather, it is about *rivalry* — and there wouldn't be any way of settling this contest, except perhaps to wait and see whose interpretations got cited and used elsewhere, whose abstractions entered the conversation, got voiced by others. In psychology, however, terms are used in ways which are methodical enough to "adjudicate" claims communally. MacDonald focusses especially on the abstraction *attachment*, which is in use in research in developmental psychology. *Attachment* is the relationship infants or small children form with their caregivers. It has many complexities and many (measurable) aspects and dimensions, and researchers ask many questions about it. But they (more or less) agree on which behaviours and attitudes to call "attachment" and which ones not to call "attachment." So, for example, if I interpreted Little Thumb's father's conflicted attitude or his mother's tearful protests as *attachment*, these researchers would not regard my statement as contributing to *their* conversation about children and families.

Where does this consensus about *attachment* and the types of *attachment* come from? MacDonald proposes that

> [...] observations of many infants and repeated studies [led] researchers to a growing conviction of what the salient patterns were. This was not research by algorithm; nor was it deductive reasoning. It involved something like induction through immersion in particular data. It may not, initially, have been very different from the process whereby a reader of Trollope [a nineteenth-century British writer] comes to have a feel for the kinds of motivation in Trollope's novels, or the reader of Shakespeare comes to have convictions about motivation in Shakespeare's plays. But attachment researchers hàd a conceptual frame to refer to in questions of interpretation. That frame allowed them to dismiss some kinds of interpretations and ask questions about others. (73)

The "conceptual frame" is the product of researchers' work to keep terms relatively stable across applications.

In *Writing Science: Literacy and Discursive Power* (1993), M.A.K. Halliday and J.R. Martin offer means of discriminating amongst the roles of abstraction in different disciplines. They distinguish between abstraction in the sciences — which, they say, is "technical," and dedicated to the project of "classifying" the world — and abstraction in the humanities — which, they say, is not technical. For example, and borrowing the example from Martin, a physical geographer uses the abstract term *abrasion* as an element of a system which classifies forms of erosion (which is itself a technical abstraction). This system distinguishes *abrasion* from other types of erosion. An historian, on the other hand, uses a term like *solemnity* to develop an interpretation of a particular event (in this example of Martin's, a memorial parade, and in fact the "historian" in this case is a student). *Solemnity* does not classify the parade technically.

Similarly, the historian writing on the unsolved murder of a Scottish nanny used "contemporary knowledge," "scientific knowledge of the day," "common sense," "dominant understandings," and, especially, "discourses" to summarize and interpret a series of events in Western Canada in the 1920s. While his interpretation could invite correction and refinement or revision, or a suggestion of a better way to look at this case, it is unlikely that someone would say, "No, that cannot be classified as a discourse because a discourse is always and in every case *x*. What you refer to is not in fact *x*." But a geographer identifying a formation in the landscape as the result of abrasion might be contradicted: it is not abrasion, it is another (possibly as yet unnamed) type of erosion. What the geographer has pointed to is properly situated at some other place in the system of classification.

Bruno Latour (2000), a sociologist of science, says that the difference between the objects of study in science and those in the social sciences is that objects in science can *talk back* to the researcher, and say "no, I am not what you have said. I am not abrasion." (Objects of study in the social sciences, according to Latour, do not so readily talk back. We will explore further the silence or reply of objects of inquiry in Chapter Six.) Hearing this contradiction from the object of inquiry, the researcher adjusts her taxonomy — her system of classifying the world. Further inquiry in marine biology could lead a pod of marine mammals to "say," "You have been calling us 'Beluga whales (*Delphinapterus leucas*)'; we are not that" — and the taxonomy is adjusted accordingly, or its application is adjusted, depending on whether we have seen or heard from marine mammals like these outspoken ones before.

We can observe some of the classificatory work abstractions do in the passage below, which is from an article that seeks to improve means of recognizing personality types. Among the terms which are in **bold**, which ones might you hear or utter in everyday, non-specialist talk? Of these, which would you estimate has a *technical* dimension in this context? Which terms seem to belong to the discipline of personality psychology, and seem unlikely to make an everyday appearance? If we referred to Little Thumb's father as prone to "hypervigilance and ruminative rationalization," would personality researchers recognize our statement?

> Although members of each of the three high-distress groups are prone to **anxiety** and **depression**, they manifest very different **personality structures**. Although sensitized individuals (i.e.,

those with high distress and moderate restraint) report experiencing **excessive negative affect**, they do not seem to be especially predisposed to particular **personality disorders** (Weinberger and Schwartz, 1990). They are hypothesized to have moderate levels of **ego development** (conformist/conscientious) in which "neurotic" concerns about the inherent conflicts between the **id** (i.e., wishes, desires) and the **superego** (i.e., internalized prohibitions) are salient (cf. Fenichel, 1945). Consistent with traditional repression-sensitization literature (Byrne, 1961), the sensitized group is likely to cope with **stress** by employing **hypervigilance and ruminative rationalization**. Paradoxically, sensitizers tend to stew about nonessential aspects of their **affects**, often camouflaging the defensive nature of behavior that may often involve **displacement**. Their attachment model is hypothesized to vary within the preoccupied or fearful spectrum, where what is salient is a concern about their own **worthiness** in **relationships** (Griffin and Bartholomew, 1994; Mikulincer and Orbach, 1995).

Finally, oversocialized individuals also experience high levels of **subjective distress**; however, they are highly restrained and very concerned about imposing their needs on others. Hence, they are often shy, unassertive, and guilt-prone (Weinberger and Schwartz, 1990). Although there has been little direct empirical investigation to date, oversocialized individuals are likely to compensate for any signs of antisocial affects through such mechanisms as reaction formation and undoing, where they feel that they can never do enough to make up for any **affective outbursts** or **egoistic behavior**. In the literature using the Marlowe-Crowne, they are often labeled "**defensive high anxious**" (Weinberger et al., 1979); in a sense, they can be conceptualized as unsuccessful repressors.

Daniel A. Weinberger 1998 "Defenses, personality structure and development: Integrating psychodynamic theory into a typological approach to personality." *Journal of Personality* 66, 6, 1061-77, 1074.

Terms are working hard in this passage to classify behaviour, and being called on to improve and refine their technicality. But even in this highly classificatory atmosphere, we still see the signs that these terms are a "social accomplishment." For one thing, we see the reporting expressions which trace these claims and terms to their origins in the research community:

- … (Weinberger and Schwartz, 1990) …
- They are hypothesized to have …
- Consistent with traditional repression-sensitization literature (Byrne, 1961) …

- ... is hypothesized to vary ...
- Although there has been little direct empirical investigation to date ...
- ... they can be conceptualized as ...

We also see appositives:

- moderate levels of ego development (conformist/conscientious)
- the superego (i.e., internalized prohibitions)

These appositive structures show the writer/researcher estimating the extent and stability of the terms (their social distribution), confirming their application for this purpose, and activating their components for this occasion. Even technical abstractions call for the cooperation and participation of readers.

We further extend this social dimension of abstraction on another plane when we observe the role of definition in perfecting research instruments. Here physical anthropologists concentrate on the technical definition of *blade* to question longstanding assumptions of a connection between human evolution and the development of techniques for producing these blades.

What Are Blades and What Have People Said About Them?

The standard morphological definition of a blade is any flake more than twice as long as it is wide, although some investigators prefer ratios of 2.5 or even 4 to 1. The technical definition is somewhat narrower, limiting use of the term to elongated blanks with parallel or slightly curving edges. Normally ....

Ofer Bar-Yosef and Steven L. Kuhn 1999 "The big deal about blades: Laminar technologies and human evolution." *American Anthropologist* 101, 2, 322-38, 323.

Here economists gather abstractions which have been used to analyse the economic behaviour *charity* or *philanthropy*: specifically, in this case, the action of making donations to colleges or universities.

A. A Theory of Giving

In the charitable giving literature, social scientists have distinguished several possible motivations for donations [4]: 1) altruism, 2) reciprocity, and 3) direct benefits. Each of these will now be discussed in a college giving context.

Thomas H. Bruggink and Kamran Siddiqui 1995 "An econometric model of alumni giving: A case study for a liberal arts college." *The American Economist* 39, 2, 53-60, 53.

These two instances of technical definition reveal different motivations for using the definitions as research instruments. In the first case, the record of the discipline's work on identifying blades will organize the researchers' critical review of traditional classifications of eras of human development and progress. (Are these people Stone Age?) In order to do this, there has to be some social consensus amongst researchers on what counts as a *blade*. In the second case, efforts to technicalize abstract names for giving money away could have practical applications in planning fund-raising drives.

Researchers get so accustomed to the particular operations of abstractions in their field that these operations can seem "natural" to them — natural, that is, rather than social, and the outcome of exchange, cooperation, and negotiation. The way they use abstractions will seem to them "logical," "accurate," "clear," "precise," whereas other uses of abstraction will seem "illogical," "inaccurate," "vague," or "fuzzy." Students, however, can have a different view. Taking courses in a variety of disciplines, they are not so likely to see the different uses of abstractions as "natural." In fact, in experiencing a range of sometimes contradictory reactions to their work, they would be justified in thinking that the acceptability or unacceptability of uses of abstraction is arbitrary, rather than natural. Sometimes what they write is logical, sometimes it's called illogical; sometimes what they write is clear, sometimes it is considered vague. Better than "natural" *or* "arbitrary," let's say "social." Different groups engaged in different kinds of research-and-writing activities (or different *discourse communities* [itself an abstraction enjoying prestige in some disciplines]) develop, through their association and communal purposes, different techniques for making and representing knowledge.

These differences can also affect the material conditions of learning in different courses. In disciplines which depend on technical abstractions, students spend a lot of time acquiring command of these terms and preparing to have their command of these terms tested. This can be hard work. But it might be even harder work, for some, to acquire facility with the prestige abstractions of the humanities, where the operation of terms is more covert and tacit, and less openly recognized as a matter of consensus and collaboration.

3.1.3 Definitions and dictionaries

People rely on dictionaries — either practically, by looking words up, or theoretically, by comforting themselves that, should any problem of meaning arise, a dictionary could settle it. Often associated with this reliance is an idea that dictionaries are responsible for meaning: they make meaning, or they make words mean what they do.

Actually, this idea is backwards. Writers of dictionaries describe what the meaning of the word already is. Or, better said, they describe **how people use a word**. So some language specialists don't talk about definition at all. Rather, they say that the "meaning" of a word is the set of circumstances under which it can be efficiently used. So, it would be inefficient for a person to use the word "chair" when he wanted someone else to hand in an essay.

Your chairs are due next week.

This seems to be one of the circumstances where it is not efficient to use the word "chair."

If we adjust our view of dictionaries, and see them as following rather than preceding use, we see that *the community of speakers who use the word is the source of its meaning*. These speakers (and writers), through their interactions and routine activities, develop and negotiate word meanings: the conditions under which a word can be efficiently used. If we go further, along lines established by current reasoning about the social order, we must acknowledge that "community" should be "communities": within the larger aggregate society, people get together in different groups, following different routines. These shared routines are sustained by shared interpretations of the world — and shared habits in the use of certain words, including the shared habits of specialist communities. No dictionary can report all these possible communities of speakers and the tacit agreements they have amongst themselves as to the appropriate use of certain words. So, while no dictionary would provide a definition of "chair" that justifies "Your chairs are due next week," a community of language users made up of wood-work teachers and their students could very well find the use of the word "chair" in this sentence appropriate and efficient under that circumstance.

Once we accept, first, that dictionaries only describe uses of words rather than establish definitions, and, second, that those recorded uses are only the most general kind, we can see that there is still work to be done — terms to be captured and refined in the account of their possible uses. (We see also that an assignment which involves definition does not inevitably call for a dictionary.)

3.2 Orchestrating voices, making arrangements for speakers

Up to this point, each of your summaries has brought one writer (or one partnership of writers, in the case of co-authored articles) to the page. You have concentrated on making arrangements for this speaker, those arrangements also signifying the position you are taking.

But, as we observed in Chapter Two in the section on "Reporting reporting," many of these writers have themselves incorporated other voices: not only the voices of research subjects when these have been the site of inquiry, but also the voices of other scholars, and often several other scholars. In fact, it is probably rather rare for scholarly writers to enter into dialogue with only one other writer. As a rule, they convene the scholarly conversation by bringing several or many other voices to the page, and arrange for these speakers to talk to one another. Sometimes these guest speakers talk all at once —

> Initial skepticism over the impact of neighborhood conditions and neighborhood contexts on the behavior of adolescents and young adults (Jencks and Mayer 1990) has spurred **considerable research purportedly documenting such effects (Aneshensel and Sucoff 1996; Billy, Brewster, and Grady 1994; Corcoran et al. 1992; Duncan 1994; Duncan, Connel, and Klebanov 1997; Elliott et al. 1996; Entwisle, Alexander, and Olson 1994; cf. Evans, Oates, and Schwab 1992).**

— apparently in unison, the common themes of their writings amounting to a chorus. Other times, two or three voices are heard in exchange with one another. Here an archaeologist first cites three writers (or two pairs and a single) on the connection between the status and position of producers of goods and the nature of social complexity in the surrounding community. Then two of the cited voices (Costin 1991 and Clark and Parry 1990) engage in conversation with each other:

> Recent studies of links between the organization of production and sociopolitical complexity have explored the importance of different kinds of craft specialization, particularly the difference between independent and attached specialization (Brumfiel and Earle 1987; Clark and Parry 1990; Costin 1991). Independent specialists "produce for a general market of potential customers" while "attached production is sponsored and managed by élite or governmental institutions or patrons" (Costin 1991). Thus inde-

pendent specialists generally produce utilitarian goods in response to a social "demand", while attached specialists typically make luxury goods, wealth items, or weaponry at the behest of powerful patrons (Costin 1991, 11-13).

There is some diversity of opinion about how broadly the general notion of craft specialization and attendant concepts such as attached and independent specialization should be defined. Costin (1991) favours fairly narrow definitions appropriate to the analysis of the productive regimes of quite complex societies. Clark and Parry (1990) use the same terms much more broadly, identifying elements of specialization even in situations of minimal sociopolitical complexity. In this respect, my discussion follows Clark and Parry more closely than Costin, but I am not particularly interested in insisting that the makers of Paso de la Amada figurines were "specialists" or "non-specialists". What I find useful in craft specialization theory is the perspective it provides on producer/consumer dynamics with respect to alienable goods — in particular, the idea that independent artisans producing goods specifically for alienation emerge as a response to consumer demand.

Richard Lesure 1999 "Figurines as representations and products at Paso de la Amada, Mexico." *Cambridge Archaeological Journal* 9, 2, 209-20, 210.

The writer gives the other speakers room to demonstrate their differences, positioning himself closer to one than to the other. But he then disengages himself from the conflict to select the overall consensus of their ideas as applicable to his inquiry into small ceramic figurines and their capacity to tell us about social organization.

The circumstances of this exchange belong to the host, and are a credit to the host: the summarizer who has called on these speakers in particular, found a point of shared or interestingly divergent interest, set the terms of the get-together. It takes some skill to make hospitable arrangements for scholarly speakers — to introduce strangers to one another, to renew acquaintances. The sections which follow offer you a chance to develop this know-how.

3.2.1 When the guests already know each other

Summary of more than one speaker can sometimes reproduce a discussion that has taken place face-to-face — or, that is, "page-to-page": *A* wrote something, and *B* responded to what *A* wrote. *A* and *B* know each other, and the summarizer reproduces this part of the conversation. The first passage in Section 3.2 above seems to be such a case:

Jencks and Mayer (1990) expressed scepticism about neighbourhoods having much effect on young people's behaviour, and then over the next six years a whole gang of researchers — Aneshensel and Sucoff (1996); Billy, Brewster, and Grady (1994); Corcoran et al. (1992); Duncan (1994); Duncan, Connel, and Klebanov (1997); Elliott et al. (1996); Entwisle, Alexander, and Olson (1994); cf. Evans, Oates, and Schwab (1992) — reacted to this claim of theirs, publishing findings "purportedly" to the contrary.

In other cases, the "face-to-face" quality of the speakers' relationship is not so immediate. It's not so much that one wrote in reaction to another, but that they are in earshot of one another. They research similar objects, address similar questions. So here a researcher who is investigating citation itself cites two writers (or a single and a pair) in the same paragraph, weaving their findings together, representing them in shared sentences (and also providing direct contact with each of the sources).

> Myers (1990) and Berkenkotter and Huckin (1995) have traced the passage of research articles through the review procedure and see the process as one of essentially locating the writer's claims within a wider disciplinary framework. This is achieved partly by modifying claims and providing propositional warrants, but mainly by establishing a narrative context for the work through citation. One of Myers's case study subjects, for example, increased the number of references from 57 to 195 in a resubmission to *Science* (Myers 1990:91). Both Myers and Berkenkotter and Huckin see academic writing as a tension between originality and humility in the community, rhetorically accommodating laboratory activity to the discipline. So while Berkenkotter and Huckin's scientist subject sought to gain acceptance for original, and therefore significant work, the reviewers insisted "that to be science her report had to include an intertextual framework for her local knowledge" (Berkenkotter and Huckin:59).
>
> (Hyland 1999: 342-43)

Differences between the cited writers are set aside, in the interests of establishing common ground: a finding confirmed by at least two studies. This common ground is mapped by the summarizer. (For another occasion, though, the *differences* might be the theme of the get-together.)

You could say that Myers and Berkenkotter and Huckin are at least passing acquaintances, and probably more than that, since the focus of their studies — how researchers revise their work to get it published — is so similar.

In the next "conversation" — which we will orchestrate ourselves — two voices address a roughly similar topic. In Chapter Two, you read a passage from Shieffelin and Doucet on creole generally, and on Haitian Creole in particular. The passage below, from the beginning of the article, is about Jamaican Creole, and attitudes toward that language.

Recent discussion among both Jamaican scholars and laypeople suggests that Jamaicans' attitudes toward Jamaican Creole (hereafter JC) are changing.[1] This change, some suggest, has accompanied the increased popularity of Dancehall culture and nationalistic "consciousness raising" efforts (Christie 1995, Shields-Brodber 1997).[2] Concurrent with these revisionist efforts, there came a call in 1989 by the (Jamaican) National Association of Teachers of English (NATE) to validate JC in the schools. This event reflected movement at an institutional, policy-making level, while the rise of Dancehall operated at the level of popular culture. Such a shift in attitudes toward "things Jamaican" marks a significant conceptual reorientation, in light of the high esteem that historically has been given to British culture, and more recently to American culture.

A history of low prestige

It has been said that language is the theater for the enacting of the social, political, and cultural life of a people, as well as the embodiment of that drama (Alleyne 1993). After roughly 150 years of Spanish occupation, Jamaica came under British control in 1655. English became the language of prestige and power on the island, reflecting the social status of its users, while the emergent Creole was regarded as the fragmented language of a fragmented people.[3] One theory of creole genesis holds that, because slaves were transported to the West Indies from a number of different ethnic groups along the western coast of Africa, they shared no common language; thus, in the new colony, they acquired a simplified variety of English in order to communicate with their British rulers and one another, while retaining no West African forms (Turner 1949; Alleyne 1984, Chap 6; Holm 1989:471-2). Historically, then, the speech of the slaves has been regarded as infantile by laypeople and linguists alike (Turner 1949) — as language that was not fully formed. It was not "proper" English; but then, because many of its lexical items resembled English ones, there was no reason to think it might be anything other than English.[4]

Language-internal clues also corroborate the low-prestige of JC. The language-internal phenomenon of pejoration, which has accompanied the emergence of many creole languages, has also figured into the history of Jamaican Creole "Patois." Lexical items from West African sources have taken on negative connotations, particularly in communities with large acrolect- or standard English-speaking populations. An example of one such pejoratized word is *nyam* "to eat", which has come to suggest an animal's way of eating rather than eating in a general sense. When used to describe human eating, *nyam* connotes sloppy or uncultivated devouring of food, as in "Don't *nyam* your dinner" (Alleyne 1976), or, "He had to *nyam* and scram!"

In a socio-linguistic investigation of attitudes toward a language variety that arose out of contact among groups of people coexisting under conditions of unequal power, it must be recognized that such social conditions affected the context of development of the new language. Research has shown that attitudes toward language can be markedly polarized and tightly held — both institutionally and personally, openly and internally.

Notes
1 Linguists tend to refer to this language as "Jamaican Creole," but it is widely referred to as "Patois" by native speakers. The two terms will be used interchangeably in this paper, particularly because the term "Patois" was widely used by respondents in the interviews reported.
2 Briefly, "Dancehall" is a largely urban working-class phenomenon in vernacular Jamaican culture, associated with styles of dance, music, clothing — and (important in this context) lyrics that strongly favor Jamaican Creole (Cooper 1993).
3 Interested readers are directed to Lepage 1960 and Cassidy 1961 for introductions to the history of the island which discuss issues of linguistic development.
4 Taylor (1963:804) gives an example of how lexical correspondence and similar phonological form have mistakenly been taken as adequate grounds for assuming that the grammatical categories of one language (French) operate in another (Martinican Creole).

Alicia Beckford Wassink 1999 "Historic low prestige and seeds of change: Attitudes toward Jamaican Creole." *Language in Society* 28, 57–92, 57–58.

Setting Wassink alongside Shieffelin and Doucet, we can find common ground: that *both linguists and laypeople stigmatize creole languages.* Wassink adds that attitudes are stubborn. We can also find claims which cooperate with one another: Wassink's historical account explains the socio-political origin of negative attitudes: colonial domination and the slave trade not only assembled speakers of different languages but also promoted English as the prestige language (Shieffelin and Doucet focus on French).

Wassink provides an example of **pejoration** (what is that? can you define this connection between pejoratives and West-African derived words?). But Wassink begins with the suggestion of change in attitudes. (Is this change the same as or different from the apparently ambivalent attitude amongst Haitians who idealize rural, "authentic" ways?)

Exercise

Write a 200-word summary of Shieffelin and Doucet (from Chapter Two) and Wassink (above). You could start the way Hyland does above ("Myers (1990) and Berkenkotter and Huckin (1995) have traced...."): "Shieflin and Doucet (1994) and Wassink (1999) observe that creole languages are...." Or you could start at a higher level of abstraction, trying something like this: "In post-colonial societies with histories of severe inequality, the stigmatization of creole languages...." (Or even higher, at a level which might connect political inequality and social judgements of speech.) Your summary might also, at or near the end, pose a question which arises from the conversation between these writers: having listened to these views, what might we want to know now?

3.2.2 When the guests live in the same district but may not know each other

Earlier in this chapter (3.1), we read a passage from Henry P. Huntington et al. about beluga whales. The passage briefly defined *traditional ecological knowledge* (TEK). Here is a passage from the beginning of an article which problematizes definitions of TEK:

> [TEK is] knowledge and values which have been acquired through experience, observation, from the land or from spiritual teachings, and handed down from one generation to another. (Definition of TEK in GNWT policy statement, as quoted in Abele, 1997:iii)

> TEK is *knowledge*. (Hunn, 1988:14, italics in original)

> In recent years, scientists have come to Nunavut in search of Inuit traditional ecological knowledge .... when Inuit

knowledge is collected ... it is almost always taken out of context, misinterpreted or given meaning different than it had in the first place (Stevenson, 1996a:3).

The first of the above statements constitutes the formal definitions of traditional knowledge as defined by the Government of the Northwest Territories. The second and third, both by anthropologists, encapsulated two important contemporary, if not necessarily harmonious, views of traditional ecological knowledge that together intimate not only why TEK has become an important intellectual issue, but also an increasingly political topic in the contemporary North.

George W. Wenzel 1999 "Traditional ecological knowledge and Inuit: Reflections on TEK research and ethics." *Arctic* 52, 2, 113-24, 113-16.

These writers obviously have something in common: TEK. They work in the same scholarly area, and there is good reason for them to get to know one another. But their claims about TEK issue from different kinds of research situations. Whereas Huntington et al. *use* TEK in their research on the migrations and movements and other behaviours of beluga whales in Alaska, Wenzel *reflects on* TEK itself. Arranging for these two researchers to speak to each other, we would need to explain the different circumstances from which their statements issue — an important occasion for putting to use your practice in characterizing the discussion you are citing. Huntington et al. (1999) is an instance of research in marine biology; Wenzel (1999) is an instance of review of and reflection on research methodology.

Exercise

(1) Develop the definition you wrote earlier in this chapter of *traditional ecological knowledge* by bringing Huntington et al. and Wenzel into conversation with one another. In doing so, you might consider Huntington et al. as an example of use of TEK, accompanied by a working definition, rather than putting Huntington et al. up against Wenzel all by themselves (for this could somewhat misrepresent the case: Huntington et al. and Wenzel are not in direct dialogue with one another). This might also be an occasion for a "but" kind of summary: we get this idea from *x, but y* shows us that this is not the whole story.

---

(2) Earlier in this chapter, you encountered materials for defining *civilizing process*. These occurred in the context of McGuire's study of capital punishment in Australia. Here is further commentary on Elias's theory of the *civilizing process* — in another research context, which is referred to at the end of the passage. Expand your definition to bring Pratt (below) into conversation with McGuire.

The Civilizing Process

What is it, though, that is meant by the term civilized? It carries with it common-sensical notions about values and practices which, in general, differentiate Western societies which are thought to make up the civilized world, from those other social formations which do not. Here, though, I am using it as a theoretical construct in the manner of Elias ([1939](1994)). For him, "civilizing" was one element in a triad of controls whereby individuals exercised self-control (the other two being control of natural events and control of social forces). The intensity of this self-control at any given time in a particular society could thus be seen as an indicator of its stage of development (Elias 1970). Importantly, then, "civilizing" in the Elisian sense did not mean "progress" nor did it invoke value judgment. Instead, it was the contingent outcome of long-term socio-cultural and psychic change from the Middle Ages onwards, that brought with it two major consequences. First, the modern state itself gradually began to assume much more centralized authority and control over the lives of its citizens, to the point where it came to have a monopoly regarding the use of force and the imposition of legal sanctions to address disputes. Second, citizens in modern societies came to internalize restraints, controls and inhibitions on their conduct, as their values and actions came to be framed around increased sensibility to the suffering of others and the privatization of disturbing events (Garland 1990). In these respects, while Elias himself used changing attitudes to bodily functions and to violence to demonstrate these claims, it also seems clear that the development of punishment in modern society follows this route and provides a helpful demonstration of the Elias thesis. One of the most important consequences of the gradual spread of these sentiments was, as Pieter Spierenburg (1984) has illustrated, a decline and tempering of corporal and capital punishments over this period — to the point where, at the onset of modernity, the public performance of such punishments had all but disappeared and their administration in private was increasingly subject to regulations and "scientific" scrutiny. As I want to show in relation to English prison development, these trends have since continued. In the course of the development of much of modern society punishment became "a rather shameful societal activity, undertaken by specialists and professionals in enclaves (such as prison and reformatories) which are, by and large, removed from the sight of the public" (Garland 1990:224).

John Pratt 1999 "Norbert Elias and the civilized prison." *British Journal of Sociology* 50, 2, 271-96, 272-73.

3.2.3 When some guests know one another but others do not

The next passage comes from a report by researchers who are studying South Africans' accounts of beaches as *places* following the elimination of apartheid and the end of segregation of beaches. Here they first provide an historical account of, as they say, the "concept of place-identity in environmental psychology." You will see that at this stage, the cited speakers "know" each other (see Section 3.2.1): the Proshansky et al. paper is a response to "earlier calls"; that paper in turn is criticized and appreciated, and its proposed concept is narrowed in definition (we can see the social process by which somewhat technical definitions are arrived at).

The concept of place-identity in environmental psychology
A key moment in environmental psychology's critique of a disembodied notion of identity was the publication of Proshansky, Fabian, and Kaminoff's (1983) paper on place-identity (cf. Groat, 1995). Although it has been subjected to various criticisms, the paper was invaluable in establishing place-identity as a sensitizing construct, bringing to fruition earlier calls for an "ecological con-

ception" of self and personality (cf. Craik and McKechnie, 1977). Adopting a general and inclusive definition, Proshansky *et al.* described place-identity as a "pot-pourri of memories, conceptions, interpretations, ideas and related feelings about specific physical settings as well as type setting" (1983, p. 60). As a distinctive substructure of the self, they reasoned, place-identity might function to underwrite some personal identities, render actions or activities intelligible, express tastes and preferences and mediate efforts to change environments.

Later researchers have found this formulation suggestive, if a little nebulous. Though using Proshansky as a theoretical resource, Korpela (1989) prefers a narrower definition of place-identity: as a psychological structure that arises out of individuals' attempts to regulate their environments. Through practices of environmental usage, he argues, we are able to create and sustain a coherent sense of self and to reveal our selves to others. At the heart of this psychological structure is a sense of belonging, for "place-belongingness is not only one aspect of place-identity, but a necessary *basis* for it. Around this core the social, cultural and biological definitions and cognitions of place which become part of the person's place-identity are built" (Korpela, 1989, p. 246, emphasis in original). In this conception, human actors are cast as imaginative users of their environments, agents who are able to appropriate physical contexts in order to create, here, a space of attachment and rootedness, a space of being. The personalization of dwellings is an oft-cited example. By this practice, "home" places are organized and represented in ways that help individuals to maintain self-coherence and self-esteem, to realize self-regulation principles.

John Dixon and Kevin Durrheim 2000 "Displacing place-identity: A discursive approach to locating self and other." *British Journal of Social Psychology* 39, 27-44, 28-29.

Then, continuing, Dixon and Durrheim introduce a stranger (Rowles 1983) to the conversation. To make it quite clear that this speaker is not responding directly (or even indirectly) to the previous contributions, the writers point to another group — "scholars working in other research traditions" — and we take the speaker who gets the floor next as belonging to this group working in an ethnographic, rather than psychological, tradition.

The importance of belonging to processes of self-definition has been noted by scholars working in other research traditions, confirming Korpela's claim that it is a central feature of place-identity (see e.g., Cuba and Hummon, 1993; Tuan, 1980). Rowles' (1983) research with the elderly residents of an Appalachian community provides an eloquent empirical demonstration of the idea. Rowles distinguished between three senses of "insidedness", expressing different aspects of his respondents' affinity with their surroundings. "Physical insidedness" designated their "body awareness" of their environment, expressed as a kind of tacit knowledge of the physical details of place (e.g., knowing how to find one's way). "Social insidedness" designated their sense of connection to a local community, a recognition of their "integration within the social fabric" (p. 302) (e.g., of knowing others and being known). Finally, "autobiographic insidedness" designated their idiosyncratic sense of rootedness. Often unspoken and taken for granted, autobiographical insidedness seemed to arise out of individuals' transactions within a place over time. It was this mode of place identification, Rowles suggested, that was especially important to his elderly respondents. Although they had witnessed considerable changes in their home town of Colton and had found their mobility increasingly restricted, they were able to maintain a sense of belonging by remembering incidents, places, contributions and relations in their personal lives there.

Other scholars writing in environmental psychology might have produced an account similar to the first two paragraphs. But after that point, Dixon and Durrheim present a voice that would be a less predictable contributor: their introduction to the conversation of Rowles' study of Appalachian elders is a novel arrangement. They have invited someone (relatively) unknown to the others in the field, and they make him welcome by telling where he comes from (an "empirical" project), giving him lots of time to speak, and especially recommending his "eloquent" contribution.

Exercise
The previous passage tells about ways in which people's sense of identity is linked to *place*, describing psychological conceptions of *place-identity* developing to include social dimensions. Another passage follows here which intersects the passage from Dixon and Durrheim above at one point at least (you may find others): around "personalization of dwellings" (Dixon and Durrheim) and "attempt[s] to personalize … space" (Counts and Counts, below).

In 200-250 words, bring these two passages into contact with each other, summarizing each to represent their distinctiveness — the different contexts for their claims about dwelling, identity, and place — and their commonality. Ambitiously, you might also refer to an earlier passage from Counts and Counts, which we read in Chapter Two, on territoriality and community.

Because interior space is so limited, RVers spend a lot of time outdoors and include the area where the rig is parked as part of their home or dwelling space. Interior space is private; most socializing occurs in the external space adjacent to the RV: in lawn chairs under an awning, at a picnic table or on the astroturf "lawn" in front of the rig. The notion that one's home or dwelling includes the out-of-doors is well known cross-culturally. In his definitive study of dwellings in many societies, Oliver observes that they do not require permanent structures. He says:

> To dwell is to [...] live in, or at, or on, or about a
> place. For some this implies a permanent structure, for
> others a temporary accommodation, for still others it
> is where they live, even if there is little evidence of
> building [....] It is this double significance of dwelling
> — dwelling as the activity of living or residing, and
> dwelling as the place or structure which is the focus
> of residence — which encompasses the manifold cul-
> tural and material aspects of domestic habitation.
> (Oliver 1987:7)

As we observed above, one distinction between boondockers and resort park residents is that boondockers refuse to accept limits that restrict them to only a few feet of external space or rules defining how they are expected to use it. Typically, the area that boondockers claim for their dwelling is more extensive than the area allowed residents of private parks and greater even than the sites in many park or forest service campgrounds. Those who return to the same site year after year may stake out a considerable area for themselves. In the Slabs, for instance, we saw a "No Trespassing" sign blocking off a dirt track leading down into a shallow ravine where a trailer was parked. When we asked our neighbours whether

individuals did, in fact, own land in the Slabs they confirmed that the sign had no legitimacy. As one said, "We're
all trespassers here."

According to Randy, to be a full-timer it is necessary to
give up notions of territoriality. "People have a lot of trouble with the fact that they don't own the land where they
are parked," he said. "You can't put a fence around the
place where you park." This is true and it is the source of a
fascinating paradox, for although they cannot own the
space outside their RV, they attempt to make it their own;
as one of our informants said, to "make it like home."

Even if they plan to be in a place only a few days, many
people attempt to personalize their outside space. They
brush it clean and hang bird feeders and baskets of plants;
they fly over it flags that proclaim their nationality (U.S.,
Canadian), affiliation (RV club), or ideology (Christian
cross, the Jolly Roger, the Confederate Stars and Bars);
they bound it with stones, bits of broken glass, small white
picket fencing or strings of coloured lanterns; they plant
flowers, cactus or vegetables; they put down an astroturf
"lawn"; they decorate it with pink flamingos, fountains,
coloured rocks, hunting trophies, cow skulls and Christmas
trees; and they build patios, campfire circles and barbecue
pits. In short, anything that might be found outside a suburban home to identify it as personal space may also be
found in the space outside an RV.

(Counts and Counts 1994:177-78)

3.2.4 When some guests are rather difficult to entertain

The next passage appears in an archaeologist's study of the role of alcohol in legitimating authority in Celtic societies: chief-sponsored drinking and feasting in the Iron Age. Some of her data are archaeological:
material artefacts recovered in physical investigation. Some of her evidence, however, is documentary: written accounts of feasting in Iron
Age societies. So you will see her bringing together speakers whose
statements issue from radically different contexts: she cites "Classical

authors" on Celtic societies and a modern author describing Tlingit (North American West Coast) society.

You will see that to bring these two types of speakers together she makes special arrangements like those of Dixon and Durrheim above: research in "**many ethnographic contexts** … [provides] **additional** information" (emphasis added) on preindustrial societies. You will also see that the Classical authors are introduced with great care, and with attention to the peculiarities of these fellows. It's almost as if difficult guests wait in an anteroom while the host explains and anticipates their odd behaviour: they fail to take account of what modern scholars would be interested in, and have a tendency to obsess over the "bizarre" and to "romanticize or demonize 'exotic' peoples" (which the Celts would have been to these Classical authors). Moreover, they can be rather unreliable reporters, from a modern point of view: when they lack data on one group of exotic people, they just repeat what has been said about some other group. In effect, the summarizer says, "Now, I've got some people I want you to meet. You can't believe everything they say, and I've heard them dwell on some things that might not interest you. But, even though they're kind of strange, I think they've got some valuable information. Here they are. Let's all be polite."

> The general formula followed by most Classical authors describing the alien cultures on their peripheries was modelled on Herodotus and consisted of several categories of information: 1) population; 2) antiquity and ancient history; 3) way of life; 4) customs (Tierney 1960, 190). Unfortunately for modern scholars the unusual and bizarre aspects of the last two categories were generally recounted in some detail, while information considered mundane, common knowledge or uninteresting was less frequently recorded. Two pitfalls facing the modern scholar attempting to derive "facts" from these accounts are "Randvölkeridealisierung" (Tierney 1960, 214) and "ethnographische Wandermotive" (Tierney 1960, 201). The first is the tendency of Classical ethnographers to romanticize or demonize "exotic" peoples. The second refers to the borrowing of descriptions of customs from accounts of one culture and transposing them wholesale or only slightly modified to a completely different group of people, whenever hard facts were lacking or could benefit from being fleshed out in a more dramatic way [....]
>
> Despite these potential difficulties, several significant themes related to Celtic drinking and feasting behaviour (both insular and continental) recur in Classical sources. Some of these themes,

particularly those also found in the later insular Celtic texts, may result from similarities between geographically and temporally different groups of the Celts (Nash 1976, 116). One such theme is that of the king's or hero's portion at a banquet, described as early as Phylarchus (Tierney 1960, 197). Another is the concept of guest-friendship, mentioned by Diodorus Siculus (Tierney 1960, 250) and again by Caesar (Tierney 1960, 274); both accounts stress the Celtic emphasis on open-handedness and generosity as important virtues.

Generosity as the defining characteristic of a good chieftain or king is a common theme in both Classical and insular texts, but also in many ethnographically recorded societies at a chiefdom level of organization. Athenaeus' account of Lavernius' banquet is a good example (Tierney, 1960, 248). The Celtic chieftain Lavernius, pleased by the praise of a poet at his feast, scatters gold along the plain behind his chariot, and "the poet picked it up and sang another song saying that the very tracks made by his chariot on the earth gave gold and largesse to mankind" (Tierney 1960, 248).

Athenaeus' verbatim transcription of four of the nine surviving extracts of Book 23 of Poseidonius' *History*, the recognized "Bible" on the Celts, describes food, drink, and heroic feasting and combat, and bardic display at great length. In fact, the passage on food and drink is the longest surviving portion of Poseidonius' Celtic ethnography. This may reflect the special emphasis on food and drink in the Celtic world observed by Poseidonius.

The symbolic as well as functional significance of feasting is documented in many ethnographic contexts (Chapman 1980, 66); such sources provide additional preindustrial configurations for modelling prehistoric social organization. The Tlingit potlatch is a good example of a society in which feasting acts as an institutionalized form of social regulation. As described by Kan, "the unity and solidarity of clan relatives were emphasized by the obligatory sharing of property and food that characterized their relationships" (1989, 65-6). The status of a Tlingit aristocrat depended on the rank and wealth of his parents (especially his mother), marriage to a person of equal or greater rank, the number and scale of potlatches sponsored by his parents in his honour, and accomplishments in activities which generated wealth and enabled him to give his own potlatch(es) or actively participate in those given by his matrikin (Kan 1989, 82).[2]

Note
2   Note the key role played by feasting in establishing and maintaining
    status in this society.

Bettina Arnold 1999 "'Drinking the feast': Alcohol and the legitimation of power in Celtic Europe." *Cambridge Archaeological Review* 9, 1, 71-93, 72-73.

Exercise

(1) Before we go on to practise bringing a far-fetched guest into the conversation, you might try to make arrangements for the discussion of Iron Age feasting (above) to speak to this passage from the study of RVers.

Ritual sharing of food

The food-giving that occurs when RVers part brings into focus another aspect of reciprocity that reinforces the feeling of community: the ritual sharing of food. RVers recognize the importance of food-sharing in establishing community (Shalins 1972:281) and the necessity of trusting those with whom one shares meals. This latter point as well as one about instant community was articulated by Karl [one of the researchers' informants]. Discussing his pleasure in the potluck dinners organized by the campground hosts at an Arizona state park, he said, "I'm not big on eating stuff made by people I don't know, but it doesn't take long to get to know these people and then it's OK."

RVers exchange and share food both formally — as part of ritual, for example, Thanksgiving and Christmas dinners — and informally. Newcomers are often given food within the first 24 hours of their arrival but not, in our experience, as part of the greeting ritual. Among boondockers especially, food-sharing has great social importance, for it permits the redistribution of an essential resource without challenging the ideal that "we're all the same here." Contrast the following accounts of the charitable distribution of free food at Slab City with the resident-run system of food-sharing at another boondocking area. The attitudes of the residents illustrates the importance of self-reliance and equality to RVers and the role of reciprocity in maintaining these attributes.

Slab City is a place with no formal organization or system of control. No park rangers or hosts patrol the area, there are no amenities and no one is required to check in or out of the area when arriving or leaving [....] The only institution linking Slab residents with the outside world and external organizations (such as state government agencies and charitable groups) is the Christian Center. The Center is staffed by a resident missionary and by Slab residents who volunteer their time. It is located in a trailer positioned near the entrance to the Slabs. People who want information are referred there, and on entering the Center's trailer newcomers are asked to register, identify the named area where they are parked and give the names and addresses of their next-of-kin in case of emergency. State officials go first to the Christian Center to locate Slab residents being sought by members of their family and to get information about rumoured illegal activities. Slab residents registered with the Center can pick up their mail there and get help for others who are ill.

Center volunteers expressed frustration over the lack of participation in the food distribution program by needy Slab City residents. In the opinion of the volunteers, many people who should have been taking food are "too lazy" or "think they are too good" to stand in line for it. Consequently, proffered food is often unclaimed and vegetables are left on the ground in front of the Center to rot.

The self-administered system for distributing free food in an LTVA area less than 50 miles from Slab city contrasts sharply to the charitable one at the Slabs. In the LTVA, the system was organized by the residents and was informal, involved reciprocal exchange and was viewed with pride. To them it exemplified their self-sufficiency, their enterprise and their ingenuity in taking advantage of opportunity.

(Counts and Counts 1994:166-67)

To make this connection, you might try to find one or more high-level abstractions to give the cited speakers a common theme to address — something to talk about: *generosity? exchange? symbolic hospitality? authority?*

(2) The following passage comes from a social historian's study of changes in ways children have been valued and interpreted in the

US in the nineteenth and twentieth centuries. For example, in another section of her book, Zelizer records how the "market" for children changed over some decades. When children were valued for their labour, the market was high for teenaged boys: they were likely candidates for adoption, particularly among agricultural families. When popular views of children and childhood changed, teenaged boys lost their high value, and infant girls were the most sought-after candidates for adoption. Here Zelizer describes the "baby farm" — an institution for managing surpluses of children.

> Recent evidence suggests that poor urban families used the Children's Aid Society as a quasi-employment agency for their children. Bellingham's analysis, for instance, shows that the most common single motive for surrendering custody of children to the children's organization was the children's need for a job: "Some wanted farm service positions [...] while others were trying to get training for a trade. Some wanted factory or domestic service jobs and a good number just wanted positions right in the city."[9] Thus, the instrumental aspects of nineteenth-century foster care served not only the interests of the employers, but those of at least a segment of the children placed. The useful child found a legitimate place in the foster household economy no less than in his own working-class family.
>
> The plight of nineteenth-century babies was the flip side of children's usefulness. If a working child was an asset, an infant was a liability. Unwanted babies, or those whose parents could not afford to keep them, were more likely to die than be adopted. Faced with almost insurmountable social and economic pressures, single, widowed, or deserted mothers had few available options. Abortion was not only expensive, but required connections, especially after the 1860s when it became an increasingly illegitimate and illegal practice. The few jobs available to women with children did not pay a living wage. Unprotected by insurance, and without the support of adequate public relief or private programs, many lower-class women abandoned their babies soon after birth in public places or in a foundling asylum where infant mortality sometimes reached between 85 and 90 percent.[10]
>
> Baby farmers offered an alternative to those who could afford their fee. These usually middle-aged women built a

profitable enterprise by boarding mostly illegitimate babies. With high rates of mortality, the turnover was quick, and business brisk. Mothers were relieved of their responsibility and assured confidentiality. One baby farmer outlined her terms for a prospective customer: "I take Infants from Berth [*sic*] up and keep them in my own home until I place them in a good home and my terms is fifty Dollars and the Balance weekly ... you will never be troubled with the child after I take full charge of It until I have it adopted into a good home ..."[11] In an account of baby farming practices, the *New York Times* explained, "The mother is pleased with the prospect of ridding herself of a great incumbrance, and at the same time securing ... a bright future for the child and eagerly agrees to the terms, even if exorbitant."[12]

The prospect of adoption for the infant, however, was seldom fulfilled. As a 1910 investigation discovered, the baby farm, "swarms with children whose numbers are added to weekly. Always they come and come, and rarely ... are they carried away."[13] A baby had limited sales value; sometimes it took no more than 25 cents to obtain one. Thus, the baby farmer made her profits by charging mothers a "surrender fee," and only rarely by placing the children. Unquestionably, it was a buyer's market. In an 1890 case, an agent of the New York Society for the Prevention of Cruelty to Children pretended interest in adopting a two-week-old baby. The baby farmer demanded two dollars but quickly settled for half. "She ... urged him to take the infant at once and at his own price, for she could not attend to it."[14]

Even agents of reputable child-placing agencies were sometimes unwilling to forgo the profits involved in disposing of other people's unwanted children. During an 1897 interrogation by the New York State Board of Charities, the witness, Rev. W. Jarvis Maybee of the Children's Home Society, a national organization that placed children in free foster homes, admitted charging parents fifty dollars for taking their child. For illegitimate babies, the fee was doubled. As Jarvis explained, "We charge more for little babies because it is harder to get homes for them while they are young; we have to keep them."[15]

Notes
9 Bruce Bellingham, "Little Wanderers: A Socio-Historical Study of the Nineteenth Century Origins of Child Fostering and

Adoption Reform, based on Early Records of the New York
Children's Aid Society," Ph.D. diss., University of Pennsylvania,
1984, p. 119. This study provides an insightful revisionist interpretation of the New York City Children's Aid Society.

10 See Peter Romanofsky, "Saving the Lives of City's Foundlings,"
New York Historical Society Quarterly 61 (Jan.-Apr. 1972): 49–68;
Roger Lane, *Violent Death in the City* (Cambridge, MA:
Harvard University Press, 1979), pp. 90–100; Paul A. Gilje,
"Infant Abandonment in Early Nineteenth-Century New York
City: Three Cases," *Signs* 8 (Spring 1983): 580–90. On social
class differentials in the use of abortion, James C. Mohr, *Abortion
in America* (New York: Oxford University Press, 1978),
pp. 93–98.

11 Mary Boyle O'Reilly, "The Daughters of Herod," *New England
Quarterly* 43 (Oct. 1910): 143. This article, based on an investigation of New Hampshire baby farms, provides an unusual insight
into the business. Although conducted in 1910, the report
reflects the traditional practices of baby farmers.

12 "Baby-Farming Practices," *New York Times*, July 22, 1880, p. 5.
Some baby farms also served as a lying-in hospital or maternity
home for the unwed mother.

13 O'Reilly, "The Daughters of Herod," pp. 144–45.

14 New York Society for the Prevention of Cruelty to Children,
15th *Annual Report*, 1890, p. 32.

15 New York State Board of Charities. Thirty-first Annual Report,
1897 (New York, 1898), quoted in Bremner, *Children and Youth
in America* II, p. 316. Maybee defended the extra premium for
illegitimate babies as a penalty to discourage immorality. For a
fee, the New York branch of the Children's Home Society also
took children from public and private agencies and placed them
in foster homes.

Viviana A. Zelizer 1994 (1985) *Pricing the Priceless Child: The Changing Social
Value of Children* Princeton, NJ: Princeton UP, 173–75.

You may remember another case of *abandonment* (and also *fertility* and *poverty*) in our readings: Little Thumb's parents conspired
to abandon their children. Can you bring these two speakers
into conversation — Viviana Zelizer and the folk narrator presented by the Brothers Grimm? A far-fetched guest, "Little
Thumb" will require some special arrangements and delicate
introduction to the scholarly context from which Zelizer's
statements issue.

3.2.5 When the guest has all the answers

In many undergraduate courses, reading assignments include (or sometimes focus exclusively on) textbooks: academic genres composed by specialists for non-specialists. Rather than make new knowledge, or take another step along a line of inquiry, or interrogate the accumulation of knowledge in a field, textbooks synthesize what is known so far.

Of course, many textbooks provide an historical view of knowledge in a discipline, or sub-field of a discipline, and in this respect bring to light the social dimension of knowledge as a product of interaction amongst researchers. In this respect, they resemble the research genres. And many textbooks offer a critical overview of knowledge in a field, implying directions for further inquiry. In this respect too they resemble the research genres.

But their position vis-à-vis their readers differs from that of the research genres. First, they construct readers as "not knowing": if anyone has a question, it's the student/reader; if anyone has the answer, it's the textbook. (In the research genres, as we have seen, writers represent themselves as sharing questions with their [knowledgeable] readers. We explore this difference in the trajectories of questions further in Chapter Six.) Second, they construct readers as listeners rather than co-conversationalists (although many textbooks will provide exercises and assignments which direct their readers to a limited role as participants in scholarly discussion).

The academic textbook genres and the research genres each have their place, and the authors of the latter often become authors of the former. Writers in the research genres can hear the difference between textbook and research article.

Exercise
What features of the research genres are missing from this passage from a textbook?

> One of the direct benefits of the end of the 45-year cold war between the United States and the Soviet Union has been a substantial decline in foreign military and political presence in the Third World. An indirect cost of this withdrawal, however, has been the acceleration of ethnic, tribal, and religious conflict. Although ethnic and religious tensions and occasional violence have always existed in LDCs [Less

> Developed Countries], the waning of superpower influence
> triggered a revival of these internal conflicts and may even
> have accelerated the incidence of political and economic dis-
> crimination. Ethnicity and religion often play a major role in
> the success or failure of development efforts. Clearly, the
> greater the ethnic and religious diversity in a country, the
> more likely it is that there will be internal strife and political
> instability. It is not surprising, therefore, that some of the
> most successful recent development experiences — South
> Korea, Taiwan, Singapore, and Hong Kong — have occurred
> in culturally homogeneous societies.
>
> Michael P. Todaro 1997 *Economic Development* New York: Longman, 34.

Students too may learn to recognize or intuit the different styles which
indicate the different circumstances under which statements are produced in these different genres, one style acting to inform, the other
style acting to inquire. However, the differing purposes of the textbook
and research genres can put students in a difficult position when gathering materials for a paper in an undergraduate course: they consult
research articles, chapters, and books — but they also still hear the
informative voice of the textbook on similar topics. If they repeat the
statements of the textbook without attributing them, taking them as
Common Knowledge and Public Truth, they fail to observe the scholarly requirement of providing the traces of statements, the footprints
which statements leave in their history of use. Yet even if they do
attribute the statements to their authors, they can still interrupt a scholarly conversation by bringing in a speaker who had prepared for a different kind of discussion. How can this speaker be accommodated?

  Just as Bettina Arnold made special arrangements for "Classical
authors" and you made preparations to receive "Little Thumb" in scholarly company, you can introduce the textbook speakers with an account
of their origins and intentions. For example, this passage —

> *Prejudice* is defined as a positive or negative attitude based on
> information or knowledge which is either illogical, unrelated to
> reality, or is a distortion of fact, and which is unjustifiably gener-
> alized to all members of a group. Although prejudice can be
> either favourable or unfavourable, psychologists use the term
> most frequently in the negative sense.
>
> J.E. Alcock, D.W. Carment, and S.W. Sadava 1994 *A Textbook of Social Psychology*
> 3rd ed. Scarborough, ON: Prentice Hall, 222.

— might be introduced to a research conversation by contextualizing it:

> In their introductory book on social psychology, Alcock et al. (1994) offer a general definition of **prejudice**: '…'. This definition suggests that prejudice could be corrected by referring to external reality, or logic.

Exercise

(1) The following passage comes from an undergraduate textbook. What features of style distinguish it from a research publication? (This time the question is harder to answer, for the writer carefully accounts for the first appearance, later refinements, and eventual acceptance of current knowledge about "tribal" diets.) If you wanted to use this information in an inquiry into Western conceptions of *health*, how would you represent your source?

> Smith correctly concluded that the lack of dental decay and tooth loss observed in the tribal peoples was due to increased tooth wear, which kept the teeth clean and polished. He attributed the increased wear to the consumption of less cooked and less refined food and the absence of knives and forks, which meant that more chewing was required, as well as the presence of grit or "dirt" in the food. It was later learned that the absence of refined carbohydrates also contributed to healthy tribal teeth. The reduced tooth wear of contemporary peoples who eat industrially processed foods is likely related to the common problem of impacted molars, as Grover Krantz (1978) has observed. People eating coarse foods wear down the grinding surfaces of their teeth, which creates enough jaw space to accommodate the third molars when they erupt. When there is no significant wear, these "wisdom teeth" often must be extracted.
>
> The association between traditional dietary patterns and healthy teeth was documented more systematically in a series of field studies conducted by American dentist Weston Price (1945), between 1931 and 1936. Price visited some of the most traditional peoples in Amazonia, East Africa, Australia, and throughout the Pacific and found that tooth decay and periodontal disease were virtually absent among self-sufficient peoples but steadily increased as they adopted the food patterns of industrial societies.

In 1956, shortly after Price's dental research, T.L. Cleave, a doctor in the British Royal Navy, used medical data on tribal peoples to isolate a single feature in the diets of industrialized people that caused what he called the "saccharine disease," a wide-ranging complex of conditions including tooth decay, ulcers, appendicitis, obesity, diabetes, constipation, and varicose veins. Like both Smith and Price before him, Cleave (1974) was impressed by the fact that tribal peoples did not suffer from many of the common ailments of civilization, and he attempted to find the special conditions that made the tribal peoples healthier. His primary finding was that the traditional foods of tribal groups were consistently much higher in dietary fiber than the highly refined complex carbohydrates consumed by industrialized peoples. Higher-fiber diets speed the transit time of food through the digestive system, thereby reducing many common diseases of civilization. It took many years for his findings to be incorporated into popular nutritional wisdom in the industrialized world, but now high fiber, along with low fat and low salt, is widely accepted as an important component of a healthy diet.

John H. Bodley 1997 *Cultural Anthropology: Tribes, States, and the Global System* 2nd ed. Mountain View, CA: Mayfield, 147–48.

(2) Sometimes course books are not textbooks designed to introduce newcomers to a discipline but comprehensive and informative representations of a point of view. The next passage comes from such a book. What features distinguish it from a research publication? How might you introduce this writer to a scholarly conversation?

It may seem incredible that anyone in the Americas should perceive the continents' impoverished, largely marginalized indigenous peoples as a threat, but individuals and states are products of their history, even if they deny it. In countries where indigenous people form the majority or a substantial minority, the white, Western elite and the governments they dominate show the classic psychology of rich exploiters who have grown paranoid through fear or greed. "They know only too well what they have done to the Indian, and are paranoid that the Indian might one day do the same to them," says one Bolivian aid worker.

A complex racism was part of the institutionalization of
the conquest, providing the historic rationale for human
rights abuse. Medieval Hispanic concepts of "purity of blood"
(*limpieza de sangre*) were transferred to the Indies, and American Spaniards became obsessed with classifying the various
permutations of race. Racism, including cultural discrimination, became the ideological framework that justified the
domination of the invaders and the subordination of the
conquered.

Phillip Wearne 1996 *Return of the Indian: Conquest and Revival in the Americas*
London: Cassell, 64.

3.2.6 When the guest is a popular guy

Here is a passage from a book on demographic trends, written by
experts but addressed to a broad audience distributed beyond the scholarly community.

A country filled with young people is one whose retailers compete predominantly on price. In such a country, anything that can
lower the average cost of production and reduce the price to the
consumer is important. A young Canada during the 1960s and
1970s enabled the big retail mall to be born and thrive, making it
possible for stores to lower costs and pass the savings on to customers. The malls won't disappear but their glory days are over.
In the 20 years to come, the demographic shift will favour a
revival of neighbourhood specialty stores supported by local customers for whom price is no longer the most important factor in
a purchase decision.

Stores that can deliver good products and good service will
dominate this new marketplace, while stores that waste consumers' time and treat them rudely will disappear. The art of customer service is something at which Canadian retailers are noto-
riously incompetent because, until the late 1980s, they were
operating in a marketplace that didn't require it. It's no accident
that countries such as Japan and Germany discovered quality and
service before we did. Their populations are much older than
ours, and their retailers had to respond to the demands of a
changing marketplace a decade or more earlier than ours did. The

Canadian retailers that prosper in the changing market place of the coming years will be those that succeed in adopting customer service as a way of life.

David K. Foot and Daniel Stoffman 1996 *Boom, Bust and Echo: How to Profit from the Coming Demographic Shift* Toronto: Macfarlane Walter & Ross.

Here is a linguist well known in scholarly circles but on this occasion writing for an audience as broad as that addressed by Foot and Stoffman above.

A similar conflict exists between [a couple I will call] Louise and Howie, about spending money. Louise would never buy anything costing more than a hundred dollars without discussing it with Howie, but he goes out and buys whatever he wants and feels they can afford, like a table saw or a new power mower. Louise is disturbed, not because she disapproves of the purchases, but because she feels he is acting as if she were not in the picture.

Many women feel it is natural to consult with their partners at every turn, while many men automatically make more decisions without consulting their partners. This may reflect a broad difference in conceptions of decision making. Women expect decisions to be discussed first and made by consensus. They appreciate the discussion itself as evidence of involvement and communication. But many men feel oppressed by lengthy discussions about what they see as minor decisions, and they feel hemmed in if they can't just act without talking first. When women try to initiate a free-wheeling discussion by asking, "What do you think?" men often think they are being asked to decide.

Communication is a continual balancing act, juggling the conflicting needs for intimacy and independence. To survive in the world, we have to act in concert with others, but to survive as ourselves, rather than simply as cogs in a wheel, we have to act alone.

Deborah Tannen 1990 *You Just Don't Understand: Women and Men in Conversation* New York: Ballantine Books, 27-28.

What features of scholarly style are missing from these two passages? If these were research publications, what would be different about them? Will these out-going, friendly speakers fit into the scholarly get-together you have arranged? Will they pay attention to the qualifications, abstractions, and uncertainties of the other guests? Or will they try to dominate? Will the other speakers object, shy away, fall silent, or get up and leave? And what is your reader going to think of this speaker who is used to the limelight or the microphone? Chances are, these popular speakers won't fit in. Their statements will not interact with others' — and the party will be over.

If you feel committed to including the popular speaker, you can take some measures, though, to introduce the new arrival to the other guests: "Writing for a general audience and addressing such-and-such, x simplifies...." "While x's claims overlook the uncertainty of evidence in this area, they do represent/speak to widely held interest in/concerns about...."

Watch out for books whose covers list "PhD" after the author's name. This doesn't mean that the PhD is a hoax or not a good one, but that the authority of the book is being recommended to a non-scholarly audience. In the scholarly community, advertising that one has a PhD is not likely to impress, since most writers participating in scholarly discussions have one.

3.2.7 When the speaker is on-line

The World Wide Web is a benefit to researchers. At the very least, it offers efficient access to library catalogues (older readers will remember card-catalogue cabinets as antiques from a bygone era). And the Web offers easy access, even at home, to indexes which were formerly published in very big books kept on library premises, never to venture into the outer world. In many disciplines, scholarly journals which used to live only on library shelves now reside on the Web in electronic form. All these changes have made research life richer.

There are some complications, though, mainly arising from the operation of browsers and search engines. These technologies can lead you to domains where research publications mingle with popular publications, and both these find themselves in the company of organizations sponsoring more or less viable points of view, and individuals promoting their own interests or ambitions for publicity. Recent amalgamations of on-line periodical indexes have, as well, tended to blur the distinction between peer-reviewed research publications and general-audience journalism.

How can you tell if you are finding speakers suitable for introduction into scholarly conversation? On-line research journals will include the circumstances of publication: names and affiliations of members of the editorial board; procedures for submission and review of articles. Look for these indications. Stand-alone publications may be harder to evaluate. But your experience in identifying the characteristic sounds of scholarly voices should be a reliable guide for you by now.

Making arrangements for scholarly conversation is a challenge for undergraduates: as newcomers to research communities, they can find it hard to prepare an appropriate list of guest speakers. But it's also a challenge for graduate students, and sometimes for professional scholars, too. Appendix B offers opportunity for more practice in this aspect of scholarly life.

Works Cited

Bhatia, Vijay K. 1993. *Analysing Genre: Language Use in Professional Settings.* Harlow, Essex: Longman.

Giltrow, Janet, and Michele Valiquette. 1994. "Genres and knowledge: Students writing in the disciplines." In *Learning and Teaching Genre*, ed. Aviva Freedman and Peter Medway. Portsmouth, NH: Boynton/Cook, Heinemann.

Halliday, M.A.K., and J.R. Martin. 1993. *Writing Science: Literary and Discursive Power.* Pittsburg: U of Pittsburg P.

Latour, Bruno 2000. "When things strike back: A possible contribution of 'science studies' to the social sciences." *British Journal of Sociology* 51(1): 107-23.

MacDonald, Susan Peck. 1994. *Professional Academic Writing in the Humanities and Social Sciences.* Carbondale: Southern Illinois UP.

Readers reading

Handbooks for writing recommend knowing your audience. This seems like sound advice. But who is your audience? How do you get to know your readers? This chapter is about readers, and ways of estimating their reception of your work.

4.1 Who do you think you're talking to?

In everyday conversation, we have a good idea of who our listener is. It's the person in front of us. Sometimes the person is a family member or a friend, and conversation is easy. Sometimes the person is a stranger, and this can make conversation more difficult. But usually we have some legitimate, acknowledged reason for addressing the stranger: they're a receptionist in a doctor's office; a tax consultant; a person enrolled in the same pottery class — information that enables us to address them usefully in the situation. In either case, once we get going, we monitor the listener's response; we make inferences, and adjust our emphases, themes, strategies of address.

Still, even face-to-face, we can sometimes struggle with inferences about our audience. Language and cognitive specialists study these efforts: Herbert Clark's work on "audience design" (1992), for example, investigates people's habits of inference in addressing others, finding that conversation keeps us busy at various levels of consciousness as we estimate the frame of mind of our co-conversationalists and others who might overhear us. We reckon others' knowledge of the world, calculating the extent of **mutual knowledge** — what can be safely assumed and what needs to be explained. Some of Wallace Chafe's studies (especially 1994) discover, in addition to these calculations, our ongoing estimates of listeners' centre of attention: what is in the spotlight for them, what has slipped into the shadows and peripheries.

When we are writing, we can't *see* our audience in front of us, to watch their reactions, but often we know so much about them that we don't need to see them. For example, working in genres like the postcard or the personal letter, we normally have a reliable picture of our reader. Also, we have received postcards and letters ourselves, so we have experience of our *own* responses to certain forms, and also of the social routines which call for postcards and letters.

On the other hand, when we are working in genres like the letter of complaint, or the letter of inquiry, or the letter of application, we have, generally, much less information about the recipient — except, probably, as a social type: a corporate employee handling public relations; a human-resources director, or a kind of "boss." If we have not ourselves received many or any letters of inquiry, complaint, or application, we have neither our own response to such documents to go on nor experience of the genre's typifications of interests and priorities, or routines of presentation. If, however, we are dedicated complainers, requesters-of-information, or job applicants, we may be familiar with typical outcomes of our writing — redress or silence, offers or brush-offs. From this history of responses, we might infer aspects of the situation and alter our techniques for the next time.

Where do student writers of university essays belong on this map of distance from or proximity to their readers? To locate the student writer, try the exercise which follows. It can help you and your instructor talk about how you interpret your situation as a student writer. It is not the only way of finding out how you picture your reader, but my colleagues and I have found that it can shed light on otherwise shadowy impressions.

Exercise

In groups of three or four, discuss your answers to the questions below. Make notes of the answers and your discussion.

- What do you do when you get a marked essay returned to you? Interpret this question broadly, mentioning any physical or mental operation you go through in handling that returned essay. (For example, do you re-read it, tear it to bits, photocopy it for your friends?)

- What do you consider typical marking commentary on essays? What kinds of things do professors typically say about essays?

Collaborate with other members of your group to compose a 300- to 400-word summary of your findings, accounting for differences and similarities in your habits and perceptions. Try to make a connection between your habits and attitudes upon having a marked essay returned to you and your ideas of professors' typical remarks. (For example, if you typically celebrate the return of the essay, this may be directly related to professors typically expressing delight at the perfections of essays.)

Using the information you have gathered, and sharing your findings with other members of the class, locate the student writer in the terms discussed above: in what sense do student writers "know" their readers — as friends, acquaintances, strangers, types? Is the student writer's experience of the academic genres like that of the writer of the postcard or like that of the writer of the job application? From the information you have collected in this exercise, what inferences would you make about academic readers? How do you picture readers of your essays? How do these readers read? What do you know about them, so far?

4.1.1 Attitudes toward language

Although I cannot predict the particular results of the exercise above, I know from experience that writers can have negative opinions about readers' sincerity and open-mindedness. And they can attribute disappointing grades to insincere efforts and closed-mindedness on the part of readers. I would not deny the justice of such opinions: in any writing context, we can find readers with agendas of their own, a bone to pick, or a chip on their shoulder.

But to dwell on idiosyncrasy and resistance is to lose sight of more productive characterizations of readers. As a first step in building a more helpful characterization of readers, we will consider academic readers' responses in a very broad context: that of **attitudes toward language** itself.

From several excerpts we read in Chapters Two and Three, we have learned that people tend to have rather pejorative — and moralistic —

attitudes toward language. Both excerpts we read about creole languages reported severe judgements about these languages and their speakers: according to popular views, creole expression is not only incorrect and corrupt but also ugly and coarse. It's worth noticing that linguists themselves can be involved in perpetrating these views, and worth reminding ourselves of the political possibilities of scholarly activity and "expertise." But it's perhaps even more noteworthy that laypeople — non-experts — are confident and ready in their judgements of the status of other people's speech. It seems that when we learn language, we also acquire instruments for ranking other users of language. Deborah Cameron (1995) considers these evaluative behaviours as entailed in the nature of language itself — which is not to say that one cannot evaluate the evaluations as more or less politically oppressive. In fact, in the second excerpt we read about creole (Wassink 1999), we heard about official campaigns and popular trends which are defying and overturning politically oppressive attitudes toward Jamaican Creole.

Just as we learn to rank others, we can also learn to rank ourselves. Pierre Bourdieu (1991) analyses people's attitudes toward language as evidence of "symbolic domination": domination, that is, which operates not through physical coercion but through psychological/social processes. Undergoing these processes, people internalize the values which subordinate some members of society to the advantage of others. In effect, symbolic domination recruits people to the service of their own domination. Through their experience of schooling especially, but also from other social experience, people learn to disparage their own speech and writing, to suspect it of errors, and to feel intimidated by the speech of those whom they have been taught to regard as exemplary — usually the members of the privileged classes, or those who have spent a long time studying in institutions of higher learning. (So we could predict that creole speakers will not only know how to speak creole but will also know how to rate their own speech as *low* in relation to that of speakers of Standard English or French.)

Outlining and reflecting on the origins and history of Standard English, James Milroy and Lesley Milroy (1991 [1985]) identify the "complaint tradition": the cultural practice of publicly deploring the state of the language, announcing its decline from an earlier perfection (this ideal time usually coinciding with the complainer's own schooldays). Young people's speech and writing in particular are often the target of complaint. Milroy and Milroy trace the complaint tradition back several centuries, and other scholars (e.g., Miller 1991) have traced North American traditions of complaint about student writing to the 1880s at least, when changes in the social order in late nineteenth-century

America resulted in new, middle-class populations seeking higher education — and meeting the disapproval of élite classes. (A passage from Min-Zhan Lu (1992) in Chapter Two reported similar disapproval from the élite in the 1970s, when, once again, social change sent new populations to university.)

Complaint tradition

Instances of the complaint tradition are not hard to find. While I was writing this chapter, I read in the newspaper the opinion of a "[j]ournalist and biographer ... author of William Shakespeare" who condemns Harry Potter books as simple and publicity-seeking only, as not deserving the excitement which attends them at the time he is writing. The Harry Potter books, he says, are not like the Alice books, or the Simpsons, or other contemporary and excellent books and programs for children. Thrown into this severe evaluation of a popular series are some claims from the complaint tradition: (1) "Britain is a country with dramatically *declining standards of literacy*, increasingly dragged down to the lowest common denominator by the purveyors of all forms of mindless entertainment"; and the object of the writer's disdain and the public's delight has (2) "a pedestrian, *ungrammatical* prose style which has left me with a headache and a sense of a wasted opportunity" (emphasis added).

The complaint tradition has a long history, and promises to persist into the future, despite scholarly efforts to discredit complainers. Either language is always and perpetually in decline, or complainers are always and perpetually complaining, no matter what. Referring to complaints and panics about standards of literacy, Milroy and Milroy also point out that there is no evidence to suggest that levels of literacy today are not higher than ever.

Nevertheless, language remains the site of stigma, pejorative, ranking, and evaluation. Following some theories of language, we could think of users of a language as agents of the language's development and survival (languages, in this sense, "use" speakers) — and then go further, to think of speakers also as agents of the schemes of evaluation and ranking which attend the political life of the language. And most commentators on this situation mention the role of education (as an institutional practice) in providing the experience and criteria for evaluating speech and writing. Without mass education, modern complainers would have fewer schemes for lament, and speakers and writers would be less intimidated, and less susceptible to symbolic domination.

From this broad perspective on attitudes toward language, we can narrow our focus to the practices of academic readers. Like anyone else — like me, like you — academic readers participate in these ideologies of language. Asked to assess written work, university professors are as liable as anyone — and maybe more liable than some — to deplore the decline in the language, to complain about usages, and to dedicate themselves to correcting what they perceive to be errors. And students, having their written work assessed, are as liable as anyone — and maybe more liable than others — to experience symbolic domination, to suspect their own writing of error, and to accept and even expect moralizing pejoratives (their writing is "sloppy," "careless," it fails to show "respect for the reader").

It's possible that some elements of the typical commentary that students get on their work are inspired by dominating ideologies of language. These aspects of commentary tend to be more informative about attitudes toward speech and writing, and about the stratifications of the social order (teaching people to know their place), than about the writer's degree or quality of success as a participant in the scholarly conversation. We can regard this as useful information: in the long run, it is probably good to come into realistic contact with evaluative attitudes toward language. As Bourdieu points out, "linguistic relativism" (any usage is as good as any other) can be "naïve" (1991:52-53). But contact with evaluative attitudes can also overshadow more practical information about readers' expectations of scholarly writing.

Exercise
This practice exercise asks you to reflect on your expectations of your marker. Sentences like these can attract some markers' attention:

(i) If an informant reported visiting their country of origin for periods of more than 120 days two or more times during the previous three years, they were classified as members of "transnational" communities.

(ii) Everyone in the group expresses their commitment to principles of equality.

These look like good sentences. Why would they be vulnerable to correction? What's wrong with them?

The marker who objects to the sentences above refers to the principle of agreement in number. Plural pronouns *they, them, their* are supposed to have plural antecedents: e.g.,

> **The hooligans** were not aware that **they** were under surveillance.

Singular pronouns *she/her/hers; he/him/his; it/its* are supposed to have singular antecedents: e.g.,

> **One** of Kabeer's subjects described **her** husband as hospitable to new ideas.

In the examples (i) and (ii) above, this principle is defied. In (i), *their* and *they* do not agree with the singular noun phrase *an informant*. In (ii), *their* does not agree with singular *everyone*. These sentences could be changed to avoid the marker's corrective gaze:

> (i) If **informants** reported visiting **their** country of origin for periods of more than 120 days two or more times during the previous three years, **they** were classified as members of "trans-national" communities.

> (i) If **an informant** reported visiting **his or her** country of origin for periods of more than 120 days two or more times during the previous three years, **he or she** was classified as a member of a "transnational" community.

> (ii) **Members** of the group express their commitment to principles of equality.

> (ii) Everyone in the group expresses **his or her** commitment to principles of equality.

It may (or may not) surprise you to know that, according to many accounts of the principles for "correct" English, they could also be rewritten this way:

> (i) If an informant reported visiting **his** country of origin for periods of more than 120 days two or more times during the previous three years, **he** was classified as a member of a "transnational" community.

(ii) Everyone in the group expresses **his** commitment to principles of equality.

In "Androcentrism in Prescriptive Grammar: Singular 'they', sex-indefinite 'he', and 'he or she'" (1998[1975]), Anne Bodine examines the history of this prescription. She observes that the *they* pronoun as singular sex-indefinite is both historical and current: for centuries people have said and written sentences like —

Who dropped their ticket?

Everyone is expected to bring their work-in-progress with them.

One owner has altered the facade: they've put up a big awning.

— and they continue to do so. Until the late eighteenth century, speakers and writers were left alone, and not harassed or criticized for using *they, their, them* in these situations. Then, Bodine reports, prescriptive grammarians got hold of this feature of English, and composed rules, these rules favouring the masculine singular pronoun. They wanted:

Who dropped **his** ticket?

Everyone is expected to bring **his** work-in-progress with **him.**

One owner has altered the facade: **he** has put up a big awning.

Expanding the domain of the long-standing linguistic privilege of the masculine (e.g., man and wife, king and queen, mankind), the rule-makers referred to the value of **number** — it was not logical to have a plural pronoun and a singular noun antecedent. As Bodine points out, they pursued one logic — of "number" — and thereby forsook another — the logic of sex: if the group with "work in progress" includes both women and men, it is "illogical" to refer to them all by the masculine singular pronoun "his." Meanwhile, rule-makers dismissed the "he or she" and "his or her" alternative as "awkward" or "clumsy."

Bodine's discussion shows us that English *does* have a sex-indefinite pronoun: *they*. People use it all the time. Jane Austen used it; Shakespeare used it. Educated speakers and distinguished figures use it today — at least in speech. But if they write it down — well, then copy editors schooled by prescriptivists will want to change it. And if students use it, some markers will correct it.

Knowing that sex-indefinite *they* is both (a) a common feature of Standard English, and (b) a feature outlawed by many handbooks, what do you think markers should do? Do you want your sentence —

Everyone is entitled to their own opinion

— corrected for *their*? If a professor corrects your sentence, would you be interested in informing them of Bodine's research?

4.2 Traditions of commentary on student writing

The theory of genres — the idea, that is, that typical ways of speaking and writing enable typical social activities — suggests that different writing situations will call for different forms of expression. By now, we are well aware that the research genres display features which are not necessarily unique to them but which are arranged in ways which distinguish research writing from other kinds of writing. And we are noticing that the research genres differ amongst themselves: marine biology has things in common with archaeology but has ways of speaking that it doesn't share with archaeology; anthropology resembles psychology in some ways but not in others. Since language, involved in the diversity of ways of being and doing, tends toward variety, complainers will find lots of occasions for their services.

The complaint tradition, on the other hand, presupposes that where variety exists, there is only **one correct form** (Milroy and Milroy (1991 [1985]). These unitary views of language produce their own genres: handbooks of usage, for example ("Improve your English with this handy and authoritative reference text!"). We could also call commentary on student essays a "genre," one traditionally supported by unitary views of language. Composition textbooks often provide their users (students and teachers alike) with marking symbol guides: *run-on, gr, awk, logic, vague, ww* (= "wrong word"), *org* (= organization), *evidence*. Designed to operate universally across genres, the symbols can suggest that "[lack of] logic" or "vagueness" is identifiable regardless of reader or situation. Similarly, a company of terms escorts markers' traditional responses to student writing: "argument" (you need one), "evidence" (you need this for your argument), and "details" (you need these to support your argument) are some of these terms. But these terms can be misleading. In her study of writing in history, Sharon Stockton (1995) found that

> "[a]ll faculty agreed ... that *argument* is the key word for good writing and that the absence of argument constitutes the central problem in students' written work" (50), but that expectations differed depending on students' level, and "[i]n fact, faculty assignments, grades, and comments on student papers seem to imply that explicit argument as such was not the central issue of concern" (51). Despite professors' calls for *argument*, "[u]ltimately, assignments and evaluations show that written sophistication in student writing was in this department a function of *narrative complexity*" — "a certain specialized form of narrative" (52). When professors said "argument," they had a variety of other things in mind. (Giltrow 2000:132-33)

In this case, traditional advice on (or complaint about) student writing was misleading. In other situations, traditional commentary can usefully represent a reader's uneasiness but fail to point to the conditions which would satisfy the reader's expectations. Asked to comment on a student's essay from a Shakespeare class, a literature professor explained to us that he had written "evidence?" in the margin next to the writer's claim that "In the absence of the romantic bond, Othello's life would lose much of its meaning, and he would revert to his role as a 'soldier for pay'" because

> "There are a number of problems there; I asked for evidence. I am asking for evidence as to whether [Othello] was ever spoken of in those terms by anyone including himself as a 'soldier for pay' because that has certain connotations to it and he is a general after all. Is 'soldier for pay' a formulation which matches someone's view of Othello in the play? Is there any evidence that he loses the romantic bond? That this would happen? That he would go back to being a general?" (Giltrow 2000:134)

Here the marginal query "evidence?" hides the reader's more complete and informative response: he needs to hear some voice from the play corroborating the writer's prediction about Othello. Using general terms like "evidence," marginal commentary can fail to express the reader's genre-specific expectations — in this case, the literary-critical expectation that the writer's statements will be woven with wordings from the text. In a different research genre, "evidence" would mean something else.

Sometimes a reader's comments can appear contradictory. For example, here an academic reader asks for "specifics" in the *presence of* specifics: a student writes in a paper for a course in the sociology of the environment, "our water comes from a metal tap and flows down a metal drain … we drive over concrete roads and highways," and the professor responds, "This is the point at which I wonder when it's going to get more specific" (reported in Giltrow 2000:136). The "specifics" the student has offered are possibly suitable to another genre: for example, the "essay" question on a language-proficiency examination.

Misleading or incomplete signals are transmitted not only to students but also to researchers themselves, when their work is evaluated. One of my colleagues, Michele Valiquette, interviewed a fine arts professor whose book manuscript had been rejected. An anonymous reviewer claimed that the manuscript lacked "supporting evidence" for its "argument."

> The writer, a professional scholar, finds these remarks about argument … baffling …: "I find that a really strange comment. I mean, I can imagine, some historians would want a kind of intricate and detailed support for the reading of certain paintings and certain texts. That's fine when it comes to canonical culture, you have everyone writing in response to that culture. But when it comes to aspects of culture that were suppressed or censored … how are you going to, I mean there were no reviews … or very few…." Struggling to negotiate these readings of her work … the writer summarises advice from a senior colleague, who told her "not to sort of bond to readers' reports, that you have to understand where the reader is coming from, try to figure out their academic practices or the research practices from what they are saying about your work." (Giltrow 2000:138)

Reading between the lines of the manuscript review, this researcher recognized the reviewer's response as conditioned by genre expectations — ways of making claims and presenting data — peculiar to one sector of the discipline. She was lucky to have an encouraging mentor to help her interpret the reviewer's commentary, for these expectations were concealed by the all-purpose terms "evidence" and "argument."

It is possible that traditional marking commentary can go on at *too high a level of abstraction* to be entirely informative to writers. This high level of abstraction and generality no doubt has its own social function:

it suggests a unanimity, a consensus about what "good" writing is (it is "clear," "coherent," "logical"; it has an "argument" with "evidence"), a solidarity amongst authoritative readers. This solidarity amongst authoritative readers is no doubt comforting to them, and can also be assuring to student writers by suggesting that at least there's no confusion about goals — if they could just figure out how to achieve them.

> General advice on writing can remind us of what Alvesson (1993) says about "mission statements" — a corporate genre. Focussing on "abstract values," explicit statements of goals and values are composed in such a way as to make nonsense of contradictions. Alvesson offers the example of IBM being credited with "respect for the individual, encouragement of constructive rebellion, and emphasis on doing what is right ... values and virtues so generally and positively described as to be almost meaningless...."

4.3 Alternatives to traditional commentary

Writers of letters of complaint or application have only the outcome of their writing — a rebate or a brush-off, an interview or a *thank-you-for-your-interest-but* — as feedback on their efforts. Student writers (and professors, when they submit their research for publication or other evaluation) have the advantage of getting direct comments on their writing. Even when challenging to the writer's self-esteem, these comments are valuable. And even when they're not entirely informative, they can still be gleaned for indications of readers' genre expectations.

But traditional commentary has its shortcomings. For one thing, it can be influenced by the ideologies of language which produce the complaint tradition — deeply held views about correctness and commitments to protecting the language from the (perceived) mess its users make of it. Taking traditional commentary to heart, writers might come to think of writing mainly as a struggle to reach an inaccessible ideal: their sentences will never be good enough; the language police are sleepless in their vigilance, forever poised to raid essays for criminal imperfections and shameful lapses. But more important perhaps is the generality of commentary, suggesting a timeless and universal standard for expression, when, in fact, even in the research disciplines, diversity and change prevail.

Rather than give up on feedback altogether, we can work on developing techniques for giving and getting useful response to writing. The techniques we concentrate on in the following sections focus on **the reader's experience of using the text**: how the reader understands, anticipates, makes meaning. We find out about how readers behave when they meet words, sentences, paragraphs. From this information, we draw a portrait of the reader.

4.3.1 Catching the reader in the act: the think–aloud protocol

People studying readers' behaviour try to find out about reading comprehension: how do readers get messages from texts? What kind of writing makes the message obscure? What kind makes it clear? You can probably imagine that this kind of research is not easy. If we want to find out about how people obey traffic signals, we can put ourselves at an intersection and watch cars speeding up, slowing down, stopping, and then going again. But how can we watch people read?

To catch readers in the act, researchers have devised ways of measuring small physical signs of reading, like eye movement. And other measures try to get at comprehension itself, as a *fait accompli*, by asking readers questions about what they have read, or asking them to do other tasks connected with their reading.

Another technique for researching the reading process is the **think-aloud protocol**. The think-aloud protocol asks subjects to report the ideas that are going through their heads as they perform a task, like writing an essay or reading one. Think-aloud reports are like eyewitness testimony of events that researchers can't witness themselves. Here is a fragment of a reader's think-aloud protocol.

Text
Many people considered him to be an example of the exinanition of classic thought, but he was, in fact, a subtle and thoroughly philosophical thinker in the best classical tradition.

Comment
1. Exinanition? Queer word
2. Well, exinanition, that is really disturbing
3. Ex, that means out or out of
4. Inan, I don't know at all what that means
5. It kind of destroys the whole text
6. So it must be something which is the opposite to being a thoroughly philosophical thinker since it says:
7. He was, in fact, a thoroughly philosophical thinker

8. What you stumble on is the word, kind of, and you want to get its meaning from other things
9. But this is the only thing it is possible to get out of this, I think

Yvonne Waern 1988 "Thoughts on texts in context: Applying the think-aloud method to text processing." *Text* 8, 4, 317-50, 342.

If a writer got the kind of response cited above from a reader, she would learn that the word "exinanition" caused her reader problems, taking up processing energy. Notice that the subject doesn't say the word is *wrong*. He doesn't utter one of the typical marking expressions: "wrong word" or "faulty diction." He simply reports what is going through his head as he comes to an understanding of what he is reading. With this kind of report available, a writer could decide what revisions might benefit readers.

The think-aloud protocol resembles forms of usability testing of documents. In the process of composing manuals, instructions, information bulletins, and other genres, technical writers sometimes test their documents' efficiency by having them read out loud — by people who might purchase software, for example, or citizens who might seek information about a government program, or car owners who might need to know about a vehicle recall. As they read aloud, the subjects report their understanding, and their difficulties. In light of these reports, and informed about where other readers are likely to have trouble, writers then revise (or not — there have been some studies on when and whether technical writers actually *do* revise after usability testing). The think-aloud protocol is thus both an instrument of research and a tool for professional writers.

It can also contribute to students' conceptions of their readers, as research conducted by Karen Schriver (1994[1992]) has shown. Gathering her subjects from senior writing classes, and dividing them into experimental and control groups, Schriver provided the experimental group with 10 transcripts, over a six-week period, of readers using written instructions for aspects of operating a computing system. In the meantime, the control group was taught audience analysis and text design by more traditional methods. The experimental group studied transcripts like this:

> *OK, now I'm going to try* ... Commands for English Text. EMACS enables you to manipulate words, sentences, or paragraphs of text. *These commands sound like the ones I'd use all the time — good.* In addition, there are commands to fill text, and convert case. *I don't know what it means to fill text. I guess it means putting data from one text into another ... that is, filling the text with what you want in it. Well, I guess I'll soon find out.*

Editing files of text in a human language *human language? Boy that sounds strange, what could they be distinguishing here? Maybe computer language or machine language from human language?* ought to be done using Text mode rather than Fundamental mode. *Well, I don't know what text mode or fundamental mode is, so how will I know which I'm in? Let's see ...* Invoke M-X Text Mode to enter Text mode. *I won't do that because I do not have time to see the other section. That's terrible to tell me to ...* See section 20.1 [Major Modes], p. 85

(Schriver 1994:4)

Testing at the beginning of the study showed that the two groups were equivalent in their ability to predict when readers would have trouble with what they were reading. Testing after six weeks of instruction found that, while the control group had not changed in their ability to predict readers' difflculties, the experimental group's ability to identify where actual readers had in fact had trouble understanding what they were reading improved by 62 per cent. Improving dramatically in the accuracy of their analyses, these students also changed in the way they talked about problems: their remarks became more reader-centred or "I"-centred ("readers might not see the connection here," "I don't understand this word") and less text-centred ("this paragraph is too long"). The control group changed much less in this dimension of analysis.

Transferring the think-aloud protocol to academic writing situations, we may conceptualize readers as **users of documents**. Like technical writers observing a person working with a draft of a software manual, we observe a reader working with an instance of scholarly writing — a summary, a proposal, a research paper. From these observations, we learn where potential readers may have problems with a particular text. But we also learn about more than just particular sentences in particular writings. As Schriver's research shows, writers can also learn from think-alouds when the read-aloud text is not their own: overhearing a reader working on someone else's writing, they gain experience which they can use to sketch their portrait of the reader. Schriver's research suggests that this kind of close-up experience of readers' behaviours can be generalized — to anticipate readers' responses to our own work-in-progress, to explain responses to previous work, to help us plan future work.

4.3.2 The sounds of think-aloud

Thinking out loud while reading doesn't necessarily come naturally. For one thing, most thinkers-aloud have long experience of traditional marking commentary and, in their first attempts, are liable to reproduce its sounds ("this is well organized," "there should be a thesis statement," "this flows"). And, face-to-face with the writer, thinkers-aloud may be tempted to praise, contracting perhaps for praise in return. It's also tempting to just read, and not comment.

Recognizing that readers may not be sure of how to break the silence, we have developed models and guidelines for thinking aloud. For research purposes, when we ask instructors to think aloud, we provide a model like this:

> The purpose of this paper will be to show how the representation of Africans can be extended to the representation of women in *Heart of Darkness* written by Joseph Conrad. *This sounds like the essay question to me. That's not terrible, but I find I don't really pay attention when I hear the sound of an essay question.* "The Heart of Darkness *written by Joseph Conrad"* — *that sounds as if I don't know Conrad wrote* Heart of Darkness. *I'd prefer something like "Conrad's* Heart of Darkness." This will be accomplished by the analysis of the inhuman role of women in the story, *"the inhuman role of women"* — *I stop there* — *the women behave in a non-human way? that doesn't seem to be right* — *oh, maybe. I'm thinking of Kurtz's "Intended"* ... *"inhuman"? oh well* ... the supremacy imposed upon them, and their physical attributes which emit a darker figure of the human woman. *"supremacy"? in what sense? I think I see what he's getting at, but it's hard work getting through this sentence: what does "supremacy" have to do with "inhuman" and then "darker figure"? "human woman"? Maybe the body* ... *there could be something here in the disparity between dark interpretations of the body and interpretations of woman as supreme ideal, but this whole first paragraph reminds me of the introduction to a five-paragraph essay: thesis statement, three points.*

We then add explicit guidelines for those who will be responding in instructional situations — students, teaching assistants, professors.

Guidelines for readers
*You are not a marker / evaluator; you are a person **using** a document. You make **no judgements**; you only report what's going on in your mind.*

Rather than...	*aim for ...*
this is ungrammatical sentence.	I'm having trouble with this There's something about it that makes me stop. I've read this sentence twice.

Rather than…	*aim for …*
	Now I'm going on but I'm still not sure about that sentence.
this is the wrong word	this word makes me stop. I'm not sure why you use this word: why do you say "social" agenda? that's a positive term to me, but you seem to be using it in a negative way.
	I don't really know what this word means: "peer review" — I stop there, I have no idea.
there's no thesis statement	OK, I'm through the first paragraph, but I can't really say what you're going to focus on. Is it the public perception, or the corporate model? I hope I find out in the next paragraph.
	I'm through the first paragraph, and I figure you see a connection between the "back-to-basics" idea and the "standardization" Zieber mentions. You're going to talk about that.
repetition	I think you already said this — or did I get it wrong? Is there something different here and I missed it?
no transition	I'm having a hard time making a connection between this paragraph and this one — this is about the university's "service agenda" and this one is about "depersonalization." Is the connection that they're both individualistic? That's my guess but I don't know if that's what you intend, and I don't feel very sure I could explain this to some one else. It's hard work here.
the main point should be at the start	Oh now I see what you're saying. I'm going to go back and re-read to see if I missed something.

Report moments when you're working efficiently — understanding, getting new ideas of your own:

> "who learns and why" yes I see that — the "who" is about access, and that's a question of social class and the distribution of wealth, and the "why" is about the role of knowledge in the society, or in the economy. I'm thinking it's also "what" — if you put the who and the why together you start to go towards the answer to the "what" — what should be taught?

*Offer frequent reports of the **gist** of what you're reading:*

> OK so far I have this main idea in mind: the Zieber article might seem more radical but it's actually more traditional. That's what I'm getting from this.

And to these suggestions for readers, we add guidelines for writers, encouraging them to take advantage of this opportunity to see what happens when their writing is out in the world, on its own, without their recommendation or apology.

Guidelines for writers
- don't explain or justify what you've done
- value the chance to watch someone making meaning from what you've written

Think-aloud can be practised on any piece of writing, for any piece of writing is a document to be *used*, in some way, and readers can report their experience of making use of it. The next example is my own think-aloud on a passage from a book (Ian Hunter [1988] *Culture and Government*).

> **Unlike classical education** *I guess I have a general idea of what this is, although I'm not sure how he sees it in this context,* **Romantic aesthetic education** *I'm stopping here, "Romantic aesthetic education", does that mean that "Romantic education" was aesthetic? or that "aesthetics" was one branch of Romantic education? I think it's the latter* **was directed at the individual's aesthetico-ethical organisation** *"aesthetico-ethical," I don't like "o" suffixes, but lots of people use them; so this would be moral development going along with learning to appreciate beauty —* **at producing** *here is an explanation* **a synthesis out of the divided "ethical substance"** *I stop there, what is that? I'm just going back, maybe I missed something, no … ;* **and this practice of**

ethical reconciliation has indeed passed into the modern teaching of English. *I don't understand the "divided substance" but I have a hunch about reconciliation — not that I could explain this to anyone, so far* **Unlike the latter, however,** *OK the romantic idea is different from the modern one* **the Romantic aesthetics of self-cultivation was for most of the nineteenth century a more or less voluntary "practice of the self"** *"practice of the self," not sure what that is but I like the sound of it, I guess it's equivalent to "self-cultivation," improving yourself, something you do on your own initiative,* **confined to caste groupings at one remove from the emerging machinery of popular education** *it was something the élite did, I think that's it, although "one remove" sounds not very far away and the élite would be very far away from the classes served by "popular education," maybe I don't use "at one remove" the proper way. OK it was élite practice, I think that's it, but I wish there were a specific — what groups of people did this, what did they do? Maybe it doesn't matter that I don't know what "divided substance" is; I'm not sure what it has to do with the élite being separate from the masses. But I get the general idea that ...*

What should the writer do? Well, he doesn't have to do anything. His book is published, and he is well known. But others who overhear this might learn about difficulties a reader can have when she encounters many complicated, high-level abstractions and no lower-level mentions.

Exercise

Two excerpts follow, each from the beginning of literary narratives. The second is written in a fairly traditional "realist" style, the first in a less traditional style. Guided by the suggestions and models above, practise think-aloud, reporting your efforts to understand, including those points where you stop, or re-read, or question and speculate.

PASSAGE 1
[beginning of "The Prologue," Keri Hulme, The Bone People *(1984)]*

He walks down the street. The asphalt reels by him.
It is all silence.
The silence is music.
He is the singer.
The people passing smile and shake their heads.

He holds a hand out to them.
They open their hands like flowers, shyly.
He smiles with them.
The light is blinding: he loves the light.
They are the light.

★★★

He walks down the street. The asphalt is hot and soft with
sun.
The people smile, and call out greetings.
He smiles and calls back.
His mind is full of change and curve and hope, and he knows
it is being lightly tapped. He laughs.
Maybe there is the dance, as she says. Creation and change,
destruction and change.
New marae from the old marae, a beginning from the end.
His mind weaves it into a spiral fretted with stars.
He holds out his hand, and it is gently taken.

★★★

She walks down the street. The asphalt sinks beneath her
muscled feet.
She whistles softly as she walks. Sometimes she smiles.
The people passing smile too, but duck their heads in a
deferential way as though her smile is too sharp.
She grins more at their lowered heads. She can dig out each
thought, each reaction, out from the grey brains, out through
the bones. She knows how. She knows a lot.
She is eager to know more.
But for now there is the sun at her back, and home here, and
the free wind all round.
And them, shuffling ahead in the strange-paced dance. She
quickens her steps until she has reached them.
And she sings as she takes their hands.

★★★

   They were nothing more than people, by themselves.
Even paired, any pairing, they would have been nothing
more than people by themselves. But all together, they have
become the heart and muscles and mind of something
perilous and new, something strange and growing and
great.
   Together, all together, they are the instruments of
change.

PASSAGE 2

[beginning of "Prologue: 1975," Rohinton Mistry, A Fine Balance *(1995)]*

The morning express bloated with passengers slowed to a crawl, then lurched forward suddenly, as though to resume full speed. The train's brief deception jolted its riders. The bulge of humans hanging out of the doorway distended perilously, like a soap bubble at its limit.

Inside the compartment, Maneck Kohlah held on to the overhead railing, propped up securely within the crush. He felt someone's elbow knock his textbooks from his hand. In the seats nearby, a thin fellow was catapulted into the arms of the man opposite him. Maneck's textbooks fell upon them.

"Ow!" said the young fellow, as volume one slammed out of his lap and back onto the seat. "Everything all right, Om?"

"Apart from the dent in my back, everything is all right," said Omprakash Darji, picking up the two books covered in brown paper. He hefted them in his slender hands and looked around to find who had dropped them.

Maneck acknowledged ownership. The thought of his heavy textbooks thumping that frail spine made him shudder. He remembered the sparrow he had killed with a stone, years ago; afterwards, it had made him sick.

His apology was frantic. "Very sorry, the books slipped and — "

"Not to worry," said Ishvar. "Wasn't your fault." To his nephew he added, "Good thing it didn't happen in reverse, hahn? If I fell in your lap, my weight would crack your bones." They laughed again, Maneck too, to supplement his apology.

Ishvar Darji was not a stout man; it was the contrast with Omprakash's skinny limbs that gave rise to their little jokes about his size. The wisecracks originated sometimes with one and sometimes the other. When they had their evening meal, Ishvar would be sure to spoon out a larger portion onto his nephew's enamel plate; at a roadside dhaba, he would wait till Omprakash went for water, or to the latrine, then swiftly scoop some of his own food onto the other leaf.

If Omprakash protested, Ishvar would say, 'What will they think in our village when we return? That I starved my nephew in the city and ate all the food myself? Eat, eat! Only way to save my honour is by fattening you!'

4.3.3 Reading on behalf of others

Consider the following first sentence of an essay:

> The four articles have in common a focus on the experience of
> marginalized identities in times of social change.

> Traditional commentary: *What articles?*

> Think-aloud commentary: *I know which articles you're referring
>   to, but others wouldn't.*

Classroom situations bring to light some special conditions of think-
aloud response. Readers who are fellow students or the instructor share
with the writer certain knowledge of the immediate scholarly situation:
readings, assignments, circumstances exclusive to that course. So the
"traditional" remark "what articles?" can seem odd. After all, the marker *knows* about the articles.

In early days of using think-aloud techniques, and trying to avoid
reproducing traditional commentary, I used to keep quiet at points like
those exemplified above. But I was uneasily quiet, because, just like the
"traditional" reader, I was reacting to "the articles," and just not saying
so, for I *did* know what articles the writer was referring to. Examining
my response, I realized that I was reading on behalf of other readers:
people who had not been in this class. I was uneasy on their behalf.
Now I report these reactions.

Similarly, encountering a specialist term which has been thoroughly
discussed in class —

> Chavez's work (1994) on undocumented immigrants offers new
> perspectives on transnational communities.

— a marker might inscribe their response with an instruction: "Define."
Since the marker was present during discussion, and has read the materials being discussed, this too can seem odd. Or it can be taken as a blanket directive to define everything in sight, no matter how apparently
well known. A thinker-aloud might also stop at this point, not because
they don't know the meaning of "transnational community" but
because they sense the possibility of another reader — another participant in scholarly discussion — coming across the term. These are the
conditions which trigger the appositives we discussed in Chapter Three.
If, thinking aloud in response to a fellow student's writing, you find
yourself concerned about others' understanding, report your estimate of
their possible difficulty.

4.3.4 Thinking "grammar" aloud

Our earlier discussion of the complaint tradition and ideologies of correctness might lead you to suppress all notice of what appear to you to be departures from Standard English — in spelling or grammar. But if you *do* notice something, say so! It's part of your experience of using the piece of writing, and useful information for the writer. If spelling and grammar turn out to be tremendous obstacles to your appreciation of the writer's intentions, and your participation in their project, then you need to report this circumstance. But you might also try to report the degree to which missing apostrophes or odd spellings are confounding your efforts to find meaning.

> *I notice that "is" comes after "institution and government" — that should be "are," I think, but it's not stopping me*

> *I've lost this sentence, I thought it was ending. Now I see a comma, so I'm going back to re-read*

By giving the writer the measure of difficulty — "it's minor, so fixing this isn't going to make much difference over all"; "it's a big block, so it had better be attended to" — you make "grammar" a matter of the reader's experience of the text, rather than a matter of living up to rules.

4.3.5 The ambiguity of questions

> According to Kabeer, following
> Giddens, community membership
> is made up of both rules *and* resources.   *What's the difference?*

Markers often respond to student writing with questions. I do so myself, and for a long time I felt quite satisfied with this practice. It seemed "interactive," and engaged. But a study (Cowan, Giltrow, Josephson, and Valiquette 1997) we conducted with five writers responding on-line to one another's work showed me the ambiguity of questions. As I worked on analysing responses, and measuring the revisions which resulted, I found that I couldn't be sure of the meaning of the questions. In the sample above, does the question mean that the reader *doesn't know* what the difference is between "rules" and "resources"?

> *What's the difference?*   = I don't know what the
>   difference is.

Or is the question an instruction, a directive telling the writer to do something?

> *What's the difference?*   = You should do what I am telling you, which is to define these terms and explain the difference.

Or is the question a sign of the reader engaging with the point?

> *What's the difference?*   = I'm thinking that the *difference* is complicated, maybe a "rule" can be a "resource" in some circumstances. I wonder if the "rule" about female seclusion could be a "resource" contributing to ethnic identity.

Now I try to specify my intentions when asking a question: I am asking this because (a) I don't know what this is; (b) I can imagine readers appreciating seeing this briefly discussed; (c) you've made me think about this, and wonder.

Questions can be ambiguous in everyday conversation too. *A* can ask *B*

> Have you paid the phone bill?

when (1) *A* is about to pay the bills and will pay the phone bill if *B* says "no"; (2) *A* knows *B* has not paid the phone bill and means to say "I do everything around here and I am mad because you haven't even paid the phone bill, it is the least you could do, etc." So sometimes we answer a question with another question, "Why do you ask?" — and then design our response to the first question.

4.3.6 Think-aloud and genre theory

Genre theory finds the regularities of writing in **readers' and writers' social experience**. Readers and writers know — or get to know — how to write in ways which will satisfy a situation, or to read in ways that include recognition of a situation through their mutual experience of types of situations. It's not rules and enforcements that make writing acceptable but *contact* with instances.

Think-aloud techniques coax out this readerly know-how. By focussing on readers' experience in efforts to understand, think-aloud articulates what would otherwise remain unspoken. And it concentrates on what works for readers, speaking to their expectations, rather than on what satisfies rules.

But what if your reader is not particularly experienced in the genre in which you are writing? What if you are inexperienced and the reader is as inexperienced as you are? What if you are asked to think aloud on a paper for a social geography course, and you have never seen a paper or taken a course in social geography before? *If you are the reader,* declare your point of departure: "I don't even know what social geography is…. I don't know anything about social geography, but still I'd say that it's hard to see how this paragraph relates to what you say in your introduction … now this seems to repeat what you've said before … OK what you're saying is…." *If you are the writer,* consider the source: this is a novice's effort to understand what you have written. The novice will have some experience of scholarly writing, and their responses will still be valuable.

Years ago, I found myself reading a lot of history papers for students, responding to their drafts. I had not been good at history myself as an undergraduate, but from my experience of other disciplines, I figured that probably these student writers needed more abstractions to manage all the details they reported. A colleague and I interviewed several history professors, and they seemed to agree with this idea. And, like Stockton's (1995) interview subjects, they recommended that students have an "argument." Eventually I realized that I was wrong in my advice. To be sure, abstractions were expected, but, in history, they were laminated with detail rather than elevated. The "argument" comprised delicate manoeuvres of abstraction which never weakened that lamination, and at the same time reached deep into the archival sources which supplied the details. Although I had conscientiously "thought aloud," and so had the historians who were our subjects, it wasn't until I had much more contact with published research in history that I *recognized* this research genre, and really *heard* the voice of the discipline.

The discipline of history has been a lesson to me. History is like other research genres — but different from them too, in very important ways. My inexperience in history could not be compensated for even by my experience in other research disciplines. And, among experts in the field, know-how was mainly ***tacit***: difficult to articulate, and potentially misleading when stated. But I also learned that this is not a hopeless situation. By paying attention to instances of the genre, and reading lots of scholarly publications in history, I eventually tuned in.

4.3.7 Reliability of readers

How far can you count on your thinking-aloud reader? Like any readers — like you, like me, like the reader of the Fine Arts professor's manuscript — the thinking-aloud reader occupies a position in the world, whose coordinates comprise that person's experience, interests, temperament, politics. Sometimes readers will come out with things which reflect peculiarities of position:

> There is a gap in our understanding of tradition and migration.
>
> *"gap," I don't like that word it reminds me of the store and khaki*

Maybe no one else on earth would have said this. (Or, on the other hand, maybe this word is being appropriated by brand mentality and will soon be captive to commercial connotations.) If no one else would have this reaction and the thinker-aloud is not the reader for whom the paper is destined, then the writer can probably leave it as is.

We still might wonder, though, how idiosyncratic responses are, over all. In the study mentioned above (Cowan et al. 1998), we were particularly interested in inter-reader reliability: to what degree did five readers' independent responses agree? We found that, during the four-month period of the study, agreement amongst readers increased. It seems that (as Schriver's study showed too) being in earshot of readers reading, thinkers-aloud developed a sense of a larger audience, and became spokespersons for that audience, which included them but also went beyond them. Without explicit coaching to do so, they began to read on behalf of others, or their ways of expressing their responses made them more representative of others' reactions. This is a limited finding, but enough to encourage the practice of listening in on other writers getting feedback: it enlarges materials for portraits of readers.

As Schriver's research on think-aloud protocols shows, writers can learn about readers by examining and considering transcripts of readers' responses to others' writing. With this benefit in mind, I asked two experienced readers of academic writing to respond to passages representative of undergraduate writing. At the end of this chapter, I present those passages and responses for your inspection and information. I also present the transcripts as *models* of think-aloud techniques of response. The readers who offer their responses are skilled in giving this kind of feedback to writers.

Before we approach those transcripts, however, I would like to give you brief accounts of some theories of reading and understanding. Perhaps one or two — or all — of these conceptualizations will particularly speak to you and give you insight into your situation as a writer addressing a reader. And these various theories may also give you language for talking about writing, as well as means of thinking about the outcomes — sometimes successful, sometimes possibly disappointing — of your writing.

4.4 Structures of reading

Over instances, think-aloud protocols reveal occasions where readers typically have trouble. Think-alouds reveal both **social** and **cognitive** occasions for trouble. For example, a reader experienced in the research genres stops at an unqualified or unattributed claim:

> For centuries, women had no alternative but to marry or go into religious orders.

> *Well that might have been true in some cases but there were alternatives, a woman could become the housekeeper of a widowed father or brother for example, and different areas of Europe…*

This response is conditioned by the reader's experience of the research genres, which privilege complexity, limitation, readiness for exceptions. Another reader, with experience of feature-article genres in popular publications and without scholarly expectations, might not stop at all at this statement.

Or sometimes a reader might stop for reasons we could see as more "cognitive" — almost anybody would stop.

> RVers have pot-luck dinners, and they exchange addresses before they hit the road again. "Private-park" RVers object to the way "boondockers" live.

> *oh…what's the connection here? pot-luck and addresses, that sounds like friendliness, but then there are objections. Maybe the boondockers don't have pot-luck dinners? Is that why the private-park people object? Or each type has the same rituals but they don't get together and that's a kind of contradiction? I don't know. I need some help.*

Like any reader on any occasion, this one looks for connections between statements: a reason for the second sentence to appear in the context of the first. Having no guide from the writer, the reader struggles on her own. This could be seen as a cognitive response — a reaction which records general efforts at reasoning.

Still, it's hard to separate cognition from sociality, for there may be cultures where pot-luck or address-exchange are not signs of friendliness, and the reasoning would go differently.

4.4.1 Abstraction, details, and readers' efforts after meaning

Work done in the early 1980s (especially van Dijk 1980, and van Dijk and Kintsch 1983) suggests that readers take cues from higher-level content in interpreting details, and in storing the meaning of those details. The passage above, for example, could be resolved for readers by abstractions which instruct them in how to use the details.

> RVers have pot-luck dinners, and they exchange addresses before they hit the road again. **Yet this** *reciprocity* **occurs alongside** *stigmatization*. "Private-park" RVers object to the way "boon-dockers" live.

Now pot-luck and address-exchange mean *reciprocity*, and *reciprocity* is posed as at least partly conflicting with *sitgmatization*. The scholarly practices of abstraction we explored in Chapters Two and Three are not just formalities: they have important cognitive functions as guides for readers and as directives to cognitive activities. As we saw in 4.4, these activities can be witnessed especially in the absence of such guides, when readers attempt a passage without higher-level terms ("macro-propositions" in van Dijk's analyses).

Still, as we saw in Chapter Three, abstractions are not purely cognitive operators. They also have a social aspect. For instance, in the humanities and some social sciences, some abstractions simply enjoy more prestige than others, having a current career in the life of the discipline. And in the sciences and some social sciences, technical abstractions can have definitions which are the product of labour amongst researchers, as they collaborate on and corroborate the circumstances in which particular abstractions can be used.

As useful as abstractions can be, not all genres call for them. We have seen that narrative may touch abstractions only intermittently, and in some cases not at all. Telephone books have high-level, generalizing titles — "Calgary," "San Diego" — and then plunge into details of names and addresses and phone numbers. How do people manage with genres like telephone books, when they seem to have trouble with mention of pot-luck dinners? The next section looks at occasions where readers manage apparently unrelated details, and compares them to scholarly writing occasions.

4.4.2 Relevance

People using telephone books don't read, stop, and say "I'm having trouble with this. What's the connection here? Is this about *community*? or *alienation*, and *fragmentation*?" They don't need high-level guides to use phone books, because they bring a question of their own to the page ("What's Binky's phone number?"). The question provides a context for interpretation, whereas readers of "RVers have pot-luck dinners" are not likely to have a context of interpretation for this statement (unless, perhaps, they were preparing for some RVing themselves, packing up their motorhome and wondering if they should include a casserole dish, or their recipe for lasagna. But then they would read a "Guide to RVing in America" rather than an academic paper).

The conditions which make a statement usable in context have been described by Sperber and Wilson (1986) as having to do with **relevance**. On the one hand, "relevance" is an everyday term which makes ordinary sense: someone might say, regarding mention of pot-luck dinners, "How is this relevant?" But "relevance" also becomes, in Sperber and Wilson's hands, a technical abstraction, accompanied by measures of degrees of relevance: a statement is relevant in indirect relation to the effort it takes to find the context in which it is meaningful. The more processing effort it takes a reader to find a context for interpretation, the less relevant the statement is for that reader. For example, in the following —

> Bingo: Binky, what's your phone number?
> Binky: 888-9999

— "888-9999" is highly relevant to Bingo because the context — Bingo's own question — is immediately accessible. It takes very little effort for Bingo to find this context. The reader who encountered mention of private-parkers' criticisms of boondockers in the context of mention of pot-luck dinners and address-exchange, however, has to make a much bigger effort to discover a larger context in which the criticism is meaningful. (This is a simplification of Sperber and Wilson's theory. They speak of "contextual implications" instead of meaningfulness, and the delicacy of their analyses would probably fill the loopholes you may see in my rough analyses.)

We can apply relevance theory to genre theory. Some genres, serving contexts which both reader and writer recognize, can in part look like the pot-luck passage, where the connection between adjacent statements — the relevance of one to the other — is not clear on the surface. In reference genres, like encyclopaedias or computer manuals, sentences next to each other can seem to bear only a general relation to one another. Here is an entry from *The Encyclopaedia of Aquarium Fish* (David J. Coffey 1977 London: Pelham) for Brachygobius or "bumble-beefish":

> A native of Indian and south-east Asia. Has a yellow body with broad, vertical, dark brown or black bands. It is most at home and spends most of its time close to the bottom of the aquarium. (70)

This is generally about the bumblebeefish, but what is the connection between the fish's origin, its appearance, and its favourite spot? Does the author mean to say that, *because* of its dark-striped yellow body, the fish lurks at the bottom? What does the fish's colour have to do with the bottom of the aquarium? However, most readers would not ask such questions. The social use of encyclopaedia genres is such that readers bring information requirements with them, and these requirements contribute to the context for interpretation of details.

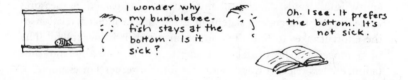

So the reader's context of understanding makes the sentence "It is most at home … close to the bottom of the aquarium" **relevant**, and meaningful. (It has immediate "contextual implications.")

It has been observed that some parts of some research genres also have a list-like structure that seems to answer unstated questions like the bumblebeefish questions. John Swales (1990) has noted this condition in the *Method* section of research articles. In Chapter Six we will see that the *Background* section of ethnography can also present patterns of connectedness (or un-connectedness) similar to that of the encyclopaedia article.

But for the most part the research genres are not like the reference genres in this respect. That is why simply offering extra information about Dickens ("Dickens was born in Portsmouth") in case your reader might be interested, or might have a question about Dickens ("*I'm making a map of the birthplaces of famous writers. I'll just read this literature essay to see if I can find out where Dickens was born"*), doesn't work. This is not to say that birthplaces of authors are not mentioned in literature papers, but that the reader will work to find a context in which the fact of a writer being born in a certain place (or even at a certain time) is meaningful.

Abstractions can also be analysed for their relevance. Some abstractions are poised at the thresholds of many easily accessible contexts in certain disciplines. They can operate powerfully to make details meaningful, although all abstractions, in academic contexts at any rate, probably contribute to relevance.

4.4.3 The mental desktop

We will explore one more technique for composing our portrait of the reader. Derived from cognitive studies, this technique pictures the reader organizing a **desktop**: a space on which statements arrive, one after the other, as the reader advances through a text.

If your actual desktop is like mine, it gets covered with piles of paper, and you end up paying attention only to what's on top — most recently arrived — until these pages themselves get covered by new arrivals. Reading can be like this, too, if what we are reading is very difficult for us: we concentrate on one sentence or a few sentences at a time. In the meantime, previous sentences disappear from consciousness.

The reader's desktop is a finite area. It can't get bigger. In other words, the reader's attention span — or short-term memory — is inelastic. No matter how hard readers try (or how much you wish they would try), they can only concentrate on a relatively small number of things at a time. This is the way the human brain works. Writers have to learn to live with this inescapable condition of reading comprehension.

This small, inelastic space for paying attention may make the reader seem like a limited being, hardly worth addressing with an interesting paper. Moreover, the limitation does not match other qualities of our own reading experience: we read articles, chapters, books, and we have a sense of remembering a lot more than the handful of items that happened to be the last ones to pass across our mental desktop.

According to the theories behind the mental desktop image, readers **manage** their desktops — successfully under good circumstances, less successfully under other circumstances. Up to a certain point, it's the *writer* who is responsible for these circumstances.

To the picture of the reader and desktop I will add a **management device**. The management device arranges and uses mental space. The mental space is furnished with, in addition to the desktop, a sort of **side-table** for temporary storage, and **filing cabinets** for long-term storage. To manage the flow of information and make the most of it, the reader operates the management device to assign statements to these different mental spaces. The reader operates the device to detect:

- those items which can be combined to form a single item, thus leaving room on the desktop for new items to be concentrated on:

    "Mitsubishi ... Toshiba ... Sumitomo ..." these three examples all show family networks associated with corporate growth ... I'll combine them as such. Now there's room for more.

- those items which can be put aside but kept nearby on the mental "side-table" as not centrally relevant at this point but liable to be necessary at any moment:

    Most of this isn't about family, *but family* is bound to come up again. I'll just put the idea of family *and* corporate growth here, *within easy reach when it's needed.*

- those items which can be neglected, left to fall off the desktop when other material arrives —

    OK, the American market is just an example, not part of the main focus

    — or sent to long-term memory files which house all we know but aren't thinking about right now:

    American markets don't seem to be important to this discussion. I won't be needing this. I'll file it.

When there is no immediate, accessible context for interpreting details, the reader can't *use* them for their contextual implications. (Here we see a **cognitive** outcome of a **structural** feature: a passage that stays low, and doesn't make higher, interpretive levels accessible, can confound a reader.)

> *Here's Mitsubishi, here's Toshiba, and now here's Sumitomo ... hmm ... Does this mean cartel? Or some other form of market domination? Is it good? Is it bad? I'm not sure. I'd better keep all this material and these possibilities here on my desk.*

Finally, when the management device is not properly directed to a clear context for interpretation, it may make some very inefficient decisions about long-term storage. Encountering a big claim early in an essay, and finding it neither developed nor repeated in subsequent passages, the device may judge that it is not important enough to keep handy. So the claim gets sent to the long-term memory files — that big, elastic capacity that houses the person's experience and knowledge of the world.

> *American markets haven't come up again. I predict they won't. I'll send this to long-term storage and make room for other things.*

Now the material is not exactly forgotten, but it is no longer in mind. And, stored in long-term files, it is relatively inaccessible compared to items on the desktop and on temporary holding surfaces. If the device has made a mistake, and it turns out that this material *is* needed, the reader has to go and retrieve the item from the long-term files.

> *Now, what's this about? It seems to presuppose ideas about American markets. Do I have something on that? Maybe in my files … where did I put that?*

The retrieval takes up attention capacity. During the time the reader spends retrieving something from long-term storage (assuming he *can* retrieve it, and hasn't simply forgotten it), the desktop gets dishevelled. When he returns, he finds that things have fallen off, and have to be recalled by re-reading.

4.5 Readers read

In this section, you will hear readers reading passages, thinking aloud as they go. Each of the two readers has long experience reading and writing in the research genres — in language studies, rhetoric, the social sciences, literary studies. The passages are representative of undergraduate writing in the humanities and social sciences. Some are taken directly from student essays; some are like those which formed the basis for Schriver's study, developed to activate and make audible readers' behaviour as they encounter particular kinds of information structures.

While there is a lot to be learned from these passages and the responses they activate, this selection is by no means exhaustive of the occasions of scholarly writing and reading. Rather, it is intended as a glimpse of what is usually hidden from writers: the sight (and sound) of readers-at-work. It may inspire you to conduct your own, further inquiries: to ask readers to read for you — your own work or others' — or to become more observant of your own reading experiences.

Each reading episode begins with the target passage. (1) Start by reading the passage, developing your own response to it, and, in light of that response, estimating the response of other academic readers. (2) Then inspect the reader's (or readers') think-aloud response: how would you analyse the reader's work on the passage? What conditions seem to be affecting the reader's reception of this writing? (Reading Episode 1 is followed by such an analysis, to suggest the kind of reasoning you might do to interpret these readers' responses.) (3) Finally, consider what changes you might recommend to the writers of these passages: how should they think about revision? (Reading Episode 1 is followed by an example of such recommendations.)

Reading Episode 1

[a beginning]

Everyone has their own definition of community. For some people it is the place they grew up. For others it is the place they live and work in. Anderson says community is "imagined" (quoted in Chavez 1994).

But what is community? Webster's (1987) defines community as "a unified body of individuals; ... the people with common interests living in a particular area; ... an interacting population of various kinds of individuals ... in a common location." What happens to a community when its original basis, the idea people have of its founding and its reason for existing, is threatened? In this paper I will investigate one such case: coastal communities where fishing has been a way of life and now the salmon stocks are greatly reduced and, in some cases the fishery has been closed.

READER A

Everyone has their own definition of community. OK I'm stopping here because I'm thinking this is a definition paper ... because I'm thinking that what's important here is the definition but what I would want is um an indication of why I'm being given this information so I was trying to supply that information in terms of it being a definition paper um ok so I have this general sense that everyone has their own definition of community I'm still at this point not sure of why I'm reading this or why this is important that I get a sense of this generalness of everyone having their own definition **For some people it is the place they grew up.** ok so um **the place they grew up** so I'm getting further distinctions in terms of definition **For others it is the place they live and work in** ok [pause] still don't have a sense ok I guess we're talking about community and different perceptions of community here [pause] that I'm not really sure what to do with these differences they seem so general I need something more focussed **Anderson says community is "imagined"** ok I have a source here so I'm thinking that the idea of community is confirmed so she'll be paying attention to this um I'm not quite sure I understand what Anderson would mean by "imagined" at this point or the significance of this. **But what is community?** ok another question! but still I'm intrigued by this "imagined" and mainly it's because as a reader of scholarly writing I'm interested in scholarly reports of things **Webster's (1987) defines community as "a unified body of individuals; ... the people with common interests living in a particular area; ...** ok people with common interests living in a particular area ok so this refers back to the kinds of definition that I read above here **an interacting population of various kinds of individuals ... in a common location."** ok so this issue of commonality is always important ... I'm still not sure why I need to answer what is community but I'll continue **What happens to a community when its original basis, the idea people have of its founding and its reason for existing, is threatened?** not quite sure what to do with this question and I'm not sure how we go from these sort of general definitions of community to something happening to community this threat and I don't know why this threat is important for the writer and I'm still keeping in mind this idea of imagined so how is that related to any of this **In this paper I will investigate** I appreciate this I feel like I'm getting a sense of what um hopefully I'll read on and get an idea of what I'm supposed to be focussing on **one such case: coastal communities where fishing has been a way of life and now the salmon stocks are greatly reduced and, in some cases the fishery has been closed.** ok I have to re-read [re-reads last sentence] **one such case —** of this threat to community **coastal communities where fishing has been a way of life and now the salmon stocks are greatly reduced** I'm assuming but I'm not being told that [pause] practices in the community are being threatened so I'm assuming that the community will change somehow I'm still not sure what the significance of this is ok so I move from these sort of general definitions of community to [pause] um some questions of what community is and an instance not the operation of community but something

happening to a community I don't know how things are adding up here, what I should be focussing on, but I get from the end of it that I should be focussing on changes in communities but I have to infer that this idea of threat and this change in the salmon stocks

Analysis of response

What do we learn from this encounter between reader and text? The reader looks for the **relevance** of the opening claim: a context in which it would have implications. She hypothesizes that the writer was *assigned* a definition (which suggests a classroom rather than scholarly motivation, possibly). But her inference is not confident: she still wonders "why [she is] reading this." She recognizes the citation as a scholarly move, but dwells on "imagined" — a complex idea. The definition from "Webster's" does not displace "imagined": the reader keeps it on her mental desktop, even though it is not called for again (in this excerpt). Seeking connections, the reader works on connecting the dictionary definition with material from the first paragraph. The writer's question and statement of intention gives the reader some confidence, but she still works to find a connection between, on the one hand, the question and statement and, on the other hand, what has gone before. For herself, she constructs the focus on *change*.

Thinking about revision

If I were advising the writer, or working on this passage myself, I would focus first on "imagined" community (which attracted the reader's interest), from Anderson, and develop this definition to establish connections which the reader struggled to make. These connections could be secured by working with Anderson's definition to involve prevailing ideas like "original basis," "founding," and "reason for being": shared themes in people's *imaginations.* And then I would look at connecting these *imaginary* conditions with the *material* conditions of daily work and "way of life" (communities not being *imagined* out of thin air). And now the question stands up: what happens to the *imaginary* when the *material actuality* changes? The coastal communities the writer refers to offer an occasion for addressing this question.

I would probably leave out Webster's definition, and the general claims about "[e]veryone [having] their own definition of community."

Reading Episode 2, in which two readers respond to the same passage

[a beginning]

In Camerons' article (1995) she observes that improper grammar can cause people to make unfair or discriminatory judgements about the speakers or writers who make these errors. Attitudes towards language are often based on social prejudice: low-class people are condemned by members of the elite for being lazy and undisciplined. As Milroy and Milroy point out (1991), prejudices that would be unacceptable to express in any other context are acceptable in talking about grammar. (Milroy and Milroy 1991)

Nevertheless, I believe that it is important for people to have the skills necessary to express themselves in ways that earn them the social respect they deserve.

READER A

In Camerons' article (1995) I'm stopping here I notice the apostrophe but I'm stopping because I wouldn't mind an indication of what the article is because this assumes I know what particular article **she observes that improper grammar can cause people to make unfair or discriminatory judgements about the speakers or writers who make these errors.** um I'm stopping on the use of improper and error because it seems that — **grammar can cause people to make unfair or discriminatory judgements** it seems that this part of the gist of Cameron's article questions the idea of improperness itself or error [pause] but still I'm getting a sense of the topic nonetheless that it's um people have ideas about language and based on these ideas about language they make judgements about people's use of language **Attitudes towards language are often based on social prejudice:** ok so this does fulfill my idea of what the topic is **Attitudes towards language are often based on social prejudice: low-class people are condemned by members of the elite for being lazy and undisciplined.** I'll just stop because I'm trying to make a connection between language **Attitudes towards language are often based on social prejudice: low-class people are condemned by members of the elite for being lazy and undisciplined.** ok so the social elite considers the language use of low-class speakers as reflections of their character [pause] their attitudes towards language would probably follow these perceptions of these other people um it's a beginning ok so I'll expect to hear more about the connection between language and this particular perception later on ok **As Milroy and Milroy point out (1991), prejudices that would be unacceptable to express in any other context are acceptable in talking about grammar. (Milroy and Milroy 1991)** repeat ok so it seems to me that this says that language becomes a site for all these other attitudes that it's perfectly acceptable to talk about these attitudes in the context of language use or grammar I'm expecting to see the period after the parenthetical citation here just because I'm trained to do that I get this information in this part of the sentence so it's unnecessary to have it here

Nevertheless, I believe that it is important for people to have the skills ok now I'll have to go back up **As Milroy and Milroy point out (1991), prejudices that would be unacceptable to express in any other context are acceptable in talking about grammar.** uh **Nevertheless, I believe that it is important for people to have the skills necessary to express themselves in ways that earn them the social respect they deserve.** [pause] ok so I sense a critical stance here in terms of what Cameron and Milroy and Milroy argue and this person is ... suggesting that people should have access to the kinds of skills that would offset these attitudes I find myself wanting to argue with the point more than anything but um maybe I'm not sure why the writer has come to this conclusion so sort of a context for this so what am I needing here [pause] not sure how the writer gets from this discussion of Cameron's article and Milroy & Milroy's work to this position here so further discussion in between would help me out and is this the complete beginning? and it seems more like an opinion maybe it's the word believe that's causing me to think that "these people say this but I disagree" [pause] without a kind of context for that position of disagreement

READER B
In Camerons' article (1995) she observes ok a couple of things they're not huge that "in" doesn't seem necessary where else would she be doing it and the "article" I can see this reference is an article anyway so just "Cameron observes" [interviewer: *interesting thing is it's not an article it's a chapter*] it's a chapter! a chapter! [pause] "Cameron observes" I'm just correcting **that improper grammar can cause people to make unfair or discriminatory judgements about the speakers or**

writers who make these errors. [pause] something about the
way that Cameron is introduced because it's an English course
you don't always know that people will be familiar so you might
want to say "linguist" but since it's a writing class uh maybe not
necessary **observes that improper grammar can cause
people to make unfair or discriminatory judgements
about the speakers or writers who make these errors** I
like the opening though with a reference to a scholarly source it
sort of grounds it for me but "improper grammar" and "errors"
no I think that that needs something like what is perceived as
improper grammar and yes especially coming from Cameron I
know that she wouldn't talk about error so I'd expect error to be
in quotation marks something to show that she must be characterizing views of others the writer of the paper hasn't conveyed
that that's another speaker ok ok **Attitudes towards language
are often based on social prejudice: low-class people** I
don't like that phrase it feels a bit bumpy to me I stop there for
sure maybe it's lower class working class I don't know there are
other phrases that don't stand out the way that one does for me
**are condemned by members of the elite for being lazy
and undisciplined.** ok **As Milroy and Milroy point out**
that's nice I like that attributed source **(1991), prejudices that
would be unacceptable to express in any other context
are acceptable in talking about grammar. (Milroy and
Milroy 1991)** there's a little bit about the set up here I don't
think I need Milroy and Milroy again in the brackets but it says
to me that this is someone who is learning to bring in sources
it's not a huge deal

    **Nevertheless, I believe that it is important for people to
have the skills necessary to express themselves in ways
that earn them the social respect they deserve.** well it's surprising to see this by itself um hmm [pause] well I don't know
I'm not sure about this at all um [pause] it strikes me that this
kind of goes against the claims in these two sources [pause] so
that's a really controversial statement that last one [pause] it's
something about not representing these sources entirely accurately so the names are in them so as someone who actually reads
in this area I'm a little uneasy about the way the writer has char-
acterised their arguments I mean I'm glad that there's citation
here but they're complicated arguments and they've been kind of
levelled here maybe sometimes it's better to use a little of the
original speaker I'm not sure

Reading Episode 3

[a beginning]

Since time began there has been a war between the sexes. In many situations, there is a power struggle between men and women. In today's society, social changes have given women more power, but research shows that they still are perceived as the "lesser" sex. The question is: "What effect has social change had on women's status?" Is the power struggle coming to an end or is it taking a new forms? In this paper I will look at the research done by Penelope Eckert (1990) and Kabeer (1994) on Bangladeshi garment workers in London.

READER A

Since time began there has been a war between the sexes. ok this will have to do with some kind of gender issue I don't even want to say "a war between the sexes" because it's such a huge category that I'm not sure how I should be focussing my reading of this I'm just going to keep reading and see how the writer focusses it for me **In many situations, there is a power struggle between men and women.** ok so it's about power struggles um between men and women um it's so general that I don't know what to do with it usually when I'm reading scholarly work I get a sense of much more specific topic um ... the scholarly discussion limits the topic if we're talking about power struggles which is so all encompassing there isn't a sense of who is talking about that or how they're talking about it how they're narrowing it um I guess I want to know here at this point is what does research say about this and I suspect that what they have to say is a lot more specific than what's here **In today's society, social changes have given women more power,** ok I'm still at this very high level of generality **but research shows** ok I'm feeling a bit of relief here **that they still are perceived as the "lesser" sex.** maybe if I had more specific kinds of research I would get at the significance of this because I know this already in a general sense this perception of women as the lesser sex so I'm wondering what the more specific scholarly discussion of this issue is **The question is: "What effect has social change had on women's status?"** hmmm it seems to be a really general question women's status has obviously changed with social change I'm not sure the specific significance of this question but it gives me a sense of what this writer is trying to focus on but I'm still not sure exactly what the focus is and if I had more indication of explicit research that might help too to limit this general topic **Is the power struggle coming to an end or is it taking a new forms?** a new form I would be tempted to say rather than a new forms um ok I'm not sure what to do with these questions they seem very big I'm kind of scared to answer them myself and I'm not sure if the writer I'm reading would be able to answer these questions **In this paper I will look at the research done by Penelope Eckert (1990) and Kabeer (1994) on Bangladeshi garment workers in London.** oh [pause] I'm assuming that Eckert and Kabeer both write this article or that's the way it appears to me but because I've read these two articles I know that they're separate that Eckert's article is about something else a different subject not garment workers so mention of her topic would be helpful here I'm also trying to go from this very high mountaintop of a discussion of social changes and women and power struggles between men and women to Bangladeshi garment workers in London it goes from very general to very specific instance of a group of women I'm assuming that they're women so it might be more helpful for me to have discussion of Eckert's research and a discussion of Kabeer's research to help um create a topic out of this particular research because at this point I wouldn't know what this was if I hadn't read the articles I go from very very general to very specific with nothing in between ... so this issue of women's status and struggle how is that manifested how are instances of that played out in these two articles. I tend to just skip over this [pointing to the first sentences of the passage].

Reading Episode 4
[a beginning]
Cameron's study of "verbal hygiene" (1995) shows that public concerns of grammar are related to political issues: controversy about grammar in school curriculum in Britain was furthered by political conflict. Milroy and Milroy (1991) show that concerns about grammar have a history and they are connected to the processes that "standardized" English. Both these sources show language in public debate. How do these concerns show up in private discussions? In this essay I will examine a study done by Verkuyten, De Jong and Masson (1994) to find cases where language is an issue for the inner-city residents talking about ethnic minorities. I will also look at ways that ideas about language are the same as or different from ideas people have about others'

lifestyles. To do this I will look at Counts and Counts' ethnographic study of RVers and the way they perceive boundaries between "them" and "us."

READER A

Cameron's study of "verbal hygiene" (1995) shows that public concerns of grammar are related to political issues: controversy about grammar in school curriculum in Britain was furthered by political conflict. ok [rereads] I'm not re-reading because it's difficult just to get a sense [rereads] ok there's this connection then between the controversy that surrounds grammar and political issues I could use just a brief specification of this political conflict just to solidify this link between grammar and political conflict what kind of political conflict is this **Milroy and Milroy (1991) show that concerns about grammar have a history and they are connected to the processes that "standardized" English.** ok so I'm getting a really good sense of the topic here in terms of this concern about grammar and its history and its link its sort of political historical links **Both these sources show language in public debate.** [rereads] I'm stumbling over the wording here show how language operates in public debate? show how language is used in public debate? what is in public debate? **How do these concerns show up in private discussions?** I'm going to go back here again a brief instance of this would be helpful ok **How do these concerns show up in private discussions?** ok so we have this instance of public debate but there's now also this instance of private I had to go back and re-read just a bit because I was kind of caught up in this publicity around grammar and politics and now I'm reading here about private discussion so I'm wondering what kind of private discussions? among families? or between teacher and student or between friends? I'm not sure what this refers to **In this essay I will examine a study done by Verkuyten, De Jong and Masson (1994) to find cases where language is an issue for the inner-city residents talking about ethnic minorities.** ok so maybe this isn't private maybe this is still public I'm fixated on this um [pause] ok so language here is linked to issues of ethnicity and particular groups of people and that links back to ideas of some kind of political conflict **I will also look at ways that ideas about language are the same as or different from ideas people have about others' lifestyles.** [long pause] ideas about language are the same

as or different from ideas people have about others' lifestyles. [pause] ok I always think of lifestyles as things like people jogging or people being vegetarians so I'm not sure what this refers to here does this refer to ethnicity is this what the writer means ? or about class or about different kinds of categories of people different stereotyping categories of people and I'm trying to make them connect now back to political conflict and different kinds of debate around this stuff ok so maybe this idea of concerns shows up in private discussions maybe this is a kind of contrast that the writer is providing in terms of here's investigation into public conflict around grammar or public discussions around grammar and this writer wants to talk about it terms of private milieux but I'm not sure how Verkuyten DeJong and Massons how that is private rather than public but maybe I'm misinterpreting the connection here **To do this I will look at Counts and Counts' ethnographic study of RVers and the way they perceive boundaries between "them" and "us."** [long pause] there is a sense or this idea about differences between people or perceived differences between people and the writer seems to be situating this in terms of language which ok and it must have some kind of political implication but I'm not sure how maybe just a bit more indication of what these articles deal with would help me understand how they're going to help the writer deal with what they're going to talk about which I'm thinking is how these concerns about language show up in private discussions because I'm still not sure it seems like an interesting area of investigation hmmm … in terms of my scholarly expectations everything is working for me but yeh hmmm

Reading Episode 5, in which two readers respond to the same passage

[a beginning]

In Counts and Counts (1992), feelings of equality co-exist with discrimination. The RVers say they are all the "same" and equal, but they notice and criticize ways that are different from theirs. Verkuyten et al. (1994) agrees with this. The residents of the old neighbourhood say that equal treatment is important but they criticize foreigners for not fitting in. A further questions arises from this; can *community* by defined only in terms of similarity or does community also include ways of interpreting differences? Another question would be; are attitudes towards others more discriminatory when the others are seen as newcomers?

READER A

In Counts and Counts (1992), feelings of equality co-exist with discrimination. [pause] **The RVers say they are all the "same" and equal, but they notice and criticize ways that are different from theirs.** [pause] this sounds like summary so I get the sense that this is what is going on in Counts and Counts they have feelings of equality and they also discriminate so I would end up if I hadn't read their article thinking that this was what Counts and Counts are feeling or this is what the writer sees them doing ... having **feelings of equality co-exist with discrimination: they are all the "same" and equal, but they notice and criticize ways that are different from theirs.** so the RVers themselves are discriminating not Counts and Counts ok **Verkuyten et al. (1994) agrees with this.** ok so if I hadn't read either one of these articles I would just automatically assume that they're actually having a discussion or have had a discussion and um but what I think the writer is trying to do is she or he is trying to position these two together so she is making them agree as opposed to um them actually agreeing so she's trying to find points of comparison she's attempting to compare two articles rather than um have them actually agreeing on something or them citing each other, which they don't do so I would use wording that's more comparative or that indicates a comparison between ideas rather than the discourse of agreement **The residents of the old neighbourhood say that equal treatment is important but they criticize foreigners for not fitting in.** so the idea here is that there are groups of people that see each other equal or expect equal treatment but in both cases with the RVers and these residents of the old neighourhood they also find ways to um differentiate between each other that's the idea that's important **A further questions arises** I'm stumbling over the wording a bit here "a further question arises" **from this** ok I'm not sure where I see the question above here so I'm going to reread to see if I've missed it **but they criticize** ok **can *community* by defined only in terms of similarity or does community also include ways of interpreting differences?** oh a question is arising from this um and this is the question yeh that's interesting so the writer is asking can we only define community based on similarity or does the notion of community almost always involve this idea of difference as well or incorporates difference **Another question would be;** um ok I'm stopping here on this semicolon on this punctuation and noticing above because I thought I had read a colon um pause I might be tempted to just skip over it I just expect certain kinds of sentence structure with these kinds of punctuation it stops me **Another question would be; are attitudes towards others more discriminatory when the others are seen as newcomers?** this person based on this observation of how community works has come up with some questions [pause] around community and how it operates so maybe um a kind of discussion of the significance of these questions in terms of Counts and Counts' findings would be helpful yes

READER B
In Counts and Counts (1992), feelings of equality co-exist with discrimination. well this disturbs me somewhat because it seems like the equality and discrimination are in Counts and Counts' article and I don't have any recollection of that article being like that so I'm wondering if this writer means "Counts & Counts explain that argue that feelings of equality coexist with discrimination" I suspect it's something like that yes! because as I go on **The RVers say they are all the "same" and equal, but they notice and criticize ways that are different from theirs.** so clearly it's the RVers who have these feelings, not Counts & Counts and that unsettles me it makes it hard to concentrate as I go on **Verkuyten et al. (1994) agrees** well that's a group so agreement thing agree agree **with this.** [pause] ok there's something about the way the two sources are being brought together that I find a little bumpy where it makes it sound as though Verkuyten et al. have read Counts and Counts and outright agreeing with them and that's not what's going on I don't think uh so I'd be happier with something that makes a similar point that shows that it's the writer of this paper who is bringing the two sources together ok back **The residents of the old neighbourhood say that equal treatment is important but they criticize foreigners for not fitting in.** ok I mean overall I like the fact that these two quite different articles are being brought into the same place I just think that I need a little more help the reader needs a little more help connecting them **A further questions arises from this;** now I'm getting a little disturbed — "the questions" — I think the writer knows that it's "question" and these little typos are throwing me off it's hard to concentrate **can** *community* **by** see another one **defined only**

in terms of similarity or does community also include ways of interpreting differences? [pause] ok [pause] ok Another question would be; are attitudes towards well see it's the punctuation thing there's a cumulative effect of small things are attitudes towards others more discriminatory when the others are seen as newcomers? [pause] well a big jump between those two questions maybe I'd like a little set up for that too I need a sense of things coming together before it opens up to other possibilities that could be addressed they're interesting questions but I'd just like them contextualized a bit

Reading Episode 6, in which two readers respond to the same passage
"Swearing: an expressive and creative form of language"
Linguistics 260

The usage of swear words has been frowned upon and held negative connotation since language's beginning. Most often considered to be a taboo act, many people find this facet of language to be offensive and an indication of a lack of intelligence or linguistic creativity on behalf of the speaker. With an examination of the functions, roles, and forms that swearing takes on in language, this paper aims to disprove this last statement and to show that in effect, swear words are an expressive form of language and their usage is a reflection of the cultural focus within the speaker's society. This focus has seen major changes over the years, and has evolved along with and at the same rate as the society in which it exists.

Origins of Swear Words in (Canadian) French and English
Bonvillain quotes Sapir in *Language, Culture and Communication* as stating that: "The complete vocabulary of a language may indeed be looked upon as a complex inventory of all the ideas, interests and occupations that take up the attention of the community" (1997:49). With this statement in mind, it is not surprising that the main subject of taboo language hundreds of years ago was, indeed, religion. Apart from an individual's occupation or means of income, religion was their main focus and took up much of their thought and time. Having good religious faith showed that they were respectable and upstanding citizens, therefore the usage of any taboo language was forbidden.

READER A
The usage of swear words has been frowned upon and held negative connotation since language's beginning. ok

so hmmm I'm having to re-read because there's a couple of points where I'm stumbling um I'm wanting to say or read the use of swear words pause um has been frowned upon ok I'm not sure why I'm reading this or why this is significant because it's very general and it's something I know already so um it's like saying a table has four legs **The usage of swear words has been frowned upon and held negative connotation since language's beginning.** the beginning of time so what I'm looking for is the level of generality things are so general for me and I'm needing a focus and I'm wanting to know what the scholarly discussion is about swear words I guess swear words is what we're talking about and the perception of swearing **Most often considered to be a taboo act, many people find this facet** facet why am I stumbling over that aspect is probably fine **of language to be offensive and an indication of a lack of intelligence or linguistic creativity on behalf of the speaker. Most often considered to be a taboo act, many people find this facet of language to be offensive and an indication of a lack of intelligence or linguistic creativity on behalf of the speaker.** I notice quite a difference between the language of this sentence and the language of this second sentence um **and held negative connotation since language's beginning.** I sense a kind of I'm not sure if it's [rereads] [pause] this seems to be that this writer here seems to be much more fluent it seems to be two different speakers and I'm wondering if this is a quotation and if this is a quotation it would be more helpful to have the source **With an examination of the functions, roles, and forms that swearing takes on in language, this paper aims to disprove this last statement and to show that in effect, swear words are an expressive form of language and their usage is a reflection of the cultural focus within the speaker's society.** ok so um pause I sense this is a scholarly discussion of the use of this type of language as taboo I'm noticing the abstractions taboo linguistic creativity the functional roles of this particular language use the cultural focus this idea of culture situated language use and this seems to contrast with this first sentence in terms of the level of generality of the discussion and sometimes it's just the wording that I'm stumbling over **held negative connotation since language's beginning This focus has seen major changes over the years, and has evolved along with and at the same rate as the society in which it exists.** ok **this paper aims to disprove this last statement and to show** [pause] **that in effect, swear words are an expressive**

form of language and their usage is a reflection of the cultural focus within the speaker's society. ok so what we have here is what some perceptions of the language are and a kind of stance in relation to this [pause] I could use kind of indication of what people are saying where these perceptions come from **This focus has seen major changes over the years,** which focus which focus **an expressive form of language and their usage is a reflection of the cultural focus within the speaker's society.** ok so the cultural focus has seen major changes over the years so [pause] **and has evolved along with and at the same rate as the society in which it exists** this sentence doesn't really do much for me as a reader it gives me a sense that culture changes and that um [pause] culture changes along with society or in relation to society but I'm not sure what to do with it in terms of the issue of this type of language use pause um ok I'm confused

Origins of Swear Words in (Canadian) French and English this is a heading so the focus will be on this use of language, of swearing [pause] as an expressive form of language rather than a form of language that indexes lack of intelligence and creativity [pause] ok so I have a sense of the focus but I don't know what the scholarly discussion is of this

Bonvillain quotes Sapir in *Language, Culture and Communication* **as stating that:** um pause I'm going to go back up here **Origins of Swear Words in (Canadian) French and English** this sort of reminds me of this kind of statement of since language's beginning way up here at the top the origins of swear words gives me a sense of this enormous time frame and I'm not sure why origins why it's important to understand the origins of swear words in relation to this and perhaps [pause] this is why the writer is talking about evolution of society and culture but I'm still not quite clear about why I need to know this stuff um **Bonvillain quotes Sapir in** *Language, Culture and Communication* **as stating that:** I'm tempted to say something around the wording a little bit to smooth it out I would read it **Bonvillain quotes Sapir in** *Language, Culture and Communication* [pause] who says that or something I guess it's fine I certainly know what the writer is trying to do I would just skip over the colon here I'm not used to seeing it in this context for quoting **"The complete vocabulary of a language may indeed be looked upon as a complex inventory of all the ideas, interests and**

occupations ok so we have Sapir talking and he says **"The complete vocabulary of a language may indeed be looked upon as a complex inventory of all the ideas, interests and occupations that take up the attention of the community" (1997:49).** [pause] so vocabulary indexes or is an inventory of the culture of the community so that's why this writer is talking about language in terms of a cultural focus above this would have been helpful information in the opening paragraph **With this statement in mind, it is not surprising that the main subject of taboo language hundreds of years ago was, indeed, religion.** I'm a little concerned because I feel like I'm going to go on a long journey through time and I'm not sure [pause] I do find it interesting this idea of taboo language and religion though I'm interested to read it but I'm not sure what are we focussing on an historical account of swear words or are we talking about the use of swear words in particular cultures which culture are we looking at I guess I'm wanting to know which time frame **Apart from an individual's occupation or means of income, religion was their main focus and took up much of their thought and time. subject of taboo language hundreds of years ago was, indeed, religion. Apart from an individual's occupation or means of income, religion was their main focus and took up much of their thought and time.** so the writer is just telling me how important religion is I'm not sure if I need this it doesn't help me at this point understand how the main subject of taboo language was religion **Having good religious faith showed that they were respectable and upstanding citizens, therefore the usage of any taboo language was forbidden.** I'm not understanding the relation between being faithful citizens or upstanding citizens and the use of taboo language as being forbidden so I'm assuming that respectability was ok in your non-use of this kind of language um [pause] is it possible that there's taboo language that isn't forbidden what would that be like? is that possible? so at this point I find everything very interesting but I'm a little concerned that I'm going to be on this long journey and I'm not sure quite what I should be paying attention to

READER B
"Swearing: an expressive and creative form of language" ok I like that title **The usage of swear words has been frowned upon and held negative connotation since language's beginning.** well first of all I'd like to know who says

that and it strikes me as a really big sweep "since language's beginning" ... something about parallelism in there isn't there that I'd like has held negative connotations it doesn't bother me too much it's mostly who says this **Most often considered to be a taboo act, many people** it's not the people who are considered a taboo act ... anyway **find this facet of language to be offensive and an indication of a lack of intelligence or linguistic creativity on behalf of the speaker.** ok that could be so but I am wondering where these things come from I'd like to know the sources of these observations **With an examination of the functions, roles, and forms that swearing takes on in language, this paper aims to disprove this last statement** oh I'll have to go back which statement? ok that's a little confusing for me I'd rather see this straightforward what this paper is going to explore I'm not sure what part of the last statement is being "disproved" **and to show that in effect, swear words are an expressive form of language and their usage is a reflection of the cultural focus within the speaker's society.** uh [pause] you know I'm not quite sure what this is going to be but it sounds quite interesting to me it's an alternative take on swearing, swear words from the way they're generally sort of viewed so I like that but I'm having a little difficulty figuring out where the paper is going **This focus has seen major changes over the years,** huh [pause] this focus what focus oh ok the cultural focus **and has evolved along with and at the same rate as the society in which it exists.** oh that takes me in a couple of little circles that are hard to figure out this paper is going to be about swearing and I think it's a different kind of take on swearing than what we might expect but I'm not sure how it's going to be doing this

Origins of Swear Words in (Canadian) French and English oh I didn't know it was going to be Canadian French and English

Bonvillain quotes Sapir in *Language, Culture and Communication* as stating that: "The complete vocabulary of a language may indeed be looked upon as a complex inventory of all the ideas, interests and occupations that take up the attention of the community" (1997:49). I like this because now I'm getting some of the uh scholarly thinking I expect on this topic I might have liked this sooner **With this statement in mind, it is not surprising that the main subject of taboo language hundreds of years ago was, indeed,**

religion. complete vocabulary [pause] gosh [pause] I'm having a little trouble making some of the connections they're great big statements and like this jump to religion I need a little help getting there **Apart from an individual's occupation or means of income, religion was their main focus and took up much of their thought and time.** the lack of citations continues to disturb me in fact it's disturbing me so much I'm having trouble paying attention **Having good religious faith showed that they were respectable and upstanding citizens, therefore the usage of any taboo language was forbidden.** can't link the first and second part of that sentence don't know what the relation between religious faith and being upstanding and "therefore" taboo language is forbidden pause I keep feeling like it's almost getting to a point but it never quite does I'm mean there are some grammatical things there but they don't disturb me all that much it's the lack of citations

Reading Episode 7
[conclusion to] **"Negotiating the Hermeneutical Landscape: K. as Land Surveyor" English 378**

The most imitable quality of Klamm is his sleepiness. The bureaucracy itself comes to embody this sleepiness. "Burgel continued, stretching his arms and yawning, which was in bewildering contradiction to the gravity of his words" (338). "No, you don't need to apologize for being sleepy, why should you? One's physical energies last only to a certain limit. Who can help the fact that precisely this limit is significant in other ways too? No, nobody can help it. That is how the world itself corrects the deviations in its course and maintains the balance" (351).

And so, the country is not so fatally strange. As many of Kafka's landscapes, *The Castle* is recognizable to the outsider in a form closely analogous to the dreamworld. It is, in fact, dream which links, for instance, the child, the poet, the schizophrenic, the foreigner and the villager in a fundamentally — and perhaps frighteningly — recognizable humanity. A special issue of *The Journal of Anthropological Research* on human rights noted: "No one has ever discovered a culture that was so vastly different as to be wholly incomprehensible or uninterpretable to outsiders." It was K.'s task, however, to interpret the country of the Castle in the most profoundly personal way imaginable — so as to understand and secure a meaningful role for himself in a foreign land. Paradoxically, in being subsumed by the dreamworld, and so, coming

closest to what had been his extraordinarily conscious goal —
Klamm — K. relinquished his role as Land Surveyor. He abandoned his pursuit of interpreting the hermeneutic landscape in
terms of absolute boundaries.

READER B

**The most imitable quality of Klamm is his sleepiness. The
bureaucracy itself comes to embody this sleepiness.**
"imitable"? but I like that I like the repetition that's nice it keeps
you on track quote **"Burgel continued, stretching his arms
and yawning, which was in bewildering contradiction to
the gravity of his words" (338).** ok so I know, I see the sleepiness in that too **"No, you don't need to apologize for being
sleepy, why should you? One's physical energies last only
to a certain limit. Who can help the fact that precisely this
limit is significant in other ways too? No, nobody can
help it. That is how the world itself corrects the deviations
in its course and maintains the balance" (351).** I really like
the quotation there it absolutely supports that point

**And so, the country is not so fatally strange. As many
of Kafka's landscapes, The Castle is recognizable to the
outsider in a form closely analogous to the dreamworld.**
um ok sleep dream connection ok I like that **It is, in fact,
dream which links, for instance, the child, the poet, the
schizophrenic, the foreigner and the villager in a fundamentally — and perhaps frighteningly — recognizable
humanity.** I found the sentence structure pleasing they're complex ideas but I'm not having to work overly hard to get at them
**A special issue of _The Journal of Anthropological Research_ on
human rights noted: "No one has ever discovered a culture that was so vastly different as to be wholly incomprehensible or uninterpretable to outsiders."** I like the way
it's now moving out into the larger issues from the consideration
of the of um the castle it's linking up with the bigger picture oh
I think that I would probably note who said that rather than citing the journal get it in there well when I look at this I think that
perhaps it's somebody who is actually in anthropology because I
think that this might be something that the writer is really familiar with that might not be so familiar to readers and writers about
literature so I might prepare the way for them a bit more [pause]
what do human rights have to do with the dream I think that I
need to see connection between recognizable humanity and
human rights I guess that's the connection **It was K.'s task,**

however, to interpret the country of the Castle in the most profoundly personal way imaginable — so as to understand and secure a meaningful role for himself in a foreign land. **Paradoxically** I like this because it's wrapping up but it's not trying to offer a single interpretation it's keeping alive the paradox and the contradiction and the I like that sense of multiple possibilities **Paradoxically, in being subsumed by the dreamworld, and so, coming closest to what had been his extraordinarily conscious goal — Klamm — K. relinquished his role as Land Surveyor. He abandoned his pursuit of interpreting the hermeneutic landscape in terms of absolute boundaries.** that is the end, I like that it does bring things simultaneously full circle in terms of discussion of this novel and at the same time it points out to the whole culture I like the use of quotation and to me it's clearly a literature paper in that use of beautiful bits of writing

Works Cited

Alvesson, Mats. 1993. *Cultural Perspectives on Organizations*. Cambridge: Cambridge UP.

Bodine, Anne. 1998 (1975). "Androcentrism in prescriptive grammar: Singular 'they', sex-indefinite 'he', and 'he or she.'" In *The Feminist Critique of Language*, ed. D. Cameron. London: Routledge.

Bourdieu, Pierre. 1991. *Language and Symbolic Power*. Cambridge, MA: Harvard UP.

Cameron, Deborah. 1995. *Verbal Hygiene*. London: Routledge.

Chafe, Wallace. 1994. *Discourse, Consciousness, and Time: The Flow and Displacement of Conscious Experience in Speaking and Writing*. Chicago: U of Chicago P.

Clark, Herbert. 1992. *Arenas of Language Use*. Chicago: U of Chicago P.

Cowan, Ann, Janet Giltrow, Sharon Josephson, and Michele Valiquette. 1998. "Feedback: Its uses, reliability, and design." Paper presented at annual meeting of Canadian Association of Teachers of Technical Writing. Ottawa.

Giltrow, Janet. 2000. "'Argument'" as a term in talk about student writing." In *Learning to Argue in Higher Education*, ed. S. Mitchell and R. Andrews. Portsmouth, NH: Boynton Cook/Heinemann.

Miller, Susan. 1991. *Textual Carnivals: The Politics of Composition*. Carbondale: Southern Illinois UP.

Milroy, James and Lesley Milroy. 1991 (1985). *Authority in Language: Investigating Language Prescription and Standardisation*, 2nd ed. London: Routledge.

Schriver, Karen. 1994 (1992). "What document designers can learn from usability testing." *Technostyle* 19 (3/4).

Sperber, Dan, and Deirdre Wilson. 1986. *Relevance: Communication and Cognition*. Cambridge, MA: Harvard UP.

Stockton, S. 1995. "Writing in history: Narrating the subject of time." *Written Communication* 12(1): 47-73.

Swales, John. 1990. *Genre Analysis: English in Academic and Research Settings.* Cambridge: Cambridge UP.

van Dijk, Teun. 1980. *Macrostructures: An Interdisciplinary Study of Global Structures in Discourse, Interaction, and Cognition.* Hillsdale, NJ: Erlbaum.

van Dijk, Teun and Walter Kintsch. 1983. *Strategies of Discourse Comprehension.* New York: Academic Press.

Waern, Yvonne. 1988. "Thoughts on texts in context: Applying the think-aloud method to text processing." *Text* 8(4): 317-50.

Scholarly styles and the limits of knowledge

5.1 Scholarly wordings

Scholarly writing is often ridiculed in the popular media. Like the speech of people who have not internalized schoolroom rules of usage, it is deplored by those who believe in "good" writing. Most scholarly expression goes on out of earshot of the rest of the world — in scholarly journals and at scholarly conferences. But when the sounds of scholarship do leak into more public settings, they can come in for some criticism and laughter. For instance, when a curriculum document reaches the attention of the popular press, those wordings which are traceable to otherwise secluded research domains make people indignant and amused. An example of such "edu-babble" is cited here:

> A certain minimum fluency is required before students are able to reflect critically on their own language use. Attention to language forms and conventions should therefore increase gradually as language skill develops and should arise specifically out of the reading and writing being done. Students are more likely to achieve good punctuation and spelling and surface correctness through extensive practice in reading and writing rather than conscious attempts to apply rules out of context.

Then it is rewritten in "plain" language:

> Students are more likely to learn correct language uses, punctuation, and spelling by reading and writing than by learning rules in isolation.
>
> (*Ottawa Citizen*, reprinted in *The Vancouver Province*, July 5, 1994, A14)

Whatever the defects of the original or the virtues of the rewrite, the rewrite gets rid of material like "certain minimum fluency is required," "attention to language forms and conventions," and "through extensive practice in reading and writing rather than conscious attempts to apply rules out of context." Such expressions bear the marks of scholarly activity. Events and attributes are turned into things (x pays attention to y = "attention to" y; x attempts to apply y to z = "attempts to apply" y to z; x is fluent = "fluency"). And agents of actions and possessors of attributes disappear (who pays attention or attempts to apply? who is fluent? who requires fluency?).

In getting rid of these features, and achieving a plain language standard, the rewrite might be said to restore "common sense" to the original. At the same time, it seems to reduce the conceptual complexity of the original.

I suggest that the original is not in itself bad, nor that the reaction is mistaken. Rather, there has been a **genre violation**: the writers of the original perhaps transferred the sounds and styles of scholarly research too directly to a non-research document. And the readers who objected and the rewriters who responded to these objections failed to take account of the fact that the curriculum document on which this newspaper article was based was addressed to professionals: teachers and educational administrators. In other words, the situation which the document served did not include all readers of the *Ottawa Citizen* or the indignant politicians whose consternation was reported.

This example illuminates the conflict between what Halliday and Martin (1993) have called the "common sense" of, roughly speaking, our everyday experience of the world and the "uncommon sense" of the learned domains of research.

From a distance, it seems tempting to vouch for common sense, and deny uncommon sense as unnatural, deliberately deceiving, or possibly pretentious. Yet common sense has also been the source of some questionable ideas: that whales are fish (to use one of Halliday and Martin's examples), or less innocent ideas, such as that women are inferior to men, or that children benefit from stern discipline, or that rivers are a good place to get rid of industrial waste. That is to say, sometimes "common sense" is only unexamined assumptions which, left unexamined, perpetuate conditions that benefit some people and disadvantage others — or benefit no one in the long run. These assumptions are so widely held — that is, so common — that they appear self-evident.

Research activities seek to expose some of those common-sense assumptions for examination, and this process of examination is represented in the distinctive language of the scholarly genres. For example, in a common-sense world, we all understand the work *think* and use it in various situations —

[Binky and Bingo are taking a car trip]

Binky: When did we get gas?	Bingo: Hmm. Let me *think*.
Binky: We're going an average of 85 kph. When will we get to Mariposa?	Bingo (looking at a map): Wait. I'm *thinking*.
Binky: What are you doing?	Bingo (looking at a map): I'm *thinking* about where we should go next.

— but cognitive scientists who want to find out about how people think would distinguish amongst these situations, seeing that one is a matter of remembering, another is a matter of calculating an answer to a particular question, and the third is a more complex procedure. For the third case, they might (and have) come up with a specialized term: *nonspecific goal strategy in problem solving*. Rarely would we hear this term outside scholarly circles — or, indeed, outside the even smaller circle of the discipline of cognitive science.

Some people complain about this kind of wording. They suggest that it is an unnecessarily complicated way of speaking. Why not just say "thinking"? They suggest that, by choosing the specialist term, writers exclude commonsense people and isolate scholars in a false distinction made of elaborate language. And some suggest that this kind of wording is not only pretentious and exclusionary, but also hard to read. We will examine the grounds for these complaints.

5.1.1 Is scholarly writing unnecessarily complicated?

Later sections of this chapter will offer broader perspectives on this question, looking at how the structure of a noun phrase like *nonspecific goal strategy in problem solving* cooperates with other features of scholarly genres to produce the discourse which typifies and maintains research activities. In the meantime, we could grant that, sometimes, scholars might be advised to say "thinking" instead of "nonspecific goal strategy in problem solving."

But we can make this concession to critics of scholarly style only in light of other considerations. In efforts to reorganize common-sense knowledge of the world into uncommon-sense, researchers analyse issues and entities into smaller parts, differentiating those parts into segments which may be scarcely visible to the untrained observer. Those segments — produced by research activity — then become objects of study, and the names for the objects of study are necessary to reporting the results of study.

Our opinion of the wording *nonspecific goal strategy in problem* solving may come down to our opinion of research activity itself. Are its products useful?

This is a big question, and further inflated by our culture's ambivalence towards "science." On the one hand, we invest heavily – materially and socially – in professional research. Tax and corporate dollars support scholars' activities; "experts" and "scientists" are called in as authorities on many matters, from family life to outer space. But, on the other hand, we not only ridicule expert language but also question both our investment in "pure" research (that without any immediately foreseeable use) and the applications of research in new technologies: we complain that they have spoiled cherished aspects of our customary ways of life. You may remember a passage presented in Chapter Two from Anthony Giddens (*The Consequences of Modernity*) which analyses "trust" in expertise. Giddens suggests that, while people generally trust scientists to know how things work, they can also regard the specialist or scientist as a "buffoon" (Giddens 88-99).

Our judgement about the complications of scholarly language would eventually have to take into account this ambivalence. For now, we might say that, if the activities which appear to depend on wordings like *nonspecific goal strategy in problem solving* have good results, then the wording is not "unnecessarily complicated." And one of these results might be a clearer picture of how people reason: how certain kinds of schoolroom problem-questions (*if A is travelling at 50 kph and B is going 56 kph in the opposite direction ...*) may trigger in children reasoning different from that which the teacher anticipates, or how a doctor's diagnostic questioning may trigger replies that obscure rather than illuminate a patient's condition.

5.1.2 Is scholarly style exclusionary and élitist?

Scholarly style does exclude many readers. Even within the larger academic community, readers who are members of one discipline can be excluded from the ongoing discourses of other disciplines. While researchers seem to be generally respectful of those working in other fields, smirks and raised eyebrows are not unknown when a researcher comes within earshot of the wordings of another discipline. The "post-modernism" of the humanities and some of the social sciences can inspire ridicule amongst those who do not work in those terms. And, equally, the classifying vocabularies of the sciences and some other social sciences can arouse suspicion amongst those who work with less technical terminologies.

Genre theory predicts that this will be so: the more highly defined and particular the situations which language serves, the more distinctive will that language be, and the more inscrutable to people unfamiliar with those situations. So we might also predict that any social group — skateboarders or pilots or childcare workers — will develop and maintain speech styles which serve and represent the routines which organize their activities. And these styles will, to a greater or lesser degree, exclude people who don't belong to the group and incur the risk of social reactions to that exclusion.

But to say that that which excludes is exclusionary is to suggest something more than just group boundaries. It suggests the operation of power — as do claims about élitism. If the effects of scholarly style are consistently to the advantage of those who use it and to the disadvantage of others, then critiques of scholarly ways of speaking need to be taken seriously. (This is a big issue, too, and one which we will examine in Chapter Six.)

5.1.3 Is scholarly style hard to read?

This question is also a difficult one, but one which we are in a better position to answer here.

Criticism of scholarly expression has sometimes focussed on what has been called its heavily **nominal** style. This characterization refers to its preference for nouns over verbs, and the way that preference results in big noun phrases like the one that we have been using as our example: *nonspecific goal strategy in problem solving* is longer than *thinking*. This difference is visible to the naked eye, and needs no special grammatical analysis to reveal it. Once nouns are preferred over verbs, noun phrases bear a particularly heavy load, carrying content that would otherwise have been distributed throughout the sentence. These concentrated loads appear likely to challenge readers on two fronts: (1) the syntactic density of noun "strings," and (2) the potential ambiguity of these strings. We will examine each of these conditions.

Syntactic density

In English, the noun phrase is capable of expanding by picking up other sentence elements. In the following series, you will see noun phrases growing by absorbing material from other parts of the sentence.

(i) *the noun phrase absorbs an adjective*
This behaviour is **criminal**.
This **criminal** behaviour...

(ii) *the noun phrase absorbs another noun*
The reports record **offences**.
The **offence** reports...

(iii) *the noun phrase absorbs a predicate — verb and adverb*
Some strategies **work forward**.
Some **forward-working** strategies...

(iv) *the noun phrase absorbs a predicate — verb and (object) noun*
Strategies **solve problems**.
Problem-solving strategies...

There are limits to what the noun phrase can absorb, but these examples don't even approach those limits. They exemplify only some of the simplest noun-phrase expansions.

You can see that the capacity of the noun phrase to incorporate other sentence elements provides one of the normal economies of English. For example, by installing "work forward" in the noun phrase (iii), the writer leaves the rest of the sentence free to carry other information:

Forward-working strategies enable the problem solver to explore the problem space to see what moves are possible.

Speakers of English use the capacity of the noun phrase all the time to achieve economies of expression. Instead of saying —

My car has broken down. It is brand new.

— the speaker can economize, presenting the same information in fewer words:

> My brand-new car has broken down.

Yet, while this *appears* to be the same information, the choice between the two versions is not entirely free or arbitrary: it has to do with **topic development**. For instance, if the speaker were to continue reporting his predicament, the second version would tend to lead to development of the "break-down" topic —

> My brand-new car has broken down. I was going along and heard this BUMP-BUMP.

— whereas the first version would *tend* to pave the way for development of the "brand-new" topic:

> My car has broken down. It's brand new. I just got it last month.

In reflecting on the noun phrase's capacity to absorb material from other parts of the sentence in ways that are patterned rather than arbitrary, let us first take a **cognitive** approach: what does the heavy noun phrase mean to readers' working conditions? That is, how does the decoding of a long noun phrase impose on readers' limited resources for paying attention?

Most theory and research in this area suggests that as readers make their way through sentences, they predict, on the basis of the word they are currently reading, the syntactic category of the following word or phrase. So, if readers encounter —

> **the ...**

— they predict, as most likely but not inevitable, that a **noun** will come next:

> **the goal ...**

(Of course, readers don't need to know the names for syntactic categories. They just need the ordinary knowledge of English that enables people to put together phrases like *the goal*, or *the barn*, or *the stove*, and avoid phrases like ⋆*the because*, or ⋆*barn the*.)

If their expectations are disappointed, and they find not a noun but an adjective —

the nonspecific ...

— they recover easily, and now predict a noun, since adjectives following determiners like *the* have a high probability of being followed by a noun:

the	**nonspecific**	**goal**
determiner	*modifier (adj)*	*nominal head (noun)*

This seems to complete the noun phrase, and readers are ready for a verb — the goal *is* something, or *does* something. They predict a verb. But what if they encounter another noun?

the nonspecific goal strategy ...

the	**nonspecific**	**goal**	**strategy**
determiner	*modifier*	*modifier*	*nominal head*
	(adj)	*(noun)*	*(noun)*

Now they revise their hypothesis about the sentence and its structure: *goal* is not the head of the noun phrase, but only another modifier. (Notice that we have not yet approached the structural limits of the noun phrase. Somebody could conceivably write "the nonspecific goal strategy research innovation project.")

Analysis of this predictive procedure first isolates noun strings — that is, nouns modified by other nouns — as the most dense site of such failed-then-revised-hypotheses sequences. Then it proposes that these recursive predictions burden readers' attention capacity. (We could see this burden as a micro version of the larger efforts after meaning we explored in Chapter Four, when we inspected that state of readers' mental desktops as they worked to construct the relevance of lower-level information to higher-level concepts.)

> **Exercise**
> These are noun phrases taken from published articles in a variety of scholarly disciplines. Analyse them along the lines of the analysis of "the nonspecific goal strategy," above: what predictive hypotheses would readers first make and then revise as they made their way through these noun phrases?

> labour supply decision-making
> voluntary employee turnover
> issues management structures
> other-race face recognition
> · eating pathology scores
> risk management science
> droplet size distribution measurements

So far, our evaluation of the syntactic density of noun phrases has been **cognitive** only: we have been estimating readers' reasoning as they meet long noun strings. But readers are more than cognitive beings. They are also social beings. And research shows that, while noun strings may cause trouble for some readers, they are no problem for other readers. Are some readers dull and others brilliant?

In fact, the difference lies in readers' different experience of the world. Readers' social milieux and the background knowledge they have acquired play a big part in their understanding of what they read (see for example many of the contributions to Davison and Green [1988], which emphasize the resources that readers bring with them to what they read). It all depends on readers' previous contact with the subject treated by the text. For example, investigating stylistic features in management studies, I came across the term *relationship marketing*. Being unaccustomed to the topic, I didn't know what that was — a dating service? professional matchmaking? Reading on, I was able to infer — from appositives, synonyms, and other elements of the co-text — that *relationship marketing* was a sales strategy which emphasizes techniques for building an enduring relationship with customers: keeping in touch after one sale had been made, building a context for future sales. Presumably, readers more familiar with these aspects of the discourse on management would not have had to experiment with the noun phrase *relationship marketing* the way I did.

Conditions people have in mind when they talk about "clarity" (and "conciseness") in the scholarly genres may have as much to do with the *identity* and *position* of the reader as they do with the style of the writing. Tracing down this possibility, a student in an undergraduate class in writing in the research genres carried out a small study of readers' level of difficulty in encountering scholarly forms of expression. She selected introductions from three articles, one each from scholarly publications in biomedical science, geography, and literary studies. She asked two readers to evaluate the passages for "clarity." The first subject, a physician, rated the biomedical passage as "most clear," and the literary studies passage as "most unclear." The second subject, a first-year student in a university-transfer program at a college, rated the literary-studies passage as "most clear," and the biomedical article as "most unclear."

Exercise

Following is a passage dealing with uses of the concept *community*, a concept whose scholarly sense you have become familiar with from readings in previous chapters. Using the think-aloud techniques introduced in Chapter Four, ask two or more members of the class to read and comment on the passage. Do the results differ according to readers' backgrounds — their area of study, for example? Ask someone from outside the class to read the passage: how does their experience of the passage compare with those of readers in the class? This passage also raises issues in the *politics of knowledge* — issues we will explore in Chapter Six. Would the people referred to in the passage ("migrant," "refugee") find it readable? I am grateful to Shanmugan Gopal for insisting, in a graduate class on ideologies of language, that there was something amiss when scholars wrote about the experiences of — in the cases he had in mind — populations of the Indian sub-continent in ways which those populations could not understand.

> I am less concerned with the conceptual aporia of community-capital contradiction, than with the genealogy of the idea of community as itself a "minority" discourse; as the making, or becoming "minor", of the idea of Society, in the practice of politics of culture. Community is the antagonist supplement of modernity: in the metropolitan space it is the territory of the minority, threatening the claims of civility; in the transnational world it becomes the border-problem of the diasporic, the migrant, the refugee. Binary divisions of social space neglect the profound temporal disjunction — the transnational time and space — through which minority communities negotiate their collective identifications.

> Homi K. Bhabha 1994 "Now newness enters the world." In *The Location of Culture* London: Routledge, 231.

Let's put the reader back together as a **socio-cognitive** being, and ask the question again: is scholarly style hard to read? Yes, it is — for some people. Students new to a discipline, for example, may find the nominal style of scholarly writing difficult to read. Perhaps students can benefit from first seeing the scholarly noun phrase as a structure which absorbs other sentence parts, and then methodically unpacking that noun phrase, understanding why it is causing them trouble but not letting it get the upper hand. Later sections of this chapter will provide some opportunities to practise this technique. As *readers*, students can overcome these obstacles once they understand the structure of the obstacle, and where the footholds and handholds are.

As *writers*, students can be wary of all-purpose rules for plain writing — or computer-style checkers — that call for verbs instead of nouns, and deplore noun "strings." Their readers will not necessarily have trouble with a heavily nominal style. But writers can also keep in mind the cognitive load imposed by noun strings. There may be times when unpacking a big noun phrase will offer cognitive relief to the reader. For example, Passage 2 below may sometimes be preferable to Passage 1 (where the target noun phrase is underlined):

PASSAGE 1
A recent comparative study of multi-family housing development and maintenance costs based on 1986 construction experience showed that three-storey buildings ultimately provided cheaper housing than high-rises.

PASSAGE 2
A study recently compared costs of developing and maintaining multiple-family housing. It was based on 1986 construction experience, and it showed that three-storey buildings ultimately provided cheaper housing than high-rises.

Ambiguity

We have seen that noun phrases are hospitable to other sentence elements: they will take in just about anything. As these bits and pieces are accommodated in the noun phrase, other elements are left behind. When parts get left behind, ambiguity can result. Sometimes the effort required from the reader to resolve the ambiguity is so negligible it is scarcely measurable. The underlined noun phrases in Passage 3, which appeared in a daily newspaper, make demands on readers that they meet almost automatically.

PASSAGE 3

The body, discovered in the basement of **a concrete building**, was identified as the remains of **a newspaper woman** who had lived in the neighbourhood in the late 1960s.

A concrete building means that the building was made of concrete. But *a newspaper woman* doesn't mean that the woman was made of newspaper: it means that the woman wrote articles for a newspaper. The noun phrases don't make these distinctions: they are lost when the noun phrase absorbs other elements. So, it's *readers* who make these distinctions, by consulting their knowledge of the world (no women are made of newspaper). And readers make the distinctions easily, without significant processing demands.

Other noun phrases can be slightly more distracting. Passage 4 comes from a news report about social conditions in the United States.

PASSAGE 4

Homeless experts say that the problem will only get worse as the summer goes on.

What is a "homeless expert"?

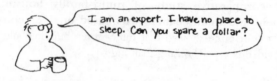

A more likely interpretation soon supersedes the less likely one.

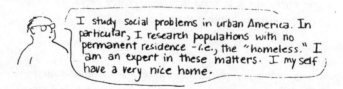

Readers resolve the ambiguity in the noun phrase by consulting their knowledge of the world.

Other noun phrases can be more stubbornly ambiguous. Like my example *relationship marketing*, the following noun string cannot be resolved by simply consulting our knowledge of the world:

police arrest information

Does this refer to information that police use when they arrest people? Or information police compile when they arrest people? Or does it refer to information about police arresting people? Without surrounding context (or maybe even with it), this noun phrase remains ambiguous.

Finally, when style is heavily nominal — that is, when information is concentrated in expanding noun phrases — an accompanying feature appears which can also contribute to ambiguity. This feature, which we have encountered at the beginning of this chapter, we will call **agent-lessness**. The doers of actions slip away when the actions are turned from nouns to verbs. So, while the verb *attend* requires (in active voice) that the doers of the action be identified —

> **Forty-five property owners and six tenants** attended the meeting.

— the noun *attendance* allows these agents of the action to withdraw from the sentence:

> Attendance was high.

Agentless writing has been condemned as both ambiguous and deceptive, an instrument of concealment. Leaving charges of deception aside for the moment, we must concede that heavy nominals which eliminate agents are liable to be ambiguous. For example, in *labour supply decision-making*, who is making the decision? (and about what?) Someone who has not read the article from which this phrase was taken might be surprised to learn that the decision-makers were Bangladeshi women in London who chose to do piece-work at home rather than look for jobs in garment factories.

The ambiguity and syntactic density of a heavily nominal style are both potential troublemakers for readers and writers. Yet scholarly style risks these troubles. This way of speaking must therefore provide some benefits, some important service to scholarly situations. In the next section we will observe these benefits and services.

Two exercises conclude this section. In the first, you can practise unpacking a heavily nominal passage — something you may want to do when revising writing of your own.

The second exercise presents a passage from non-academic writing that exhibits many of the features we have been talking about as typical of scholarly writing. It is a description of a management position in the private sector. You will be asked to assess its cognitive and social profile: how does its grammar call on reader's reasoning capacities and their knowledge of the world? At the same time, it demonstrates a condition often overlooked by criticisms of scholarly writing: that the boundaries around scholarly expression and research communities are permeable, and the language of scholarship can seep out into surrounding communities. While *labour supply decision-making* may seem like an entirely specialist term, peculiar to academic circles, a term like *dysfunctional family* may once have seemed so too, yet is currently in constant use in the public media and in private conversation. This is a case in which, through being useful to a culture's routines, research has found its way out of scholarly communities and into other circles.

Exercise

(1) Screen the passage below for heavy noun phrases. Rewrite by unpacking them, spreading their elements out into other parts of the sentence and other sentences. (Note that the rewrite will not necessarily be an improvement — merely another version, less nominal, possibly more friendly to readers in certain situations.)

Sample:
Incarceration-based measures are the most common in national prison-use assessment.

Rewrite:
Some measures are based on the frequency with which criminals are incarcerated. These rates are the measure most commonly used to assess the way nations use prisons.

> The Australian basic-wage Royal Commission of 1920, seeking working-class standard-of-living criteria, was chaired by a widely-read and respected living-wage champion, husband of a controversial family-planning advocate. Despite the liberal-reform inclinations of the Commission's chair and its nearly 40% recommended basic-wage increase, one of the main legacies of the Commission was the unquestioned equation of the "family" wage with the male-provider wage.

Adapted from Kerreen M. Reiger 1989 "'Clean and comfortable and respectable': Working-class aspirations and the Australian 1920 Royal Commission on the Basic Wage." *History Workshop* 27, 86–105.

---

(2) The advertisement below appeared in the Career Opportunities section of a national newspaper. Other advertisements in this section included descriptions of positions available in engineering, private- and public-sector administration, personnel and sales management.

Screen the style of this text for features we have identified as belonging to scholarly expression: that is, nouns that represent actions or events, and in doing so lose agents (doers) and objects (done to). What questions might someone ask about who does what to whom? Evaluate this passage for its potential ambiguity and syntactic density. Speculate on why these ways of speaking, which seem characteristic of research genres, turn up here in a business genre.

SENIOR CONSULTANT
Automotive marketing

Blackburn/Polk Vehicle Information Services (BPVIS) is Canada's leading supplier of motor vehicle and marketing information services to the automotive industry and its allied businesses. We are looking for a Senior Consultant to work with our clients to market our full range of products and services.

We require an individual with the following skill set:

- knowledge of the automotive market and its information requirements
- general understanding of geo-demographics and market research
- general knowledge of direct marketing.

Our services for the automotive industry include market performance evaluation and benchmarking, network planning and location analysis, customer profiling studies, and support services for direct communication and customer retention programs.

The successful candidate will have strong presentation and interpersonal skills and be self-motivated.

Compensation is performance related and is commensurate with experience. Please apply in confidence to _____.

5.2 Sentence style and textual coherence

Here are four scholarly passages which can arouse questions:

PASSAGE 5

What appears increasingly clear is that educational attainment is not synonymous with skill requirements in the workplace, and that a single years-of-schooling measure cannot serve as an adequate proxy for the variety of working capacities required by an industrialised society.

Keith Burgess 1994 "British employers and education policy, 1935–45: A decade of 'missed opportunities'?" *Business History* 36, 3, 29-61, 31.

Who gets educated? Who requires skills? Who measures what? Who works? Who has — or lacks — capacities?

PASSAGE 6

During this period [1880–1920] a latent nativist, anti-immigrant tendency in American society and politics grew rapidly, in response to economic problems, urban growth and changes in the nature and scale of immigration.

Mark Ellis and Panikos Panayi 1994 "German minorities in World War I: A comparative study of Britain and the U.S.A." *Ethnic and Racial Studies* 17, 2, 238-59, 239.

Who tended? Who responded? Who had problems? Who moved to cities? Who immigrated?

PASSAGE 7

The insertion of a Fourth World of indigenous populations who have a distinct vision of their place in a world that until recently has ignored them (Graburn 1976) cultivates an awareness of the political potential of submerged nationalities that are emerging once again in the postmodern world. This belated recognition of submerged ethnicities comes in the wake of the demise of the Second World, which no longer provides the paradigmatic base for analyses, as the structures of capitalism, socialism, and imperialism are undermined.

June Nash 1994 "Global integration and subsistence insecurity." *American Anthropologist* 96, 1, 7-30, 8.

Who inserts a Fourth World? Who is aware? Who belatedly recognizes? Who analyses? What nationalities and ethnicities are these? Who or what submerged them?

PASSAGE 8

Our study advances and tests a model incorporating both institutional and resource explanations for why firms adopt certain structural modifications, namely, issues management structures. The study ... provides a model to account for variation in the development of issues management structures across firms.

Daniel W. Greening and Barbara Gray 1994 "Testing a model of organizational response to social and political issues." *Academy of Management Journal* 37, 3, 467-98, 469.

Who explains? Who modifies what? Who manages? What are the issues and what does it mean to manage them? Who develops structures?

These samples — all heavily nominal — seem to confirm the view that scholarly writing is difficult. But they all appeared in respected journals. This style must in some way benefit scholarly writers and readers, and serve scholarly situations.

Halliday and Martin (1993) argue that this "language of the expert" gives priority to **taxonomy**: that is, to schemes for classifying and ordering phenomena. Such schemes depend on **names** for things. So, in Passage 8, the action *modify* becomes the noun *modification*, which can then take an attribute ("structural"), which will distinguish it from other "modifications." The action or event stabilized as a noun can then be worked into an arrangement with other named phenomena, "institutions" and "resources." These arrangements, Halliday and Martin argue, are designed to reveal relations of **cause**. This is evident in Passage 8, where the authors explicitly ask "why?" In this ordering search for causes, the grammar of research genres ends up with heavy nominalizations.

We might also note tendencies in current scholarship in many disciplines to **integrate** — to bring together theories, conditions, analyses, dimensions. So, for example, *labour supply decision-making* names an effort to combine — or integrate — analyses of labour supply (availability of workers) with analyses of how people and households make decisions about what jobs they will seek, or keep, or quit. The grammatical outcome of this research initiative is a big noun phrase.

To this social analysis of nominal expressions we can add a cognitive, or socio-cognitive, dimension. In Chapter Four we imagined readers working with passages of sentences, seeking higher-level terms in which to understand stretches of detail, or to understand the **relevance** of statements in context. Not all genres instruct the reader's efforts after meaning in the same way, and not all genres produce relevance in the same way. The scholarly genres typically maintain coherence and relevance by repeated instatements of high-level, abstract topic entities.

Other genres — like newspaper reports, thank-you notes, or computer manuals — don't do this.

With these conditions in mind, we can begin to see the role of heavily nominalized expressions in supporting these recursive hierarchies of language, repeated movements between abstract and concrete, generalities and detail. If, over several paragraphs, I were to write about a number of cases where employers preferred to train young employees on the job and tended not to hire people with secondary-school diplomas, I could compress these many cases into *skill requirements in the workplace* and *educational attainment* and specify the relation between them: **not synonymous**. These expressions eliminate the employers who hired and taught and the workers and students who learned or failed to learn. But they also provide an ascent to the high level of abstraction that will hold this section of the discussion together, and then serve as tokens for this section as the discussion develops over 10 or 20 pages. These abstract terms — the nominal versions of actions and events — can be reinstated at each of those points when the academic reader's desktop needs instructions on managing information. While the details on particular firms and industries and school curriculum can be filed away, the high-level terms should be kept handy.

So, as the article on German minorities (Passage 6) proceeds, particular historical episodes of persecution can be assumed under *nativist, anti-immigrant tendency (*and, in the process we learn more about what *nativist, anti-immigrant tendency* meant in America between 1880 and 1920, and the term becomes fuller, richer). In the article on subsistence economies (Passage 7), *awareness* and *belated recognition* become names for the author's stories (from 30 years of fieldwork experience) of her own changing understanding of the relation between *submerged ethnicities* and established but now inadequate ways of analysing those communities anthropologically. In the article on issues management (Passage 8), *variation in the development of issues management structures across firms* is the name that holds together extensive data of 451 firms in three industries, *issues management structures* recurring repeatedly. (In my study [Giltrow 1998] of the language of management research, I found that a noun phrase of this type — abstract, topically high-level — could occur as many as 12 times in two paragraphs.)

Scholarly writers seem to need a concentrated expression they can reinstate to bind together parts of their discussion and to control extensive stretches of lower-level information. These expressions are like elevated platforms from which the extent of the argument can be captured in a glance. There is not much standing-room on these platforms, so, when the arguments are complex, the expression can be dense. In the article on Bangladeshi garment workers, *labour supply decision-making* has to capture at once the article's distinctions as a contribution to the analysis of labour markets. The author examines labour as offered by workers rather than required by firms — hence "labour supply." And she examines the conditions which determine the decisions people make about work in an immigrant community where husbands' wishes about the wives' work may not coincide with the women's wishes, and where both sets of choices are hemmed in by racial attitudes in the surrounding community. *Labour supply decision-making* is the platform from which expanses of statistical and interview data can be viewed.

These viewing platforms are situated throughout the scholarly article, often working to incorporate summary of other writers' statements. Below, in an article on *voluntary employee turnover* (people quitting their jobs), *employee turnover* is ground shared by the other writers and the current authors, while the expressions *job alternatives* (if I quit will I be able to get another job? will it be a good one?) and *job satisfaction* (am I happy in my work? do I get along with my boss? will I be promoted?) themselves compress information. And these abstractions not only point back to accumulated reasoning but also can be extracted from the publication and indexed as **key words** — to signal to researchers the site of scholarly conversation on a topic shared in a research community. Abstractions sum up previous research attention and the current episode — and they point forward too, as reference or orientation for other researchers' future work.

PASSAGE 9

In a major conceptual advance from previous research directions, Hulin and colleagues (1985) recognized that job alternatives and satisfaction could have substantially different effects on employee turnover across various populations. For example, job alternatives but not job satisfaction might have a substantial and direct effect on turnover among marginal and temporary employees (often described as the secondary labor market). In contrast, both alternatives and job satisfaction might have significant effects on turnover among permanent and full-time employees.

Thomas W. Lee and Terence R. Mitchell 1994 "An alternative approach: The unfolding model of voluntary employee turnover." *Academy of Management Journal* 19, 1, 51-89, 54.

Nominal expressions also tend to appear as writers end one section of argument and move on to the next stage. Here, the writer concerned with subsistence economies concludes a three-part account of the "world crises" affecting the "submerged ethnicities." She uses three expressions which nominalize verbs (and remove their agents) to compress the preceding discussion and make it portable, able to be carried forward compactly to the next section:

PASSAGE 10

These world trends of **integration of economies, dependence on finance capital**, and **erosion of subsistence security** have profound consequences for the societies we study, whether they are located in core industrial countries or in developing areas. I shall illustrate their implications in three case studies of integration into the **global economy** where I have carried out fieldwork.

(Nash 1994:13, emphasis added)

Unlike many other genres, scholarly genres must live up to demanding coherence requirements, hinged on abstraction and spread through deep descents to specifics and sharp ascents to generality. We could say that these large patterns of abstraction and specificity at text level determine smaller patterns at sentence level.

In 5.1 we asked what benefits come from long expressions which many measures would estimate as cognitively costly (hard to read). Now we have the answer: cognitive cost at the level of sentence and phrase for a profit at the level of textual coherence.

Yet the model of the reader's mental desktop warns us that those sentence-level costs can be high — to readers who give up, and to writers who can't get through to exhausted readers. So you will find academic writers stopping to unpack a passage and relieve some of the congestion on the desktop.

PASSAGE 11

Pleck suggests that Afro-American women worked more as a reaction to their greater long-term potential for income inadequacy than to immediate economic deprivation. It was as if they were taking out insurance against future problems.

James A. Geschwender 1992 "Ethgender, women's waged labor, and economic mobility." *Social Problems* 39, 1, 1-16, 7.

Sensing perhaps that *immediate economic deprivation* (being poor? not having enough money?) and *long-term potential for income inadequacy* (worry about not having enough money later?) are complicated ways of speaking, the author rephrases these expressions in everyday language.

In other words, while the grammars of the research genres privilege the heavily nominal phrase — for reasons we have just examined — they also privilege corrections to the socio-cognitive conditions produced by their own styles. We practised one of these stylistic correctives in Chapter Three: the appositive expression. The appositive says it again, in other words, giving the reader a second chance at an important but difficult concept. For instance, the writer in Passage 11 above says again "long term potential for income inadequacy." Seeded throughout research writing we find two tiny expressions which signal writers' efforts to say it again: *i.e.* and *e.g.* The expression *i.e.* (*id est*) signals that an element in the preceding statement (or statements) will be repeated: *i.e.* works *laterally*, putting an additional expression next to the one which the writer estimates as important but difficult, or important and complex, and deserving further attention. Synonymous with *i.e.* are *that is, namely, in other words, that is to say*.

On the other hand, *e.g.* (*exempla gratia*) signals that an element in the preceding statement will be exemplified, at a lower level of generality; *e.g.* works *vertically*, descending from high levels to lower levels of specificity. Synonymous with *e.g.* are *for example, for instance*. Both *i.e.* and *e.g.* can work as appositives — enriching readers' understanding of a term, inviting their cooperation in its use in the particular context.

By these means, writers can reduce cognitive costs of heavy nominal expressions to the reader. But what can readers do when they face imposing clumps of nominals? Rather than give up, they can unpack those clumps for themselves, finding the everyday wordings that would represent the ideas at stake, and trying to think of examples of what the writer is talking about.

Exercise
Take Passages 5 to 8 and unpack them for yourself. Try to answer the questions posed about these passages. Question Passage 10 similarly, and answer the questions you come up with. In each case try to construct concrete examples of what the writers are talking about. Using i.e and e.g., rewrite the passages, incorporating answers to the questions.

5.3 Messages about the argument

In the previous sections we saw that the research genres are distinguished by nominalizaton and the superstructure of abstraction that it builds. Both nominalization and abstraction can appear in other genres (in an exercise above, agentless nominalizations appeared in an employment advertisement; abstractions can show up in that genre too, as for example, when employers ask for "commitment" or "initiative" from potential employees). But they do not work in the same way they do in the research genres, where they consistently enforce the special coherence of scholarly writing and attach individual research contributions to an on-going scholarly conversation. The features we will inspect in this section — messages about the argument — also distinguish the academic genres.

PASSAGE 12

... the study of gender issues generally in rural areas remains relatively neglected (Little 1991).

This paper is an attempt to begin to redress the balance by concentrating on the gender divisions apparent in the material collected by the Rural Church Project, and aims also to highlight the need for further specific study of gender and the rural church. After a brief discussion of the history of staffing in the Church of England, we consider recent published studies on gender roles in the Church and our own material from the Rural Church Project survey on the staffing of parishes in five dioceses. We then turn to rural parishioners and consider the influence of gender on church attendance and religious belief, together with attitudes towards women priests. Our conclusion is an attempt to reconcile the very different pictures of the rural church which emerge from the information on staffing on the one hand and attendance, belief and attitudes to women priests on the other.

Susanne Seymour 1994 "Gender, church and people in rural areas." *Area* 26, 1, 45-56, 45.

This passage, from a geography journal, exhibits several features we will investigate: it refers to itself ("This paper"); it refers to the author ("We"); it forecasts the argument to follow; it situates itself in relation to what other studies have said — or not said.

To sharpen your sense of these features as distinctive, call to mind other genres, familiar from everyday life. Would you find a newspaper report or a thank-you note referring to itself?

| This report provides information on protest at the legislature. | This thank-you note expresses gratitude for two gifts received last week. |

Probably not, although instances of some other genres (very formal business letters, for example, or legal documents) can refer to themselves. Would you find a newspaper report or thank-you note referring to the author in this (limited) sense?

| I/we present a series of quotations from participants at the protest. | I/we describe the gift in favourable terms. |

Probably not, although the thank-you-note writer may refer to himself in other senses ("I have been very busy at school and look forward to the holidays"). Would you find a newspaper report or thank-you note forecasting its discussion?

| These quotations will be followed by quotations from political figures responding to the protest. | Following the description of the gift, brief news about the recipient's family will be presented. |

Probably not. And it is hard to construct a situation where either of these everyday genres would situate the current utterance in relation to what others have said, or not said.

| Little information about this event has been published, since it only happened yesterday. | No one has so far expressed gratitude for this gift in writing. |

Later in this chapter, we will look at this last feature, which situates the utterance in relation to other utterances. In the meantime, we will examine the other features which distinguish the cited passage from — at least — newspaper reports and thank-you notes.

5.3.1 The argument refers to itself

The emphasized wordings in the following passages each refer to the text being written/read. What patterns do you detect in these moments when the article mentions itself?

PASSAGE 13

Over **the following pages** we aim to challenge this view and demonstrate that restrictive practices of this type have been nowhere near as common or serious as some have argued.

Nick Tiratsoo and Jim Tomlinson 1994 "Restrictive practices on the shopfloor in Britain, 1946-60: Myth and reality." *Business History* 36, 2, 65-84, 65, emphasis added.

PASSAGE 14

This study explores the possible cognitive bases for Justice Jackson's conundrum, by closely relating what happens in legal advocates' minds while composing to what happens in court readers' minds as they grapple with a case decision. **The study** directly compares, for the first time, the thought processes of professional appellate attorneys as they researched, composed and revised a brief for litigation with the subsequent thought process of two independent appellate court readers, charged with pronouncing a decision. Through **this comparison** of advocates' with decision-makers' "on-line" processes, the purpose of **the study** is to explore alternative theories for why appellate advocates experience difficulties in forming successful rhetorical strategies for their briefs. In particular, **the comparison** permits one to explore empirically why these advocates may fail to perceive accurately the effects of their chosen strategies upon judges and court staff readers.

James F. Stratman 1994 "Investigating persuasive processes in legal discourse in real time: Cognitive biases and rhetorical strategy in appeal court briefs." *Discourse Processes* 17, 1-57, 1-2, emphasis added.

PASSAGE 15

Two main hypotheses are addressed in **this study**: (1) that unidentified and untreated learning difficulties may be related to teenage girls becoming pregnant, deciding to raise their children, and dropping out of school, and (2) that teenage pregnancies may *not* characteristically be "unintended."

(Rauch-Elnekave 1994: 92, emphasis added, italic emphasis in original)

What we can learn from these samples is that reference to the thing being written/read often coincides with the expression of a major claim or promise, and/or with a forecast of the order of the upcoming discussion. We can therefore speculate that such references will be a helpful signal to your readers (accustomed as they are to the sounds of the scholarly genres) to pay close attention.

We might also note that in the second and third samples the writers might very well have used *I* or *we*: "I directly compare ..."; "I address two main hypotheses..." Are these entities — *paper, study, analysis* — stand-ins for the writer? Surrogates in a situation that disallows *I*? Not exactly, for Passage 13 shows that the first person *we* can accompany reference to the thing being written/read. And we see in the next section that, contrary to many people's ideas about prohibitions against *I* in academic writing, the first person occurs frequently in published scholarship.

Exercise

Inspect essays you have written recently or are currently drafting: do you find expressions which refer to the essay itself? (Keep in mind that such wordings appear at points where writers make major claims or promises.) How do you feel about saying, "This study focusses on three explanations for ..."? Would you feel better saying, "This paper ..." or "This essay ..."?

5.3.2 The *discursive I*

Although *I* occurs in the scholarly genres with nowhere near the frequency that it does in daily conversation (where it is a favoured sentence-opener), it is by no means absent from published scholarship.

Sometimes students ask their teachers if they want them to use *I*, or to avoid it. This question is often accompanied by a question as to whether the teachers are interested in the students' own opinions. In the long history of the teaching of writing, *I* and "opinion" have become connected.

However, in conventional, mainstream scholarship, it would be hard to connect *I* with the ordinary sense of "opinion," in light of the constraints under which it occurs. We will now examine these constraints.

Here are some occurrences of *I* in published scholarship. See if you can infer the constraints which control the use of *I*. (Analysis follows, but try to make this out for yourself before looking at the analysis.)

PASSAGE 16
Lesbian theory and feminism, I want to suggest, are at risk of falling into a similar unhappy marriage in which "the one" is feminism.
★ ★ ★

I intend to begin this section by expanding on the argument against reducing the institution of heterosexuality to (a part of) the institution of male dominance.

(Calhoun 1994: 573)

PASSAGE 17
Let me conclude by returning to the title of this paper.

Naila Kabeer 1994 "The structure of 'revealed' preference: Race, community and female labour supply in the London clothing industry." *Development and Change* 25, 307-331, 329.

PASSAGE 18
... I shall focus upon expectations and evaluations regarding the participation of married women, with husband present, in the waged labor force. I begin with a discussion of the "cult of domesticity," explore ethnic variations in commitments to the cult, examine the causes and consequences of its decline in influence, and evaluate the consequences for ethnic groups of difference in rates at which married women work for wages. I close with a consideration of policy implications.

(Geschwender 1992:1)

PASSAGE 19
This article has two purposes. The first is to show that ability grouping in secondary schools does not always have the same effect, and therefore it is worth seeking ways of using it more effectively than commonly occurs. A brief review of earlier studies, and a reinterpretation of the conclusions of an earlier synthesis, provide the support for this claim. The second goal is to explore instances of relatively successful uses of ability grouping, in the sense that high-quality instruction fosters significant learning among students assigned to low-ability classes. What characterizes such classes? To address this question, I draw on evidence from earlier studies by other authors, and I provide two new illustrations taken from a larger study of eighth- and ninth-grade English classes in 25 midwestern schools. Although these examples are far from conclusive, common elements emerge that, taken together, may help to characterize effective instruction in low-ability classes in secondary schools.

Adam Gamoran 1993 "Alternative uses of ability grouping in secondary schools: Can we bring high-quality instruction to low-ability classes?" *American Journal of Education* 102, 1-22, 1.

PASSAGE 20

The author decided to investigate the academic achievement levels of the teenage mothers with whom she was working after
being told repeatedly that their favorite subject in school was
math — an unexpected and perplexing finding because girls are
generally reported to feel they are not good at, and thus dislike,
math (Parsons, Adler, and Kaczala, 1982).

(Rauch-Elnekave 1994:97)

On the one hand, the *I* of the writer in these passages seems to hover
on the vanishing point. In virtually every case, the *I*-construction could
be eliminated without depleting content. It could simply disappear
("Lesbian theory and feminist theory are at risk of ..."), or be replaced
by one of the text-referring words like "study" ("this section begins"),
and Passage 19 mixes such words ("article," "review") with instances of
I. One (20) has actually transformed the first-person *I* into third-person
"the author"/"she."

So we might look at the typical habitat of *I*: what does it occur with?
Then we notice that all the verbs that have first-person subjects refer to
some **discourse action**:

I want to suggest
I begin with
I shall focus
I explore, examine, evaluate
I close
I draw on evidence
I provide
Let me conclude

Analysts who specialize in the study of the research genres would distinguish among these verbs, finding different categories of discourse
action. But, for our purposes, it is enough to note their general similarity: they all describe the speaker in his or her capacity as a writer/
researcher. Let us call the *I* of the scholarly genres the ***discursive I***.

As a writer in the scholarly genres, you can refer to yourself, pointing yourself out to your reader. But, as we have seen, your identity is
limited, and attitudes to these limitations run to extremes. So many students have told me that their teachers and professors have instructed
them not to use *I* that I think there must still be some *I*-avoidance
afoot. Perhaps this can be explained by the limitations on *I* when it
occurs in scholarship. Those who would disallow *I* translate the limits
into a blanket prohibition.

Taking a different view, some scholars criticize the research genres for the limits they put on *I*. Conventions which limit writers to the *discursive I* erase elements of identity that are, in fact, relevant to research and its results. Such criticisms propose that who we are, as social and political beings, influences what we choose to study, how we gather information, and how we interpret that information. The *discursive I* obscures those influences and limits not only the surface expression of scholarship but its deeper character as well. In Chapter Six we will consider the larger arguments to which such reflections contribute.

Exercise

(1) Passage 17 above — "Let me conclude ..." — resists elimination of the first person. Can you think of any way of putting this differently? What aspect of the expression makes any change difficult? From this example, can you infer any general features of the *discursive I*?

(2) What do you think of Passage 20's "The author decided...."? Does it help you to know that this paper was written by a psychologist? Can you devise any other way of writing this passage — without using *I*?

(3) Inspect essays you have written recently or are currently composing: how do you represent yourself when you write an academic paper? Are you happy with this representation? Would your friends and family recognize you? What options do you feel you have? Do the options vary according to the discipline you are working in?

5.3.3 Forecasts and emphasis

Like references to the text itself, the *discursive I* of scholarly writing often occurs along with forecasts: statements about how the argument will be organized, what readers can expect.

PASSAGE 21

First, I will summarize prior research indicating that instruction is typically inferior in low-ability classes. **Second**, I will briefly show that new data from a study of midwestern secondary schools mainly conform to this pattern. **Third**, I will give four examples — two drawn from past research, and two original cases taken from the study of midwestern secondary schools — that illustrate that high-quality instruction can occur in low-ability classes. **Finally**, I will consider the limitations and implications of these illustrations.

(Gamoran 1993:4-5)

Forecasts can also show up in agentless forms — that is, without either the text itself or *I* promising a particular course of discussion.

PASSAGE 22

Before proceeding to a more precise description of the research methods used and a detailed discussion of sample matched reader-writer protocols, the relevance of this study to current theoretical disputes over appropriate rhetorical techniques and planning processes for appellate advocates should be put into sharper focus. Two basic issues will be addressed:

1) What rhetorical techniques in briefs do current brief writing theories recommend appellates use, and what conflicts exist between these theories?

2) What problems has empirical research investigating these theories encountered?

(Stratman 1994:7)

This passage achieves its agentlessness by using the **passive voice**: "the research methods **used**" (*who* used the methods?); "the relevance ... should **be put**" into sharper focus" (*who* should do this?); "two basic issues will **be addressed**" (*who* will address the issues?).

The passive voice has been condemned by many, and defended by few. Despite its bad reputation amongst people who compose rules-for-writing, however, it is very common in scholarly expression, as well as elsewhere. In the three passive constructions listed above, for example, the themes of the sentences ("the research methods," the relevance," and "two basic issues") are more important than *who* is "using," "addressing," or "putting them into sharper focus." Passive voice enables this functional thematization.

While we do not run across forecasts so often in everyday life —

| Binky: What have you been up to? | Bingo: In addressing your question, I will first express my philosophy of life. Next, I will show that philosophy operating in my recent activities. Finally, I will describe my plans for the future. |

— they are extremely common in the scholarly genres. It seems that forecasts play an important role in helping readers manage the contents of their mental desktops. Forecasts instruct the desktop's information-management device. They guide readers in determining when one section is finished and another beginning — determining, that is, when to file lower-level information, compacting its gist into higher-level statements that can be kept handy as the discussion goes on to other areas.

Readers are also served by statements of **emphasis**. Here are some examples.

PASSAGE 23

The **crucial point** for this essay is that between 1939 and 1944 the organization attracted *popular support*.

★ ★ ★

Our **main interest** here is the style of the printed language — how did it reconcile with the everyday language of the predominantly oral world?

Thiathu J. Nemutanzhela 1993 "Cultural forms and literacy as resources for political mobilisation: A.M. Malivha and the Zoutpansberg Balemi Association." *African Studies* 52, 1, 89-102, 92-93, emphasis added, italic emphasis in original.

PASSAGE 24

The **general point here** is that there are instances — this [campaigns for non-sexist language] is one — where we can locate the specific and concrete steps leading to an observable change in some people's linguistic behaviour and in the system itself.

(Cameron 1990: 91, emphasis added)

PASSAGE 25

What I want to **highlight** in Wittig's explanation of what bars lesbians from the category "woman" is that it claims both too much and too little for lesbians as well as reads lesbianism from a peculiarly heterosexual viewpoint.

(Calhoun 1994:563, emphasis added)

Many guides to "good" style disallow sentences beginning with *it*. These sentences are said to be boring or "empty." Yet *it* in English serves a built-in grammar of **emphasis**, known as the cleft. Notice how *it* works in these ordinary, conversational sentences to stage the importance of a particular part of the sentence.

Binky brought the cookies. [not anybody else]   It was Binky who brought the cookies.

A speaker could use intonation — "BINky brought the cookies" — to achieve emphasis. Writers can't use intonation — but they can (and do) use the **cleft** form of the sentence. (Notice how, if you say the second sentence above, stress falls on "Binky.") If the speaker or writer wanted to emphasize the contribution rather than the contributor, they could say or write:

It was the cookies that Binky brought [not the lasagna].

In research writing, cleft sentences beginning with *it* can accomplish emphasis, e.g.,

It was Foucault's work that mobilized research of institutions under the "surveillance" theme.

The "end-weight" principle

And, while we are thinking about sentences beginning with *it*, we can also observe that on many occasions the tendencies of English will shift heavy material to sentence-end, leaving the sentence beginning "empty." Of the following pair, (1) is more likely to be produced by English speakers and writers.

(1) It may be argued that this neglect is due to a lack of scholarly interest in the rural church rather than in gender relations in the Anglican Church as a whole.

(2) That this neglect is due to a lack of scholarly interest in the rural church rather than in gender relations in the Anglican Church as a whole may be argued.

The reason that (1) is preferred is that it obeys the "end-weight" principle in English: a tendency for sentences to tilt, letting heavy material slide to the end, and producing what's called anticipatory-it or it-extraposition. Like the passive voice, sentences beginning with it have been criticized by authorities on "good" style, but there seems to be little basis for these criticisms.

Some research articles provide neither forecasts nor emphasis pointers. Movements along the hierarchy of generalization — from high-level abstraction to specifics and back again — themselves convey implicit messages about the argument, messages that will alert experienced readers to important points in the text. Nevertheless, many do use expressions of emphasis, and most seem to offer some kind of forecast.

Similarly, most instances of *I* could be removed, and the expression in which they occur adjusted to get across equivalent information. But *I* occurs nevertheless, with some frequency. Perhaps both techniques not only benefit readers' desktop-management devices but also provide writers with greater control over the use that readers make of their texts. Perhaps forecasts and emphasis pointers would have, on some occasions, controlled some of those unruly readers/instructors who missed your point. While we could speculate that both forecasts and emphasis (and the associated references to the text itself and its writer) are signs that scholarly genres are domineering or overpowering in their measures for controlling readers' interpretive work, we can perhaps also sympathize with writers' desires to overrule the hazards of misunderstanding.

The scholarly genres can seem aloof productions, remote from the personal contact and proximities of more mundane genres or of everyday conversation. Yet the features we have looked at in this section all summon writer and reader to the same spot, putting the writer in close touch with the reader.

Exercise
Imagine a reader from outside the academic community encountering the passages below (both of which are first paragraphs of introductions). How could you prepare that reader for contact with these examples of scholarly expression? How would you explain the features of these passages so the imagined reader would understand them as functional expressions of the academic

community's routines and procedures? (It might help to imagine a particular reader — a friend, family member, neighbour, co-worker, or maybe yourself at an earlier stage of your education.)

PASSAGE A
Recent research in the history of nineteenth century psychiatry has explored the expanding powers of the medical profession and the proliferation of the asylum, that "magic machine" for curing insanity. This medicalization of madness has usually been portrayed as a "top-down" process: "social control imposed from above with greater or lesser success on a population now the unwitting object of medical encadrement." But as historians have begun to study individual asylums and the complexities of committal, more emphasis is being placed on the role played by families in the process. Asylum doctors, it has been suggested, merely confirmed a diagnosis of insanity already made by families, by neighbors, or by non-medical authorities. Consequently, as the American historian Nancy Tomes has argued, "the composition of a nineteenth century asylum population tells more about the family's response to insanity than the incidence or definition of the condition itself." Such arguments imply a more "dynamic and dialectical" interpretation of the process of medicalization, one that requires a careful assessment of family demands for medical services and the degree to which these demands were met, willingly or unwillingly, by the emerging psychiatric profession. In the present stage of research on mental illness and its treatment, it is vital to expand the range of institutional studies.

Patricia E. Prestwich 1994 "Family strategies and medical power: 'Voluntary' committal in a Parisian asylum, 1876-1914." *Journal of Social History* 27, 4, 799-818, 719.

PASSAGE B
It is now well known that optimizing governments face a credibility problem when agents form rational or model-consistent expectations because of the time inconsistency of the resulting policy (Kydland and Prescott, 1977). A time-inconsistent policy is one which is optimal at the beginning of the planning period but becomes sub-optimal at subsequent times thereby creating an incentive to renege. Assuming that

the private sector has complete information of the nature of the policy-maker's calculations, the incentive to renege can be anticipated. Thus time-inconsistent policies may not be believed in the absence of some institutional arrangements which force policy-makers to precommit.

Paul L. Levine and Joseph G. Pearlman 1994 "Credibility, ambiguity and asymmetric information with wage stickiness." *The Manchester School* 62, 1, 21-39, 21.

5.4 The state of knowledge: limits, conditions, positions

When research findings are reported to the public, in the genres of the broadcast media or the general-circulation print media, they are normally "popularized." Specialist, technical terms are translated, or replaced with ordinary ones. We can expect that, thereby, some meanings are lost — careful distinctions produced by technicality itself.

But we might also expect that some other meanings, equally important, are also lost in popularizations. Research genres not only report findings but also represent the **state of knowledge** itself: its limits, the conditions under which it was produced, the positions from which statements issue. In popularizations, statements of research findings lose some of these indicators (and we might ask why these qualifications are not functional in popular genres).

The following sections, to the end of this chapter, focus on features which index statements for their status as knowledge — and distinguish research discourse from popular genres, and also from some forms of school writing. We discover these features as they occur in important structures of the research genres, sections which **organize** scholarly discussion.

5.4.1 Introductions: generalization and citation

Most people would probably agree that introductions typically begin at and sustain a relatively high level of generality. For the schoolroom essay, generality itself is often enough to get the essay under way.

Throughout history, humans have sought their identity.

Or:

Imagination is a powerful force in our daily lives.

But if we transferred this habit of generality directly to the academic essay, we might find that academic readers' expectations are not entirely satisfied by generalities like these. Academic readers are used to beginnings like the one below, from the *issues management structures* article which has already provided us with some examples. The article does begin with some general statements —

> In the last 20 years, business organizations have been increasingly held accountable for their corporate social performance in a variety of areas (Wood, 1991). Firms have been confronted by an organized, activist, and concerned set of stakeholders (Ansoff, 1975; Freeman, 1984) clamoring for improved corporate performance on a wide range of social and political issues, from clean air and nutritional labelling to equal employment opportunities.
>
> (Greening and Gray 1994: 467)

— but those generalities are attributed to particular people. Why? It seems to me that most people — including the writers — already know that public consciousness of business and industry has changed, and corporate spokespersons appear on TV, and are often quoted in the print media to answer complaints about their products and practices. But, even though these circumstances seem to be part of common knowledge, this passage attributes their mention to particular writers. Did the authors of the present article not know about this development in business domains until they read the three articles cited? This seems unlikely. Why are statements that could easily be justified as belonging to the present writer attributed to other writers?

John Swales (1990), in his study of the introductions to research papers, observes that one of the moves writers typically make is to confirm that they are carrying on a **tradition** of inquiry. This topic has been ratified, as the parenthetical citations show. It is not just anybody who mentioned that firms must deal with social issues — it is published researchers who have said this. In the academic community to which this article is addressed, people recognize this topic as something to be studied. The citation shows that the claim attached to it is verifiable by measures valued in research communities rather than simply coming from "common knowledge," which can turn out to be in some way mistaken (see 5.1).

"Common sense" threshold

Where is the threshold which separates commonsense (stereo)typifications from research-supported typifications? Here a psychologist cites ethnic typifications produced by research, rather than common sense:

> Some investigators have attributed ... low rates of delinquency and other behavior disorders [among "people of Asian descent in North America, particularly those of Chinese heritage"] to culture-related factors. That is, Asian culture emphasizes conformity, family solidarity, harmonious relationships, and respect for authority, especially the unconditional respect for parents, or filial piety (Fong, 1973; Hsu, 1981). The North American culture, on the other hand, emphasizes freedom and individualism. Consistent with this notion of cultural differences, Kelley and Tsang (1992) reported that Chinese parents in North America used more physical control over their children and more restrictive child-rearing practices than did their non-Chinese counterparts.
>
> Siu Kwong Wong 1999 "Acculturation, peer relations, and delinquent behavior of Chinese-Canadian youth." *Adolescence* 34, 133, 107-19, 107-08.

As well as putting a check on common sense — on widely held views — attributing generalizations to others can also put a check on personal perceptions. We may notice, in our daily life, that the servers at fast-food outlets are young people. So we construct a generalization: "The fast-food franchise industries hire young people." But what if it is only the one or two outlets that serve the fried chicken we like that actually do hire young people? What if, in the next district or province, most servers are elderly? Our limited experience — our particular position in the world — has distorted our knowledge of the situation. And what if our experience is limited in another way, by attitudes and interests? Maybe we have a grudge against young people, and feel the world is overrun with them. We see them everywhere. Our unchecked personal perception would produce an unwarranted generalization, one which reflected our position in the world, our point of view. So, in academic writing, we find generalizations which typify sections of the population secured with citation:

> This article analyzes labour supply decision-making for a particular group of women workers in a particular segment of the Lon-

don clothing industry. It takes as its starting point the concentration of Bangladeshi women in the homeworking sector of the East London rag trade (Mitter, 1986a).

(Kabeer 1994:307)

This example suggests, too, that citation can be a check on stereotypes as well as on personal perceptions. Citation indicates that the generalization has been produced in a context of scholarly exchange, and that context includes the anonymous, expert reviewers who evaluated the research before publication: assessed its methodology, its interpretation of data, its account of other work in the field.

Anonymous review

Before a scholarly article or book is published, it gets reviewed by experts in the field who are selected by the editor of the journal or scholarly press to which the manuscript has been submitted. The identity of the expert reviewers is not disclosed to the author, and the experts do not know the identity of the author of the book or article.

Anonymous review is an element of the situation which composes the research genres. Considering what we've just seen about generalizations, what would you say is the function of the anonymous review? Although researchers (and, indirectly, the public) rely on anonymous review to assure quality, not everybody is crazy about it: can you think of what critics of anonymous review might say against it?

Exercise

Here are two examples of generalization occurring in opening sections of research articles. What would be the "commonsense" versions of these generalizations? Why is the commonsense version not adequate to the scholarly situation? That is, why are these generalizations secured by citation?

PASSAGE A
Just as people are unable to ignore discredited information in making personality judgments (Wyer and Budesheim, 1987; Wyer and Unverzagt, 1985) or revising social theories

(Anderson, Lepper, and Ross, 1980), so mock jurors are unable to ignore evidence that had been ruled inadmissible (Carretta and Moreland, 1983; Sue, Smith, and Caldwell, 1973; Thompson, Fong, and Rosenhan, 1981; Wolf and Montgomery, 1977). As new information is presented, it is immediately processed into people's ongoing belief revisions, or schemata, which are then resistant to change and colour the evaluation of subsequent evidence and instructions (Wrightsman, 1991, Ch. 13).

Brian H. Bornstein 1994 "David, Goliath, and Reverend Hayes: Prior beliefs about defendants' status in personal injury cases." *Applied Cognitive Psychology* 8, 233-58, 235.

PASSAGE B
Gender is one of the most important categories — if not the most important category — in human social life. The dichotomy between female and male is of crucial relevance to virtually every domain of human experience (Bem, 1981; Huston, 1983; Ruble and Ruble, 1982). All known cultures specify that female-male is a fundamental distinction. They provide terms to distinguish boys from girls and men from women. More importantly, they associate men and women with different sets of characteristic features and with different sets of behavioral expectations (see Williams and Best, 1990).

Thomas Eckes 1994 "Features of men, features of women: Assessing stereo-typic beliefs about gender subtypes." *British Journal of Social Psychology* 33, 107-23, 107.

Introductions in the schoolroom-essay genre and in the research genres share a tendency for high-level beginnings. Both genres, it seems, strive thereby to establish **common ground** with readers. The difference between them is that "common ground" extends in a different direction in the schoolroom essay. There, introductory generalities seem to cast such a wide net as to grab any reader in sight — the blanket generality is perennially functional in the schoolroom essay. The research genres, on the other hand, compose introductory generalities not to cast a wide net but to initiate scholarly conversation — to resume the collaborative consideration of topics that research communities are working on. Accordingly, reported speech is the start-up mechanism of many scholarly introductions.

5.4.2 Introductions: reported speech

As we saw in Chapter Two, reported speech is so crucial a feature in scholarly discourse that the research genres have developed their own distinctive ways of incorporating the speech of others. And supporting systems of documentation — footnotes, endnotes, lists of works cited, parenthetical clusters of names and dates — are intricate and rule-governed, although the rules vary from discipline to discipline.

Equally intricate are the systems that direct writers to quote a lot, or not much, or quote directly, or to paraphrase, or to put other writers' names in the reporting sentence, or to put them in parentheses, or even to leave the other speakers unidentified. In the passages which follow, we may find some *guides* to this system, but we will not find the kind of *rules* that govern, for example, the preparation of a "Works Cited" page or the punctuation of a parenthetical citation in a certain discipline. Instead, we will find tendencies and signs of preferences, traces of the habits of academic communities.

So we observe, for example, that, while reported speech can occur at any point in a scholarly essay, it is most likely to occur in the introduction, somewhat less likely to occur in the conclusion, and least likely to occur in the space between. Not all of the samples we will look at show up at the very beginnings of the articles, but most are part of the writers' introductory moves, playing a big role in getting writers started in their address to their readers.

5.4.3 Reported speech: direct and indirect

When we say what someone else has said, we have choices as to how to go about it. We can use the exact words the other person used:

Binky to Bingo: No matter how often I went over this clause of the contract, they still didn't understand.	Bingo to Flo: So, when I asked Binky about those clients, he said, "No matter how often I went over this clause of the contract, they still didn't understand."

This is called direct speech. In writing, direct speech is supposed to be verbatim; in talking, as some research has shown, people are often not accurate in their repetition of others' words.

Instead of direct speech, we can use our own words — which can be more or less close to the original:

Binky to Bingo: No matter how often I went over this clause of the contract, they still didn't understand.

Bingo to Flo: Binky said that no matter how often he explained that clause of the contract, they still didn't understand.

OR

Bingo to Flo: Binky said that his repeated explanations of the contract clause had no effect on the clients' comprehension.

This is called indirect speech. When you are summarizing, you can often find yourself using indirect speech: the exact words of the original are transformed to fit into a smaller space, and a different context.

You may notice that my second example of indirect speech moves toward the nominalized style of scholarly writing: "he explained" becomes "explanations"; "they ... understand" becomes "clients' comprehension"; and these two noun phrases are linked by a cause relation — "no effect." Not all indirect speech will take this nominal route, but in the scholarly genres — especially where longer chains are compacted, as in summary — we may find indirect speech heading this way.

Reported speech, mostly in indirect form, can take another step toward nominal style by transforming the reporting verb itself into a noun. So —

he	**suggests** **assumes** **argues**	that ...

— can become:

his	**suggestion** **assumption** **argument**	that ...

The choice between direct and indirect speech is reflected in questions students sometimes ask about their writing. How much should I quote? Do I quote too much? Do I need more quotations?

These are good questions, for it appears not only that there are certain tendencies in the proportion of direct to indirect speech, according to the function of the summary (to confirm what has been said, to dispute it, to go further), but also that direct speech is used differently in different disciplines. Greg Myers (1989) finds, for example, that direct speech is used ironically in the samples of articles in the biological sciences he analysed: that is, writers quote directly when they don't agree with the original source. You will see that this finding does not hold for our passages.

5.4.4 Reported speech: identifying the speaker

The simplest, base-line case of reported speech — both direct and indirect — is "*x* said *y*."

Blink to Flo: The shopping is great. I got so many bargains.	Flo to Bingo: Blink said, "The shopping is great. I got so many bargains." OR Flo to Bingo: Blink said that the shopping was great and he got a lot of bargains.

Or "*x* said" can be replaced by a characterization of the utterance, and followed by the gist, and here, with a bit of direct speech retained.

> Flo to Bingo: Blink expressed enthusiasm about shopping opportunities and reported getting "bargains."

Research writing can often depart from these base-line cases. Commonly, the reported speaker can leave the sentence itself and relocate in parentheses.

> The shopping is good, and bargains are available (Blink 2000).

This form can eliminate the speech verb (*say* and its many substitutes, such as *report, suggest*, etc.) as above, or retain it:

> It has been reported that the shopping is good, and bargains are available (Blink 2000).

Sometimes the speaker or speakers can disappear entirely: the act of speech is represented as agentless:

> It has been reported that the shopping is good, and bargains are available.

This form of expression seems to defy the research community's practice of attributing statements. Yet our samples will show that indirect speech can occur without an identifiable speaker. On non-scholarly occasions, agentless reports of statements may tend to make the statement seem more valid — coming from not just one person (who may or may not be reliable) but from more widely distributed sources.

> The Prime Minister is said to be considering tax cuts.

So the agentless report of speech can suggest some consensus. Inspecting the samples of reported speech below, you will have a chance to see if this is the case in scholarly publications.

In a variation on the agentless report of speech, statements can sometimes be attributed to a **typified group** — "researchers," "linguists," "neo-classical economists," for example, in the scholarly genres; "experts," "officials" or "business leaders" in other genres. So our example, in a "group-speaker" form, could be rewritten as:

> Consumers report that the shopping is good, and bargains are available.

When statements are presented as reported speech, their quality as knowledge is indicated: the statement has been produced — somewhere. At first it may appear that, in the scholarly genres, to present a statement as coming from a position other than that of the present speaker may implicitly ratify the statement as true: "this is not just my idea." But, as we saw in Chapter Two, things are more complicated than this. Statements are reported not simply to ensure that only true things get down on paper. Writers also report statements to sketch a community of speakers producing knowledge in a particular area. Reported statements produce a map of that knowledge domain. And a main concern of scholarly writers, as we will see, is to locate themselves on that map — maybe close to some speakers, or far away from others, maybe starting in densely populated locales where a lot has been said, but heading out into sparsely settled regions from which few statements have been transmitted so far.

5.4.5 Reported speech: naming the speech action

We have called the simplest or "base-line" case of reported speech "*x* says *y*." In the variation on the shopping example, we picked up the verb report (which could turn into a noun, producing "the report that shopping is good"). But *report* is by no means the only other verb for reporting speech. *State, propose, suggest, maintain, claim* are some others. And associated with verbs of speech are a set of verbs we could call "knowledge-making." Among the knowledge-making verbs we find words like *analyse, investigate, examine, discover, find, identify, observe.*

> **Analysing** shopping opportunities, Blink (2000) **found** that bargains were available.

Like the verbs of speech, these verbs can be turned into nouns. So we might come across sentences like this:

> **Analysis** of shopping opportunities has led to the **identification** of bargains (Blink 2000).

Where a range of wordings presents choices, the different choices tend to be associated with different functions. So, in everyday speech, to use *claim* as a reporting verb may in some situations have the effect of discrediting the statement, or at least suggesting that it needs review.

> Binky to Bingo: Well, Blink claims to have found bargains.

It is not clear whether *claim* — as just one example — has the same function of negative evaluation in scholarly writing. Nor is there extensive evidence as to which kinds of reporting verbs position the writer near the reported speaker (in agreement) or far away (in some form of disagreement). But some research (e.g., Thomas and Hawkes 1994) has found some correlation between the choice of reporting verb and the position of the writer vis-à-vis the sources reported.

Choice of reporting verb can also be influenced by the discipline in which the writer is working. In his study of citation practices in eight disciplines (molecular biology, magnetic physics, marketing, applied linguistics, philosophy, sociology, mechanical engineering, electronic engineering), Ken Hyland (1999) found diversity in reporting expressions used. For example, marketing is distinctive for its "particularly high degree of author tentative verbs, with *suggest* accounting for over half of all instances" (350); philosophy and marketing are more likely than the other disciplines in the sample to name the cited author outside parenthetical references (358-59); physics favoured the reporting verbs *develop, report, study*, while sociology preferred *argue, suggest, describe, note, analyse, discuss*. In the sample, none of the science papers used direct quotation (348). Hyland suggests that different citation practices in different disciplines "serve to reinforce the epistemological and social understandings of writers by conveying an orientation to a particular ethos and to particular practices of social engagement with peers" (359). In other words, part of what people learn when they learn to participate in the activities of a research community is a discipline-specific understanding of how scholarly work is organized, and how knowledge is made. Techniques for reporting the speech of others display this understanding.

Exercise

(1) Below you will find five samples of scholarly writing which report the statements of others. The samples illustrate the range of expression and function described above: the summoning of the voices of others to gesture to a Big Issue or established line of research; the variation between direct and indirect speech; the naming, obscuring, or typifying of other speakers; the characterization of the production of statements with various words for speaking and/or making knowledge.

Examine each sample to identify these features. From these limited data, can you generalize your results? What do you notice about the reporting of statements in scholarly prose? Can you see any correlation between the features you identify and the disciplines in which the writers are working?

PASSAGE A

One topic of recurring interest in the analysis of written discourse has been the identification of various text types. This identification has frequently involved linking a rhetorical "mode" or "aim" of discourse with the particular linguistic categories which realize that mode or aim in a text (Jakobsen, 1960; Hausenblas, 1966; Barthes, 1970; Benveniste, 1971; Colezel, 1973; Werlich, 1975; Faigley and Meyer, 1983). In that this method links discourse functions to linguistic features, it continues the Prague School tradition of functional linguistics begun by Mathesius (1975; see Vacheck, 1964) and Mukarovsky (see Garvin, 1964; Burbank and Steiner, 1977) and associated today with the work of Danes (1964, 1974), Firbas (1964), Sgall and Hajivoca (1977, 1978). There are also strong analogues to the Prague School method in the functional analyses of texts performed by British linguists in the neo-Firthian school (especially following Halliday, 1976a, 1976b) and by American linguists working with Longacre's

(1976) version of tagmemics. While there have been functional analyses of specifically scientific texts by neo-Firthian linguists — most notably Widdowson (1974), Widdowson and Allen (1978), and MacKay (1978) — there has thus far been no comparable analysis of scientific texts using Longacre's tagmemic taxonomy.

Edward L. Smith Jr. 1985 "Text type and discourse framework." *Text* 5, 3, 229-47, 229-30.

PASSAGE B

In the second paradigm, gender is construed as a global personality construct. The concepts of masculinity, femininity and androgyny exemplify this approach (see, e.g., Archer, 1989; Cook, 1985; Morawski, 1987). In reviewing the literature concerning the sex-differences and the gender-as-a-personality-construct approaches, Deaux and Kite (1987) come to the following conclusion: "The scientific record on questions of sex differences, based on either biological or psychological distinctions, is shaky at best [...]. Yet despite evidence of considerable overlap and situational specificity of gender-related behaviors, beliefs in sex differences are held tenaciously" (p. 97).

Researchers adopting the third and most recent approach conceive of gender as a social category, that is, as a category on which perceivers base judgements, inferences and social actions. The central research issue here is not "how men and women actually differ, but how people think that they differ" (Deaux, 1984, p. 110).

Thomas Eckes 1994 "Features of men, features of women: Assessing stereotypic beliefs about gender subtypes." *British Journal of Social Psychology* 33, 107-23, 107-08.

PASSAGE C

Although lesbian feminist theorizing has significantly contributed to feminist thought, it has also generally treated lesbianism as a kind of applied issue. Feminist theories developed outside of the context of lesbianism are brought to bear on lesbianism in order to illuminate the nature of lesbian oppression, and women's relation to women within lesbianism. So, for example, early radical lesbians played off the feminist claim that all male-female relationships are dominance relationships. They argued either that the lesbian is the paradigm case of patriarchal resister because she refuses to be heterosexual or that she fits in a continuum of types of patriarchal resisters.[2] In taking this line, lesbian theorists made a space for lesbianism by focusing on what they took to be the inherently feminist and antipatriarchal nature of lesbian existence. Contemporary lesbian theorists are less inclined to read lesbianism as feminist resistance to male dominance.[3] Instead, following the trend that feminist theory has itself taken, the focus has largely shifted to women's relation to women: the presence of ageism, racism, and anti-Semitism among lesbians, the problem of avoiding a totalizing discourse that speaks for all lesbians without being sensitive to differences, the difficulty of creating community in the face of political difference (e.g., on the issue of sadomasochism [s/m]), and the need to construct new conceptions of female agency and female friendship.[4]

Notes
2   On the former, see, e.g., Charlotte Bunch, "Lesbians in Revolt," in her *Passionate Politics, Essays 1968-1986* (New York: St. Martin's, 1987); and Monique Wittig, *The Straight Mind and Other Essays* (Boston: Beacon, 1992). Regarding the latter, see Adrienne Rich, "Compulsory Heterosexuality and the Lesbian Continuum," in *The Signs Reader: Women, Gender, and Scholarship*, ed. Elizabeth Abel and Emily K. Abel (Chicago: University of Chicago Press, 1983).
3   For instance, Jeffner Allen states in her introduction to the anthology *Lesbian Philosophies and Cultures*, ed. Jeffner Allen (Albany, N.Y.: SUNY Press, 1990), "The primary emphasis of this book is lesbian philosophies and cultures, rather than lesbianism considered in relation to or in contrast to, patriarchy, or heterosexuality" (p. 1).
4   See e.g., the recent anthology, Allen. ed., *Lesbian Philosophies and Cultures*; as well as Sarah Lucia Hoagland's *Lesbian Ethics: Toward New Value* (Palo Alto, Calif.: Institute of Lesbian Studies, 1990; and Janice G. Raymond's *A Passion for Friends* (Boston: Beacon, 1986).

(Calhoun 1994: 558-59)

PASSAGE D
Many commentators on post-war Britain have suggested that the workforce and its unions must accept a large part of the responsibility for the country's continuing economic ills.

British workers may or may not have been unusually strike prone, but they have certainly long colluded, it is believed, in a range of restrictive practices on the shopfloor, thus increasing costs, curtailing output and drastically limiting the scope for necessary industrial modernisation. As the distinguished Anglo-German academic Ralf Dahrendorf has recently put it, working people in Britain have tended to "stretch their work so that it begins to look like leisure".[1] In this situation, the inevitable consequence has been economic stagnation.

Over the following pages we aim to challenge this view and demonstrate that restrictive practices of this type have been nowhere near as common or serious as some have argued.

Note
1 R. Dahrendorf, *On Britain* (1982) p. 46.

(Tiratsoo and Tomlinson 1994: 65)

PASSAGE E
The diverse ways in which people of areas considered peripheral to advanced capitalism confront the problems of survival force us to rethink theories of the crisis that take into account subsistence systems and the question of survival in a holistic context. Economists of the neoclassical school have always left subsistence production out of their equations, and they have done little to update their supply-demand functions to explain the present crisis except to invent a term, stagflation, for why their market theory does not work. Marxists start with the proposition that the cyclical crises of capitalism result from the decline in the rate of profit as the organic components of capital (technology and administrative expenses) rise in relation to the variable component (labor costs); but they end with a critique limited to national policies. Neo-Marxists have extended the analysis to show how countries with mature economies, trying to overcome their own cycles of recession, tie peripheral economies into an unequal exchange that subverts their development (Amin 1970; Frank 1967, 1980; Wallerstein 1983). Some have demonstrated how, since the decade of the 1960s, the expansion of investments in low-wage areas throughout the world has intensified competition among workers, thereby

depressing wages and reducing the basis for organization in the worksite (Frobel et al. 1980; MacEwan and Tabb 1989; Nash and Fernandez-Kelly 1983; Safa 1981).

(Nash 1994: 8)

(2) Examine essays you have written recently or are currently drafting. How do you go about stating the generalities which introduce your work? How do these generalities resemble or dif-. fer from those in the sample passages?

(3) The passages which we have been examining are typical: that is, they conform to general tendencies in introductions in research genres, and they compactly display distinguishing features. (That's why I chose them.) In your scholarly life, you will find many variations on these features and their arrangement. In one discipline in particular, you are likely to find significant and fairly frequent variation from the patterns we have been observing. Below are two sample introductions from articles in history journals. Examine these introductions and describe the ways they depart from what we have come to regard as typical of scholarly introductions and their way of establishing the generalities that frame the writer's contributions to research.

PASSAGE A

Toward the end of the eighteenth century, a young Philadelphia merchant confided to his uncle that a recent series of business reversals had "wholly unmanned" him. Another, writing in 1798 to a friend who was in debtors' prison pending a bankruptcy hearing, dubbed his friend's creditors "relentless harpies" and congratulated him for "driving" them "off."[1] Philadelphia's eighteenth-century merchants punctuated the voluminous correspondence upon which much of their trade depended with narratives of business failures that used gender imagery in striking ways. The cumulative effect was a sustained meditation on the precariousness of manly identity and reputation, a precariousness linked not only to the competitiveness and volatility of markets but also to the difficulties of defining a reputable self within the world of patronage and connection that still structured market relations. This essay undertakes a close reading of those narratives of failure as a way of illuminating the history of male subjectivity and the formation of gender conventions in a specific market milieu.

The essay focuses on the correspondence of Philadelphia's largest wholesale merchants — men who traded actively in the Caribbean and overseas to London and southern Europe. They were, for the most part, among the wealthiest of the Philadelphia merchants. Most amassed sufficient wealth to appear among the richest 15 percent of all wholesalers active in the last half of the eighteenth century, a group defined by a net worth of at least fifteen thousand pounds in 1770. Such wealth allowed these men, albeit with difficulty, to "emulate, if not quite duplicate the lives of the lesser gentry of England."[2] The history of these merchants' subjectivity is thus bound up not only with the creation of — or obstacles to the creation of — an occupational ethos but also with the formation of an elite identity.[3] Moreover, the merchants were implicated in the articulation of a conservative and deeply masculinist discourse of civil inclusion and exclusion that circulated among elites, some of whom dominated the national leadership after the Revolution, at least for a time.

Notes

1 Robert Lamar Bisset to Henry Hill, July 2, 1794, correspondence file, 1790s, Lamar, Hill, Bisset, & Company Box 1, Sarah A.G. Smith Family Papers, 1732-1826, collection no. 1864 (Historical Society of Pennsylvania, Philadelphia); Charles Young to Henry Banks, Sept. 12, 1798, correspondence file, 1798, box 4, Ball Collection, collection no. 28, ibid.

2 Thomas M. Doerflinger, *A Vigorous Spirit of Enterprise: Merchants and Economic Development in Revolutionary Philadelphia* (Chapel Hill, 1986), 20-22, es. 21, 25-26, 31-32. See also Gary B. Nash, *The Urban Crucible: Social Change, Political Consciousness, and the Origins of the American Revolution* (Cambridge, Mass., 1986), 256-59; Frederick B. Tolles, *Meeting House and Counting House: The Quaker Merchants of Colonial Philadelphia, 1682-1763* (New York, 1948), 109-14, 131-34; Gordon S. Wood, *The Radicalism of the American Revolution* (New York, 1992), 110-20.

3 These merchants also mediated between Philadelphia's elite and traders of the middling sort. Although mercantile wealth became more concentrated in the late eighteenth century, wholesale trade remained open to new recruits from among shopkeepers and artisans. Doerflinger, *Vigorous Spirit of Enterprise*, 20-40, 51,

126-34; Nash, *Urban Crucible*, 120-21. Elite merchants,
interacting with fellow traders, suppliers, and purchasers who were
at ease in the social and cultural milieu of mechanics and shopkeepers, experienced diverse, class-related cultural styles. As a result, individual merchants were prone to hesitate between, alternate between,
or amalgamate styles in ways that contributed to the interesting
bricolage qualities of their writing.

Toby L. Ditz 1994 "Shipwrecked; or, masculinity imperiled: Mercantile
representations of failure and the gendered self in eighteenth-century
Philadelphia." *The Journal of American History* 81, 1, 51-80, 51-53.

PASSAGE B

In October 1888 the Colonial Office expressed deep disquiet
at news that an officer of the Gold Coast Constabulary,
Inspector Akers, while involved on an expedition to subdue
Krepi, had inflicted harsh sentences of flogging upon men
under his command who were accused of attempting to
strike an NCO, drunkenness and cowardice. The nine accused
Hausa constables were flogged publicly before the whole
force, the worst offender receiving 72 lashes. Both the
method of flogging and the number of lashes given were
extremely severe and contrary to the standing orders of the
Constabulary. In an enquiry that consumed a considerable
amount of Colonial Office time and paper the matter was
thoroughly investigated and Akers, an officer with "many
good qualities" but "having a violent and hasty temper," was
invalided home.[1]

European use of physical violence, even excessive violence,
against African subordinates was not particularly unusual in
the late nineteenth and early twentieth centuries. However,
the Akers case, coming less than ten years after flogging had
been abolished in the British Army, marks an approximate
point at which the Colonial Office began to exercise concern, and seek to regulate, the extent and severity of officially
sanctioned corporal punishment inflicted on African soldiers
and also labour. A discussion of official and colonial attitudes
to the use of corporal punishment in British Africa is a large
subject and beyond the compass of a brief article. What is
attempted here is much more manageable: a discussion of the
attempts by the Colonial Office, over a period of more than
sixty years, first to regulate more closely and then to bring to
an end corporal punishment in the African Colonial Forces.

Colonial Office officials were agreed on the need to regulate corporal punishment; those advocating abolition steadily increased with the progress of the century. Both regulators and reformers in London had to contend with military officers and colonial administrators who argued that corporal punishment was necessary for the control and discipline of African troops, especially when on active service, and the steady pressure from various humanitarian lobbies in Britain denouncing severe practices in the colonies.

Note
1   Public Record Office, Kew [PRO], CO96/197/3064, 31 Dec. 1888; and CO96/197/3080, Griffith to Knutsford, conf., 30 Nov. 1888.

David Killingray 1994 "The 'rod of empire': The debate over corporal punishment in the British African colonial forces, 1888-1946." *Journal of African History* 35, 201-16, 201.

5.5 Documentation

Reporting expressions like the ones we have been inspecting summon a community of voices, and position the present writer amongst them. But everybody knows that these expressions are only part of the system that situates research amidst other research. Like the leafy, above-ground part of a plant, they are secured by an underground part, a root system of documentation — footnotes, endnotes, lists of "References" and "Works Cited."

It is also well known that styles of documentation differ from discipline to discipline. So the distinctive appearance of the two passages cited in the exercise above is characteristic of publications in history. Most disciplines do not use the heavy footnotes characteristic of history publications. Rather, they use some variation on a system of parenthetical expressions in the body of the text which are keyed to an alphabetical list at the end. So, these entries in a section called "References" —

Linn, R.L. (1987). Accountability: The comparison of education systems and the quality of test results. *Educational policy* 1 (2), 181-198.
Madaus, G., West, M.M., Harmon, M.C., Lomax, R.G., and Viator, K.A. (1992). *The influence of testing on teaching math and science*

in grades 4-12. Chestnut Hill, MA: Boston College Center for
the Study of Testing, Evaluation, and Educational Policy.
Madaus, G.F. (1985)."Can we help dropouts? Thinking about the
undoable." In G. Natriello (Ed.), *School dropouts: Patterns and
policies* (pp. 3-19). New York: Teachers College Press.

— are signalled by parenthetical expressions in the body of the text:

> The idea of using assessment as a lever for school change is not a
> new one: many accountability tools in the 1970s and 1980s tried
> to link policy decisions to test scores (Linn, 1987; Madaus, 1985;
> Wise, 1979).

The parenthetical "(Linn, 1987)" sends the reader (if he or she is interested) to the first entry above, while "(Madaus, 1985)" sends the reader to the third rather than the second entry under "Madaus." (If
Madaus had two entries, both by himself and both from 1985, the
writer could have distinguished them as "1985a" and "1985b.") While
documenting systems vary in detail, they all operate to achieve one
principal effect: the reader's easy movement from the body of the text
to the full documentation in the "References" or "References Cited"
or "Works Cited" pages. So, although this entry in an anthropology
journal —

> Rouse, Roger
> 1991 Mexican Migration and the Social Space of Postmod-
> ernism. Diaspora 1:8-23.

— looks a little different from the ones in an education journal, it nevertheless operates the same way, as an easy-to-arrive-at destination for
the reader of this passage in the body of the article:

> Although many examples exist, a recent example was presented
> by Rouse (1991), who carried out ethnographic research among
> immigrants from the Mexican community of Aguililla living in
> Redwood City, California. In developing the notion of "transna-
> tional communities," Rouse presents a novel challenge to spatial
> images, highlighting the social nature of postmodern space.
>
> (Chavez 1994)

Making arrangements for the readers' "easy movement from the body
of the text to the full documentation" is part of the writer's larger

orchestration of the scholarly conversation. Most obviously, it enables readers — if they choose — to find the source in a library or elsewhere, read it, and join the conversation themselves. Less obviously but equally important, the full documentation provides more information about the circumstances under which the cited statement was produced. A reader who may not in fact get the original and read it can still find relevant information about the conditions of the statement's production: did the cited statement appear in a book or an article? If it was in a book, was it a chapter in a collected edition? Who edited the book? If it was an article, in what journal did it appear? What was the title of the book or chapter or article (i.e., how did it announce what it was about)? And, most important, when was the statement produced?

Exercise

Below are four samples of entries from reference pages at the end of articles in scholarly journals. Inspect these samples to determine the points at which they vary (e.g., punctuation, use of capitals, order of information, and so on).

Referring to the samples below or to a sample of articles you have collected from the discipline you are majoring in, answer these questions: How do scholars document a source that is (a) an article in a journal? (b) a book? (c) a chapter in a book? (d) an article in a book?

From a "Works Cited" list in *PMLA* (a literary-critical journal, *Publications of the Modern Language Association of America*):

Baudrillard, Jean. *For a Critique of the Political Economy of the Sign.* Trans. Charles Levin. Saint Louis: Telos, 1981.

Eisenstein, Sergei. "Dickens, Griffith, and the Film Today." *Film Form.* New York: Harcourt, 1949. 195-255.

Geertz, Clifford. *The Interpretation of Cultures.* New York: Basic, 1973.

Gilbert, Elliot. "The Ceremony of Innocence: Charles Dickens's A Christmas Carol." *PMLA* 90 (1975): 22-31.

From a "References" list in *Environment and Planning*:

Frobel F, Heinrichs J, Kreye O, 1980, *The New International Division of Labor: Structural Unemployment in Industrialized Countries and Industrialization in Developing Countries* (Cambridge University Press, Cambridge)

Johnson H T, 1991, "Managing by remote control: recent management accounting practices in historical perspective," in *Inside the Business Enterprise: Historical Perspectives on the Use of Information* Ed. P Temin (University of Chicago Press, Chicago, IL) pp. 41-70

Monden Y, 1981, "What makes the Toyota production system really tick?" *Industrial Engineering* (January) 36-46

From a "References" list in *Language and Communication*:

AUDEN, W.H. 1962 Dingley Dell and the fleet. In *The Dyer's Hand and Other Essays*, pp. 407-428. Random House, New York.

JAYNES, J. 1976 *The Origin of Consciousness in the Breakdown of the Bicameral Mind*. Houghton Mifflin, Boston.

JAYNES, J. 1986 Consciousness and the voices of the mind. *Canadian Psychology* 27, 128-137.

LAWSON, L. 1989 Walker Percy's prodigal son. In Crowley, J.D. (Ed.), *Critical Essays on Walker Percy*, pp. 243-258. G.K. Hall, Boston.

From a "References" list in *Genetic, Social, and General Psychology Monographs*:

Eisenstadt, S. (1989). *Israeli society* (2nd ed.). New York: Stockten.

El-Sarrag, A. (1968). *Psychiatry in northern Sudan: A study in comparative psychiatry. British Journal of Psychiatry*, 114, 946-948.

Spiro, M.E. (1983). Introduction: Thirty years of kibbutz research. In E. Krausz (Ed.), *The sociology of the kibbutz: Studies in Israeli society II*. New Brunswick, NJ: Transaction Books.

5.6 Introductions: the knowledge deficit

Investigating the role of reported speech in getting the scholarly discussion under way, we observed that, when statements are presented as issuing not from the present writer but from other writers, they include an implicit comment on their status as knowledge. They were produced by someone; they came from a site in the research community.

If we take this perspective on scholarly statements, we can see reported speech as mapping a set of positions in the territory of knowledge producers. On this map, no spot is occupied simultaneously by more than one publication: in some sense, each position on the knowledge map is "original."

Some disciplinary locations on the map are very heavily populated. Competition for space is keen, and researchers vie for position. In the "hard" sciences, in particular, groups of researchers address (relatively) the same questions about (relatively) the same phenomena: their work is concentrated in areas densely occupied by researchers (so these disciplines have been called "urban" [Becher cited in MacDonald 1994:23-25]). In the "softer" sciences and the humanities, where abstractions are non-technical or less technical, researchers and their activities are more spread out (so these disciplines have been called "rural" [Becher cited in MacDonald, 1994:24-25]). Here, researchers may not be addressing the same question so much as related or similar phenomena. In these sparsely populated areas, researchers may even go to some trouble to point out that their question or the phenomenon they are studying *is* related or similar to other researchers' questions or objects of inquiry. (Hailing others across rural fields, researchers in "diffuse" disciplines [Toulmin cited in MacDonald 1994:31] conduct their research in more solitary circumstances. Meanwhile, researchers in urban, "compact" sites work in close proximity to others, always in earshot of on-going conversations, and not needing to raise their voices to be heard by neighbouring researchers.) These different circumstances for scholarly work — different schemes of association amongst workers — also contribute to different techniques for locating one's work in relation to others' work, but we can observe some shared tendencies.

One way researchers can locate themselves on the map is by claiming to add to existing knowledge: a space that has been recognized as unoccupied or only tentatively claimed gets filled up with new data and further reasoning. Sometimes the space has not yet been recognized: it has gone unnoticed by others. Another way scholars get title to a position on the map is to evict the current occupant: they show that previously established knowledge cannot hold that ground because it is faulty or incomplete in some way. (In Chapter Six, the discussion on "Research Questions" also reviews ways in which the Western scholarly traditions imagine inquiry, and the need to know more.)

Knowledge deficits

Knowledge deficits can also be discipline specific: that is, patterned to reflect the types of inquiry that go on in a particular research community which shares interest in core questions about the world. Here, an archaeologist's introduction first describes a site:

> The Moose Creek archaeological site is situated on a hilltop point near the confluence of Moose Creek and the Nenana River (Fig. 1). The site faces southwest on the eastern side of the river and is located 210 m above the modern floodplain on a terrace of the Nenana gravel formation (Wahrhaftig, 1958; Hoffecker, 1996). The highest known archaeological site in the region (Hoffecker, 1996), it affords a commanding view of the entire southern half of the valley.

But the existence and position of this site is not enough to motivate inquiry. The site also poses an **archaeological question** generally — "the cultural-historical affiliations of [its] components" — and questions peculiar to this site.

> The site was discovered in 1978 by J.F. Hoeffecker and C.F. Waythomas (Hoffecker, 1982) during the North Alaska Range Early Man Project.[...] Because there were no microblades in the lower component, it was tentatively assigned to the Nenana complex (Powers and Hoffecker, 1996). However, concerns persisted regarding both the validity of associating the assemblage with the radiocarbon dates obtained from soil organics and the absence of diagnostic Nenana complex tools, such as Chindadn "points" and scraper planes similar to the ones discovered at the nearby Walker Road and Dry Creek sites (Hoffecker et al., 1993). To address these lingering problems, the Moose Creek site was re-excavated in 1996.
>
> G. Pearson 1999 "Early occupations and cultural sequence at Moose Creek: A Late Pleistocene site in Central Alaska." *Arctic* 52, 4, 332-45, 332-33.

In making moves on the knowledge map, the writer identifies a **knowledge deficit**. There is something we don't know, some space on the map where there is a gap, a spot where no one has so far settled to take careful account of the place. The only way such a deficit — a gap, a space unsurveyed or inadequately surveyed — can be identified is through a review of what is known, or taken to be known. Reported speech — the whole practice of citation and summary — **constructs the deficit**. While on the one hand reported speech warrants the speech of the current writer *positively*, by connecting it with ratified statements and established concerns, it also, on the other hand, warrants the speech of the current writer *negatively*, as a response to a deficit. The samples in the exercise which follows show various ways writers identify knowledge deficits.

Exercise

Inspect the following passages and identify the ways each one establishes the writer's (or writers') right to speak positively (i.e., by connecting the present work with established concerns) and negatively (i.e., by identifying a knowledge deficit).

PASSAGE A

In this article, we examine the cultural categories and the conceptual logic that underlie the orthography debates about kreyòl that have taken place over the last 50 years. In Haiti, as in many countries concerned with nation building, the development of an orthography for vernacular literacy has been neither a neutral activity nor simply about how to mechanically reduce a spoken language to written form. The processes of transforming a spoken language to written form have often been viewed as scientific, arbitrary, or unproblematic. However, the creation of supposedly arbitrary sound-sign (signified/signifier) relationships that constitute an orthography always involves choices based on someone's idea of what is important. This process of representing the sounds of language in written form is thus an activity deeply grounded in frameworks of value.

(Shieffelin and Doucet 1994: 176)

PASSAGE B

[This] study directly compares, for the first time, the thought processes of professional appellate attorneys as they researched, composed, and revised a brief for litigation with the subsequent thought processes of two independent appellate court readers, charged with pronouncing a decision.

★ ★ ★

[T]he large professional and academic literature on writing effective appeal briefs has appropriately emphasized that briefs lie at the "headwaters" of judges' and their staff attorney's [sic] decision-making process.

Despite this emphasis, the thought processes of opposing brief writers while they compose has never been systematically studied in real time (Stratman, 1990a). Similarly, the thought processes of appellate judges and their supporting staff as they actually read and evaluate these briefs have never been directly studied (Becker, 1964; Benoit, 1981, 1989; Benoit and France, 1980; Hazard, 1982; Jones, 1976; Llewellyn, 1960; Schubert, 1964; Wassertron, 1961). Most of the extant theories abut the difficulties real brief writers face in understanding court readers' response to their text are drawn from secondary data, primarily commentaries by judges. These commentaries have rarely, if ever, presented a real-time account of what thinking occurs in the readers' minds during brief review. The neglect of the brief-reading process in empirical research not only hinders the development of theory describing appellate judges' decision-making processes, but also hinders the development of a theory of the skills and strategic decision processes required to successfully compose appellate briefs (Ashley and Rissland, 1985; Lundeberg, 1987; Rissland, 1984, 1985; Skinner, 1988; Stratman, 1990b).

(Stratman 1994: 1-2)

PASSAGE C
Despite the vociferous debate surrounding the ordination of women to the priesthood of the Church of England, the issue of gender and the rural church has been remarkably little studied. Whilst it may be argued that this neglect is due to a lack of scholarly interest in the rural church rather than in gender relations in the Anglican Church as a whole, even the recently published Faith in the Countryside pays noticeably scant regard to the issue of gender (ACORA 1990). Furthermore, the Rural Church Project from which the material for this paper has been drawn, was set up primarily to address the dearth of information on rural churches, and gender did not

form a specific focus (Davies et al 1990a, 1990b, 1990d; Davies et al 1991). Indeed this lack of research supports Little's assertion that, despite recent work, the study of gender issues generally in rural areas remains relatively neglected (Little 1991).

This paper is an attempt to begin to redress the balance by concentrating on the gender division apparent in the material collected by the Rural Church Project, and aims also to highlight the need for further specific study of gender and the rural church.

(Seymour 1994: 45)

PASSAGE D

There are several studies which have analyzed the discourse functions of quotation. Some researchers have analyzed languages other than English (e.g., Larson 1978; Besnier 1986; Glock 1986). Other have analyzed English, but most did not examine discourse samples to determine if their analyses are actually supported by data (e.g., Wierzbicka 1974; Halliday 1985; Li 1986; Haiman 1989). Additionally, these studies have not addressed the question of whether direct quotations are really quotations. In other words, how authentic are direct quotes? Do they represent actual previous utterances, or are they inventions of the speaker? This paper focuses on these questions as well as on the functions of quotation in informal spoken English. Unlike these other studies, my analysis is based on discourse samples.

Patricia Mayes 1990 "Quotation in spoken English." *Studies in Language* 14, 2, 325-63, 326.

PASSAGE E

In many ways, the influenza pandemic of 1918-19 is the "forgotten" epidemic; forgotten, at least, by scholars studying British Columbia's First Nations. Much attention has been paid to the timing and severity of late eighteenth- and early nineteenth-century epidemics for what they tell us about the proto-historic and early contact culture and population change. Scholars have argued the significance of these epidemics in softening up indigenous societies for the onslaught of colonization. Few, however, have examined later disease patterns for what they tell us about the nature of cross-cultural relations in the early twentieth century.

Mary-Ellen Kelm 1999 "British Columbia First Nations and the influenza pandemic of 1918-19." *BC Studies* 122, Summer, 23-47, 23-24.

Titles

Sometimes titles identify the knowledge deficit by asking a question (a technique you might consider in your writing): for example,

"What is Beyond the Big Five?"
[of personality descriptors in psychology]

"Where Do Migrants Go?"

"Where Does Newness Come From?"

As a student writer, you may be reluctant to say that nobody has ever studied this before, or that everybody has got it wrong so far. But, with some adjustments, you can still replicate the move which identifies a knowledge deficit. So, for example, Passage D in the exercise above could be recast to show that there is something interesting to be found out:

> Although speakers often resort to sayings which they attribute to other speakers, and listeners accept these sayings as appropriate elements of conversation and other speech genres, we might still ask what role such quotations play in these speech acts. What conditions motivate speakers to repeat others' claims? Is the repetition exact or approximate? authentic or fictionalized? In short, how and why do we represent our own speech as originating with someone else?

Or it could be recast to mark the writer's position in relation to one other speaker (instead of seven):

> Halliday (1985) provides a useful account of the functional grammar of reported speech, but his analyses do not explain the role

of quotation in conversation and other speech acts. What conditions motivate speakers to repeat others' claims?

That is, where a professional version of the statement of the knowledge deficit would summarize many (if not all) published claims about a research entity, the student version can summarize one or two.

In some situations, student projects may cite no other speaker. In those cases, the introduction can instead propose plausible ideas about the object of inquiry and then show that these ideas, reasonable as they seem, are problematic: they leave some questions unanswered. The example below in effect invokes possible statements about the object of inquiry, bringing these statements into a kind of conversation with one another, and allowing a question to emerge from this conversation.

> *As For Me and My House* can be read as a system of concealment: Mrs. Bentley skips days at a time, shifts her focus suddenly to the weather, offers little information about her own background while she relentlessly exposes her husband's personal history. Yet the idea of concealment suggests an audience — and *As For Me and My House* is represented as a diary, a genre which assumes no audience but the writer herself. If the narrative is indeed a pattern of withholdings, how can we reconcile this condition with the book's generic presuppositions about audience? From whom is the missing information being concealed? Perhaps by revising the idea of concealment, and recasting it as a system of attention to painful matters, we can understand Mrs. Bentley's diary on its own terms, as a diligent, deliberate — and sometimes desperate — personal inquiry into the circumstances of her life.

You will see from these examples that a question tends to follow the problematizing activity, or the identification of a knowledge deficit. In Chapter Six we explore the **research question** further — its design, its characterization of the knowledge deficit.

And, for student writers and professional scholars alike, arrangements for speakers — those schemes of scholarly conversation we investigated in Chapter Three — can take the writer to the verge of a knowledge deficit, and incite questions. Introducing *speaker x* to *speaker y*, and summarizing the statements of each one, the writer arranges for a new, so far unheard-of exchange between these positions. For example, *moral panic* is described by Deborah Cameron in relation to public excitement about grammar. Scott Kerwin's account of the Janet Smith bill describes another episode of public excitement — about race in a colonial society. Are these panics similar, or are there telling differences? The action of bringing Cameron and Kerwin together to speak to one another in itself raises questions.

5.7 Making and maintaining knowledge

Consider for a minute what it means to make knowledge. Say Binky felt a need to know, on a particular summer day, if that day was warmer or cooler than the day before. He might consult his own sensations, and find that, yes, this day was hotter. Reporting his sensations, he gets some corroboration.

Binky: Whew. It's hot.   Bingo: Yes. A real scorcher.
This is the hottest day.   This is the hottest day.

We could say that Binky and his corroborator have made some knowledge of the relative temperatures of the season in question. (They might go on to compare this season to others, and generalize about climatic conditions.)

But say both Binky and his corroborator had, the day before, gone for a long swim in a mountain lake. The swim cooled their bodies, and they found the air temperate, not scorching. You could say that their position — their point of view, their experience of the world — had affected their findings about relative temperature. Aware of variables like swimming in glacial waters, the next time Binky constructs knowledge of relative temperatures he looks for some sign outside himself and his closely positioned corroborator.

Binky: This is the hottest   Bingo: Yes.
day. The butter's melting. It
didn't melt yesterday. This is
the hottest day.

Now they could be said to have made knowledge by consulting a sign (butter), reading it (it's melting), and citing this evidence. But Bingo might question Binky's evidence.

Bingo: *Our* butter melted a bit yesterday too. Where do you keep your butter? How much did it melt?

So, Binky has made some knowledge of relative temperature (it's hot enough to melt butter), but it is vulnerable. Or, to put it another way, this knowledge is not conclusive: it provokes further knowledge-making.

Finally, if Binky wanted to make knowledge that was independent of his position — his swimming experience, his habits in storing and observing his butter — he might consult a widely recognized and respected instrument of measurement: a thermometer.

> Binky: This is the hottest day. It's 33 degrees. It was only 31 degrees yesterday.

This may seem to put an end to knowledge-making on this topic, but someone could go further (claiming a knowledge deficit), questioning Binky's instrument or its use.

> Bingo: Are you sure? Did you move the thermometer? I keep mine in the shade. Have you had your thermometer checked?

Or someone could question the use of the instrument itself.

> Bingo: Yesterday was hotter for me. I was tarring a roof. I've never been so hot in my life. It's very well to say it's the hottest day, but you aren't taking into account the experience of roofers.

In this sequence of knowledge-making actions, we have, very roughly, travelled through the range of **methods** of the research disciplines, from "soft" (so-called "subjective" interpretations of data corroborated by members of a community occupying similar positions) to "hard" (so-called "objective" interpretation sustained by research instruments which produce quantitative readings of the world) and back to what we might call "critical" (sort of "reflexive-soft" interpretations which question whether any knowledge can ever be produced independent of the interpreter's position).

Even without the critical techniques of current theory, we can see that knowledge-making procedures differ from discipline to discipline. These differences are reflected in stylistic differences: different ways of representing the production of knowledge. The most conspicuous of these differences is that which distinguishes publications with lots of numbers from those with no numbers. This difference has been characterized as the difference between **quantitative** and **qualitative** study — a distinction we will encounter again in Chapter Six. Along these lines that distinguish quantitative from non-quantitative study, research genres are also distributed according to whether they make provision for a "Methods" section — an explicit account of how the researchers produced the knowledge they are now reporting — or leave method implicit. (We will look at some examples of "Methods" sections in 5.7.1

below, and look again at the description of methods in Chapter Six, when we investigate the genre of ethnography.)

Despite these differences, however, the research genres share a concern for the sources of knowledge, and an interest in tracing the production of knowledge. The prominence of reported speech is an obvious sign of these interests and concerns. But it is not the only sign of them. Appearing with some regularity throughout reports of research are typical expressions which signify that knowledge is under construction, and in the process of being made, and that it comes from a position in the research community. In 5.7.2 we will inspect some of these expressions, and try to arrive at generalizations about their use. First, though, we will glance at the research genres' most explicit demonstration that knowledge is made.

5.7.1 Methods

Method sections expose the procedures by which knowledge has been produced.

> Binky: Method: A thermometer was placed on an east-facing wall of an average-size dwelling. Readings were taken from the thermometer on two successive days at midday. The readings were compared.

The rhetoric of method sections has been much studied, for these sections show some interesting stylistic features. For one thing, they tend towards agentless expressions. So you will find in one of the samples in the exercise below these wordings: "[t]he conversations to be examined here ..."; "[t]he groups were formed after consultation with the children's teachers." In these cases, the people who examine, form groups, and consult with teachers are missing from the statement. This feature of style has excited a lot of commentary, and sometimes it is interpreted as a way of persuading readers that the researchers' methods were very "scientific" and "objective," and not open to personal bias.

Another interesting feature of method sections is their unusual pattern of coherence: although sentences are all, roughly, about "method," sometimes the relation between sentences is obscure, if measured by ordinary standards of connectedness. So, in the first sample in the exercise below, you will find:

> The participants in this study were educationally and socially advantaged, middle-class, urban children who were predominantly

white. The children attended the day-care centre for full days, year round, and had known each other for 1-3 years.

If this were not a method section, a reader could very well ask, "what is the connection between, on the one hand, race and socioeconomic status and, on the other hand, full-time attendance in daycare? Is it a causal connection? And what does any of this have to do with the topic of the article?" But it is a method section, so readers don't ask these questions.

Exercise

(1) Six samples of method sections appear below. (None except Passage F is complete; Passage E is in an account of a series of experiments, and relies on the reader having gone through a much longer description of the method of another experiment.) Analyse these samples for agentlessness and connectedness. Then consider the overall function of these passages: if you were to generalize from these limited data, what would you identify as the main concerns of researchers composing an account of their methods? What kinds of questions are the researchers answering about their work? Can you detect differences in these questions in different disciplines?

PASSAGE A

To measure the effects of herbivores on belowground and aboveground vegetation we devised an experimental design following Chabreck et al. (1983). Four types of exclosures (treatments) were constructed using 1-m high fences constructed of vinyl-coated poultry wire with 40-mm diameter hexagonal openings. The exclosures take into account the behaviour of vertebrate herbivores. The specifications of the exclosures were a 40 m X 50 m area, with fencing buried 20 cm, allowing waterfowl to fly into the exclosure and graze while excluding mammals — primarily nutria (waterfowl-grazed, abbreviated WG): a 2 m X 2 m area, with fencing bottom 30 cm above the substrate, allowing nutrient to enter underneath the fence and graze, but excluding waterfowl (nutria-grazed, or NG); a 2 m X 2 m area, with fencing buried 20 cm excluding both waterfowl and nutria from grazing (ungrazed, or UG); and a 40 m X 50 m unfenced control area set off with corner posts, allowing grazing by both nutria and waterfowl (openly-grazed controls, or OG).

In fall 1985, we constructed, on each of two islands in the Atchafalaya Delta (Hawk Island and Arrowhead), duplicate sets of the treatment exclosures (designated as north and south) in expansive homogeneous stands of S. latifolia. Likewise, we constructed, in January 1986, two sets of exclosures in Wax Lake Delta — one each on opposite sides of a tidal channel, on Long and Manhatten islands. Because of the co-dominance of the two Sagittaria species on both islands in Wax Lake Delta, the two large treatment areas (WG and OG) were constructed to contain both S. latifolia- and S. platyphylla-dominated areas, with the dominant species accounting for over 80% of the aboveground biomass in that particular area of the exclosure. On these islands the number of small exclosures (UG and NG) of each replicate was doubled so that one set contained S. latifolia and the other S. platyphylla. Thus, we had six complete sets of exclosures in the Wax Lake Delta to accommodate both S. platyphylla- and S. latifolia-dominated stands.

[additional paragraphs on reasons for choosing study sites; measuring of vegetation; measuring belowground biomass; measuring waterfowl; and a bit on mammals]

D. Elaine Evers et al. 1998 "The impact of vertebrate herbivores on wetland vegetation in Atchafayala Bay, Louisiana." Estuaries 21, 1, 1-13, 1-2.

PASSAGE B

The sample consisted of adult patients (over the age of 18 years) who met one of the selection criteria: (a) surgery in the past 24-72 h and pain in the last 24 h, or (b) diagnosis of cancer, care in oncology units or hospice units, and pain in the last 24 h as assessed by the research assistant. Two hundred thirty-four patients were recruited for this study, including 100 postoperative patients, 100 oncology patients, and 34 hospice patients. The response rate was 94% for the surgical group, 89% for the oncology group, and 68% for the hospice group. The sample size of the hospice group is small because some hospice patients were too fragile or even cognitively impaired at the time this study was conducted. Of these 234 patients, 49% (n=115) were male and 51% (n=119) were female. The age range was from 18 to 87 with a mean (SD) of 52.8 (15.9) years. Sixty-five percent of the participants (n=152) were married. Their religious affiliations included Buddhist (51.7%), Taoist (12.4%), Catholic (1.0%), Jewish (7.7%), and none or other (27.2%). Twenty-seven of these patients had a high school-equivalent education and 44% had completed college education. Demographic characteristics of the patients in each of the study groups are presented in Table 1.

2.3 Instrument

The outcome questionnaire of this study was adopted from the study by Ward and Gordon (1994). This questionnaire was translated into Chinese by using a translation and back-translation method to ensure correct translation. The questionnaire was based on the American Pain Society Standards (Max et al., 1991). This questionnaire included (1) patients' assessment of pain severity and satisfaction with how pain was managed by physicians and nurses, (2) patients' perceptions of the time between a complaint of pain and receipt of medication, and (3) patients' perceptions of the time between a complaint of inadequate medication and the receipt of different or stronger medication. Patients were asked if their doctors or nurses discussed with them the importance of pain management. The specific items in the outcome questionnaire, based on the PAS standards, are listed in Table 2. Finally, a one-page demographic sheet covering basic information, such as age, gender, and education was included in the questionnaire.

2.4 Procedure

Patients who met the selection criteria were approached individually by the research assistant. Patients who met criterion (b) (diagnosis of cancer) were approached within 72 h of admission to the unit. The research assistant described the study and obtained oral consent. Special emphasis was made that the patients' confidentiality would be protected and that their care providers would not know any individual's answers. Patients were asked to complete the questionnaire without assistance from others. If a patient [....]

Chia-Chin Lin 2000 "Applying the American Pain Society's QA standards to evaluate the quality of pain management among surgical, oncology, and hospice inpatients in Taiwan." *Pain* 87, 43-49, 43-44.

PASSAGE C

The conversations to be examined here are from an extensive research project with 3- to 5-year-old children at a day-care center in a large midwestern city. The children were grouped into 12 same-sex triads on the basis of friendship and age. The groups were formed after consultation with the children's teachers. The participants in this study were educationally and socially advantaged, middle-class, urban children who were predominantly white. The children attended the day-care center for full days, year round, and had known each other for 1–3 years.

The triads were videotaped during the regular day-care day in one of the children's usual play areas, which was separate from the larger group. The only children in the room were those being filmed. They were not supervised by an adult, although an assistant and I sat somewhat out of sight in a play loft above and behind the children's play area. The children knew we were there. They were videotaped on three separate occasions, each time playing at one of three types of activities. Each group was videotaped for a total of approximately 75 minutes (25 minutes per session).

Amy Sheldon 1990 "Pickle fights: Gendered talk in preschool disputes." *Discourse Processes* 13, 5–31, 12–13.

PASSAGE D

We analyzed a corpus of 15 "high-brow level" articles (see Huddleston 1971) distributed as follows: 10 CR [case reports] (making up a total of 13,958 running words) and 5 RP [research papers] (making up a total of 11,871 running words). The articles, all published between 1980 and 1990, were drawn from leading medical journals such as *The British Medical Journal, Annals of Internal Medicine, The Lancet, Archives of Internal Medicine* and *The New England Journal of Medicine*. These journals were chosen because they are considered to contain the best medical journalism.

The number of hedging devices was recorded in each rhetorical section in each article separately, and the percentage of hedges (with respect to the total number of running words making up each rhetorical section in each article) was computed. The results were analyzed by means of $x2$ tests. The alpha value was set up at .05.

For the reasons stated in the Introduction and in order to identify hedges as accurately as possible, we carried out a rigorous contextual analysis (both from a linguistic and medical standpoint) of the linguistic expressions commonly considered as hedges. This is why the taxonomy we adopted in this research (see below) considers both formal and functional criteria. Obviously, such a procedure does not guarantee a 100% reliability rate in the ascription of a given linguistic form to a hedge, but we believe that it is much more reliable than a "blind" (i.e., non-functional, purely formal) identification which would undoubtedly lead to the distortion of the data both in their quantity and their distribution.

Françoise Salager-Meyer 1994 "Hedges and textual communicative function in medical English written discourse." *English for Scientific Purposes* 13, 2, 149-70, 153-54.

PASSAGE E

Observers. Caucasian volunteers were recruited from the University of Texas at Dallas undergraduate psychology program and again received a research credit for a core course as compensation. Each observer participated in only one of the rating subexperiments. Twenty-five observers rated faces for typicality, 20 observers rated familiarity and repetition, and 20 observers rated memorability and attractiveness.

Stimuli. The stimuli were the recognition test sections of the videotapes described above. Each tape contained all 240 faces, blocked by race. The order of rating Japanese versus Caucasian faces was counterbalanced across the observers in each of the subexperiments.

Procedure. Observers were tested in groups of 1 to 5 and were given response sheets to make the appropriate ratings. Again, because of the length of the list, the observers were given breaks periodically.

Alice O'Toole, Kenneth A. Deffenbacher, Dominique Valentin, and Hervé Abdi 1994 "Structural aspects of face recognition and the other-race effect." *Memory and Cognition* 22, 2, 208-24, 211.

PASSAGE F

Subjects

The subjects were 64 girls, ranging in age from 12 to 17, who voluntarily enrolled in a comprehensive program for teenage mothers and their infants that was provided by the local public health department in a large city in North Carolina. Of the 64 girls, four were white and 60 were African-American. They had been sexually active from a young age, the average age at first intercourse having been 13.3 years (range 10 to 16, median 14). Average age at the time of first birth was 15.5 years (range 12.5 to 17; median 15). One girl who gave birth at the age of 12 1/2 years had been raped by her mother's boyfriend. Less than half of the girls' mothers had been teenage mothers themselves. Although 43% of the fathers frequently participated in the care of their infants, 19% maintained only minimal contact, and 38% had none. Half contributed to the support of their child. Although school attendance by parenting teenagers was encouraged in the school district, 12 of them (18%) were not attending school at the time of initial intake into the program.

Procedure

Girls were required to attend the clinic at regular intervals, depending upon the age of their infant (i.e., mothers of younger infants attended more frequently), although many appointments were not kept. Efforts were made to administer a structured interview and a measure of self-esteem (Piers-Harris Children's Self-Concept Scale). In addition, the records of some of the girls' performances on the California Achievement Tests (CAT) were obtained from local public schools ($N = 39$). The scores reported were those most recently completed by each girl. They include the results of testing done in the sixth ($N = 9$), seventh ($N = 8$), eighth ($N = 20$), and ninth ($N = 2$) grades between 1984 and 1988.

The Mental Scale of the Bayley Scales of Infant Development was administered to infants at their 9th and 18th month clinic visits, where possible. Because of logistical difficulties (e.g., missed appointments, attrition) all data are not available for every girl.

(Rauch-Elnekave 1994: 93)

> (2) Practise writing in "method-section" style: describe how you found out what your bank balance was; how you came to a decision about how to vote in a recent election; or how you determined the cost of an airline ticket to a holiday destination.

As we noted above, not all disciplines use method sections. Research in disciplines in which scholars do not share recognized instruments and procedures do not explicitly expose the means by which knowledge has been made. So, in literary criticism, you will not find:

> The novel was read and notes were taken. Annotation took place at each point where the annotator could detect mentions which might signify something.

But even in disciplines where methods are tacit — generally but silently understood, and not much talked about — there can still appear implicit traces of method. In these disciplines, theories and concepts take the place of instruments and procedures, producing knowledge by operating on a particular set of data.

5.7.2 Modality and other limiting expressions

Earlier in this chapter we met the *discursive I*: the being who arranged and forecast discussion, who pointed to parts of the text, summing up and emphasizing. *Discursive I* can also become the knowledge-making *I*, although this being is perhaps more shy than the *discursive I*. For example, in summarizing the views of another writer, this writer appears in the surface of text as a reasoning being, evaluating the statements of others:

> Because lesbians and heterosexual resisters must have, on [Wittig's] account, the same relation to the category "woman," there can be no interesting differences between the two. This, **I think**, is a mistake, and I will argue in a moment that lesbians are in a quite special sense not-women.
>
> (Calhoun 1994:564, emphasis added)

Since the scholarly genres impose so many restrictions on the presentation of the writing "self," we might well scrutinize this special appearance of the writing self to find out what conditions permit it.

What we will find is that the *I think* in the passage above is by no means an isolated case. Rather, it is a variation on a set of expressions that are in fact abundant in the research genres, and that tend to occur in just such situations as the passage above exemplifies: situations where the writer is taking a step beyond established knowledge, moving to offer new statements to the research community. To develop some perspective on this set of expressions and their range of occurrence, we will first see how the grammar of *I think* is related to the grammar of some other expressions which are related to it in function.

Estimates from positions of limited knowledge

Say Binky is inside on a dark night. He hears a sound on the roof. He reports to Bingo:

> It's raining.

Since he is inside, where it is dry, he is **inferring** that it is raining. Another way of reporting his finding would mark his statement as such an inference — an estimate from a position of limited knowledge.

> I think it's raining.

Or the speaker could mark his statement as such an estimate by other means. He could say:

> It seems to be raining. / It must be raining .

Or, if the speaker and his companion are new to the area, and less certain about local night sounds, he could express his estimate with less certainty:

> Bingo: What's that noise?   Binky: It could be rain / It might be rain / Maybe it's rain.

Embedded in the statement, all these expressions — along with others like *evidently, apparently, perhaps, possibly, appears* — condition the statement as the product of inference from a position of limited knowledge. They **modalize** statements. Roughly speaking, they are equivalents of *I think*. Although they erase *I* from the surface of the expression, they nevertheless maintain the sense of the statement in which they occur as being knowledge under construction from a certain location: the speaker's or writer's position in the world.

> **Obviously ...**
> *Must* can seem like an expression of certainty but it is in fact a sign of strong but not infallible conviction attending an inference. For example, *It must be nearly 4 o'clock* suggests that the speaker does not have a watch and so can't say for sure what time it is. Along with *must*, *obviously* can seem like an expression of certainty, but the next examples show that speakers can use obviously (like *must*) in the presence of doubt, or uncertainty:
>
> > ...obviously you grew up, although this might not be the case, in a family that encouraged this interest [in music]
> >
> > (Rex Murphy, *Cross-Country Check-up*, CBC, 23 April 2000 talking to a constitutional expert about music)

From a distance, we might think that the research genres would be the ones *without* these markers of limitation, which indicate possibility rather than certainty, *maybe* rather than *yes* or *no* — and even subjectivity in that these expressions indicate the writer's reasoning, inference, speculation. If we think of research and the sciences, from hard to soft, as sources of authority and ultimate fact, we would not expect these traces of indeterminacy in the research genres. But in fact they are abundant. As the examples we examine below will show, they occur especially, but not exclusively, in introductions and conclusions.

> **Indeterminacy and reported speech**
> Perhaps we would not be surprised at this abundant indeterminacy in the research genres if we thought of the research genres' distinctive dependence on reported speech. In a way, the expressions which make a statement indeterminate by showing that it is the speaker's inference from incomplete evidence are something like the statements which are reported as coming from someone other than the writer. So, to return to our rain example, the speaker could also make a claim about the weather by reporting the speech of someone else.

Binky: Tanya says it's
raining.

Bingo: Oh.

If the speaker's companion knows that Tanya has just come in from outside, then he is likely to credit the statement as valid. It seems to come from a reliable position. On the other hand, if Tanya has not been out, and is only speculating, and tends to interpret all noises as rain, the addressee might not be convinced. The context in which the reported statement was produced — the speaker's identity and situation, the timing of the statement — helps the listener to evaluate the statement. Similarly, reporting expressions, documentation, characterization of the source — all these features of scholarly citation help readers evaluate reported statements.

Modality in introductions

One place we might expect to find modal expressions signifying that the statement is only an estimate of knowledge is in writers' formal statements of their **hypothesis**: the statement which is deemed plausible, but which is so far untested and will be shown to be tested in the course of the article. And, in fact, modalized expressions do show up in such locations.

> Two main hypotheses are addressed in this study: (1) that unidentified and untreated learning difficulties **may** be related to teenage girls becoming pregnant, deciding to raise their children, and dropping out of school, and (2) that teenage pregnancies **may** *not* be characteristically "unintended."
>
> (Rauch-Elnekave 1994:92, italic emphasis in original, emphasis added)

But many research publications do not specify the hypothesis in this way, and still make use of modal expressions. So, rather than attach modality simply to the hypothesis, it may be better to locate it in the larger process of constructing a knowledge deficit. Here we spot it showing up as a writer poses his research question about "low-ability" classes where "high-quality instruction fosters significant learning among students":

> What characterizes such classes? To address this question, I draw on evidence from earlier studies by other authors, and I provide two new illustrations taken from a larger study of eighth- and

ninth-grade English classes in 25 midwestern schools. Although these examples are far from conclusive, common elements emerge that, taken together, **may** help to characterize effective instruction in low-ability classes in secondary schools.

(Gamoran 1993:2, emphasis added)

The question identifies an as yet unoccupied location on the knowledge map: we don't know what goes on in these classes. Plotting his approach to this space, the writer moves speculatively. Conceding the limits of the evidence available to him, he says his work "may help" to make this unknown area known. Compare the unmodalized, unqualified version of the same statement:

Common elements emerge that characterize effective instruction in low-ability classes in secondary schools.

While the unmodalized version may actually be more in keeping with the traditions of the schoolroom essay, where students are often advised to take a stand and be decisive, the modalized version is more typical of scholarly writing, where knowledge is laboriously constructed, and statements trail behind them traces of their sources and status. In scholarly writing, statements leave footprints.

To confirm that we do not in fact know enough about what goes on in classes where less successful students, grouped together, do enjoy success, this writer must first, as he says, "[reinterpret]" standing ideas that "low-ability" grouping does not benefit students significantly, or, at least, has no regular effect on overall achievement. To identify the knowledge deficit, he must show that the current state of knowledge is inadequate.

According to this view, observed differences among studies in the effects of grouping are due to chance; taken together, the studies indicate that no real effects on achievement exist.

Another interpretation **seems** equally **plausible**. The inconsistent findings **may** have resulted from uncontrolled differences in the way ability grouping was implemented in the various school systems under investigation.

(Gamoran 1993:3-4, emphasis added)

In moving to show that a published view from a respected source comes up short, and leaves the state of knowledge in this area unfinished, the writer does not simply deny the view ("This interpretation is wrong"). He doesn't even say that "another interpretation is equally plausible," or "more plausible" — it only "seems equally plausible." And the reinterpretation is itself modalized: "inconsistent findings may have resulted from uncontrolled differences" rather than "inconsistent findings resulted from uncontrolled differences."

These traces of reasoning from positions of limited knowledge are typical of scholarly expression. They signify the research community's persistent interest in the production of knowledge. On the one hand, they permit the individual researcher to move into unconfirmed territory — a lone explorer, estimating and reckoning — and, on the other hand, they signal respect for the community's cooperative work of corroborating and recognizing established positions.

So strong is this tradition of respect for properly established positions that even when the current researchers are evidently impatient with the dominance of accepted views, and when their own research defies those views, they still identify knowledge deficits through modalized statements. So, when two researchers report extensive evidence to overturn the standing idea that trade-union activities have a lot to do with Britain's post-war economic circumstances, they nevertheless approach the standing view with signs of respect, expressed through modality. Here they treat the work of a distinguished and widely cited scholar:

> Olson's work demands to be taken seriously, yet it, too, **seems** to be flawed. Olson has attracted considerable support from economists and economic historians because his methodology conforms to the tenets of individual rational action theory inherent in neo-classical economics. However, this choice of approach **can** be criticised because it encourages a misleadingly simplified view of reality.
>
> ★ ★ ★
>
> It **may** be right to conclude about Olson, therefore, that what he has produced is not an explanation, but merely an historical set of abstractions. His theory **seems** to provide little more satisfaction than the offerings of far less sophisticated analysts.
>
> At this point, it **appears** wise to turn from the current literature and re-examine the contemporary evidence. Many recent authorities have argued, as we have shown, that restrictionism was strongly evident on Britain's shopfloor after 1945, but not much of what has been written, it **seems** fair to conclude, is very persuasive.

(Tiratsoo and Tomlinson 1994:67, 69 emphasis added)

The modalizing expressions of introductions situate the present writer in relation to others working nearby. Each of the modalizing expressions emphasized above says, in effect, "from our position of limited knowledge, we think that...." As Greg Myers (1989) suggests in his study of "politeness" in scientific articles, these situating moves are intensely social — they represent relations among members of the research community, and between individual members and the larger collective.

Knowledge is not only a product of the community; it is also an index to the standing of individual members of the community. As is true of most social situations deeply cultivated with politeness expressions, power and the competition it inspires operate at these moments when one researcher identifies current knowledge as inadequate, or mistaken, and offers his or her own knowledge products as a replacement for current knowledge. In scholarly writing, politeness takes a particular form — signs of inferences from a limited position. These signs attach themselves to statements in the form of reporting expressions (the statement issues from the position of other writers) or modality (the statement issues from the position of the present writer).

Only when a generalizing statement is widely accepted in a particular research community does it appear without reporting or modalizing expressions. Then it is "fact." (In *Laboratory Life: The Construction of Scientific Fact* (1986 [1979]), Bruno Latour and Steve Woolgar offer analyses of the linguistic signs that a statement has achieved the status of fact.) Of course, these "facts" can be subject to revision or rejection by later generations of the research community.

But before generalizing statements are treated as "fact," their expression triggers the type of complex politeness behaviours we have just seen. (We can speculate that student writers unaware of this etiquette could seem "rude" to academic readers.) This form of politeness could be called **epistemic** — having to do with knowledge.

Expressions of epistemic modality cluster around the researcher's step away from the reported statements which summarize the current state of knowledge in the field and towards the statement of the knowledge deficit. They also show up as researchers explain how they go about addressing a knowledge deficit: how they intend to proceed from a position of limited knowledge, and take it upon themselves to advance into unconfirmed spaces.

Exercise

Identify the modalizing expressions in the following passages. How do they limit the speakers' claims for the knowledge they will produce?

PASSAGE A

Human representations offer archaeologists the possibility of investigating ancient social categorization and differentiation from within. Of course, we are given only a very partial view. Figurines do not provide maps to complete social systems. Instead, they encode only very selected themes. The anthropomorphic figurines of Early Formative Paso de la Amada [Mexico] appear to be stylized human images depicting idealized social categories or roles (Lesure 1997). Their specific uses are unknown. Most were deployed, broken, discarded in household contexts. They were probably grouped into sets or scenes in which not only the individual representations but comparisons between them became important (Flannery and Marcus 1976, 382; Marcus 1989, 1996). It therefore seems likely that the message conveyed by the use of figurines involved statements not only about social categories, but about relationships between categories.

(Lesure 1999: 209)

PASSAGE B

An objective way to determine the current nature of the field of personality psychology is to examine what gets published in various journals over a fixed period of time. This is not a foolproof system, since more papers are rejected for publication than are accepted. The ones that do get accepted might thus represent a biased sample. Journal editors serve as "gatekeepers" and therefore what is accepted might not necessarily be the best but rather may reflect the biases of journal editors and referees or the zeitgeist of psychology. Nevertheless, what is published in personality journals is probably the closest approximation of the true nature of research in the area, and is certainly a good indicator of what is currently being disseminated.

Norman S. Endler and Rachel L. Speer 1998 "Personality psychology: Research trends for 1993-1995." *Journal of Personality* 66, 5, 621-69, 621.

> PASSAGE C
> Aggregate data from the regions of Southern Italy are used to test whether risk is a significant determinant of the decision of where to emigrate, abroad or within the country. This indeed appears to be the case for both foreign and domestic migrations, after controlling for unemployment and wage differentials and other plausible variables.
>
> Francesco Daveri and Ricardo Faini 1999 "Where do migrants go?" *Oxford Economic Papers* 51, 595-622, 622.

Expressions of epistemic modality also cluster around the researcher's concluding statements, as in Passage C above, where the newly-constructed knowledge product is presented in its final form. For instance, after the hypotheses on teenage motherhood are screened through the available evidence, the writer estimates their status as knowledge using the features we've been looking at in this chapter.

> The findings of this study, although preliminary in nature, **suggest** that learning issues **may** represent a significant contributing factor to the high rate of births to teenage girls in the United States. That is, unidentified and untreated learning difficulties **may** be a factor that is common both to becoming pregnant and deciding to raise one's child, and to dropping out of school. Further, the findings **suggest** that substantial numbers of teenage pregnancies **may** not be "unplanned," but represent choices that conform to current peer values and pressures. If these observations are correct, school failure **may** not *result* from girls' pregnancies and early parenthood but **may** — like the pregnancy itself — bear a close relation to unidentified and untreated learning problems.
>
> (Rauch-Elnekave 1994:101-02, italic emphasis in original, emphasis added)

Modalized statements can show up in the long approach to the conclusion, as researchers arrive at interpretations of their data. Here, a writer offers an interpretation of evidence she has presented as to the conditions of labour after the abolition of slavery in Brazil.

> It was this process that Peter Isenberg called "modernization without change" and that has generally been interpreted as implying a crushing continuity of dependence and poverty for

former slaves. While this is in one sense quite accurate — indeed, rural northeasterners **may** have been even more malnourished after emancipation than before — an overemphasis on continuity **may** obscure the importance of the access to land that many former slaves did achieve....

Even though the physical work performed by labor tenants **might** differ little from that performed by slaves, the orbits of their lives now had a somewhat different shape. While slaves had lived in a centralized set of quarters under direct supervision, moradores usually built their huts "at scattered points on the estates." An even more general dispersion of the population was **probably** prevented by the development of central mills, but the small-scale dispersion within estates **could** be of crucial importance to the development of a life oriented toward family and neighbors rather than employer. And, to the extent that freedom of movement could be maintained, it provided some constraint on the exactions that could be imposed on rural dwellers.

Rebecca J. Scott 1994 "Defining the boundaries of freedom in the word of cane: Cuba, Brazil, and Louisiana after emancipation." *American Historical Review* February 70-102, 96.

In the next example, the writer has just presented the results of her interviews with Bangladeshi women on their decision to work at home, using a combination of the women's own words (direct speech) and summary of what they said (indirect speech). Now she combines a mention of the text ("To summarize this section") with direct-speech reports of "other studies" in the context of modalized interpretation of the interview data ("it appeared," "It seems clear"):

To summarize this section, therefore, it **appeared** that for the majority of the women interviewed, the chief advantage of homework was its compatibility with the different cultural dimensions of being a housewife within the Bengali community — primarily looking after children and keeping the house in order, but also servicing the needs of male breadwinners, usually husbands, and fulfilling the family's hospitality obligations. This finding echoes those of other studies of homeworkers, which have included women from a variety of majority and minority ethnic groups.

Any explanation of why it is mainly women who do homework ... cannot ignore the family roles of these women .... All the women in our sample considered housework and child-care to be their responsibility and regarded help from their husbands as a generous concession. (Hope, Kennedy and de Winter, 1976:8-9)

The explanatory emphasis put on the care of young children obscures what is a life-long experience of women, namely that of servicing others on an unwaged basis. (Allen and Wolkowitz, 1987:79)

(Kabeer 1994: 315-16)

Other markers of the status of knowledge

Modal expressions are perhaps the most obvious way of marking a statement as issuing from a position of limited knowledge. But they are not the only way. Just as modality is linked to the practice of reporting statements of others, it is also linked to a set of expressions which some research (Chafe 1986) has shown to characterize the speech of academics. So, while the opening generalization of the passage below appears at first to defy the modalizing and reporting tendencies we have been observing —

> During the course of the twentieth century relationships between minorities and dominant societies have fundamentally altered in wartime....

— on closer inspection we will see that it in fact conforms to traditions of marking statements for their status as knowledge.

> During the course of the twentieth century relationships between minorities and dominant societies have fundamentally altered in wartime, an assertion which applies to all states. The position of minorities usually deteriorates, particularly if they represent a group which has acted as the traditional scapegoat for the dominant society, or if they are identified with the state facing their land of settlement in war. In such a situation the minorities almost invariably face persecution, varying from controls on movement and expression to internment and even genocide. The response of the dominant group varies according to the political traditions upon which it is grounded. A liberal democracy will usually retain traces of tolerations, while an autocratic state will exercise more arbitrary anti-minority policies (Panayi 1990b). Few exceptions exist to this state of affairs, although in some cases opportunities may arise that allow a minority to make some socio-economic progress. The experience of Afro-Americans and American Indians in the first world war provides an example (Dippie 1982, p. 194; Grossman 1989).

(Ellis and Panayi 1994)

The writers seem to be aware of the risk they take in offering a generalization that is neither reported nor modalized, for they quickly move to characterize it and insist on its generality:

> … an **assertion** which applies to **all** states.

Then, as they develop this generality, they gradually and slightly reduce the application of its parts: *all* gives way to *usually, almost invariably, usually, [f]ew exceptions exist, some cases*. Each of these expressions conditions the statement in which it occurs as in some way **limited**. The writers do not commit themselves to saying that this is universally true. That would be too much.

Limiting expressions

This statement is from an article reporting results of an experimental study of ability to remember and learn a written style:

> [T]he subjects **demonstrated a trend toward** mentioning more rules for the marked forms than for the unmarked forms for all three style characteristics.
>
> Jennifer Zervakis and David C. Rubin 1998 "Memory and learning for a novel written style." *Memory and Cognition* 26, 4, 754-67, 764, emphasis added.

How would this statement sound without the limiting expression?

In effect, expressions like these control the extent of statements' application, reducing and monitoring their power to apply to all cases, leaving spaces around them to signify the limits of knowledge. Given the scholarly genres' preoccupation with the status and production of knowledge, we could expect expressions like these —

usually	**in part**
most	**at least**
some	**partly**
many	**often**
generally	**sometimes**
roughly	**typically**

— to cooperate with reporting and modality to sketch the limits of knowledge. And notice the effect that the insertion of appropriate limiting expressions can have in conditioning a broad statement for use in a research setting. Compare —

> Family-wage campaigns supported both patriarchal and corporate interests.

— to:

> Generally, family-wage campaigns supported patriarchal and corporate interests.

And inspection of the passage on former slaves' access to land reveals just such a cooperation of reporting, modality, and limiting expressions:

> "**in one sense quite** accurate"
> "**many** former slaves"
> "**somewhat** different shape"
> "**usually** built"
> "**some** constraint"

All these expressions and the modals and reporting expressions they occur with, limit the scope of the statement. In that respect, they are pointers to the statements' status as knowledge, and to the writers' limited position: they are not in a position to say such-and-such is true for all cases.

Exercise

(1) In the passage below, the writers begin to reinterpret evidence. Identify the modal and limiting expressions they use as they begin to evaluate available knowledge.

> Taken together, these various accounts appear to constitute a formidable indictment, yet closer inspection once again exposes flaws. Some industrial correspondents did, of course, have good contacts in business and may have accurately reported what they were told. Nevertheless, it is not certain what employers' complaints really added up to: grumbles from the boardroom were, of course, nothing new. Moreover, some of the press accounts have a formulatory ring and may well have been shaped more by the pressure to grab the reader's attention than the desire to present accurate facts.
>
> (Tiratsoo and Tomlinson 1994:69-70)

---

(2) Inspect essays you have recently written or are currently drafting. Do you find the modalizing and limiting expressions we have been examining in examples of published scholarship? If you find them missing, can you explain their absence? (That is, does your writing situation differ from that of professional scholars in ways that lead you away from such expressions of position and limitation? Or have you been unaware of the role these expressions play in making statements in the research genres?) If you find modalizing and limiting expressions missing from your academic writing, try introducing them at appropriate points, and observe the effect.

Linguists have described these limiting expressions as belonging to a larger family of wordings all of which index statements for their status as knowledge. If we see these expressions as part of a larger family of sayings, we can regard them as establishing writers' attitudes toward or opinions of the statement they are offering. And we find scholarly writers favouring not only attitudes about the limits of statements but also about their obviousness. So we have seen writers using words like *suggest* or *indicate*. We see them saying —

Certainly, *x*
It is evident that *x*
Surely *x*
Apparently *x*
Undoubtedly *x*

— as well as *possibly*, *may*, *might*, and so on. They can even combine apparent confidence with seeming reservation. Summarizing the research of "social investigator Ferdinand Zweig," these writers say —

> He concentrated on five main sectors (building and civil engineering, cotton, engineering, iron and steel, and printing) and found that restrictive practices of various kinds were **certainly sometimes evident**.
>
> (Tiratsoo and Tomlinson 1994:70, emphasis added)

— rather than:

> He ... found restrictive practices of various kinds.

This complex trace of reasoning — the phenomenon is "evident" (to an observer/interpreter), but only "sometimes," but then "certainly" — indicates the status of this statement as knowledge.

To say that something is *evident* — or *apparent*, or *observable*, or *recognizable* — is to say that is so to someone. Remembering that scholarly writing makes big efforts to attach statements to their sources, we might confront wordings like these and ask, well, *who* finds something evident or apparent, or *who* observes it or recognizes it? At first, these wordings might seem vague, and at odds with other features we have been looking at. But we can account for these typical wordings by noticing how they resemble some other forms we have seen. *Observable, evident, identifiable* are agentless: they take away the person who observes, identifies, or finds something evident. So they are like other agentless forms we have seen, for example:

it is known that *x*
***x* is acknowledged as ...**

Agentless expressions
In this passage, which expressions are agentless?

The problem of deep oceanic convection induced by localized surface cooling has received considerable attention in the last years. Results from field observations (e.g., in the Greenland Sea or the Gulf of Lions), laboratory experiments, and numerical simulations have led to some theoretical predictions concerning the structure of the convective region like plume scale, chimney scale, and rim current by, for example, Klinger and Marshall (1995), Send and Marshall (1995), and Viseck et al. (1996). The comparison of these scaling arguments with real ocean data on deep connection is somewhat restricted due to the lack of detailed measurements of convective plumes and chimneys, although field experiments have provided very impressive cases of deep ocean convention (e.g., Morawitz et al. 1996; Schott et al. 1996).

S. Raasch and D. Etling 1998 "Modeling deep ocean convection: Large eddy simulation in comparison with laboratory experiments." *American Meteorological Society* 21, 1786-1802, 1786.

Expressions like *it is known that...* seem to distribute knowledge: it is not just the present speaker who sees this or knows it. Similarly, in the case of expressions like *evident* or *observable*, the commentary on the status of knowledge includes not so much an estimate of its probability (as *possibly* or *may*, for example, would provide), or not only a trace of its source (something someone reported), but a measure of the position from which x is known. As —

it is known that x
x is acknowledged as ...

— suggest that more than one person knows this, so —

evident
apparent
observable
identifiable

— suggest that, from any reasonable position, people would see this ("reasonable position," however, by now should occur to us as a social rather than purely cognitive [and universal] measure. In scholarly circles, reasoning goes on in social contexts, among people of similar experience).

These markers of obviousness can take the form of *evident*, or *apparent*, *recognized/recognizable*, or *observed/observable*, or the more pronounced forms of *surely, certainly, clearly,* which insist that the statement should be acceptable to reasonable readers. Most compelling, perhaps, of these forms is *of course*. *Of course* signals that the statement is so evident that readers are only being reminded of what they already know.

> It is now well-established, of course, that the majority of British employers looked to the apprenticeship system rather than formal education in the classroom as the appropriate training for the bulk of their employees.
>
> (Burgess 1994: 32)

Of course signals that the writer takes his readers as already knowing that it is known that British employers favoured apprenticeship training. *Of course* describes that status of this knowledge as widely distributed in the community which forms the audience for this article.

In a way, *of course* is an expression of politeness: it constructs readers as knowledgeable, as not needing to be told something they already know. But what if you *didn't* know that apprenticeship was the preferred form of training? In this case, *of course* would inform you that the topic is **common ground** for the intended audience, a well-known consensus in that community.

Yet, while markers of obviousness can create the impression of consensus, they can also suddenly alienate a reader. On the one hand, you should be aware of the power of certain expressions to appear to distribute knowledge: you can use them in your own writing to signal to your readers that you know you are not delivering brand-new ideas, but, rather, ideas that are broadly entertained in the community. On the other hand, these expressions incur some risk that your reader may not find something as clear, evident, or matter-of-course as you suggest.

> Binky: Clearly, Dickens'   Bingo: Wait a minute.
> verbal art is a precursor of   That's not clear at all.
> cinematic art.

While *of course* and related expressions say "this statement is in keeping with what you and I (and others like us) know about the world: it's what we would expect," words like *surprisingly* say "this statement is *not* in keeping with what you and I (and others like us) know about the world."

> Most analyses of the various proposals to date (including the so-called Flat Tax, a national sales tax, the "USATax," etc.) have concentrated on the distributional impact of the plans, along familiar lines of progressivity and regressivity. **Surprisingly** little critical attention has been paid to the macroeconomic implications of these tax reform plans, particularly to the claims about saving.
>
> (Buchanan 1999: 60)

Of course, obviously, surprisingly signify a solidarity amongst those in the milieu convened by the utterance. In scholarly communities, these identities and identifications project shared attitudes and experiences in research disciplines — and also may distinguish the disciplines from one another. Lilita Rodman (2000) has recently reported on differences in disciplines' use of words indicating a stance or attitude toward the statement in which they are included. She found differences in patterns of *important, significant, interesting, clear* and *obvious* in the disciplines of chemical engineering, physics, mineralogy, civil engineering, and medicine. For example, *obvious* was used in chemical engineering and mineralogy at least twice as often as in the other disciplines (and, in the sample, it was not used at all in medicine, and very rarely in civil engineering). These findings suggest that the expressions themselves are sensitive to the knowledge-making assumptions of each discipline: ideas about how things come to be known.

We could also see expressions like *of course, obviously, surprisingly* as expanding the identity of the *discursive I*, for they manifest a position — from which something is well known (*of course*) or clearly to be seen (*obviously*) or never seen before (*surprisingly*). Although academic writing is often considered impersonal, or neutral, or anonymous, in fact there are many markers of **subjectivity** in scholarly style: expressions of attitude — and even feeling (of a sort). Here two economists are "[astonishèd]" by something which might not stir such feeling in people who do not share their position in the world.

> From 1929 to 1932, Argentina imported severe deflationary pressures and adverse terms-of-trade shocks from the international economy: the external terms of trade declined by 24 percent and the foreign (U.S.) price level fell by 26 percent.
>
> In this context it is **astonishing** that the Argentine Great Depression was so mild and short-lived by international standards.
>
> Gerardo della Paolera and Alan M. Taylor 1999 "Economic recovery from the Argentine Great Depression: Institutions, expectations, and the change of macroeconomic regime." *Journal of Economic History* 59, 3, 567-98, 569.

Exercise

Identify in the following passages signs of attitude (something is good, or bad) and feeling (something has taken the writers by surprise).

PASSAGE A

In many less developed countries the government resorts to minimum wage laws in a bid to raise the living standards of the workers. In India, for example, the Minimum Wages Act of 1948 laid down standards of minimum wage. The objective was "not merely ... the bare sustenance of life but ... for some measure of education, medical requirements and amenities."[1] In other countries also, such laws and regulations were motivated by similar concerns.

Unfortunately, however, there is little concern about the possible detrimental effects of such laws on the level of employment, as these laws may induce the firms to cut down on the number of workers employed.

Note
1 Committee for Fair Wages appointed by government of India,
1948.

Saikat Datta and Prabal Roy Chowdhury 1998 "Management union bargaining under minimum wage regulation in less developed countries." *Indian
Economic Review* 33, 2, 169-84, 169-70.

PASSAGE B
The complex and often fitful transition from central planning
to the market in China and the Warsaw Pact countries has
been a hot topic during the past decade. Notably, the United
States made a similar transition after World War II. Indeed, the
reconversion from a wartime command economy to a mar-
ket-oriented postwar economy, a transition accomplished
with astonishing speed and little apparent difficulty, constitutes one of the most remarkable events in U.S. economic
history. Nevertheless, economists and economic historians
have devoted little attention to that episode, and their explanations of it are, on close inspection, extremely problematic.

Robert Higgs 1999 "From central planning to the market: The American
transition, 1945-1947." *The Journal of Economic History* 59, 600-23, 623.

PASSAGE C
Unfortunately, this methodological assumption treats the
media as passive "channels" of communication or neutral and
objective observers and recorders of events, a view that for
some time now has been rejected by scholars of the media
(e.g., Gans 1981; Herman and Chomsky 1988; Shoemaker
and Resse 1991), as well as refuted by studies of the media
coverage of collective events (Danzger 1975; Franzosi 1987;
McCarthy, McPhail, and Smith 1996; Meuller 1997a; Snyder
and Kelly 1977).

(Oliver and Myers 1999: 39)

5.8 Time and space

We have inspected instances of scholarly writing describing itself —
"this discussion proposes" — and pointing to itself — "the point here
is...." Reflecting on these "metadiscourse traffic signals" or "text-

diacritical statements" (291) (statements, that is, which provide infor-. mation about how the text is organized, what it is doing), and finding them especially evident in "academic writing," Suzanne Fleischman (1991) suggests that speaking resorts to metaphors of time to organize references to itself ("as we *learned* in last week's episode"), while writing uses both metaphors of space ("in the example *above*") and metaphors of time ("*now* we turn to counter-examples").

However, whereas speakers seem to be fairly consistent in the genres which refer to themselves (storytelling, broadcast information), writers and readers are not always in agreement about what is proper; in fact, Fleischman's study was inspired, she says, by a copy-editor's corrections of her own scholarly writing (corrections which irritated her). In representing their written discourse as unfolding in time, writers appear to have the option of referring either to *their* time ("I *have provided* several examples in the next chapter") or the *reader's* time ("several examples *will be provided* in the next chapter"). At these points, where time can pivot to centre on the writer (already having made the examples) or the reader (yet to encounter the examples), the time metaphor is unstable. Like Fleischman, you may find readers' marking commentary "correcting" your timing. Perhaps, eventually, English will stabilize these expressions — but maybe not: because writing, unlike speech, survives its historical moment of production, time will remain ambiguous. So *now* — "now we examine" — can mean both the writer's time and the reader's time, even though these are different moments.

This characteristic of writing — its ability to survive its context — can also account for the privilege enjoyed by the simple present tense in research writing, with its salient habit of citation.

5.8.1 Tense and citation

Most of the reporting verbs we have been looking at seem to prefer the **simple present** form in the research genres.

> Rouse **presents** a novel challenge to spatial images, highlighting the nature of postmodern space. He **points out** that members of a "transnational migration" circuit can be parts of two communities simultaneously. However, he **argues** ....
>
> (Chavez 1994:354)

Although, clearly, the speech actions of arguing or pointing out occurred in past time (before Chavez wrote the above), they are presented in present tense.

In a sample summary in Chapter Two, I followed the trend and used the simple present too:

> To explain the means by which heterosexual society produces heterosexuality as "natural," and produces "negative social reality" for lesbians and gay men, Calhoun (1994) **catalogues** the social practices (e.g., dating, sex education, erotica) which construct sex/gender dimorphism, and the social conventions (e.g., joint gifts and invitations to husband-and-wife) and legal and economic structures (e.g., adoption procedures, spousal health benefits) which produce the "single unit" of intimately bonded man and woman.

If this were changed to —

> To explain the means by which heterosexual society produces heterosexuality as "natural," and produces "negative social reality" for lesbians and gay men, Calhoun (1994) **catalogued** the social practices....

— an academic reader could stop, or mis-step, hearing something out of tune. It appears that simple present is an eager servant in bringing scholarly conversations to life.

Simple present can play this role in conversational citation too:

> So this guy comes over and **says** is that your car and I'm like yeah and he **goes** you gonna leave it there and I'm like — *what???*

Studies of simple present (e.g., Chafe 1994) in conversational citation suggest that it coincides with speakers' evaluation of what they are saying as particularly impressive: they dramatize their report of important moments by switching to simple present, creating an effect of immediacy. In its preference for the simple present, scholarly "conversation" may be borrowing some of this immediacy.

However, this is not the whole story of tense and citation. Simple present can be, in some instances, overtaken by **present progressive** ("ing" forms of the verb):

> Here x **is questioning** the ....

This may be likely to occur with direct-speech citation — where the other speaker is quoted in their own words — and the present progressive intensifies the moment of the conversation, improving even on the immediacy provided by the simple present. But it occurs in other situations too, like this one:

> ... the latent structure of childhood negative emotions **is** only **beginning** to be conceptualized in detail (e.g., Joiner, Catanzaro, and Laruent, 1996).
>
> (Chorpita et al. 1998: 74)

More common than present progressive is **present perfect**.

> The bulk of the empirical work on migration determinants **has studied** how wage and unemployment differentials affect migration flows under the Harris-Todaro (1970) hypothesis of risk neutrality of an individual migrant. [...] The role of other factors than expected wages **has been emphasized** in the new migration literature.
>
> (Daveri and Faini 1999: 595)

Present & past perfect

Does present perfect (*has eaten, has reported, have suggested*) sound to you like a past tense? Compare it to past perfect to see that present perfect is in fact a present tense.

Binky offered [simple past] Bingo tortilla chips. But Bingo **had** just **eaten** [past perfect].

Present perfect is a sensitive form in English — second nature to speakers of English as a first language, perhaps, but difficult to explain — and called on to execute speakers' perception of what is close or distant in time. In conversation, it says something is done, but only *just* done — recent enough to be still an aspect of the present situation (and often occurs with "just"). Writers in the research genres sometimes select the present perfect, as we see above and in the next example:

> Premack and Woodruff (1978) asked "Does the chimpanzee have a theory of mind?" Since it was posed 20 years ago, Premack and Woodruff's question **has dominated** the study of both social behavior in nonhuman primates [...] and cognitive development in children, but progress in the two fields **has been** markedly

different. Developmentalists have established empirical methods to investigate children's understanding of mentality, and forging links with philosophy of mind and philosophy of science, they **have mustered** the conceptual resources for disciplined dispute about the origins [...], on-line control [...], and epistemic stance [...] of human folk psychology (e.g., Goldman 1993; Gopnik 1993; Gopnik and Wellman 1994). In contrast, those working with primates **have continued** to struggle with the basic question of whether any primate has any capacity to conceive of mental states.

C.M. Heyes 1998 "Theory of mind in nonhuman primates." *Behavioral and Brain Sciences* 21, 101-48, 101.

But the example above also shows that writers in the research genres can also pick the simple past for reporting verbs: "Premack and Woodruff (1978) *asked* 'Does the chimpanzee have a theory of mind?'" The next writers begin their article on a new model of social interaction by citing a prominent contributor to such study, and use the simple past in conjunction with a positive evaluation ("celebrated") of the work's reception:

In his celebrated essay on "The Architecture of Complexity," Herbert Simon ([1962] 1969) **developed** the argument that all complex systems shared certain structural features. These features emerged, he **showed,** by virtue of what appeared to be a universal partitioning principle — the tendency for strongly interacting entities to group together into subsystems.

Thomas S. Smith and Gregory T. Stevens 1999 "The architecture of small networks: Strong interaction and dynamic organization in small social systems." *American Sociological Review* 64, 403-20, 403.

Similarly, writing about undocumented immigrants in the US, Leo R. Chavez cites the ancestral, founding statements of social theorists:

Classical theorists **wrestled** with the notion of community, particularly the forces that held together complex societies. For Marx (1967 [1867]), the community or society **was** the arena within which interest groups defined by their relation to the means of production, competed .... Early anthropological work on tribal societies, the "classic" ethnographies of Malinowski (1961 [1922]), Evans-Pritchard (1972 (1940]), and others **were concerned** with issues of social solidarity and village life, social structure, and organization. It was Redfield (1956) who ... **brought** the notion of the "little community" into full anthropological gaze.

Eventually, the record emerges from history and touches the present:

> The subfield of human anthropology, drawing on both Redfield and the Chicago School, **has produced** a wealth of interesting research on communities around the world (Hannerz 1980).
>
> (Chavez 1994: 54)

But when does the present begin? in 1980? or in 1950, as in this article from meteorology?

> By combining surface observations, cloud-motion winds, and upper-air observations from kites and balloons, Bjerknes (1919) and Bjerknes and Solberg (1922) **set forth** the conceptual framework for understanding three-dimensional air-flows and associated weather within cyclones and about fronts by establishing the "Norwegian frontal-cyclone model." Inspection of even earlier observational analyses over North America (e.g., Bjerknes 1910; Rossby and Weightman 1926; Palmn and Newton 1951; Sanders 1955), however, reveals that frontal-cyclone evolutions over the central United States do not always mirror the conceptual model developed in Northern Europe. Recognition of the differences in topography and land-water distribution between northern Europe (where the Norwegian cyclone model originated) and the central United States **has** subsequently **led** to more complex conceptual models of surface frontal-cyclone evolutions and their attendant precipitation systems (e.g., Newton 1950, 1963; Carlson 1980; Hobbs et al. 1996).
>
> Paul J. Neiman et al. 1998 "An observational study of fronts and frontal mergers over the Continental United States." *Monthly Weather Review* 126, 2521-52, 2521.

Inspecting the second example a little more closely, we might notice that the present begins when the research question arrives — when the current writer *replies* to the reported statements, and initiates a new stage in the conversation.

> The subfield of human anthropology, drawing on both Redfield and the Chicago School, **has produced** a wealth of interesting research on communities around the world (Hannerz 1980) ....

Suffice it to say that despite all the work that has been carried out on communities, the question still **remains**: What **underlies** a sense of community? Anderson (1983) **examined** this question and **suggested** that communities are "imagined." Members of modern nations ....

Such a view allows for a redefinition of *community*. Since it is imagined, a sense of community is not limited to a specific geographic locale (Gupta and Ferguson 1992). Immigrants **are said** to live in "binational communities" (Baca and Bryan 1980), "extended communities" (Whiteford 1979), "transnational communities" in "hyperspace" (Rouse 1991), and "transnational families" (Chavez 1992). These concepts **highlight** the connections migrants maintain with life in their home communities ....

(Chavez 1994: 54)

What can we learn from this? Past tenses seem to occur in reporting expressions as a writer represents founding statements which led to other statements: so, after reaching the present in 1980 (and the chance to ask a question), we are back in the past with "Anderson (1983) examined." Or we might reckon that reporting expressions in scholarly writing favour the present tenses, for these ones seem to signal an essential motivation for scholarly work: the scholar listens to what is being said; from his or her position, has a question to ask, and takes his turn in the conversation. The present tenses cue the writer's motivation.

Although simple present is the most common form for reporting expressions in the research genres, it is joined by other forms of the present tense, and also by the past tense. With this array of tenses, scholarly writers tell the story of statements occurring, staging or dramatizing the making of knowledge. In this story, knowledge is not timeless and immutable, but historical, located in time.

Sometimes, markers write in the margins of student papers

Watch your tenses!
Tense!
Be consistent in tense

— suggesting that academic readers are sensitive to these signals which indicate the story of knowledge being made. Staging the construction of knowledge, the verb forms writers use also indicate their version of this story: their sense of the sequence of knowledge, its contexts of production, the remoteness in time of some statements (remote but still audible, and enduring or echoing despite the passage of time) and the proximity of others (some so nearby in time that they are re-spoken as if in the present moment). On the one hand, the staging of statements in time is a dimension of a writer's particular perspective on the scholarly conversation. On the other hand, it displays the writer's familiarity with the progress of knowledge in the discipline. This perhaps explains readers' sensitivity to tenses, and to (what may seem to them) misrepresentations of the progress of knowledge, and may also explain the difficulty newcomers to the disciplines can have in locating statements in time − choosing among present and past tenses, simple and perfect aspects − in ways that make sense to readers very familiar with the scholarly conversation.

"Science" writing is sometimes regarded, from some positions, as representing knowledge as timeless and unchanging (rather than located in history, as a "social accomplishment"). So simple-present-tense verbs, as in this case,

> The chemical signature of an odour **is** first **detected** by neurons in the nose. The signals **are** then **collated** by the main olfactory bulb in the cortex of the brain. The olfactory bulb **relays** the odour signature to other parts of the brain.

are analysed as rendering the claim as timeless. And it is true that one function of the simple present is to represent something which, from the speaker's point of view, is "always" true, and not at all tied to the time of speaking.

> Bingo, in August: Spring **comes**.
> Bingo, to Binky, on the bus: I **play** the piano.

In both these instances, the "present" does not mean "now." Spring is not "coming," or at least is not around the corner in August, and Bingo is not playing the piano on the bus. These statements can be made at any time, and remain true (although Bingo's life career might one day make the second utterance unusable). Simple present therefore is summoned for types of authoritative statements — like the ones in science writing, as well as maxims and other magisterial expressions that transcend sociohistorical limitations:

> A man **forgets** the loss of his father sooner than he **forgets** the loss of his patrimony.
>
> (adapted from Machiavelli)

Critiques of the authority of "science" sometimes target this timelessness. But these critiques miss the point that the statements themselves are embedded in complex reporting situations — not only the researchers' reports of their own procedures and limitations but also in their reports of others' statements. In the passage above, reporting expressions show scientific knowledge as emerging over time ... and still (and perhaps always) under construction.

> **Exercise**
> The passage above about fronts and frontal mergers is an instance of "science" writing. Identify the verb forms in this passage. In what respects do they depart from the "timelessness" often attributed to scientific statements?

5.9 Presupposing vs. asserting

In the last section we saw that tense and citation configure the writer's interpretation of knowledge unfolding – and enduring or giving way, monumental or temporary. Markers like *of course* and *obviously* also project the writer's interpretation of the state of knowledge – the distribution of knowledge, its rarity or commonness. *Of course* draws boundaries around knowledge communities: people who belong to these communities know the topics marked with *of course* and other signs of obviousness; they don't need to have things explained. At the same time, as we noticed in Chapter Three, explaining a term, defining it appositionally or even more elaborately, does not necessarily mean that you take your reader to be uninformed. Instead it can be a means of negotiating or confirming common ground. Sometimes things should not be taken for granted, and should be attributed, defined, or explained, to show that the writer respects certain ideas as having been painstakingly constructed by the research community. But other times writers appear to satisfy their readers by representing things as understood, and by not explaining.

In the meantime, as if it were not already challenging enough for newcomers to estimate the distribution and obviousness of knowledge in the disciplines, we find that *of course* and the other signs of a statement's obviousness are not the only ways of signalling that knowledge is shared. In the example which follows (the first sentences of an article), the writer makes several assumptions about readers' knowledge of the topic, through **definite expressions** — *the* or *this* phrases.

> Recent research in **the history of nineteenth century psychiatry** has explored **the expanding powers of the medical profession** and **the proliferation of the asylum**, that "magic machine" for curing insanity. **This medicalization of madness** has been portrayed as a "top-down" process ....
>
> (Prestwich 1994: 799, emphasis added)

An alternative version of these sentences shows just how much the original takes for granted and assumes as already known by the reader.

> Psychiatry was practised in the nineteenth century. In the nineteenth century, the powers of the medical profession expanded, and asylums proliferated. Madness was medicalized.

Whereas the original version **presupposes** this knowledge, the alternative version **asserts** it. Perhaps you can hear how the first version constructs the reader as *knowing*, and the second constructs the reader as *unknowing*, and needing to be told.

In any social situation, the choice between presupposing and asserting can be tricky, for, as we see, it conveys messages about the speaker's ideas of the addressee's state of knowledge. It can also convey messages about the speaker: by always asserting, the speaker can seem naive or can appear to have just learned something that is in fact well known. In the research genres, the choice between presupposing and asserting can be particularly tricky in that "knowingness" is crucial to status and power. And it seems that students can sometimes make the mistake of starting too far back, explaining too much, and thereby offending their expert readers. John Swales (1990:204-08) reports a case study of just this situation, where a PhD student's dissertation in the biological sciences explained too much, presupposed too little, and excited sarcastic and impatient comments from her readers. At the same time, however, readers can react negatively to a writer's offhand mention of a complicated concept, and can appreciate an explanatory account of it. (In the sample above, for example, what does it mean, exactly, for something to be "medicalized"? These days, lots of people are finding instances of "medicalization" here or there, but we may have been neglecting the concept itself, taking too much for granted.)

Presupposing expressions can take many forms (proper nouns, for example — to say simply "Chomsky" rather than "Noam Chomsky is a transformational linguist" presupposes that readers know who Chomsky is, and can identify him for themselves). We will not go into all these forms here. Nor can we come to any conclusions about what kinds of knowledge students should presuppose and what kinds they should assert, for, at this point, we don't know a lot about this aspect of the style of the research genres — or any other genres. What we do know, however, is that readers are sensitive to patterns of presupposition, and that these patterns signal information about the state of knowledge and its distribution.

Exercise

The first four of the following statements are opening sentences from articles in a variety of disciplines; the fifth occurs at the end of the first paragraph of an article. Some (but not all) presupposing expressions are underlined in each. To develop your awareness of the effect of these expressions, rewrite each passage to **assert** what the original presupposes. You may find yourself resorting to *there* expressions (e.g., "the three aspects of readability" becomes "there are three aspects of readability"); *there* expressions in English are specially designed for asserting. You may also notice that many of the underlined expressions are **nominalizations**: a stylistic feature we have become familiar with in our study of the research genres.

PASSAGE A

In recent years, **the school reform movement** has engendered widespread efforts to transform **the ways in which students' work and learning are assessed in schools**. ·

Linda Darlington-Hammond 1994 "Performance-based assessment and educational equity." *Harvard Educational Review* 64, 1, 5-30, emphasis added.

PASSAGE B

Scholars have long noted, often with disapproval, **the tardiness of the introduction of printing to the Muslim world**, but **the consequences of that introduction on the production, reproduction, and transmission of knowledge in Muslim societies** are now only beginning to be understood.

Adeeb Khalid 1994 "Printing, publishing, and reform in Tsarist Central Asia." *International Journal of Middle East Studies* 26, 187-200, emphasis added.

PASSAGE C

When Margaret Fuller's Woman in the Nineteenth Century first appeared in the winter of 1845, few readers were prepared to accept **her uncompromising proposition that "inward and outward freedom for woman as for man shall be as a right, not yielded as a concession".**

Annette Kolodny 1994 Inventing a feminist discourse: Rhetoric and resistance in Margaret Fuller's *Woman in the Nineteenth Century. New Literary History* 25, 2, 355-82, emphasis added.

PASSAGE D

During the 1980s and 1990s a number of factors emerged in various countries of western Europe to raise anew questions about **the meanings of national identity. The finally acknowledged presence of settled immigrant populations** (as opposed to transient-worker populations), **the arrival in western Europe of large numbers of asylum-seekers from southern and eastern Europe and from the Third World** and, most recently, debates in the countries of the European community about some of **the provisions of the Maastricht Treaty** have been among the most significant factors that have fuelled controversies about national identity.

Christopher T. Husbands 1994 "Crisis of national identity as the 'new moral panics': Political agenda-setting about definitions of nationhood." *New Community* 20, 2, 191-206, emphasis added.

PASSAGE E

To put it bluntly, **the new cultural politics of difference** consists of creative responses to the precise circumstances of our present moment — especially those of marginalized First World agents who shun degraded self-representations, articulating instead **their sense of the flow of history** in light of **the contemporary terrors, anxieties and fears of highly commercialized North Atlantic capitalist cultures (with their escalating xenophobias against people of color, Jews, women, gays, lesbians and the elderly). The thawing, yet still rigid, Second World ex-communist cultures** (with increasing nationalist revolts against **the legacy of hegemonic party henchmen**), and

> **the diverse cultures of the majority of inhabitants on the globe smothered by international communication cartels and repressive postcolonial elites** (sometimes in the name of communism, as in Ethiopia) or starved by austere World Bank and IMF policies that subordinate them to the North (as in free-market capitalism in Chile) also locate vital areas of analysis in this new cultural terrain.
>
> Cornel West 1990 "The new cultural politics of difference." In *Out There: Marginalization and Contemporary Cultures*, eds. Russell Ferguson, Martha Gever, Trinh T. Minh-ha, and Cornel West. Cambridge, MA: MIT Press 19, emphasis added.

5.10 Conclusions

Looking at conclusions from a cognitive perspective — that is, examining the role they play in readers' understanding — it is best to think of them as **confirming** what has gone before. The conclusion is the writer's last chance to make sure that connections between parts of the discussion are secure in readers' minds; it is the last chance to invoke the complex, high-level abstractions which motivated the discussion, commanded its specifics, and activated the on-going scholarly conversation. The samples provided below will show scholarly writers using their conclusions to confirm their arguments.

A cognitive perspective also predicts that conclusions which merely restate the introduction can be troubling for readers. Such conclusions can sound strange, for the reader who is addressed at the end of an essay is not exactly the same reader who is addressed at the beginning. At the end, the reader is familiar with the details and course of the argument: he or she has just been through it. To simply repeat the introduction suggests that the reader hasn't heard a word you said.

Repetition and ambiguity

Binky: What time is it?

Bingo: Nearly four o'clock.

Binky: Hmmm.

Bingo: Nearly four o'clock.

Binky: You said that.

Repetition is indispensable in scholarly writing — for reinstating the large abstractions which help readers manage their mental desktops, bringing material back to readers' attention. But repetition is also potentially ambiguous. In the exchange above, Binky has some interpretive work to do. Does Bingo think Binky hasn't heard? Is there something significant about "four o'clock" — time to prepare for the cocktail hour? time to call a cab? Does Bingo think Binky should get a watch?

When academic readers encounter in a conclusion the exact repetition of an introductory statement, even after the several pages that might separate an introduction from a conclusion in a student essay, they are liable to experience these ambiguous conditions for meaning.

But, all along, we have tried to keep in mind that reading is not only a process of reasoning and understanding, not only a cognitive process. It is also a social process. Like any use of language, scholarly reading and writing maintain the values and practices of the communities these readers and writers belong to. In conclusions, scholarly writers not only see to their readers' cognitive needs, but also advance their claims in ways that are in keeping with the representations of knowledge typical of the research genres.

In that the conclusion advances the writer's claim in its final form, we might expect that it will be seeded with modality and other signs of limits. So here, in the last paragraph of their article on plain language, researchers are still speculating and inferring:

> As in the case of consultation between health-care professionals and consumers, it is **possible** that legal concepts are difficult to understand because, even when explained in plain language, they are complex or because they are in conflict with folk theories of the law. The subjects in this study (and lay people in general), **may** have been relying on inaccurate prior knowledge of the law or on their own intuition about justice, which **frequently** does not reflect the legal reality. These results **suggest** that plain language drafting alone will take us only part way to the goal of making the law more broadly understood. It must be supported by other measures such as public legal education and individual counselling of persons faced with legal obligations.
>
> Michael E.J. Masson and Mary Anne Waldron 1994 "Comprehension of legal contracts by non-experts: Effectiveness of plain language redrafting." *Applied Cognitive Psychology* 8, 67-85, 79, emphasis added.

We could say that, in the research genres, conclusions are not conclusive. While scholarly articles begin with the identification of a knowledge deficit, they can also end by gesturing towards what is not known for sure. One way of accomplishing this is by using modals, as in the last passage. Another way is by explicitly remarking on what we don't know.

> Through his association of writing with speech, Malivha immersed *Inkululeko* in the pre-existing forms of communication, and thus ensured the paper's accessibility to its audience. As *Inkululeko* was read some fifty years ago, we are at a disadvantage in getting a clearer picture of how readers interacted with the newspaper. Questions about how the paper was distributed, read and discussed among the people would undoubtedly enrich our understanding of the role played by *Inkululeko* in mobilising for the ZBA, but what is left of these today will certainly be general impressions and memories.
>
> In spite of these limitations, it is hoped that this essay has highlighted issues otherwise largely overlooked by existing social-historical studies seeking to understand questions of popular responses to political mobilisation in the countryside. The processes of forced removal, dispossession, and community destruction undoubtedly generated political consciousness which varied with region and time. But a focus on these processes alone, this essay argued, ignores a host of other factors which can also help explain questions of popular responses to political mobilisation in the countryside. Using the ZBA as a case study, the essay focused on how ideas about these process were communicated to the Zoutpansberg people by looking at the language and style of mobilisation, and the methods as well as the media of communication the organisation used. We believe that a more detailed and thorough research in this direction will enrich our understanding of how some organisations are able to attract popular following in the countryside.
>
> (Nemutanzhela 1993: 100-01)

As well as confirming the main point of the essay, and the knowledge deficit it addressed, this conclusion directly refers to its own "limitations" by mentioning them, and indirectly refers to limitations by saying what still has to be done.

After getting under way by identifying a knowledge deficit, and then labouring to correct that deficit, many scholarly articles end by sketching a *new* knowledge deficit, gesturing to the future and the on-going process of constructing knowledge. So we find:

> The findings of this study, although **preliminary in nature**, suggest ....
>
> (Rauch-Elnekave 1994:101, emphasis added)

And, accompanying such a gesture towards the future, we can find promise for greater knowledge still, as above in the conclusion to the article about the ZBA, or here, from an article on gender stereotypes:

> ... **it might be of some interest** to explicate the relation between the cognition of gender subtypes and the cognition of situations in which they are assumed to function. Two-mode clustering **seems** to be particularly well suited to the study of such topics. Alternatively, one **might** be interested in introducing a third mode, for instance the sample of subjects providing type-by-feature co-occurrence data, and investigating the construal of interactions between classes of types and classes of situations specific to classes of individuals. Research into these diverse and fascinating issues **promises** to yield important new insights into the intricate nature of social stereotypes.
>
> (Eckes 1994: 121, emphasis added)

Exercise

(1) Examine this conclusion to the fear-of-crime study, from which you read an excerpt ("Interview with Mae") in Chapter Two, for signs of *in*conclusiveness.

> We would argue [...] that the important research question in fear of crime research is not "How rational is people's fear of crime?", a question which we have argued is far too simplistic, and indeed, patronizing. Rather a series of questions may be substituted which examine the local and global, the conscious and unconscious, the discursive and extra-discursive and the material and symbolic dimensions of fear of crime, while acknowledging that each of these pairs of terms are not binary oppositions but instead are sides of the same coin.

To us the way ahead with analyses of fear of crime and media would seem to lie with a combining of Douglas' view on risk perception as a hermeneutic and symbolic product, Hallway and Jefferson's emphasis on the psychodynamic aspects of people's responses to crime, Sparks' focus on fear of crime as a dynamic interplay of perception and cultural representation, Taylor et al.'s focus on the cognitive and emotional scripts inhering in "long-established memories and beliefs" (1996:314), and the kind of analysis of lay knowledge and the dialogic use of micro-circuits of communication we have attempted to develop in our own research.

(Lupton and Tulloch 1999: 521-22)

(2) Inspect essays you have recently written or are currently drafting. Do your conclusions sketch the limits of your findings (through modality or limiting expressions)? Do they gesture toward other opportunities for study? If not, try rewriting them to adopt these attitudes of limited knowledge and unfolding possibility for knowledge-making. (For example: "This essay has examined only one episode in the current controversy over the judicial treatment of young offenders. While it suggests that expressed attitudes toward young offenders may be linked to broader political trends, investigation of other episodes may reveal further complexities. Moreover, further study may reveal connections between public attitudes towards young offenders and public attitudes towards other policy issues, such as welfare reform.")

As the example from the article on gender subtypes shows, conclusions also tend to return the reader to the highest level of abstraction: there, "the intricate nature of social stereotypes." Cognitively, this move makes sense because it puts the finishing touches on the product on the reader's mental desktop. But it makes sense socially too, for these abstractions are often the high-status terms that gave the introduction rhetorical force — the Big Issues which warrant claims on readers' attention and identify the writer as someone in touch with established concerns.

Accordingly, it is mainly in conclusions that we see the rather rare appearance of what we could call "moral" statements. While the research genres are generally relatively free of statements of moral obligation like these —

The government **ought** to put a stop to this.

People **should** learn to respect the environment.

We **must** preserve our neighbourhoods.

— there are nevertheless some occasions when obligation is expressed. Sometimes these obligations are about research itself. Something needs to be examined more closely; something should be explained in relation to something else. We can see an example of such an expression of obligation here, in the last sentence of the article on the experience of German minorities in Britain and the US in World War I (notice as well the major abstractions — *xenophobia, control, intolerance* — that are invoked by this ending):

> In each case, the experience of the German minority **needs** to be placed within traditions of xenophobia in the two countries, but, more especially, the war atmosphere which led to increasing control of all citizens towards and a growth of more general intolerance towards all perceived outgroups.
>
> (Ellis and Panayi 1994:255-56, emphasis added)

Sometimes the expression of obligation extends to the *application* of the research, as in an example we looked at above. Plain language redrafting is not enough to make legal documents understandable:

> It **must** be supported by other measures such as public legal education and individual counselling of persons faced with legal obligations.
>
> (Masson and Waldron 1994:79, emphasis added)

And, sometimes, researchers can conclude with statements that resemble the calls to specific action or attitude we find in other genres, such as newspaper editorials or partisan political briefs. This is from a conclusion the writer has labelled "Policy implications":

> Human capital differences may be addressed by establishing programs to help women complete their education. We **should** offer

scholarships and financial aid for women at both the high school and college levels. We **must** also establish programs to allow women who were forced to drop out of school to return and complete their education. These educational programs **must** be supplemented by others that provide job training and retraining. Many women worked prior to leaving the waged labor force to bear and/or rear children. Their occupational skills often became outdated during their absence and **must** be brought up to date. Other women may never have developed relevant occupational skills because they grew up in an era or community where it was not expected that women would work for wages and will need to develop initial job skills. Programs of job training and retraining will be expensive without any possible source of funds other than the federal government.

My own analysis has revealed that young children in the home are a major barrier to married women's participation in the waged labor force. It is possible that this reflects a negative evaluation of mothers with young children working outside the home, but it could also reflect the absence of safe, affordable day care. We cannot or perhaps **should** not do anything about the former possibility, but we can certainly address the latter. We **must** establish federally funded and federally supervised day care centers. It would be especially desirable if these day care centers could combine custodial with educational functions to provide a "head start" where needed.

(Geschwender 1992: 12, emphasis added)

This conclusion seems to me strongly stated. It goes further toward real-world action/application than many research genres would permit. But the preceding (and following) examples show that "moral" statements are not entirely missing from the scholarly genres — although they may occur in different degrees and with different focus in different disciplines. (Moreover, we should keep in mind that high-status abstractions — *ethnicity, class, gender, community*, for example — which exert rhetorical force can also carry with them their own moral force as they expose circumstances of inequality or disturbing applications of power, or risks to valued ways of life.)

Different disciplines have different kinds of connections with the world beyond the research domain — and the variations in "moral" statements (what *should* be done) we have observed in the samples in this section are signals of these different connections. In the conclusion to an article from the journal *Estuaries*, for example —

The recent decline in fur demand has depressed the industry so that nutria-trapping in Louisiana's coastal marshes is no longer economical, yet control of nutria populations is essential to maximize growth of newly created marshes. Marsh creation is a major policy objective of the state of Louisiana and of the Federal government. Dealing with the population size of an introduced mammalian species is a part of that policy issue.

We have shown that an introduced species — the nutria — alone or in combination with native migrating waterfowl can seriously retard marsh development in the deltaic environment. This demonstration of the importance of herbivory in the Atchafalaya Delta has practical applications for the northern Gulf of Mexico coast where coastal wetland loss rates are the highest in North America (65 km^2 year, Britsch and Dunbar 1993).

(Evers et al. 1998: 12)

— "marsh creation" is a positive goal — a *good* — and conditions which "retard" advance towards this goal are *ills*. The nutria population is an obstacle, so "control of nutria populations is essential to maximize growth of newly created marshlands" (nutria *should* be reduced in numbers). (Notice that the arguments recommending marshland as *good* are presupposed rather than reviewed here, captured in the claim that "[m]arsh creation is major policy objective of the state of Louisiana and of the Federal Government.")

Some disciplines or sub-disciplines can trace their origins to real-world exigencies. Susan Peck MacDonald (1994) observes that attachment studies in psychology, for example, emerged to answer questions about the psychological health of children orphaned or displaced by World War II (57), and about how their well-being might be addressed. Nowadays, attachment researchers are unlikely to provide direct instructions on how to care for babies ("babies should be picked up when they cry"), but others may derive suggestions for child-rearing or public child-care policy from research results.

Each discipline might be analysed for its internal ethos — its way of thinking about what is desirable or undesirable. From this ethos its scale of imperatives develops: ranging from claims about what research should be done next to claims about what interventions should be undertaken in the world beyond research domains.

Exercise

(1) The passage below comes from the conclusion of the article on the effects of "low-ability" grouping. Identify the expressions that limit the researcher's findings.

In this passage, "Mrs. Turner" and "Mrs. Grant" were two of the successful teachers of low-ability classes observed by the writer.

> Yet another limitation of this study, also a form of narrowness, is that it relied on higher-than-expected achievement as a sign of effectiveness without considering other sorts of outcomes. Critics of ability grouping, however, maintain that low-track assignment is stigmatizing, producing harmful social outcomes apart from effects on achievement (see, e.g., Schwartz 1981; Oakes 1985). Cases studied by Valli (1986) and by Camarena (1990) seemed to open the possibility of counteracting this problem. However, in this study, Mrs. Turner commented in the year-end interview that assigning students to a remedial class stigmatizes them and depresses their motivation, and she views this as reason to avoid assigning them to a separate class. In fact, both Mrs. Turner and Mrs. Grant told us that, although they see the ability-grouping question as complex and multisided, on balance they both prefer mixing low-track students with other students. Thus, our examples of teachers who succeeded with low tracks — at least with respect to instruction and achievement — would actually prefer to end that arrangement. Perhaps, then, these are simply examples of good teachers, who would be effective regardless of how students were assigned. In any case, given the likelihood that ability grouping will continue to be used, we need to know much more about how to use it well.
>
> (Gamoran 1993:18-19)

(2) How would you rate the "imperatives" — what **should** be done, what is **good** or **bad** — in the passages below? What kind of outcomes are in sight?

> PASSAGE A
> There are at least four reasons why studying gaze aversion and disengaging from the environment may be of more than

passing interest. First, the behavior is so frequent as to be characterized as "commonplace" (Kundera, 1996). Second, the results bear a family resemblance to the irrelevant speech effect (LeCompte, 1994) and to the analysis of attentional demands on retrieval (Craik, Govoni, Naveh-Benjamin, and Anderson, 1996). Third, this sort of behavior has been noted as relevant by investigators in at least two other domains: social behavior (Argyle and Kendon, 1967), and law enforcement. In the latter context, Fisher and Geiselman (1992) recommend closing the eyes as a component of the cognitive interview designed to facilitate accurate recall of information from eyewitnesses to crimes.

Finally, Glenberg (1997) has proposed that disengaging from the environment may be a significant source of individual differences in cognition. That is, planning, recollective memory, and language all seem to require some ability to disengage from the current environment. If there is reliable variability in the capacity or skill needed to disengage (see Ehrlichman and Weinberger, 1978, for data on this), this variability ought to be systematically related to the execution of a wide variety of cognitive and behavioral skills.

Arthur M. Glenberg, Jennifer L. Schroeder, and David A. Robertson 1998
"Averting the gaze disengages the environment and facilitates remembering."
Memory and Cognition 26, 4, 651-58, 657.

PASSAGE B

In short, saving-inducing tax plans are attacking a problem that does not exist, with a mechanism that will not work, in order to achieve a goal that would harm the economy. It would be much better to design tax policy to achieve other goals such as raising revenue and redistributing income. Instead, many elected officials cloak support for regressive tax changes in the rhetoric of high-sounding theory that is known to be false. A more cynical mind might think that they know exactly what they are doing.

(Buchanan 1999:74)

PASSAGE C

The rewards of working with TEK are commonly expressed using the future tense. While improvements are certainly possible, available methods of documenting TEK, such as the one used in this study, are effective. What remain to be developed are better means of integrating TEK approaches with those of Western science, better ways of using TEK in resource management, and a better understanding of how TEK can help conservation, including sustainable use of living resources.

This research shows that an effective methodology used in a collaborative research process with elders and hunters can document a wide range of useful land detailed information. The benefits of such research include a better understanding of the ecology of a region or a species, as well as cooperation in research, which aids the cooperative management strategies that are increasingly common in Alaska and elsewhere in the Arctic. Effective processes for applying documented indigenous knowledge to management, conservation, and biological research, however, remain elusive, and require additional investigation.

(Huntington et al. 1999: 59)

Works Cited

Chafe, Wallace. 1994. *Discourse, Consciousness, and Time*. Chicago: U of Chicago P.

Chafe, Wallace, and Johanna Nichols, eds. 1986. *Evidentiality: The Linguistic Coding of Epistemology*. Norwood, NJ: Ablex.

Davison, Alice, and Georgia M. Green, eds. 1988. *Linguistic Complexity and Text Comprehension: Readability Issues Reconsidered*. Hillsdale, NJ: Erlbaum.

Fleischman, Suzanne. 1991. "Discourse as space/discourse as time: Reflections on the meta-language of spoken and written discourse." *Journal of Pragmatics* 10: 291-300.

Giddens, Anthony. 1990. *The Consequences of Modernity*. Stanford: Stanford UP.

Giltrow, Janet. 1998. "Modernizing authority: Management studies and the grammaticalization of controlling interests." *Journal of Technical Writing and Communication* 28(4): 337-58.

Halliday, M.A.K. and J.R. Martin. 1993. *Writing Science: Literacy and Discursive Power*. Pittsburgh: U of Pittsburgh P.

Hyland, Ken. 1999. "Academic attribution: Citation and knowledge." *Applied Linguistics* 20(3): 341-67.

Latour, Bruno and Steve Woolgar. 1986 (1979). *Laboratory Life: The Construction of Scientific Facts*. Princeton, NJ: Princeton UP.

MacDonald, Susan Peck. 1994. *Professional Academic Writing in the Humanities and Social Sciences*. Carbondale: Southern Illinois UP.

Myers, Greg. 1989. "The pragmatics of politeness in scientific articles." *Applied Linguistics*. 10: 1-35.

Rodman, Lilita. 2000. "Disciplinary differences in the use of *important, significant, interesting, clear,* and *obvious*." Paper presented at the meeting of the Canadian Association of Teachers of Technical Writing. Edmonton.

Swales, John. 1990. *Genre Analysis: English in Academic and Research Settings.* Cambridge: Cambridge UP.

Thomas, Sara, and Thomas P. Hawkes. 1994. "Reporting verbs in medical journal articles." *English for Special Purposes* 13(2): 129–48.

The politics of knowledge and the case of ethnography

Part of this chapter examines **ethnography** — a type of scholarly writing that develops from firsthand observation of a social group and its ways. Ethnography is an important member of the family of research genres. It also offers an opportunity for students to take an authentic research position. So this chapter assigns an ethnographic project, along with practice in two genres that often accompany research activities: the **proposal** and the **oral presentation**.

This chapter also reviews criticisms of scholarly expression, bringing together issues which have come up throughout our discussion of the research genres. It is not accidental that ethnography and criticism of research discourse appear together in this chapter. Ethnography has been a focus of scholarly innovations that seek to correct some of the conditions under which research makes knowledge. Yet, historically, it has also been one of the most powerful genres in producing just the kind of distortions in our knowledge of the world that leave scholarly practices open to serious political criticism.

The first sections of this chapter review some of the more general concerns about scholarly expression, developing a political direction for our approach to ethnography. In a certain sense, we reconsider the "readability" issues of the last chapter, this time placing them in a larger context — one which takes into account the occasions on which research discourse leaves its well-defined settings in research institutions.

6.1 "Readability" and "objectivity"

I have been tempted to regard "readability" and "objectivity" as separate issues — names for separate themes of complaint about scholarly discourses. Readability issues are usually raised from *outside* research communities; objectivity issues are usually raised from *inside* research communities.

The readability issue names complaints about scholarly writing we have already contemplated: it is too difficult, unnecessarily complicated and obscure, inaccessible to outsiders. (Or, to put it another way, its difficulty makes outsiders of too many people.) We replied to these complaints with genre theory. The styles of scholarly writing are suited to research activities. If scholarly styles drift out of research situations, they can indeed alienate people. But, when we justify scholarly style by referring to the knowledge-making situations they serve, it's hard to see how research discourses could be changed to make them more readable by more people.

Objectivity issues on the other hand arise, mostly, *inside* research communities, when scholars insist on knowing the relations between the authority of "expert" statements and the authority of privileged interests in the social order. This has seemed to me a matter separate from readability.

But, reflecting on these matters, I have come to wonder if a broader concept of "readability" in fact points to some of the tensions between research reasoning and the public reasoning of the cultures which endorse research by paying for it — and by citing it in non-scholarly contexts: how do scholarly statements perform outside their research habitats? How do they sound? How do people hear them and use them? Do they like what they hear? While we can justify scholarly styles by referring to their contexts-of-use, we may thereby imagine research as sealed off from adjacent contexts — and thereby ignore the actual traffic between research domains and the social and political occasions which surround them. Complaints about "readability" may be just the tip of the iceberg — a signal that this traffic does flow, that outsiders overhear, that research sectors are not entirely reclusive but out-going too and also hospitable to visits from outside influences. The critique of objectivity identifies this dimension of sociality in research communities — a social and political plane of influence on which research speaks to other sectors, and is spoken to by them.

The critique of objectivity emerges from reasoning we can roughly label "post-modern" — although that term is itself open to criticism for referring to too much and saying too little. We will customize the word for our present purposes, and take post-modern reasoning as those attitudes which regard knowledge as "socially constructed." Such reasoning challenges views of knowledge as fact — existing independent of the people who make it, know it, say it, use it, and exchange it. Postmodern analyses of knowledge suggest that the "objectivity" of the products of research is, at worst, a hoax, and at best a useful illusion. Any statement, the argument goes, issues from some position in the social order, and is contingent on that position. (From a different position, some other statement entirely might be transmitted.)

Let us look at this claim at the micro level. Again and again, our investigations of scholarly style turned up agentless expressions. We found good explanations for this agentlessness (nominalizations of verbs and qualities tend to eliminate the agent of the action or the possessor of the quality; nominalization in turn contributes to the distinctive patterns of abstraction and connectedness in scholarly writing). But, on the whole, agentlessness can tend to erase from the surface of the expression the people who act, and the people acted upon — all the experience of the event described. So the expression

voluntary employee turnover

directs our attention away from some active elements of the thing referred to: people quitting their jobs when they get fed up, or disappointed, or look for more meaning in life, or hate bosses who impose on them or harass or bully them. At the same time, the expression itself seems to observe this thing from a *manager's* position: it is hard to figure on an *employee* walking away from her desk and heading out the door, and looking at the event as "turnover."

So, even as the expression seems to promise an abstract objectivity, creating an entity that can be measured and analysed, it is "subjective" — that is, it is an observation *from a certain position in the social order* (and, in this case, the position is one of relatively greater power). From this, two lines of reasoning develop. The first credits knowledge on the basis of that very subjectivity. The second tends to discredit knowledge. We will look first at the ideas which embrace subjectivity.

6.2 Embracing the subject

Although many might disagree with what I am about to propose, I will risk it anyway: it is feminist reasoning, at the end of the twentieth century, which has most sincerely invited the subject — the thinking, feeling being, experienced in the complexities of daily life — back into scholarly writing. Feminist reasoning has criticized research practices for being carried out from a *masculinist* position or point of view, and then representing that position as *universal*. So feminist research would be inclined to dismantle the form of knowledge constructed by traditional research practices, and expose that knowledge as not only not "objective" but also as serving the interests of those who work at it. But some tracks of feminist research would also do more than expose the subjectivity of established regimes of knowledge. They would acknowledge the impossibility of the independent "fact" (and possibly even deny its desirability), and require that the researcher identify himself or herself. Fleshed out beyond the *discursive I* we met in Chapter Five, the "subjective" researcher would expose the relevant social and political — *personal* — elements of his or her experience of the world. These elements would constitute the full **subject position** from which the researcher speaks. The "knowledge" which the researcher then offers would be contingent on that position: not absolute or universal, but relative to that position.

It is hard to say how far this project for remodelling scholarly writing has advanced. Publications in disciplines which deal with gender-related topics are still perhaps the most likely to invite the fleshed-out subject to the page (and even then, in the presence of gender issues — as we have seen from the many excerpts from articles on gender-related topics in previous chapters — the traditional scholarly voice can still prevail). But, even amongst the articles which we have consulted for samples of standard scholarly expression, and which are not about gender issues, we can also find the writer stepping out from traditional styles and saying who she is, and what happened to her, personally, to make her think the way she does now.

> In the forty years that I have been doing fieldwork in Latin America and the United States, my own awareness of how the events I recorded are related to the world around them has expanded along with (and sometimes belatedly to) that of my informants. This follows trends in the field as the unit of investigation has progressed from one of bounded cultures where the task was to recapture a traditional past to a multilayered, historically situated inquiry where the authoritative stance of a privileged observer was no longer condoned. In tracing my own enthnographic journey, I shall try to capture some of those experiences in which I was forced to encounter the world dimensions of everyday struggles for survival. (13)
>
> ★ ★ ★
>
> I found interpretation of these events [homicides in a village in the Mayan area of Chiapas, Mexico] difficult, given the dominant

paradigm of structural functionalism in the field of anthropology.
(14)

★ ★ ★

When I completed the monograph on the Maya, I felt the need
to escape the involuted conflicts of Mayan semisubsistence farmers and work in a society where the hostility was turned outward
against class enemies. I visited the mining communities of Bolivia
in the summer of 1967, just three weeks after the massacre of San
Juan in Siglo-XXCatavi. (17)

★ ★ ★

I borrowed some books from my informants and acquired a
library of publications by current Latin American theorists to
cope with the confusion of ideological currents and social movements that I found in the mining community.

★ ★ ★

Clearly, all of this turmoil [coup, debt crisis] exceeded the anthropological models available for analysis of field data. I tried to keep
the life of the community at the center of my thinking about
what was coming in, allowing it to be filtered through the people's sense of what was happening. The life narratives that I
undertook with a few of my informants provided the ballast that
kept me from sliding into metatheories concerning the consciousness of workers. (19)

(Nash 1994: 13-19)

This article is not about gender issues, yet perhaps its style has been
influenced by the feminist reasoning which suggests that researchers
identify themselves. It's interesting too that this researcher represents
herself as changing — as a thinker and observer — over time. She
knows things now that she didn't know before; she has been influenced by others, she has changed her mind. Just as knowledge is
located in time and changes over time, so are knowledge-makers
located in time, and subject to its influences. It's worth noting further that Nash is writing in the discipline of anthropology — for,
besides feminist reasoning, the other radical interrogation of scholarly authority in the late twentieth century has come from **post-colonial** positions. Post-colonial reasoning has challenged the authority
of Western researchers to produce knowledge of other cultures, and
exposed traditional anthropological knowledge as saturated with
colonial values.

Exercise

Three excerpts from scholarly articles follow — the first two from the beginning of introductory sections, the third from a conclusion. Examine them to determine how each writer steps beyond the traditional role of the *discursive I*. (The second excerpt comes from a co-authored article innovatively structured as a dialogue.)

PASSAGE A

About 2 years ago, I conversed with an American business-man in Mexico about how difficult replacement parts were to come by in that country. Over the next several months, he formed an alliance with Mexican and American partners and investors and formed a company, one with a more specific business goal, namely, to provide rebuilt engine parts from the U.S. to commercial transportation fleets in Mexico.

During meetings over the following year, the American and Mexican partners saw me in action, doing what linguistic anthropologists naturally do — mediating worlds — sometimes in English, sometimes in rusty Spanish, sometimes in both. We mutually decided that I would spend the summer in Mexico City to help start up the company. I dealt with Mexican and American partners, government offices, lawyers, and customers. I worked in the cracks between two different "cultures," cracks described in recent books on Mexican-American relations, books whose titles foreshadow the examples to come: *Distant Neighbors* (Riding, 1985) and *Limits to Friendship* (Pastor and Castaneda, 1988).

Kismet turned me into something I had never been before — an "intercultural communicator." The rest of this article is dedicated to figuring out what, in light of that experience, the phrase might mean.

Intercultural Communicator

After my baptism by fire, I returned to the university in the autumn and approached the library with a naive question in mind: "What is the field of intercultural communication all about?" The question was naive because the literature is huge, diverse, without agreement on any particular unifying focus (see Hinnenkamp, 1990, for a related concern with the fundamentals of the field).

Michael Agar 1994 "The intercultural frame." *International Journal of Intercultural Relations* 18, 2, 221-37, 221-22.

PASSAGE B
I. INTRODUCTION: MULTIPLE OPENINGS
WITH(IN) A DIALOGUE
What, then, are the limitations of our practice? How is
our practice complicit with certain established societal
structures?
— Ming-Yeung Lu

MING-YUEN S. MA: This quote brings up many of the
questions that keep coming up in my mind as I work on this
project, and I think that they point out the uncertainties in
my motives: who am I, a first generation Chinese gay man,
who was born but did not grow up in the United States,
whose higher education was enabled by my privileged,
upper-middle-class background, to write about Asian lesbian
and gay writers? What is my placement in the text? What
does it mean for us to be writing about works by persons of
Asian and Pacific Islander descent in a language that is not
our own — though most of us communicate by it?

ALICE Y. HOM: As a second-generation Chinese American,
raised in a working-class immigrant family but educated in
an Ivy League college, I think there are some complexities to
the language issue. Many second-, third-, and fourth-genera-
tion Asian Americans do not feel their native language is an
Asian language. When talking about Asian Pacific Islander lesbian and gay writing, we have to address the definition of
"Asian Pacific Islander." In this case we are speaking of Asian
and Pacific Islander immigrants and those born in the United
States. The diaspora is limited to the United States although
some of the Asian Pacific Islander lesbian writings are coming
from Canada. For the most part, we will concentrate in this
United States-centred context because most of our research
and experiences are from here.

Alice Y. Hom and Ming-Yuen S. Ma 1993 "Premature gestures: A speculative
dialogue on Asian Pacific lesbian and gay writing." *Journal of Homosexuality*
26, 2/3, 21-31, 22.

PASSAGE C
A concluding point: the ideological structuring of place-
identity has a practical implication for how the topic is inves-

tigated. It forces researchers to become reflexive about their own positions in the world. The authors of this study, for example, are White men who grew up in South Africa, who lived in segregated areas, relaxed on the country's exclusive beaches and in this sense were co-opted into the geopolitical order of apartheid. They have found interrogation of the materially advantaged and ideological position to be a vital analytic resource. Too often researchers ignore the politics of their own place identifications and therefore sustain power relations through their academic practices.

(Dixon and Durrheim 2000: 40)

6.2.1 Unanimity and dissent, unity and division

In this book, we have encountered many instances of **multiple-authored publications** — two, three, or more writers putting their names to research. Some theorists of knowledge and ideology have analysed this practice as implying unanimity amongst the writers — seamless agreement and unified outlook. This analysis suggests further that the appearance of unanimity misrepresents the nature of research knowledge: rather than reveal it as unstable and contingent, and vulnerable to dissent, it presents it as a solid, impermeable front, supported by speakers-in-unison.

These criticisms may tend to come from "rural" disciplines, where research activities are less likely to organize workers in collaborative groups. But collaborative work can also take place in those softer, "rural" disciplines, too, and some writers in those disciplines have experimented with stylistic means of representing the nature of collaborative knowledge-making, as we see in the second example in the exercise above. In the next example, the co-authors of a book explain at the beginning of one of their chapters that they could not agree on the points to be made in that chapter and, as a result, allotted it to one of them to write on her own. (Since the writers themselves cannot agree, we might see this as an invitation to agree or disagree with the chapter's claims, rather than simply accept them as "fact.") Moreover, they also decided not to pretend that they had written it together. Instead, they announce their differences, and thereby acknowledge the divisions potential to research knowledge. (And you might notice that they also refer to themselves by their first names — expanding the repertoire of grammatical possibilities for representation of the *discursive I*.)

> This chapter focuses on the political context in which any public act of writing is embedded. As authors, we are not always in agreement on what, in the broader political sense, is in the best interests of the majority of people and what is said to be 'in the national interest.' We have therefore found it impossible to present this chapter in a way that represents both our political stances. The chapter is written mainly by Romy, and represents her positions on some issues which are not always shared by Roz. The main points of disagreement are over whether a liberal democracy and free market economy are or are not in the interests of the majority of the people and over whether the Falklands/Malvinas War and the Gulf War were or were not in the 'national interest', and we have not committed ourselves to a shared position when discussing these issues. However, this does not affect our shared conviction that writing is at the centre of political struggle, and making this point we have been comfortable to write 'we'. The very fact that joint authorship is leading us into ideological struggles is part of the point we want to make about the place of writing in struggles over meaning.
>
> Romy Clark and Roz Ivanic 1997 "Writing, politics and power." *The Politics of Writing* London: Routledge, 20.

In exposing the *making* of their chapter, Clark and Ivanic expose knowledge as something *made* — by particular people with particular political attitudes. In exposing the making of their chapter, Clark and Ivanic say who they are.

Perhaps in your career as a scholarly writer, you have also wanted to say who you are. Perhaps the roles available to you as a scholarly writer — and the topics and assumptions that accompany those roles — have not been quite the right ones for you. Maybe you quit your job one day, in frustration or in hopefulness, and you have something to say about *voluntary employee turnover*. Maybe you know something about what makes a woman decide to do piecework at home, and you have something to say about *labour supply decision-making*. But the arrangements of the scholarly genres don't seem to give you space to speak, or permission to identify yourself. Perhaps the changes suggested or inspired by feminist reasoning would allow you to speak up, from a position closer to home.

From the ground laid out by feminist reasoning, we might also see the structures of the research genres as hospitable to some kinds of knowledge and inhospitable to others. In earlier chapters we noted that other writing and reading situations don't call for the same laborious descents from high-level generalities to specifics, or the persistent restatements of abstractions to hold the parts of the text together. There may be some important kinds of knowledge that can't be captured in the controlling claims of introductions and conclusions where high-level abstractions command details. Those controlling abstractions may distort some details, or eliminate others that won't fit or that want to wander off and suggest other notions or fraternize with different ideas.

Moreover, the structures of the research genres exert strict authority over readers' work, controlling their response to every passage of text, managing readers' mental desktops with a firm hand. Some writers may not want this authority. It may seem to misrepresent not only their own character and view but also the character of the knowledge they want to present. Sometimes questions remain open, even after careful inquiry; sometimes answers defy one another.

If the research genres were to speak in their own defence, they might say that these criticisms are satisfied by features we have identified as typical of scholarly expression. They would point to the system of reported statements with their repertoire of reporting verbs that get scholarly discussion under way by summoning a community of (often competing) voices. They would point to the system of modality which renders claims as issuing from the writer's limited knowledge. Supporters of the techniques of the research genres might argue that the *discursive I* is more tangible and active than people think. And they would say that all these features — reporting, modality, *discursive I* — constitute **position**, and **subjectivity**.

To adjudicate between arguments which say that scholarly writing conceals subjectivity and those which say it adequately represents the subject, we may have to look to the second line of reasoning, which questions the political result of research practice and its expression in writing.

6.3 Knowledge and power

It may be commonplace to say that knowledge gives us power. The more we know about the world around us, the better we are able to manage it, or control it, or at least ward off some of its more harmful effects on us.

Suspecting that there is more to knowledge than this simple benefit, many thinkers in the last part of the twentieth century have inspected the relations between knowledge and power. Findings in this area may not be welcome news to everyone, and they are quite complex. To establish their relations to academic writing, we will start with a familiar instance.

Say you feel sick and visit your doctor. You tell her how you feel; she takes your blood pressure, looks down your throat, listens to your heart, maybe sends you for x-ray, or other imaging, depending on the nature of your complaint. Consulting her expert knowledge of the human body and its frailties, she tells you what is wrong with you, and what to do about it. You must subject yourself to a regime of medication; you must alter your diet, temporarily or permanently; you must stay in bed, or get up and move around, depending on the complaint. You must come back next week to be checked. You both hope you will get better soon.

You have been subjected to the modern knowledge of human health: products of the investigative practices of many researchers, products which are reported in many publications. If you get better, we could say that knowledge has given you power (at least for a while) over the hazards to which human flesh is prone. But reflect for a minute on that visit to the doctor's office. If you look at it from a social point of view, as an instance of typical interaction (and a number of researchers have in fact inquired into patients' visits to their doctors as a genre), you may sense that power resided with the doctor. With her expert knowledge, she read the signs of illness — deviations from the norms of health — interpreting them as you could not, and, from the interpretation, directed your behaviour, achieving (depending on your compliance) even some physical control over your body. From a social point of view, knowledge conferred power on the *doctor*, not the patient. The doctor enjoyed some advantage over the patient, and patients' often submissive behaviour in the doctor's office may signify recognition of this power differential.

Now let's take an example closer to the site where knowledge is actually produced. The previous chapter excerpted passages from a psychologist's article on teenage motherhood. We could say that the researcher "constructed knowledge" of young women who become pregnant and drop out of school. She made this knowledge by interviewing a group of young women who fit this description, by reviewing their scores on the California Achievement Tests, by measuring their babies' development with the Mental Scale of the Bayley Scales of Infant Development, and by measuring their self-esteem with the Piers-Harris Children's Self-Concept Scale. (You could say that these tests are like the x-ray machine or other imaging device that produces knowledge of conditions otherwise detectable only by intuition, or perhaps entirely undetectable.) The psychologist found that a significantly high number of these young women had "untreated learning disabilities." (If the young women, in the meantime, found out anything about the psychologist, these findings have gone unreported, or, at least, unpublished.) From this new knowledge about teenage mothers, we might expect some activity to follow. If this knowledge gets institutionalized, we might find teenage mothers routinely checked for learning disabilities — and subjected to a regime of treatment. Without the tests and the new "knowledge" about teenage mothers, people like the subjects of this study might be left alone, to continue their lives without this intervention.

Moreover, while the researcher identifies teenage motherhood as a recognized "social problem," the interviews revealed that the young women did not see it this way. Nor did their families, on the whole. Yet once the research community identifies the life condition of this population as a "problem" and develops more detailed, expert knowledge of the problem (it is associated with learning disability, also a "problem"), we can imagine that programs and policies will develop to capture this group and its potential members in more detailed, expert systems of testing, surveillance and treatment — implementing more exhaustive systems of control.

Knowledge has been produced from the subject position — or point of view — of the researcher. The young women are the object of knowledge, and as such become susceptible to the exercise of power. Perhaps they will resist, and go their own way. What they won't be able to do is construct publishable counter-knowledge of the research community which studies them.

And, even when specific interventions are not on the horizon, accumulations of knowledge can in themselves tend to project differentials in the social order. We might recall, in this respect, the first scholarly passage we inspected in Chapter Two, reporting on the influence of neighbourhoods on young people's behaviour. Although the perspective of that article is not openly moralizing, we might nevertheless detect disapproval of some kinds of behaviour — early childbearing, in particular. This disapproval lurks in an unspoken characterization of some neighbourhoods as having a bad influence on the young people who live in them. The researchers do not report where they themselves live, but we might speculate that they do not live in the kind of "bad" neighbourhood they investigate through quantitative methods. Research activities, and accumulations of research knowledge, tend to produce or reproduce middle-class positions — positions that include assumptions about early childbearing. Do middle-class positions — and Western, urban, masculinist ones — monopolize research conversations?

Bruno Latour (2000) offers us some materials for thinking about the economy of research statements. We met Latour briefly in Chapter Three when we discovered differences between abstractions in the "hard" sciences and those in the "softer" disciplines. He told us then that, in the hard sciences (or the "natural" ones, as opposed to the "social" ones), objects of inquiry can "talk back" to the investigator, denying statements made about them. This "objecting" object, Latour says, is the essence of "objectivity" (115). In his view, the social sciences do not have this "objectivity": human subjects tend not to "talk back" to social scientists employing current methods of inquiry (and tend, instead, to comply, or naively cooperate in the social scientist's project. To get the picture here, imagine the fed-up employees quitting their jobs, or the teenaged mothers being overtaken by systems of explanatory abstractions — *voluntary employee turnover* or *learning disability* — which are inaudible or invisible to them, known only to experts. In the meantime, the employees' own actions would be contributing to statistical surveys of turnover, and the young women's own answers on the testing instruments would be contributing to statements about them as a social "problem").

What would it sound like if subjects/objects did *talk back*, in Latour's sense? What kind of conversation would count as *back talk*?

> If social scientists wanted to become objective, they would have to find the very rare, costly, local, miraculous, situation where they can render their subjects of study as much as possible able to object to what is said about them, to be as disobedient as possible to the protocol, and to be as capable to raise their own questions in their own terms and *not* in those of the scientists whose interests they do not have to share! Then, humans would start to behave in the hands of social scientists as *interestingly* as natural objects in the hands of natural scientists. One has just, for instance, to compare the pre-feminist sociological literature on housewives and gender-roles with the literature generated after feminism had rendered recalcitrant most of the potential interviewees, to see the difference between a pseudo-objective science which had only the appearance of scientificity, with a startling set of discoveries on gender which might not always have the trappings of the natural sciences but certainly have its objectivity, its "objectity," that is, its ability to propel novel entities on the scene, to raise new questions in their own terms and to force the social and natural scientists to retool the whole of their intellectual equipment. (116)

Some commentators and theorists have examined the social and political boundary between the ones who research and the ones who are researched from another perspective. They ask, how are people distributed between the two groups? Who gets to be a researcher? Who gets researched? Who gets invited into a research community and who gets invited to answer a questionnaire? Romy Clark and Roz Ivanic (1997) (from whom we heard in the previous section, as they announced their inability to come to an agreement on the substance of one of their chapters) draw to our attention the experiences of university students who come from social groups whose members have not traditionally joined research communities. They propose that students' diverse origins — life histories, class or ethnic backgrounds — will bring them to different positions in relation to the authority rooted in academic styles of writing. Taking this line of inquiry further, Ivanic (1997) focusses particularly on student writers whose route to higher education has not been like that of "[t]raditional undergraduates" who have "experienced a steady, gradual apprenticeship in the language of education over a period of 14 years full-time schooling between the ages of 4 and 18" (5). In Ivanic's view, non-traditional students negotiate their position differently from traditional students, and the case studies she presents suggest that these students may not so readily identify with the middle-class (and white and heterosexual) positions assumed in research discourses. Min-Zhan Lu (1992), from whom we read a passage in Chapter Two, discussing "gatekeepers'" attitudes towards non-traditional students, also investigates the conditions under which those marginal to the class and ethnic centre of research communities negotiate their positions. Lu argues that to seek simply to erase or suppress the non-conforming aspects of identity is to forsake prospects for change in scholarly practice — and, we might add, scholarly authority. In the long term, then, we might see the recruitment to research communities of members of previously unrepresented groups (teenaged mothers, people from "bad" neighbourhoods, working-class felons, elders who are fearful of crime ...) as promising to disturb or perforate the boundary between those who research and those who are researched.

6.4 Qualitative research

Moved by intellectual currents like those which have carried feminist thought and the analysis of power and knowledge, other critics of scholarly practice have suggested that research with a strictly **quantitative** emphasis produces distorted versions of people's experience of the world. Once phenomena — events and attitudes, and the people who are involved in those events or harbour those attitudes — are translated into units which can be counted, and the numbers are subjected to routines of statistical interpretation, they get separated from the meaningful complexities of real-life contexts. So a study of, for example, "learning outcomes" in a hundred classrooms might identify three relevant conditions: the socioeconomic identity of the learners (as measured by a standard scale), their learning styles (as measured by a standard taxonomy), and their performance in a subject area (as measured by a standardized, norm-referenced test). The results could lead to changes in curriculum or teaching strategies.

Critics of this kind of research argue that such quantifications erase the classroom moment, the experience of students and teachers, the complex interactions amongst them. Research quantifications produce a limited or possibly skewed version of the world, and their applications can be unrealistic. In place of or in addition to quantitative research they propose **qualitative** research.

Qualitative research can take various forms. One overall way to look at it is to say that it distinguishes itself from quantitative research by replacing the **many** instances (open to statistical interpretation) with **one** instance or a few instances. The one instance is examined in detail. The long-distance panoramas of quantitative research are replaced by close-up views. So, in the qualitative version of the *learning-outcomes* study, researchers would locate themselves in one classroom, and watch — for days, months, even years. They would record what they saw, taking notes, using video or audio tapes; they would collect documents and artefacts (the teacher's lesson plans, tests, students' work, and so on); they would talk to the teacher and to the students. Unlike quantitative researchers, who arrange measurable situations (controlled instruction, perhaps; tests administered solely for the purpose of the study), qualitative researchers try to leave things as they are. The only change is the presence of the researchers themselves.

Back at their desks, the qualitative researchers interpret the material they have gathered. Surveying their data, they look for patterns and regularities, and, consulting the theoretical tools available to them, they develop explanations for what they have observed.

Both quantitative and qualitative techniques seek generalizations, but they establish the *authority* of their generalizations by different means. While quantitative studies represent their validity by numerousness and recognized means of manipulating numerous instances to coax out statistically significant results, qualitative studies have only the one instance (as in a "case study") or the one group (such as a group of young women who read teen romance fiction). So, while much has been made of the "objective" style of quantitative research, and the rhetorical force of that style, qualitative research may actually be even more dependent on *style of reporting* to persuade readers to accept generalizations developed from limited instances. Moreover, as qualitative study generates an abundance of detail, the means of controlling these data, and transforming them into text that readers can understand, are perhaps more demanding for writers than the customary techniques used for producing text to report quantitative research.

Qualitative techniques show up in various disciplines, and, while many scholarly journals are exclusively quantitative in the submissions they publish, and some tend toward qualitative research, many others publish both quantitative and qualitative work. You will also find individual pieces that are themselves a mix of quantitative and qualitative techniques. Given this variety in form and occurrence, it would be rash to list rules for reporting qualitative research. But we can observe some regularities, especially if we focus on the genre of **ethnography**. This focus also leads us to a research genre particularly hospitable to student writers: ethnography offers them a research position from which they can conduct and report original inquiry.

6.5 Ethnography

In the last 15 or 20 years, ethnographic research has illuminated many otherwise obscured situations. For example, Shirley Brice Heath's *Ways with Words: Language, Life, and Work in Communities and Classrooms* (1983) was a landmark contribution that changed views of learning and language among researchers in several fields: education, sociolinguistics, rhetoric and composition. In step with developments pending in these fields and others, Heath contributed to changes in thinking through her method of making knowledge about the lives of the people in two communities in the Piedmont Carolinas. She spent ten years associating with families in the two communities, participating in their activities, and observing and recording their ways of using oral and written language. The products of her techniques — those of a **participant-observer** — revised attitudes about the success of Afroamerican children and Euroamerican children in public schools, showing that Afroamerican children's relatively less successful performance could be attributed not to deficits in their home environments but to differences in ways of valuing and using language. (Her study tends to credit the linguistic habitat of the Afroamerican community as richer and more complex than that of the Euroamerican community.) Heath's qualitative findings corrected knowledge constructed by quantitative research: large-scale testing and statistical measurement of the school performance and socioeconomic profile of large populations. Whereas quantitative research instruments maintained the researchers' distance from the object of inquiry, qualitative, ethnographic instruments brought the researcher into close contact with the people and situations she was studying.

6.5.1 Post-colonial views of ethnography

While major ethnographies like Heath's, or Bruno Latour and Steve Woolgar's *Laboratory Life: The Construction of Scientific Fact* (1979) (which reports two years of observation of the behaviours, routines and beliefs of workers in a neuroendocrinological lab), appear to have initiated a new era in social research, ethnography is in fact not new but very old. And, while ethnography appears to correct many distortions in research practice, in its history are many episodes which, nowadays, look politically suspect.

We can trace ethnography, first, to the eras of "discovery," when Europeans set out to explore areas of the world unknown to them, and, second, to the periods of imperial expansion and colonization which followed. When navigators and explorers encountered people in distant places, they wrote down what they saw. So, when Jacques Cartier, exploring what was to become known as the Gulf of St. Lawrence, came across an indigenous community, he wrote down what he saw:

> While making our way along the shore, we caught sight of the Indians on the side of a lagoon and low beach, who were making many fires that smoked. We rowed over to the spot, and finding there was an entrance from the sea into the lagoon, we placed our long-boats on one side of the entrance. The savages came over in one of their canoes and brought us some strips of cooked seal, which they placed on bits of wood and then withdrew, making signs to us that they were making us a present of them. We sent two men on shore with hatchets, knives, beads and other wares, at which the Indians showed great pleasure. And at once they came over in a crowd in their canoes to the side where we were, bringing furs and whatever else they possessed, in order to obtain some of our wares. They numbered, both men, women and children, more than 300 persons. Some of their women, who did not come over, danced and sang, standing in the water up to their knees. The other women, who had come over to the side where we were, advanced freely towards us and rubbed our arms with their hands. Then they joined their hands together and raised them to heaven,

exhibiting many signs of joy. And so much at ease did the savages feel in our presence, that at length we bartered with them, hand to hand, for everything they possessed, so that nothing was left to them but their naked bodies; for they offered us everything they owned, which was, all told, of little value. We perceived that they are people who would be easy to convert, who go from place to place maintaining themselves and catching fish in the fishing-season for food.... I am more than ever of the opinion that these people would be easy to convert to our holy faith.

From *The Voyages of Jacques Cartier, 1534*, trans. H.P. Biggar 1924. In *Literature in Canada, Vol. I*, ed. Douglas Daymond and Leslie Monkman. Toronto: Gage, 3.

Cartier took this report home, and it played a role in "constructing knowledge" of the faraway people: the "Other," the exotic, foreign, strange, non-European inhabitants of a distant place. (Perhaps you can see from this short excerpt how Cartier's point of view, or subject position, determines the kind of knowledge he constructs about the people of the Gulf of St. Lawrence. What is the relevance, for example, of the inhabitants' interest in "hatchets, knives, beads and other wares"? What aspects of Cartier's sociohistorical context might have directed his attention to this aspect of the complex scene before him?)

As colonizers followed, and settled and dominated regions which explorers had pointed out, they too wrote about the people who originally inhabited those regions. Some colonizers and colonial travellers made a specialty of describing local people, dispatching their reports of the "Other" to a home audience, and developing the writing traditions that became a basis for the anthropological genres. Like Cartier, they wrote from a European point of view: a position, increasingly, of dominance and economic interest. (So, for example, as colonizers in the Pacific Northwest needed land for settlement, natives of the area were described as having no sense of land title. This "fact" became part of the knowledge made about these people.)

While many people who produced reports about non-European communities were amateur observers, others adopted a professional or "scientific" stance. They published their reports in journals devoted to the study of faraway peoples, founded associations, and organized meetings. In other words, they developed a research community, and ways of writing — genres — which served and embodied the research routines which characterized their work. As we encounter ethnography now, we encounter the descendants of these genres which are traceable to the interests of imperial domination. So it is reasonable to ask, as many people have, whose interests are served by the ethnographic genres? How is the writer's position embodied in the style of ethnography, and what is this position? Is it still a position of dominance — to the advantage of the writer and the interests he or she represents, and to the disadvantage of the social group described?

Addressing such questions, we also need to take into account changes to ethnographers' typical itineraries, for the objects of investigation have tended, in recent times, to move closer to home. While the traditional anthropologist/ethnographer made a long trip to a remote place (the longer the trip and the more remote the location, the more valuable the knowledge), ethnographers in current practice often don't go very far. Sometimes they just go across town, or to a classroom around the corner. Do these foreshortened journeys change the political implications of ethnography?

In this chapter and previous ones we have pursued the idea that a genre's style — the language itself — represents the routines and values of the situation the genre serves. So one way we can approach this question about the political implications of current ethnographic writing is to examine its style. How does the wording transform people and groups into research objects? Is the transformation to the advantage of the researcher? What does research practice — which values "uncommon sense" — *do* to the people it operates on? If knowledge is power, in the simple sense or the complicated sense, where does power accrue as a result of knowledge being constructed about a particular social group? Are generalities illuminating typifications or demeaning stereotypes? Here, for example, in an ethnographic account of a social group typified as RVers, the commonsense term *potluck dinner* is transformed into the "uncommonsense" abstraction *ritual food-sharing*.

> Among RVers the most common food-sharing ritual is the potluck dinner. Weekly potluck dinners are a regular event at resort parks, at many Arizona state parks during the winter season and at RV parks of all sorts at Thanksgiving and Christmas. RVers who are away from their families during the holiday season may pool their funds to buy a turkey and share a holiday meal. Some RVers travel every year to the same park where they meet friends to share Christmas or Thanksgiving dinner. Finally, any important celebration — such as a wedding — includes a potluck dinner. Newcomers join the community by participating in ritual food-sharing.
>
> (Counts and Counts 1992: 167-68)

The word the RVers themselves use — "potluck dinner" — is replaced by a term at a higher level of abstraction — "ritual food-sharing" — which is a word the RVers themselves would probably never use.

Hi! Come over later.	Hi! As a newcomer, you
We're having pot-luck.	can join the community by
	participating in ritual
	food-sharing.

The transformation moves the description away from the social milieu of the RVers themselves — moves it to another social circle, where the wordings *community* and *ritual* are valued ways of speaking. Out of earshot of RVers, ethnographic style turns them into a distant tribe, remote as African nomads (to whom they are eventually compared). We could speculate that RVers will not read "'They're my family now': The creation of community among RVers," just as African nomads, or other foreign peoples who were the object of colonial accounts, did not read what Europeans wrote about them. Could we think of this reconfiguration of *potluck dinner* as a hidden aspect of readability issues constituting popular complaints about scholarly expression? Is it that RVers *can't* read Counts and Counts — or that they *don't* read Counts and Counts? Why is *ritual food-sharing* an eccentric or ridiculous wording in the RV park?

Here (and everywhere) genre instates the social order — an order which separates RVers from professional researchers, making RVers into the "Other," and objects of knowledge. In colonial times, this separation was mapped across power differentials: ethnographers were allied with the political and economic interests of European peoples. In post-colonial times, questions about knowledge and power persist, and challenge scholarly writers to account for the political dimensions of the research routines represented and maintained by the research genres.

Exercise

Following are three excerpts from ethnographic descriptions of social groups, products of qualitative research practices. (Passage A is from an account of the experience of one of the author's students in an "undergraduate feminist theory class.") Inspect each passage for its ways of transforming the people described into objects of knowledge: look for abstractions which belong to the research community rather than the group described (that is, "words these people would never use to describe themselves"), and for typifications which you would estimate that the described people would not apply to themselves. Consider how the interests of the researchers are represented in their ways of speaking. How are these people made into the "Other"?

PASSAGE A

In her opening entry E.L. reveals the first stage of Lacan's stages or "patterns" of psychoanalytic transference by identifying with the "teacher," suggesting, at this early stage, as Ragland-Sullivan notes, that "the emphasis is on likeness and the analyst [in this case the teacher] is perceived as a counterpart" (37). She assumes that her "ideas and interests," her desires, correspond to those of her teachers and that this correspondence gives her a kind of control or mastery over the process of writing.

E.L.'s reaction five days later to her own first exploratory efforts at producing feminist theory reveals the fragility of her own hard-won sense of identity, of control and mastery.

> I think [the assignment to write an exploratory essay on the topic chosen for the term project] distracted me from my original idea. That is fine, I guess — but I don't like being confused. I like knowing what I am trying to say when I write. I don't think I knew what I was trying to say in that essay.

This was to become a persistent theme in E.L.'s diary. The harder she pressed me to reveal "what kind of paper I wanted," the more unwilling or unable I was to tell her what she wanted to hear. I say this without complacency because it was both frustrating and embarrassing to realize that perhaps I did not know myself what I wanted. In the psychoanalytic situation, as the ideal "subject supposed to know" is revealed as an illusion, an "imaginary projection," there is a parallel "disintegration of the analysand's supposition of knowing." Ragland-Sullivan describes this process in the analysand as a disintegration of the self. Because the unified *moi* (the ideal ego) gives the subject a sense of "self cohesion," "any unraveling of the strands that went into weaving that identity as a conviction of 'being' causes a debeing of being: a sense of fragmenting" (37).

Laurie Finke 1993 "Knowledge as bait: Feminism, voice, and the pedagogical unconscious." *College English* 55, 1, 7-27, 21.

PASSAGE B

Jankowski's study is unique in that he studied gangs as organizations, addressing a void in the literature. His work is limited, however, because of his adoption of the rational choice model: Both the gangs he studied and their individual members made rational decisions based on self-interest.

Organizational theorists have found rationality of decision making in even formal organizations to be "rare in nature" (Weick 1976; also cf. Zey 1992; March and Olsen 1976). There is a deep literature describing organizations as "myths" (Meyer and Rowan 1981), as being "loosely coupled" (Weick 1976), or even comparing them to "garbage cans" of solutions waiting for the proper problem to solve (Cohen et al. 1972). Any of these theories might fruitfully be applied to a study of gangs, but Jankowski chose not to examine perspectives other than rational choice. One serious deficiency is his neglect of those theories that look at the relationship of the environment to organizational type.

For example, Jankowski's (1991) claim that gangs with loose organization fade away and only those with "tight structures" endure is inconsistent with contingency theory, one of the main strands of organizational thought. Lawrence and Lorsch (1969) point out that vertically structured organizations are better suited to stable environments, whereas more decentralized or loosely organized structures are more appropriate for dynamic environments. The main thesis of their classic work, *Organizations and Environments*, is that organizations do not perform well if their organizational structures do not fit the environment they face.

Overall, the environment where drug dealing takes place is as "dynamic" as anything in the organizational literature. The fear of police raids, customers who are erratically acting addicts, potentially violent competition from other dealers or gangs, surveillance by hostile neighbours, and uncertainty in maintaining supplies are everyday occurrences. The task of drug dealing is also far from routine. The fear of violence or arrest makes every sale risky and demands varying methods of getting supplies, bagging or cooking the cocaine, and safely delivering the goods to the house or corner salesman. Even the location where the product is sold might suddenly have to change.

John M. Hagedorn 1994 "Neighborhoods, markets, and gang drug organizations." *Journal of Research in Crime and Delinquency* 31, 3, 264-94, 267.

PASSAGE C

... Masciarotte (1991:90) analyses *Oprah Winfrey* in terms of the feminist debate over women's voices and empowerment, claiming that "talk shows afford women the political gesture of overcoming their alienation through talking about their particular experience as women in society." These commentators see the genre as offering more opportunities than dangers for the audience, countering the undermining of the authentic self which critical theorists see as the effect of the mass media. The genre draws on the ways in which feminism has "redefined the relationship between the public and the private," transforming the political towards a reliance on the "circulation of discursive practices [rather] than on formal political agendas" (Carpignano et al., 1990:51-2). Masciarotte concurs: "Oprah Winfrey is not a simulated self, and so a fetish for the endless lack of consumer desire, but a tool or a device of identity that organizes new antagonisms in the contemporary formations of democratic struggle" (Masciarotte, 1991:84).

Access and public participation genres are growing in number, spreading into prime-time as well as more marginal slots in the schedule. The operation of different interest groups who gain representation through these genres and the rules of engagement which regulate their interaction in a mass media public sphere have consequences for the public expression of women's experiences, for assumptions about rationality and for the gendering of social spaces (Benhabib, 1992) and social representation (Moscovici, 1984). Audience discussion programmes may be seen to act communicatively as a forum for the expression of multiple voices or subject positions, particularly because they confront members of powerful elites with the lived experience of ordinary people.

Sonia Livingstone 1994 "Watching talk: Gender and engagement in the viewing of audience discussion programmes." *Media, Culture and Society* 16, 429-47, 432-33.

6.5.2 Talking back, taking power

Talk shows. In Passage C above, in the last exercise, the talk show is talked about. It is said to be a site for

- transforming the political towards a reliance on the "circulation of discursive practices [rather] than on formal political agendas"
- the operation of different interest groups who gain representation through these genres and the rules of engagement which regulate their interaction in a mass media public sphere.

But does the talk show *talk back*? If it heard these scholarly abstractions, would it have anything to say? And if it *did* speak to those who research it, would those words be once again seized for defamiliarization and more abstraction? It seems that a Big Space, an irregular frontier, separates the language of the expert from the language of the objects of inquiry. What is in this Big Space? From one side of it, and according to Plain Language advocates concerned about readability, we might see only the thickets of impenetrable wordings that should be cleared away: thorny and forbidding growths of technical or abstract language. Yet further exploration could discover other features too: intersections of conspiring interests, currents of resistance, swarms of common sense tracking the uncommon sense of expertise.

In Chapter Five and in this chapter, we have considered the possibility that scholarly language is exclusionary: non-experts can't understand what experts are saying. (This is the thicket theory for explaining the Big Space.) Another way to investigate this possible exclusion is to ask whether there can be dialogue between researchers and those who are researched. While such exchange may be rare, it is not unheard-of. The researcher whose interpretation of folk stories in South India you read in Chapter Two includes in her report an account of subjects' resistance to her questioning. When she asks them to tell her local stories, they add what she calls a "performative message" by which they disavow their own answers to her questions.

> The performative message to which I refer, repeatedly expressed as a prologue to tales of sacred siblings, is typified by the statement, "Of course, you know that no one actually *believes* these stories."
>
> (Dempsey 1998:65)

The performative message could be seen as an attempt to *control the results* of the research, and *have a say* in how these stories are interpreted. Dempsey continues her discussion by telling a story of story-telling. One of her informants relates a tale of another Western visitor, one who appropriated "data" collected from her visit to Kerala (South India), and interpreted it in her own colonizing interests.

> The meaning behind this performative prologue that attempts to discredit sibling stories is no doubt varied. One significantly political layer of meaning was spelled out to me by an Orthodox Syrian middle-aged man who insisted he related a story of his own before acquiescing to tell the "silly stories" I wanted to hear.

His story of choice involved another young woman from New York, a missionary, who comes to visit Kerala for a short while. Upon return to New York she reports to her church authorities that the backward folk of Kerala are in need of her help. She describes traditional Malayali eating habits — in which people sit on the floor and scoop up food using bare hands and banana leaf "plates" — to convince them that these primitives indeed require domestication. As a result of her appeal, she is given the necessary funding to return. Aghast at this story, I assured Dr. Joseph that I was indeed appalled by this woman's audacity and, furthermore, by her complete misunderstanding of cultural differences. He thus kindly proceeded with the stories I had requested.

Although I was able to "convince" Dr. Joseph that I was indeed not one of those imperialistically ignorant foreigners about whom he reads in the newspaper, *I* was not completely convinced. Had his perceived divide between us really been diminished through my assurances and, related to this (and even more unsettling), was I entirely unlike the other irrefutably demeaning woman from New York who knew what was "best" for Keralites?

(Dempsey 1998:65)

Dr. Joseph *talks back* — Dempsey hears him, incorporating his rejoinder in her research report, and at the same time questions her own position as a researcher. Dempsey analyses this situation as a "turning (or twisting) [of] some of the ideological tables of the colonial project" (66). Her Keralite informants thought that her inquiries would privilege a "rational," empirical point of view — one which they took to be typical of Western researchers and which they expected would discount folk knowledge. To protect themselves from this critical gaze, they disavowed their own stories as "silly." Dempsey's project, however, was informed by current assumptions in ethnography and in fact valued the poetic and metaphoric aspects of folk knowledge. Her analysis of the "divide" suggests that parties on both sides of it (stereo)typify the "Other."

Sometimes, nowadays, informants can be identified as research collaborators or co-authors. This technique offers some representation for the Researched. Their words are not simply expropriated — carried off to the other side of the "divide" and hoarded by the research monopolists — but sort of "on loan" to the researcher. In his report on traditional ecological knowledge of beluga whales, Huntington (1999), for example, includes his indigenous informants collectively in the authorship of the article.

"Traditional Knowledge of the Ecology of Beluga Whales
(Delphinapterus leucas) in the Eastern Chukchi
and Northern Bering Seas, Alaska"

Henry P. Huntington and the Communities of Buckland,
Elim, Koyuk, Point Lay, and Shaktoolik

But the issues of appropriation are not entirely resolved by these means. In Chapter Three, we encountered a second treatment of TEK, in the form of an excerpt from Wenzel's (1999) discussion of TEK itself, and the political implications of its appearance in research reports. Speaking from a point of view which we can probably take as representative of some research positions, Wenzel identifies several matters which complicate the use of TEK. While he recognizes the trend toward identifying indigenous informants, he also notes that confidentiality can be impaired by these practices. (And we might ask, do informants really *want* to be identified with research projects? Could their donation of their names be only another form of compliance?) Moreover, Wenzel notes that, while "southern"(notice how, in discussions of Arctic research issues, "Western" is replaced by "southern" as the dominant position and colonizing ideology) conceptions of traditional (or "northern") knowledge tend to idealize it as belonging to the whole community, individual informants do have individual, private perspectives: one person's statements on land use, harvest, or resources should not be generalized to all (116). Reflecting on complaints that TEK is gathered "piece-meal," reported out of context, and thereby misinterpreted (any interpretation by a non-Inuit being a "misinterpretation"), he recommends more systematic use and study of TEK. (But here we might see a further colonizing, in that the abstraction *TEK* is itself a product of "southern" research practices.) While Wenzel acknowledges critiques of "southern" research practices, he maintains that scientists *have to* "interpret" data — that's their job. So he will not go so far as these other commentators whom he cites:

> Southerners come north, do their field research over a number of months, usually the summer, get to know people in the community, then go south and write and publish their findings. They are acknowledged as the "experts," more so if they have included Inuit in the data collection and can cite them in their research.
>
> (Flaherty 1995, cited in Wenzel 1999:118)

Inuit own intellectual property rights to their ecological knowledge, even if much of it has yet to be written down. No

researcher has the right to document or use Inuit knowledge
without Inuit permission. And, when their knowledge is recorded by outsiders, Inuit have the right to insist that it not be taken
out of context or misrepresented .... Inuit have the rights to own
and control access to their ecological knowledge. [...]
    Many Inuit view the extraction of their TEK from its broader
cultural context as a form of theft ....At best, piece-meal extrac-
tion of Inuit TEK ... invites misrepresentations and misinterpretation. At worst, it represents a form of misappropriation and cultural exploitation.

(Stevenson 1996, cited in Wenzel 1999:118-19)

Are these ethical issues purely abstract, remote from daily practicalities?
Not really, for the knowledge constructed by "experts" — "southern"
researchers in a variety of disciplines — contributes to the shape of
development in the north, and the social and material conditions of the
lives of its inhabitants. Along these lines, we might also ask how gener-
alizable are these positions taken by critics of "southern" research in the
Arctic: do the teenage mothers, for example, *own* their answers to the
standardized tests the way the Inuit are said to *own* their traditional
knowledge of the Arctic?
    Subjects *talk back* — and interrupt the scholarly conversation. Inuit
speakers break into the circles of "southern" science. They interrogate
or disavow this knowledge-making, suspicious of the relations between
knowledge and power. The ethnographic genres have been particularly
vulnerable to such interruption, as political reconfigurations in post-
colonial times have repositioned the "Other." Dara Culhane describes
developments in the discipline of anthropology:

    The post World War II growth in Aboriginal political strength has
    had a significant impact on anthropology. The contemporary gen-
    eration of anthropologists, having come of age in the same era,
    have had to come to terms with Indigenous critiques that have
    charged, and often proven by their own ethnographic endeav-
    ours, that many of the descriptions written by previous genera-
    tions of ethnographers were at best limited and partial, and at
    worst inaccurate and insulting .... The emerging recognition of
    the "native point of view" in anthropology and other disciplines,
    and of the right of Aboriginal people to represent themselves, is
    primarily a consequence of the ongoing struggle Aboriginal
    peoples have engaged in since the advent of colonialism. Many
    Aboriginal groups now demand significant participation in and

control of ethnographic research conducted among them, a process they identify as "the decolonisation of anthropology." (1998:129)

Culhane's observation appears in her study of judicial reasoning in Canada regarding aboriginal land claims — an occasion inviting reflection on knowledge and power, and the interanimation of discourses of research expertise, common sense, and public authority. None of these discourses, it turns out, is sealed, or silent to the others. I will conclude this section on the politics of knowledge by summarizing Culhane's work for the opportunity it offers to inspect complexities where these domains fold over one another.

Experts are cited…

Culhane's study focusses on the land claims of the Gitksan and Wet'suwet'en peoples of northern British Columbia, but situates the case in a larger context of comparable claims and argument in the twentieth century throughout the former British Empire and also the United States. In this context, precedents established a "social evolutionary" measure of the validity of land claims (67ff.). Produced by research of the times, and complicit with dominant interests, social evolutionary theories classified and ranked cultures according to their social and economic development. People belonging to a culture "below" a certain level were considered to lack the socio-political sensibility to understand land "title" and could not be said to "own land," only to be vaguely associated with it, by roaming in the vicinity, superficially. So, if someone from a "higher" level of social and economic development came by, and took over, the "lower" people would have no claim. As you might expect, the political culture which sponsored the theory — and its experts, and its supporting classifications — was lucky to be ranked "high" on the scale and thereby entitled. Looking back, we can see knowledge and power conspiring: clearly the research conversation overheard the political conversation and contributed statements to it.

…and speak to positions of power

Social evolutionary theories, however, were, over time, exposed to *back talk*: the objects of low classification contradicted the theoretical construct (as well as the research activities that substantiated it). When the Gitksan and Wet'suwet'en went to court in 1987, social evolutionary notions had been mainly discredited in scholarly circles.

Research subjects talk back…

But this is not the end of the story, for social evolutionary theory had also spoken to (dominant) "common sense" of the time, informed it and been informed by it. Common sense does not necessarily disappear once specialist research knowledge is revised. Enjoying an incalculable half-life, common sense endures, and continues to operate. Culhane cites cases in the last decades of the twentieth century — including the Gitksan and Wet'suwet'en case — where judges reverted in their deliberations to this common sense of "higher" and "lower" cultures, "more civilized" ones and "less civilized" ones. Moreover, research communities in the meantime offered another classification which concentrated the attention of the court. "Periodization" (194) — another expert construction — was called on to help answer crucial questions: where were the Gitksan and Wet'suwet'en and when? Whereas social evolutionary theory ranked aboriginal cultures in relation to the "high" standards set by colonizing cultures, periodization *located* aboriginal peoples in space and time according to the advent of Europeans. Locations of the Gitksan and Wet'suwet'en which could be determined before contact with Europeans were *prehistoric*; those determinable in periods when European influence was experienced indirectly were *protohistoric*; those determinable from records produced by Europeans who were in direct contact with (in this case) the Gitksan and Wet'suwet'en were *historic*. Now, we might notice here, where experts and courts alike

…but common sense prevails

New expertise is cited

Knowledge is constructed from a limited position...

limitations are overruled...

...by the commonsense notions of "fact" and "objectivity"

are far away from moments and conditions they seek to define, that *any* statement about sites of occupation — and title — comes from a position of limited knowledge.

Even those statements deriving from "historic" records must be interpretations of those records, which were produced for different purposes, in different contexts, and informed by different interests. The language of research is designed — as we have seen — to inscribe statements for their *limitations*. In fact expertise — specialist knowledge — manifests itself through the management and articulation of those limitations. But in the courtroom, as Culhane shows, the limitations took a different meaning. The judge seized on them and, in his reasons for judgement, rejected the inferences drawn by experts called by the Gitksan and Wet'suwet'en, especially identifying oral history as unreliable — preferring the inferences drawn by Crown witnesses from other sources, although these were also obviously limited. While oral histories have themselves been both ratified and challenged in scholarly discussions, the court's reasoning in rejecting them in this case seems based on a naïve notion of scholarship. Like a judge in an earlier case which Culhane analyses, who found that experts testifying on behalf of aboriginal plaintiffs failed to live up to an ideal of "the uninvolved scientist" (94), this one also found experts called by the Gitksan and Wet'suwet'en — those who, that is, listened to subjects of ethnography *talk back* — "more advocate than witness" (McEachern 1991, *Reasons for Judgement, Delgamuukw v. R.*, cited in Culhane 272). The judge substantiated his finding by citing the "statement of ethics of the American Anthropological Association," which declares anthropologists' responsibility to "those [they study]." In other words, the discipline's own measures for ensuring the validity and correcting the bias of its knowledge-making procedures become grounds for, as Culhane says, the court's "absolute power to arbitrarily interpret and evaluate expert evidence according to its own rules, at its pleasure" (341). Evidence from the Crown's main witness, however, was recognized by the judge, even though her statements also issued from a position of limited knowledge, and were, as Culhane points out, "highly theoretical" (275).

The cited expert speaks, again, to positions of power

In their stylistic refinements, the research genres monitor speakers' participation in knowledge-making conversations, and they limit the extent and recognize the contingency of statements. Some research genres even provide for *back talk*, further refining their knowledge claims and respecting the contingencies of position. Yet, when expert statements are cited outside scholarly contexts, they come into dialogic contact with other discourses — and they take their chances. When we ask the scholarly community — *is it safe to eat this food? Will there be an earthquake? What will happen if the minimum wage is increased? What kind of people commit crimes? Have the Gitksan and Wet'suwet'en occupied this territory since time immemorial?* — what are the outcomes of our query?

6.6 Constructing ethnographic topics

The preceding sections have focussed on social and political complications of expert knowledge, and, particularly, the relations between inquiring experts and groups inquired into. While all research genres map zones of expertise which make strangers of non-experts, the ethnographic genres are especially likely to dramatize the relations between research communities and other social sectors. We (and others) ask, where do ethnographers stand in relation to the people they study? Are their interests located with the site of inquiry? Or elsewhere, with other positions? How does the style of ethnography itself represent the researcher's position?

This section and following ones also focus on the ethnographer's position, but in more practical, working terms: how does the ethnographer turn a classroom or an RV park or a gang's hangout into a research site? How do teen readers of romance fiction or prison inmates studying French or people watching *Oprah* become objects of scholarly interest?

One step in this transformation of everyday sites into research sites is a process we are already familiar with: a scholarly abstraction enters the picture. So, the researchers who investigated the customs of RVers invoke *community* and *social change*, citing these high-level abstractions from contexts of scholarly conversation.

> There is a concern that social change has resulted in the destruction of community in contemporary North America (Bender 1978:4). For instance, Bellah et al. argue that although North Americans value mobility and privacy, these values "rob us" of "opportunities to get to know each other at a reasonably intimate level in casual, unforced circumstances" (1985:135). North Americans' high regard for these values have, in other words, robbed them of a sense of belonging — of a sense of community. If this is true, we would expect RVers, who choose their lifestyle at least partially *for* its mobility, to be isolated, lonely people who have difficulty in establishing a network or a community to help them cope with crisis. Such is not the case.
>
> (Counts and Counts 1992:154-55, emphasis in original)

An ethnographic study of the behaviours and routines of workers and clients in a credit union invokes *literacy*, and people's functioning in "modern society":

> During the last decade there has been a good deal of public outcry over the problem of literacy skills. In particular, this discussion has come to focus on the literacy skills individuals must possess in order to function in modern society. This competence, known as *functional literacy* (cf. Pattison 1982), entails skilled interaction with such materials as apartment leases, job applications, and product instructions. Many have argued that the unintelligibility of these written materials has contributed significantly to the absence of literacy.
>
> Deborah Keller-Cohen 1987 "Literate practices in a modern credit union." *Language in Society* 15, 7-24, 7.

The ethnographic study of readers of teen romance fiction summons *ideological struggles, social control, social identities; gender, class, ethnic, age, and sexual identities*:

> An important theme in this volume is the cultural role played by written texts in ongoing and ideological struggles for students'

hearts and minds. School texts have often been a mode of social control through the "selective tradition" contained within their pages, which elevates the stories of powerful groups to the level of canon. However, students are not some tabula rasa upon which the text inscribes their social identities. Rather, students approach texts from the position of their previously acquired gender, class, ethnic, age, and sexual identities.

Linda K. Christian-Smith 1991 "Readers, texts, and contexts: Adolescent romance fiction in schools." In *The Politics of the Textbook*, ed. Michael W. Apple and Linda K. Christian-Smith. New York: Routledge, 191-212, 191.

Like those we have observed in other introductions, these abstractions come with a reputation: they are recognized topics in the research community. They have been addressed before, and the current writers cite instances from other research publications. The investigators of RVers' ways report the statements of other commentators on community; the writer who researched the practices of a credit union attributes statements about literacy to other researchers. And even here, where the invoked abstraction — *racism* — is so compelling as to warrant an opening generality unsecured by citation, the authors soon turn to reported statements.

> To combat racism it is necessary to understand its complex features and underlying themes. In Britain it has recently been argued that such understanding is lacking in many anti-racism strategies (see Gilroy 1990; Rattansi 1992).
>
> (Verkuyten et al. 1994: 253)

This example also shows ethnographers — like researchers using other techniques of inquiry — establishing a knowledge deficit: there is something we need to understand; and this understanding is "lacking." The rest of this first introductory paragraph goes on to weave together the dominant abstractions *racism* and *anti-racism*, the statements of others, and persistent gestures toward the gap in our knowledge.

> Anti-racist understanding of racist thinking is not very sophisticated. Cohen (1992), for instance, typifies anti-racism as the disavowal of complexity for the sake of pursuing moral certainties. Anti-racism appears to be lacking in effectiveness because of its doctrinaire form and its lack of powerful arguments which go beyond a moral appeal to tolerance. What seems to be required is

a more complex understanding of the nature of racism and critical reflection on the ideas and approaches used in anti-racist work.

(Verkuyten et al. 1994:253)

Like other researchers, ethnographers sketch a map of existing knowledge, showing routes currently under construction, and desirable destinations not yet reached. In the sample above, the mapping of knowledge begins to turn several evenings of conversation among people living in Rotterdam into a research site, and a matter of scholarly interest.

Sometimes the statement of a knowledge deficit can be as brief and decisive as the traditional anthropologist saying, "No one has written about this faraway island before." For instance, after explaining that her work "falls into the tradition of narrative inquiry," the writer who investigates prison inmates studying French points to the as-yet unvisited spot she will journey to:

> Although not labeled as such, narrative inquiry probably accounted for *Life in Classrooms* (Jackson 1968). This portrait of schools serves as a benchmark in educational research. Ethnographic studies have also examined life in jail (Spradley 1979, 1980). No studies, however, have examined the interactions of these two institutions — school and prisons — and that is the intent of this research.
>
> Ann Masters Salomone 1994 "French behind bars: A qualitative and quantitative examination of college French training in prison." *The Modern Language Journal* 78, 1, 76-84, 77.

Student writers could feel wary about making such a claim about the state of knowledge — "*no* studies ..." But they can take a position nevertheless by pointing to the *limits* of other, related research. So, for example, in establishing a knowledge deficit that will be filled by a study of undergraduates' in-class note-taking, a student writer might offer a summary of Heath's *Ways with Words* (1983), invoking abstractions like *literate practice*, and then show a route not taken by Heath.

> While Heath's account of each community's use of written aids to memory provides some basis for speculating on differences between men and women in this literate practice, she neither collected nor analyzed her data with a view to illuminating gender distinctions. This study explores a comparable literate practice — in-class note-taking — with the specific intention of discovering whether some of the gender differences we glimpse in Heath's work show up in other settings.

Equally, once the scholarly abstraction is established, the student writer may be able to secure it by reporting statements of as few as one or two other writers. While the authors of theses and honours essays will need a much denser network of published voices to invoke the community of knowledge-producers, the writer of an assignment such as the one to which these sections are leading can take a scholarly position by reporting the statements of one or two others.

6.6.1 Representing ethnographic method and background

Ethnographers can spend weeks or months or even years amongst the people they are observing. In the reports of their research, they represent these periods of their lives in terms which focus on the experience as a research activity. So, under the heading "Research Methods and Sources of Data," the investigator of "Neighbourhoods, markets, and gang drug organization" identifies himself as a researcher, outlines the research relationship between himself and his objects of study, and defines part of that research population in terms he takes to be relevant to the current topic.

> The interpretations presented here draw on observations and extensive field work over a number of years, specifically on data from studies in 1987 and in 1992. During the early 1980s, the author directed the first gang diversion program in the city and became acquainted with many leaders and other founders of Milwaukee's gangs. He has maintained a privileged relationship with many of them during subsequent years. The confidential interviews in this most recent study were conducted in late 1992 and early 1993. As in the original study, the research follows a collaborative model (cf. Moore 1978), in which gang members cooperate with academic staff to focus the research design, construct interview schedules, conduct interviews with their homeboys, and interpret findings.
>
> As part of our current study, we conducted 3-hour interviews with 101 founding members of 18 gangs: 90 were male and 11 female; 60% were African American, 37% Latino, and 3% White. Their median age was 26 years, with three quarters between 23 and 30 years old.
>
> (Hagedorn 1994: 269)

Reading between the lines, we might catch sight of enduring and complicated relationships — and the routes of personal and professional life that led this researcher into the midst of gangs and drug dealing. But, on the surface, these matters are reduced, deleted, or transformed into a subject position constituted from research practice. (Even the *discursive I* is transformed into "the author"/ "he.") Agentless expressions —

I observed	"observation"
I interpreted	"interpretation"
I worked extensively in the field	"extensive field work"
I conducted interviews	"interviews ... were conducted"

— turn the spotlight on the research activity rather than on the researcher, whose role is assumed rather than asserted. While both researchers and research objects are typified ("academic staff," "gang members"), there is more classifying information about the latter than about the former: although we know the principal researcher is male, we don't know his age or his ethnic category.

At the same time, however, this researcher's subject position is refined by mention of a "collaborative model": a set-up which invites the objects of knowledge to take part in the making of knowledge. Such a model replies to the post-colonial criticisms of ethnography, which would be suspicious of a research project investigating non-"White" people who were poor.

Exercise
Here are three samples of method sections in ethnography, showing a range of representations of ethnographic method. Compare the rhetorical and stylistic features of these passages: that is, how do these convince readers that the researchers' methods produce reliable knowledge? At the same time, you might consider political implications which could arise from these techniques of inquiry.

PASSAGE A
Research Method
Our field research on RVers was conducted between October 1 and December 15, 1990. Our goals were to interview as many different kinds of retired RVers as possible and to focus on Canadians travelling in the United States. We attempted to live and be like the people we wished to study. Our age and

---

appearance facilitated this (we did not alienate potential informants by our youth, a problem encountered by some researchers attempting to work in retirement communities; see Streib, Folts and LaGreca 1984). We rented a 12-year-old, 25-foot Prowler trailer and pulled it from British Columbia to the U.S. southwest with an aging van. We stayed in private and public RV parks in British Columbia, Nevada, Arizona and California. We boondocked on U.S. Bureau of Land Managment (BLM) land in the southwestern desert and (with hundreds of others) we trespassed on an abandoned World War II Army training base — popularly known as The Slabs or Slab City — near Niland, California. We slept overnight in private parks, in public campgrounds, in roadside rest areas and in the parking lots of truck stops. In short, for two-and-one-half months we became RVers.

We conducted 50 interviews with retired RVers, some who were singles and others who were couples. Of our interviews, 34 were with full-timers and 16 were with part-timers; 25 were with Americans, 24 with Canadians and 1 was with a British couple. Of the 24 Canadians, 16 were full-timers, while 18 of the 25 Americans were full-timers. We were able to ascertain the ages of 81 of our informants: 2 of these (both women married to older men) were in their 40s, 13 were in their 50s, 45 in their 60s, 19 in their 70s and 2 in their 80s. Our youngest informant was 46, the oldest 86.

We followed an interview guide and asked everyone the same questions, although not necessarily in the same order (also see Kaufman 1986:22-23). We did not tape our conversations, which were informal and intended to encourage people to talk in a relaxed context about what was important to them. Some of our informants were curious about our project and asked us as many questions as we asked them; others seemed delighted to find an audience interested in RVing and talked with enthusiasm about their RVing experiences. Some of the interviews were brief, lasting only an hour or so. Others lasted for hours over several days. People were interested in our research and most were extremely co-operative and helpful. Many spoke of a need for the general population to know more about RVing and some hoped that wider exposure would dispel a lingering stereotype of RVers as "trailer trash." Others labelled themselves as trailer trash or "trailerites," with irony and fierce pride, as if daring the world to despise them. A number of people said they had thought about writing a book on RVing themselves. Some brought us magazine articles relevant to our research; others introduced us to people whose stories they thought we should hear; and some sought us out to discuss the advantages of RV retirement. One couple even led us to a park 45 miles from where we and they were camped to show us where we could find Canadian boondockers.

We initially intended to supplement interviews with a questionnaire asking about age, former occupation, estimated income before and after retirement, length of time retired, type of RV selected, etc. Many people were suspicious of the questionnaire and resisted it. Some flatly refused to fill it out. Others declined to answer particular questions — especially the ones about income: "I forget," we were told .... [One] couple commented that they did not mind answering questions in conversation because this made us all equals and they could ask *us* questions too. They would, however, respond to a questionnaire either by throwing it away or by lying. And one man, when asked to fill out a questionnaire, inquired "Are you going to ask me if I eat dog food?" In his experience, he said, this was the sort of question asked by people who pass out questionnaires. We abandoned the questionnaire after two weeks.

(Counts and Counts 1992:156-67)

PASSAGE B
Analyzing the audience of audience discussion programmes
Sources of data concerning audience reception
The empirical research reported in this article is based on a multi-method project on audience discussion programmes which consisted of twelve focus group discussions following viewing of an audience discussion programme, a series of individual in-depth interviews with viewers and programme participants, and a survey questionnaire from some 500 respondents from a diary panel. Each was considered in conjunction with textual analysis of a wide range of audience discussion programmes (see Livingstone and Lunt 1994a for details). These diverse sources of audience reception data are

analyzed specifically in relation to gender for the present paper. Methodologically, the intention is for these different kinds of data to support one another, trading off considerations of sampling and interpretive validity to arrive at a multi-faceted picture of audience reception for the genre.

(Livingstone 1994: 433)

PASSAGE C

Triangulation of data to support the narrative was achieved by collecting information in several ways: my daily journal, college inmate-student evaluation instruments, the inmate-student newspaper, informal conversations with inmate students, and inmate-students' written work.

(Salomone 1994:77)

Sometimes the representation of method calls for an account of **background** — a description of the observed group's social and/or physical context, their habitat. Background seems to be somewhat discretionary in ethnography. Sometimes researchers leave it out; sometimes they figure it is relevant. And the grounds for this estimate of relevance can stay submerged, or tacit. For example, here, where the ethnographer of credit-union practices combines background and method, it is hard to say what is significant about staff reductions: how are we to see this circumstance in light of the larger topic of *literacy* or *literate practice* and in light of later findings regarding the use of documents?

At the time of this study, the membership of the credit union was approximately 15,000 and was drawn from three institutions: a large midwestern state university, a community college, and a nonprofit research concern. Slightly more than 50 percent of the credit union's membership were nonacademic employees (e.g., trade, technical, clerical). The proportion of nonacademic members was great among borrowers of CU funds, where they comprised two-thirds of that group. Initially, the target site had thirty-three full-time and eleven part-time employees. Due to rising costs, staff size was trimmed to twenty-four full-time and eleven part-time employees during the period in which the data were collected. Over the bulk of the project, there were five major departments in this credit union: Loans (including Collections), Office, Operations, Education/Marketing, and Accounting.

(Keller-Cohen 1987:9)

We saw in Chapter Five that method sections can depart from the rule of dominating (or domineering) coherence in the research genres, and background sections of ethnography also seem exempt from the strictest patterns of connectedness and relevance. The account of background doesn't have to openly demonstrate its relevance to other sections or to higher-level abstractions that control the discussion. So the writer who tells about inmates learning French also tells about where they live —

> *The institution.* Originally built for half as many prisoners as it now holds, this medium security prison suffers from overcrowding to perhaps a dangerous extent. Housed in red brick buildings over fifty years old, inmates sometimes have their sleeping quarters in hallways. The men are "counted" six times a day at approximately three-hour intervals. They eat in a common dining hall, have movies once a week, and engage in organized sports. Educational programs are available to qualified inmates: a General Education Development (GED) program serves those working toward a High School Equivalency Certificate; a college program leads to Bachelor of Arts, Bachelor of General Studies, and Bachelor of Science degrees.
>
> (Salomone 1994:77)

— although it is not clear how these statements are to be interpreted in relation to the study's overall findings and concerns: the transferability of established foreign-language-teaching techniques to prisons. Moreover, if we looked for the kind of tight, local connectedness typical of most research writing, we would come up with uncertain results: what, exactly, does being "'counted'" have to do with once-a-week movies, or Bachelor's degrees? What is the gist of this paragraph?

Sometimes, background sections make a more explicit point, as here where the neighbourhoods of Milwaukee gangs are described under a heading which itself interprets statements about the habitat of the observed social group:

Background: Gangs And Decreased Legitimate Opportunities

Before we look at variation between neighborhoods, we need to briefly sketch the background for the growth of Milwaukee gang drug sales in the mid- to late 1980s. Economic conditions deteriorated in Milwaukee during that time. Manufacturing jobs declined precipitously in the 1979-83 recession and did not ever completely recover. During the 1980s, Milwaukee lost 19% of its manufacturing job base (McMahon, Moots, and White 1992). Of the large firms that paid high wages and where many minorities had been hired (Trotter 1985), 37% were shut down. The Milwaukee area lost 42,000 manufacturing jobs while gaining 100,000 service jobs. The majority of all metropolitan jobs are now located in the suburbs, accelerating spatial mismatch of Milwaukee's "hyper-segregated" minority population with new jobs (Kasarda 1985).

These trends hit Milwaukee central city neighborhoods especially hard, with 1990 African American male unemployment rates exceeding 45% (Rose, Edari, Quinn, and Pawasarat 1992) compared to less than 3.7% of all area workers. As African American and other youths who founded Milwaukee's gangs in the early 1980s reached adulthood, they found few good-paying jobs (Hagedorn 1988). Most of the founders of Milwaukee gangs bobbed in and out of conventional employment and periodically sold cocaine as a means of survival (Hagedorn 1994). But there were major differences between neighborhoods in the organizational form of gang cocaine sales as well as the rise and fall of a notorious citywide drug gang. We will begin our examination of variation in gang drug organization by examining Milwaukee's infamous "Citywide Drug Gang."

(Hagedorn 1994:271)

In this example, background is organized to demonstrate its relevance to the study's concerns, and it would not be hard to construct the gist of these paragraphs. But, on the whole, statements in background and method sections are under much less pressure to maintain connectedness than other sections of the research genres. Some have suggested that the list-like quality of method sections is a sign of readers' assumed familiarity with research practice: they can fill in the missing parts with their background knowledge of research routines. (And to explain too much would spoil the effect of scholarly solidarity on knowledge-making techniques.) Perhaps something similar could be said for background sections. Reading a list-like set of statements about a prison, or an urban community in economic decline, or a financial institution, we fill in the gaps for ourselves, from our knowledge of the world, and get an implicit or tacit feeling rather than explicit propositions about the research population's habitat.

Besides this tendency to list-like flatness, background sections, and other parts of ethnography, can have the effect of making the familiar strange, and unfamiliar — an effect something like that which comes of transforming "potluck dinner" into "food-sharing ritual." So Shirley Brice Heath's ethnography of "ways with words" in two communities includes this account of a living room, attending to the elements of this cultural space as carefully as if they were a remote people's ritual artefacts:

> The screen door on the front porch of this first house on the street opens into a living room filled with showroom-like matching furniture: a suite of sofa and chairs, two end tables, and a coffee table fill the small room as they once did the display window of the furniture store. There have been a few additions: starched stand-up doilies encircle the bases of end table lamps, ashtrays, and vases. Flat crocheted doilies cover the arms of the chairs and sofa and the headrest position of the chairs. A hand-crocheted afghan in the suite's colors is thrown over the back of the sofa. A huge doily of four layers, and a large vase of plastic flowers top the television set. The wooden floor is covered with a large twist rug, and several small matching scatter rugs mark the path to the hall which leads to the bedroom and kitchen.
>
> Shirley Brice Heath 1983 *Ways with Words: Language, Life, and Work in Communities and Classrooms.* Cambridge UP, 30-31.

Or the ethnography of literate practices in a credit union can make familiar occasions (going to the bank) seem new and somewhat unfamiliar:

> At the time this research project began, the money machine service was a relatively new one at the credit union ....The money machine document was presented to new members at the time they enrolled for services at the credit union. The document has two parts: a single page application (3.5" x 8") to use the automated teller and a ten-page foldout section (of equal paper size) describing the rights and obligations of a money machine user. In order to use the money machine you need only fill out the application; it is not necessary to read the agreement .... Many mem-

bers left the agreement on the Coordinator's desk when the application procedure was complete. Some gave it a perfunctory treatment — picking it up, turning it over, and placing it back down on the desk.

(Keller-Cohen 1987:18)

Defamiliarization can also overturn the brand names that direct our attention as we regard the marketplaces of our everyday experience. So a *Tastee-Freeze* might become a "roadside shop offering iced confections and grilled meats with condiments." Released from its accustomed associations, the Tastee-Freeze could now be compared with roadside shops world-wide and exotic, in Goa or Beijing or Costa Rica.

Perhaps this defamiliarization is the modern descendant of ways of writing which got their authority from describing the truly unfamiliar — ways and customs of people remote from the European societies which used the early ethnographic genres. Perhaps, in now applying this technique closer to home, modern ethnographers inherit some of that authority.

Exercise
(1) Here is a chance to try the defamiliarizing techniques of modern ethnography. Suppose you are writing an ethnography of routines of speaking (or not speaking) in food markets in the area where you live. Write a "background" section to account for the context of these uses of language.

(2) If you were to conduct such a study, what techniques of inquiry could you use? Describe those techniques in ways comparable to the method sections we have examined. One more such section follows, combining method and background, and showing one way of representing research method.

The Research Context
During an eight-month period in 1985-86, I studied teen romance-fiction readers in three schools in a large American midwestern city that I will call "Lakeview." Once dominated by the automobile, farm-equipment, and alcoholic-beverage industries, the economic crisis of the late 1970s left its imprint on the city and surrounding communities. Plant closings have transformed Lakeview from a smokestack city to

---

one of empty factories and glittering strip malls. Most new businesses are in the service sector, such as fast-food and insurance companies, and employ the bulk of the working- and middle-class women and men in Lakeview.

Lakeview School District is a large district that draws students from the inner city and some of the outlying areas that were annexed to the city thirty years ago. My sites of research were Jefferson Middle School and Sherwood Park Middle School, two outlying 7–8 schools, and Kominsky Junior High School, an inner city 7–9 school. At the time of the study, Lakeview was in the process of converting the junior high schools into middle schools. Jefferson and Sherwood Park each had about three hundred students. Sherwood Park's student population was mostly White. Like Sherwood Park, Jefferson was predominantly White, but had three Chinese students as well. Kominsky's 700+ student body was about one-half White, one-quarter each Black and Hispanic, with a small Vietnamese and Asian Indian population. Both Jefferson and Sherwood Park split their students into three tracks (low, medium, and high) for reading instruction. Reading placements were based on the results of the following: district-wide and individual-school standardized reading test scores, teacher recommendation, and students' previous grades. Kominsky and Sherwood Park also had an additional reading support service through the federally funded Chapter I program, which enrolled one-half and one-quarter, respectively, of their students.

In order to study readers and their romance novels I used a variety of methods combining ethnography with survey research. An initial sample of seventy-five young women from the three schools was assembled through interviews with teachers and librarians regarding who were heavy romance-fiction readers and by personal examination of school and classroom library checkout cards and bookclub order forms. A reading survey was given to all seventy-five young women. From this survey, I was able to identify the heaviest romance-fiction readers, some twenty-nine young women, whom I interviewed individually and in small group settings. These twenty-nine young women had five teachers for reading in the three schools. I observed these classes and interviewed the teachers. This chapter stems from the written reading survey of the seventy-five young women, and from observation of and interviews with the twenty-nine young women and their five teachers.

(Christian-Smith 1991:194)

(3) Again, if you were to conduct a study of routines of speaking in food markets, what abstractions could you invoke to begin the transformation of everyday, "commonsense" experience into an object of scholarly interest?

The researchers whose writings we have examined report having spent quite long periods observing the group targeted for study. Student writers are not likely to be able to spend so much time collecting data. But their representations of method can nevertheless construct an equally scholarly position. By specifying the ways data were collected (interviews, questionnaires, observation, analysis of documents) and recorded (by hand in notebooks, for example, or by audiotape), and specifying the number and duration of research episodes (two one-hour periods of observation, for example, or a half-hour interview with each of three informants), and by typifying the research population and setting (shoppers in a large retail food outlet catering to a suburban neighbourhood in a Canadian metropolitan area of 2.3 million), student writers can establish as valid the sources of the knowledge they have made about the social group they have studied. A properly designed and managed "method" and "background" can transform your real-life, commonsense, everyday experience — as a shopper — into a research project that produces well-grounded research knowledge.

6.6.2 Interpreting ethnographic data

Months and years (or even just hours) spent observing people's ways and talking to them about their ways can produce a lot of material, some of it recorded, and some of it stored in memory. And this material is not only plentiful; it is also waiting to be transformed from its everyday, "common sense" forms, as it originally occurred, into the "uncommon sense" forms of scholarly writing. So the ethnographer of the credit union had to convert the documents, routines, and values of the credit-union community into forms other than those in which she had originally experienced them.

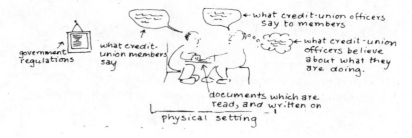

Some aspects of the ethnographer's experience — her research activities and the research population's habitat — have already been converted in method and background sections. These sections begin to reorganize and segment experience, and further operations continue that reorganization and segmentation. Although some ethnography adopts a narrative form, telling the story of the researcher's encounters with the research population, most ethnography *partitions* experience, dividing its specifics into segments and naming their gist with a high-level abstraction. So, the results of a year and a half of observing activities in a credit union produce these abstractions, which *interpret* the data in terms relevant to the topic: "literate practices" and the limits on or opportunities for communication that arise from them:

LITERATE PRACTICES: INSTITUTIONAL
Characteristics of document availability
The structure of interactions
Attitudes and beliefs
    Compliance versus membership size
    Efficiency
    Consultative aids
    Conflicting views

LITERATE PRACTICES: CREDIT UNION
MEMBERS' DISCUSSION

Evenings of discussion among eleven residents of Rotterdam are reorganized under a series of headings which pick out abstractions which the authors argue are entertained by *both* anti-racist *and* racist talk.

Equality: Equal treatment
                Equal opportunities
   Merit
   Rights
   Freedom
   Rationality

Two and a half months of life on the road with RVers produce abstractions which, serving as headings for sections presenting results of the study, interpret details:

   Equality, Community and the Good Life
   Community and Reciprocity
      Exchange of Personal History
         Ritual Sharing of Food
         Community, Space and Place
         RVers and the Problem of Limited Space

In the study of working-class male offenders' ways of representing their crimes, the researchers analysed the findings under headings some of which cite the subjects' own words —

   'We're meant to be criminals, but they're the biggest criminals'
   Men as family breadwinners
   It's 'time to build your own lifeboat'
   'Robin Hood, Robin Hood ...' [sung]

— although the "Discussion" section interprets the findings in abstractions which the subjects would probably not use. For example:

> ... in their discussion of the relationship between unemployment and **economic crime** generally, the men in this study justified involvement in economic crime, drawing upon **dominant** and, the authors would argue, **gendered patterns of discourse**.
>
> (Willot and Griffin 1999:456, emphasis added)

All these sets of interpretive headings (introducing abstractions which in turn control the lower level material which follows) are the products of operations which up-root information from its narrative sequence —

> The first place we went was in Oregon. When we were setting up, a woman named Vanessa came over and invited us to potluck.

We told her what we were doing and arranged to interview her. She told us that some people have very expensive RVs and stay in private camps with many restrictions. She showed us her photo album.

— and reorganize it into interpretive orders characteristic of scholarly writing. The reordering establishes the hierarchical structures of generality which we have identified as characteristic of the research genres.

So a moment with Vanessa, or a particular utterance on a Rotterdam evening, doesn't *disappear*, but, rather, withdraws to re-emerge in a characteristically interpretive and hierarchical structure. Accordingly, the passage below establishes abstract concerns — *rite of passage* and *community* — in generalizing about RVers' custom of divesting themselves of their belongings, and then descends to a specific case and a particular moment of the research project.

> Giving up home and possessions is a rite of passage, especially for full-time RVers. Those who have done it share a unique experience that sets them apart, even from other RVers, and creates among them a sense of community. As onlookers we witnessed, but could not participate in, the comradeship shared by full-timers as they swapped stories about how they decided to give up their homes, how they established priorities in determining which of their possessions to keep and the difficulties of actually carrying through with their decision. Most full-timers said they spent a long time deciding to do it and many took several years and more than one start before they completed the process. As Randy expressed it:
>
>> People who want to go full-time have a set of problems. The first is letting go of their house. You can't have a nest. You must strip your belongings down to the bare essentials and get rid of the rest. You can't take a lot of things with you. Too many people try to hang onto their house and rent it out. Renters tear the place up and they lose their shirts. I tell them, "Give it up and sell."
>
> (Counts and Counts 1992:176)

Notice that we don't know *when* "Randy" said what he is reported to have said. Although this passage occurs near the conclusion, the researchers may have met Randy on their first day on the road. Converting two and a half months of travel to a research document, the writers re-order time.

Similarly, the remarks of some young women talking about characters in a teen romance are excerpted from the researcher's eight-month experience amongst them, and re-introduced under the heading "Creating and Pondering Femininity." Then they become elements relevant to the abstractions "reading practices" and gender and "social identities":

> Although readers' life experiences are important in constructing meaning when reading, the text still exerts a measure of control over those meanings. In this regard, Iser claims that the text's control happens through "blanks" or gaps in the text. Many times the threads of the plot are suddenly broken off, as happens between chapters. Or they continue in unexpected directions. These textual features prompt readers to "read between the lines." The blanks call for combining what has been previously read with readers' own life experiences and expectations. Although teen romance novels are not characterized by many unexpected twists and turns, they nevertheless require a certain amount of constitutive activity on the part of readers. When female readers encounter blanks in romance texts that involve matters of femininity, two things occur. Readers are offered models of femininity, but are also given opportunities to think about femininity. I will exemplify this dynamic by recounting the readings by three young women of Marshall's *Against the Odds*.

★ ★ ★

Annie filled the blanks in this manner:

A: It was fun trying to figure out what Trina and the other girls would do to get back at those boys. I thought that they would sneak into the boys' locker room and do something to their sports equipment. Marsha had the guts to do something like that.

LKCS: Was that something you might have done?

A: Are you kidding? No way! I'd never have the guts. Well, you'd have to do something, that's for sure. Hmm, I'd probably start a rumor about the guys or every time me and my friends would see them we would make like we were talking about them. They can't stand that!

Marcy's responses to the same passage also set up a conflict between who she is and who she would like to be:

M: I figured Trina and Laurie would come up with something fantastic. I never thought in a million years that they would stuff confetti drenched in cheap perfume into the boys' lockers.

LKCS: Would you do that, get even in this way?

M: Well, I'd like to do something like that, to get even with some of the boys in my math class who are real pains. But I'd get chicken and probably just fume.

LKCS: Can you tell me more?

M: It's kinda difficult, I mean, well, I guess I don't want to be seen as a girl who's too pushy with boys. You have to be careful about that. But then you can't let boys push you around. I don't know.
(Christian-Smith 1991:202-03)

The paragraph which follows the sections of transcript goes on to convert them to research knowledge by deeply interpreting the young women's remarks in abstract terms valued by the scholarly community: "reader-text-context relations," "femininity," "gender tensions" (203). When research subjects' words are released from their original context and place-in-time, they enter into exchange with the abstractions of research reasoning.

Ethnographers' "Conclusions" sections recombine the abstractions which have interpreted the data or re-ordered experience.

Conclusion

In her discussion of the Gabra of Kenya, Prussin observes that the repetition of fixed spatial pattern reinforces the cognitive structure of interior space for nomads (1989). We would take this further and argue that when RV nomads set up at a new site, their repetition of spatial patterns reinvents and reinforces their cognitive structure of home, society and community. Although RVers carry with them the form of their social structure, the form is empty. Because they share no history with their RV neighbours, there is no one to fill the status of "neighbour," "friend" or "family," but the ideal content of these forms is shared knowledge. Therefore, when a newcomer pulls in, the strangers who are instant neighbours immediately begin to perform the roles of friend and family by sharing substance and labour. They help the newcomer set up, bring food, give advice and exchange information and personal history. This sharing and exchange allows RVers, who have no common past, to recreate the structure of history from one park to another and to embed themselves in a familiar social structure given substance. Like the Gabra, their reconstruction of history and society enables them to insulate themselves from a hostile environment — the "Crazies" out there — and to transform the stranger who might "rip you off" into the friend who will look after you in your time of need.

(Counts and Counts 1992:179)

And before going on to speculate on the implications of their findings for developing effective strategies against racism ("how prejudice and racism should be approached in an old inner-city centre"), the researchers who observed evening discussions in Rotterdam recombine and confirm the interpretations that were expressed in the ordering abstractions:

Conclusions

We have tried to show that there are basic principles which are being shared and used in an anti-racist as well as in a more racist discourse. Notions such as equality, freedom, human rights and rationality are used by Dutch local residents in their daily thinking and arguing about ethnic minorities living in the same inner-city quarter. In the discussions these principles are acknowledged and used by all participants: those who present themselves as anti-racists as well as those who describe themselves as racists.

(Verkuyten et al. 1994:265)

6.7 Assignment: ethnography

Finding a research site

Ethnography involves researchers in the lives of others — sometimes marginally, sometimes deeply. We have discussed political implications which follow from this involvement. In developing an ethnographic project, you will have to take account of the politics of the position you assume in relation to the people and situations you observe, monitoring the transformations which turn them into objects of knowledge.

At the same time as ethnography intervenes in the lives of others, it also calls on ethnographers themselves to consult their own lives and experience for possible research sites. Although ethnographic style can conceal the personal connections between the researcher and the research site, it is often the designs of life itself that destine a researcher to investigate one site rather than another. Was the "modern credit union" Deborah Keller-Cohen's own bank? Did she notice how a bank official explained a loan agreement to her, and decide there was something there worth investigating? Did she have a friend working at the bank? Did Dorothy Counts and David Counts know some people who sold their home, divested themselves of their possessions, and set out to roam the American interstates? Did their friends suggest the research itinerary? Or were the Counts planning a trip anyway? Both Ann Salomone and John Hagedorn had jobs that led them to the situations that became the sites of their research: Salomone taught French in a prison; Hagedorn directed an inner-city social program.

In choosing a site for your research, examine your daily life for the access it may provide to situations where people behave in interestingly characteristic ways: situations you have witnessed or situations you may yourself be involved in. Here are some examples of situations students have written about using ethnographic techniques:

- sports-card trading sessions among pre-adolescent boys
- interactions between servers and Asian-Canadian patrons and between servers and non-Asian-Canadian patrons in a dim-sum restaurant
- purchase of sea-bus tickets from an automated wicket
- question-and-answer routines during a guided tour of an aquarium
- instruction-giving by instructors to novice and experienced divers on a dive boat

(You may notice that four of these research sites have a regional quality to them. Developed by students living on the west coast of Canada, they arose out of their life experience.)

Research sites need to meet certain criteria. First, you must have an opportunity to gather data. You need to be able to situate yourself to watch, take notes, use a tape recorder, and gather any relevant documents. Second, the situation needs to be narrow enough to permit firsthand observation. So, interesting as the site "planning a wedding in a post-feminist era" might be, you may not have time to gather data on all phases of this often elaborate and prolonged procedure. (You might, however, narrow it to "selection of the bride's ceremonial costume.")

Third, your research population (even if it is only one person) has to agree to be observed and written about. You need to be able to explain to them the purpose of your investigation, and to assure them of confidentiality: that is, you will write about them in such a way that readers will not be able to identify them. (Often, ethnographers use fictitious names for their subjects, if proper nouns make the reporting go better. Some even use fictitious names for the geographical location [e.g., "Lakeview"] or identify the place in general, typifying terms [e.g., "a small western Canadian city with a resource-based economy"].)

Ethical review and research permission
Research and teaching institutions monitor the research activities of their members. "Ethics" committees review research proposals principally to ensure that no harm comes to research subjects – physical harm in the case of, for example, clinical trials, but also social harm in cases where the publication of observations or information disclosed in interviews could be to the disadvantage of the research subject. These harms can also be reckoned in the broader sense of socio-political permission: the research subject must understand the purpose of the inquiry, and willingly participate in the knowledge-making project. Ethnographic researchers need to secure and record permission of subjects by explaining the project and its methods, and asking the subject to sign a permission form.

And, finally, your research site must be a place where you can cultivate abstractions relevant to other published scholarship. The Counts' article, for example, isn't only a report of RVers' ways. It also addresses a research question about *community*, one which has been addressed by other researchers whom they cite. Verkuyten, de Jong, and Masson don't just listen in on what people say about their neighbourhood. They address research questions about *racist and anti-racist discourse*, which they frame by citing other writers on racism and on the social psychology of "commonplaces" ("principles which speak for themselves and are not questioned as such" [Verkuyten et al. 1994:254]).

Criteria for selecting a research site in effect combine two facets of your experience: (1) the avenues of your daily life that reveal behaviours and situations around you and give you access to these situations; (2) the course of your life as a scholar and reader, which has brought you into contact with the research concerns of the academic community.

So the sample research sites listed above tended to centre around the abstractions *literacy* and *genre*, issues addressed in publications we studied in the courses in which students arrived at these topics. Citing and summarizing Deborah Keller-Cohen and Shirley Brice Heath, the student who wrote about sports-card trading sessions interpreted three eleven-year-olds' use of documents to support their evaluations of the cards and their bids and counter-offers. (One of the eleven-year-olds was her son.) The student who wrote about ordering in a dim-sum restaurant cited and summarized Heath and Carolyn Miller ("Genre as social action" 1984) to invoke the abstraction *tacit knowledge*: the role of unspoken but mutually understood assumptions in defining group boundaries.

These are delicate negotiations between scholarly experience and everyday experience. And they offer important insights into the nature of this kind of inquiry. Let me give an example. The student who wrote about tourists and commuters getting sea-bus tickets from an automated wicket was interested in how people coped with written instructions for a procedure that had been traditionally governed by an oral genre (spoken interactions between traveller and ticket-seller). After observing people using the wicket, successfully or unsuccessfully, and watching them confer with other travellers or with station attendants, and interviewing some of the sea-bus patrons, she drafted her introduction. The major abstraction she invoked was *transportation technology*. She made it a Big Issue by remarking on the need for attention to transportation in the context of population growth and environmental concerns. But this Big Issue stalled when the writer turned to cite relevant research and sketch a knowledge map with the gaps and spaces her work would occupy: Heath, Keller-Cohen, and Miller on literate practice and the role of genre in housing common knowledge of social routines. It was hard to get from *transportation* to the domain of knowledge represented by the other writers she would cite to ratify her topic and situate herself amongst the voices of the research community. Inspecting this stalled essay, we saw that the writer's Big Issue was not transportation technology but *genre* and *literacy*. On those topics she was an expert — able to cite relevant statements by others. That is, *transportation* was a high-level name for her *research site*, not her topic.

Similarly, the student who wrote about communication between dive-boat instructors and novice and experienced divers also first invoked a Big Issue that seemed compelling but finally would not sustain the conventions of the research genres. A dive-boat instructor herself, she referred to and developed the topic *safety* in her introduction. This seemed to be an automatic Big Issue: everybody wants to be safe. But, despite being a dive-boat instructor, she was not in fact an expert — in the research sense — on safety. She was an expert on routines of communication — that was her *topic*. The dive-boat, along with the safety issues involved in its operation, was her research site.

6.7.1 Research questions

Amongst customary ways of talking about writing in school situations, we come across the idea of "finding a topic." (Once this topic is "found," it is often then "narrowed.") I would not dispute the importance of having a topic (and I would not dispute the importance of getting it "narrowed"), but I have come to wonder if there might not be better ways to think about this stage of academic writing processes. I suggest that, instead of thinking of themselves as "looking for and finding a topic," writers might think of themselves as developing or "designing a research question." Having listened to the scholarly conversation in a certain area, and having joined the conversation as a summarizer taking a position in relation to others' statements, the writer prepares to take her turn by asking a question which arises — one which appears as a result of the position she has taken.

In this context, "research question" has a special meaning, one which needs to be distinguished from other meanings it might have in other contexts. In some classroom situations, and in some other life situations, "research" means "find out (and write down) what experts say" about something. For example, I might want to know (or have been assigned to want to know) about clear-cutting of forests — what specialists say about the practice of taking all the trees off some hectares of land, and then replanting the land with seedlings. I don't know anything about this, except maybe what I have seen from a highway, or heard from people who have gone tree-planting, or read in the newspaper. To get more complete information, I consult experts publishing their findings in scholarly journals in forest sciences. I am ignorant; they are knowledgeable. I ask them, "What's the story about clear-cutting?" I research the topic. The knowledge deficit is all on my side.

In the scholarly genres, however, the knowledge deficit is *shared*: the community of experts collectively doesn't know something (yet), and the research question identifies the something — isolates it, points to it — and proposes a technique for at least addressing if not conclusively answering the question. The person posing the research question is situated *amongst* the experts, and is in conversation with them.

This situation may seem inaccessible to students, but this is not so. Simply by bringing speakers together, you can — expertly — arrange for a question to emerge. For example, you might bring together Shieffelin and Doucet (1994) and Wassink (1999), both of whom write about creole, and identify their commonality, finding in this get-together a question from Shieffelin and Doucet with which to interrogate Wassink: are the idealizations of "nation" in the Haitian situation precursors of the changing attitudes Wassink discovers? Further, you could introduce Cameron (1995) on "moral [grammar] panic" and Milroy and Milroy (1991[1985]) on the "complaint tradition" to the conversation, and ask of these writers whether the post-colonial conditions Shieffelin and Doucet describe are significantly different from those which Cameron and Milroy and Milroy describe as producing pejorative attitudes towards language. Any uncertainty which arises from conversation amongst scholarly voices can be grounds for a research question.

In the Western tradition of scholarship, research questions tend to favour certain lines of inquiry. Things are often imagined as

- **hiding** — as concealed, so far, from view (*Research has shed little light on … What remains unexplored is …*). A variation on this is something appearing to be one thing but possibly being something else.
- **needing to be combined** with something else. Especially, research methods themselves are thought of as likely to benefit from having another method added to them. We saw an example of this in Chapter Three, where psychoanalytic and non-psychoanalytic psychologists needed to get together. In an analysis of the language of management studies, I found that scholarly articles in this area repeatedly called for "**integrated** — or 'simultaneous,' or 'dynamic,' or 'interactionist' — models of inquiry" (Giltrow 1998).
- **being more complicated** than we thought. Whereas in the "hiding" questions things may not be as they seem, in the "more-complicated" questions, things are not only **x** *but also* **y**.
- **having escaped notice** — "Economists and historians have devoted little attention to that episode." Here, for example, a researcher finds that the light of scholarly inquiry has shone on one spot — and left other areas in darkness.

In many ways, the influenza pandemic of 1918-19 is the "forgotten" epidemic; forgotten, at least, by scholars studying British Columbia's First Nations. Much attention has been paid to the timing and severity of late eighteenth- and early nineteenth-century epidemics for what they tell us about the proto-historic and early contact culture and population change. Scholars have argued the significance of these epidemics in softening up indigenous societies for the onslaught of colonization. Few, however, have examined later disease patterns for what they tell us about the nature of cross-cultural relations in the early twentieth century.

(Kelm 1999: 23-24)

Fahnestock and Secor (1991) offer a witty but also illuminating analysis of the **topoi** — the customary "places" to go to get arguments — in literary criticism. Among the literary-critical topoi they discover are (1) the "appearance/reality dichotomy"; (2) "ubiquity" or "everywhereness" (an image, theme, idea, wording is *everywhere* — in books, in poems, and so forth); (3) "paradox" — opposites are surprisingly reconciled; and (4) "*contemptus mundi*" — the modern world is a mess.

6.7.2 Suggested areas of inquiry

Genre and literacy

Because we have repeatedly consulted theories of genre in this book, and because you have been involved in analysing the written expression of research communities and its role in maintaining the values and routines of research communities, you have become (perhaps inadvertently) expert in *genre* and *literate practice*. You can exploit this expertise in an ethnographic project by focussing on a typical real-life situation in which people interact in routine ways, consciously or unconsciously complying with recognizable norms of expression. So, for example, you might secure the cooperation of two or three of your fellow students and observe their note-taking techniques in class, and their transformation of this genre into the essay genre. Or you might observe two or three of your friends who use e-mail — a genre emerging from technological change. Observing these behaviours, collecting relevant documents, and possibly interviewing your subjects, you will collect enough data for speculative and tentative generalizations about *learning*, *language*, and *authority*, or about *technological change* and *literacy*.

If you decide on a project related to genre and literacy, I suggest the following sources:

Coe, Richard, Lorelei Lingard, and Tatiana Teslenko, eds. 2002. *The Rhetoric and Ideology of Genre: Strategies for Stability and Change*. Cresskill, NJ: Hampton.

Devitt, Amy. 1993. "Generalizing about genre: New concepts of an old concept." *College Composition and Communication* 44: 357-86.

Freedman, Aviva, and Peter Medway. "Locating genre studies: Antecedents and prospects." In *Genre and the New Rhetoric*, ed. A. Freedman and P. Medway. London: Taylor & Francis.

Heath, Shirley Brice. 1983. "Chapter Six: Literate traditions." In *Ways with Words: Language, Life, and Work in Communities and Classrooms.* Cambridge: Cambridge UP.

Keller–Cohen, Deborah. 1987. "Literate practices in a modern credit union." *Language in Society* 16: 7-24.

Miller, Carolyn. 1984. "Genre as social action." *Quarterly Journal of Speech* 70: 151-67.

Swales, John. 1990. "Chapter Two: The concept of discourse community" and "Chapter Three: The concept of genre." In *Genre Analysis: English in Academic and Research Settings.* Cambridge: Cambridge UP.

Appearing in well-known journals or in books from widely distributed publishers, these should be available in your university library. Summary of two or three of these sources will enable you to invoke the voices of the research community, and to take a position amongst these voices. (Remember that, to identify the knowledge deficit you will address, you need only describe the limits of these sources: they propose a general framework which can direct your inquiry in a research site they do not explore.)

Gender and language — politeness and other speech behaviours
Many of this textbook's examples of scholarly expression have dealt with gender issues: these attract attention in many disciplines. At the same time, much of our inquiry into scholarly expression could be characterized as having to do with **politeness** — especially if we define politeness as the encoding in language of mutual recognition of social status. (So Myers [1989] has accounted for salient features of research articles in science journals as features of politeness — a configuration of relative distribution of power and a concern for the community's solidarity.) Reporting and modality, features we looked at in Chapter Five, are often associated with politeness: reporting and modalized expressions leave space open around the speaker's statement — space available for a listener to occupy. By making statements somewhat indeterminate, reporting and modalizing expressions help speakers appear not to impose on addressees. So, instead of uttering the command —

Bring me a glass of water

— a polite speaker might say:

I **wonder** if you **might be able** to bring me a glass of water.

Or a speaker who wanted to express an opinion about his or her addressee's appearance might avoid the directness of —

Your trousers are too short

— and select instead a form that modalizes and minimizes the opinion:

Your trousers **might possibly** be **just a little** too short.

Folk theories of gender and politeness seem to associate politeness with women: people think women are more polite than men. Some research tends to confirm the folk view; other research does not. The following is a very brief list from the extensive research into differences in women's and men's speech and can provide a basis for inquiry into gender difference in communicative situations. (Myers [1989] may also be useful to you. And you will find in Sheldon, below, especially, some definitions of speech styles that go beyond just "politeness.")

Brown, Penelope. 1990. "Gender, politeness, and confrontation in Tenejapa." *Discourse Processes* 13: 123-41.

Coates, Jennifer. 1986. "Chapter Six: Sex differences in communicative competence." In *Women, Men and Language*. Harlow, Essex: Longman.

Dubois, B.L., and I. Crouch. 1975. "The question of tag questions in women's speech: They don't really use more of them, do they?" *Language and Society* 4: 289-94.

Giltrow, Janet. 1996. "Ironies of politeness in Anita Brookner's *Hotel du Lac*." In *Ambiguous Discourse*, ed. K. Mezei. Chapel Hill: U of North Carolina P.

Sheldon, Amy. 1990. "Pickle fights: Gendered talk in preschool disputes." *Discourse Processes* 13: 5-31.

Summary of two or three of these sources (or any others you discover) will enable you to define an issue, a topic ratified by research. To investigate the topic, you can turn to the academic world around you: classroom discussion, comments addressed to university lecturers, responses to commentary on marked essays, for example, or to life beyond the academic world: the workplace or marketplace, or the home.

Disciplines and their discourses

Traditionally, ethnography has involved researchers in some degree of face-to-face contact with the groups they have undertaken to study: on-site observations and interviews, or some other form of limited participation in the group's activities. But, for the purposes of this assignment, we could include research that involves no face-to-face contact with the groups targeted for inquiry. So differences in different disciplines' styles of expression could be investigated by examining a selection of articles from scholarly journals. After all, genre theory tells us that communities leave traces of their values and practices in the documents they typically use. Accordingly, these articles will be a source of knowledge about the social groups which produce them.

This book offers some guides for examining documents representing the habits and routines of different academic communities. Concentrating on introductions and conclusions, you might attempt to characterize

- the role and qualities of generalities
- the quality of "prestige abstractions"
- the use of reported statements and the practice of documentation
- the use of modality and limiting expressions
- the ways a knowledge deficit is identified
- the presence and quality of descriptions of method
- the presence of *discursive I* and messages about the argument (including headings and other types of partitioning)
- the presence or absence of recommendations for action in the world.

To position yourself as a researcher, you could cite and summarize one (or more) of the studies listed above as frames for studying genre (Devitt, Swales, Freedman and Medway, Freedman and Coe, or Miller would be most relevant), and cite and summarize the findings of

MacDonald, Susan Peck. 1994. "Chapter Two: Patterns in disciplinary variation." In *Professional Academic Writing in the Humanities and Social Sciences.* Carbondale: Southern Illinois UP.

Myers, Greg. 1989. "The pragmatics of politeness in scientific articles." *Applied Linguistics* 10: 1-35.

Swales, John. 1990. "Chapter Seven: Research articles in English." In *Genre Analysis: English in Academic and Research Settings.* Cambridge: Cambridge UP.

Establish as your research site articles selected from scholarly journals in sciences, psychology, business, criminology, economics, education, history, anthropology, communications, literary criticism, or other fields which are relevant to your own academic goals and interests. You could concentrate on just one field, or you might find comparison of two or more fields more revealing. You might also consider an historical inquiry, investigating changes in a discipline's typical discourse over a period of decades.

Or you might compare scholarly accounts of a topic with popular accounts of similar matters. Still referring to the features listed above, you might compare a sample of the public discourse in the popular media on immigration to the account offered in —

Chavez, Leo R. 1994. "The power of the imagined community: The settlement of undocumented Mexicans and Central Americans in the United States." *American Anthropologist* 96(1): 52-73.

— or a sample of the public discourse on crime to —

Hagedorn, John M. 1994. "Neighborhoods, markets and gang drug organizations." *Journal of Research in Crime and Delinquency* 31(3): 264-94.

Lupton, Deborah, and John Tulloch. 1999. "Theorizing fear of crime: Beyond the rational/irrational opposition." *British Journal of Sociology* 50(3): 507-23, 516-17.

Willott, Sara, and Chris Griffin. 1999. "Building your own lifeboat: Working-class male offenders talk about economic crime." *British Journal of Social Psychology* 38: 445-60, 451.

— or popular description of eating disorders to —

Apter, Alan, et al. 1994. "Cultural effects on eating attitudes in Israeli subpopulations and hospitalized anorectics." *Genetic, Social, and General Psychology Monographs* 120(1): 85-99.

and other publications cited by Apter et al.

Or you might compare citation practices in a sample of articles from a research discipline with citation practices in news reports in print or broadcast media: how are knowledge and knowledgeable speakers represented in these genres? How is "fact" represented?

6.8 Preparing a proposal

Proposals (also called "abstracts" or "abstract proposals") are a widely used genre in academic communities. Seeking a place on a conference program, or a spot in a collection of essays that will be published on a particular topic, scholars answer "Calls for Papers" with a proposal.

(Think of the proposal as a *bid* to enter an actual, face-to-face conversation.) Conference chairs or the editors of collections evaluate the submissions they receive on bases we have become familiar with. They look for the Big Issue: topics that excite interest in the research community. They look for evidence that the author of the proposal is in touch with established positions on the topic: statements reported from recognized sources. They look for mention of a knowledge deficit: an estimate of the limitation of what has been said so far. They look for some account of method: how knowledge will be constructed on this topic. Chairs and editors also try to estimate the proposal's feasibility: can the researcher actually accomplish what he or she promises? Is the research site appropriate and manageable? Will it yield relevant data that can be usefully interpreted?

Proposal and rejection

When students propose topics which instructors reject, they can interpret the rejections as dictatorial, or a constraint on self-expression. So it can be useful to think of course assignments as being like calls for papers: the instructor is like the chair of a conference, or the editor of a collected volume. Giving the go-ahead on a topic, the instructor estimates whether it will enter into conversation with the speakers and statements composing the course. An acceptable topic/research question will have the timeliness of "answering" a call, an invitation.

If I were interested in the Big Issue *gender and language*, I might compose a proposal which identified the issue and cited some previous research on the topic —

As Coates (1986) and others have observed, there is a long history of commentary on women's speech, commentators having, through the centuries, detected and interpreted features which they believed to be peculiarly feminine. More recently, studies such as Sheldon (1990) and Eckert (1990) have attempted to interpret identifiable features of women's speech in relation to the social context in which they occur, referring to larger theories of power and dominance in the social order. Christian-Smith (1991) has added reading practice to speaking practice in looking for significant patterns in the gendering of language.

— and then identify a knowledge deficit and a research question:

> Yet all these studies focus on one kind of social context: the school. We might wonder whether educational settings exert particular influence on the interactive styles of speakers, and whether the features identified in these studies occur in other institutional settings, such as the workplace, or other public contexts.

It is all very well to wonder about this, and my reader might feel a spark of interest, but he or she — as someone responsible for the success of a conference or a volume of collected papers — would need to know more before accepting the proposal. What am I going to *do*? My reader might accept the claim that —

> This paper will investigate language and gender in settings beyond the school.

— but still not accept my proposal, having no idea how I will find my way in this vast research site called "settings beyond the school." But if I specify the research site, show that it is relevant to the topic, and explain how I will construct knowledge from the data it offers, my reader will feel more confident that my project is feasible:

> This paper will report data gathered from a public institutional setting with a decision-making goal: transcripts of two meetings of a municipal Board of Zoning Variance, on which two men and three women serve. I will examine conversational turn-taking, topic shifts, personal narrative contributions, and mention reading of documents such as by-laws and site plans to discover whether the "cooperative" speech styles of girls and young women in school settings are also evident in this more overtly political context.

(Notice that I am not an expert on city planning or municipal politics: zoning decisions are only my research site, not my topic.)

Proposals have many of the stylistic and rhetorical features of scholarly introductions. And both genres — proposals and research articles — serve the values and routines of the research community. But they differ in function in that, in many disciplines, the proposal describes work that has not yet been completed — perhaps only planned, or barely begun. If a scholarly paper were actually to come from my (fictitious) proposal, its introduction might differ significantly from the proposal, reflecting what I found when I actually carried out the research. Conference chairs and editors know this: they know that the work may not have been done yet, and that the actual product may differ from the one predicted by the proposal. (So at scholarly conferences, you can observe a by-product of the operation of the proposal genre: people standing up to present their work and saying, "First I have to tell you that my title has changed ....") But the proposal gives chairs and editors confidence in the process: the researcher is aware of relevant research in the area; has a specific research question in mind; has a manageable research site and productive techniques for constructing knowledge.

Assignment

Write a 200-300 word proposal for the paper you are working on to fulfill one of the assignments suggested above, or for another paper you are working on. Ask your instructor to go through his or her files to find examples of proposals he or she has submitted or received: inspect these examples to determine the salient features of the genre. Or follow this plan:

- **Title** (including major abstraction and reference to research site, e.g., for my imaginary project above: "Gendered styles in institutional settings: Interactions in meetings of a decision-making panel")
- **The Big Issue** and Prestige Abstraction which warrant this project
- **Existing knowledge** (statements reported from other researchers)
- **Knowledge deficit** (limits of existing knowledge)
- **Research question** (addressing these limits)
- **Research site** (the "place" where you will conduct this research — which does not have to be a geographical location but can be a *textual* location if you are examining documents)
- **Method** (how you will construct knowledge — gather, organize, and interpret your data)

6.9 Making an oral presentation

A main event in the life a research community is the **conference**. Conferences — organized, programmed series of oral presentations of research results — abound in the academic world. Their abundance is a sign of their usefulness in the knowledge-making professions. Conferences summon several speech genres: the keynote address, the introduction of speakers, the roundtable discussion, the audience response to research reports, for example. But the most important one is the paper presentation.

Professional scholars and students have in common the genre of the oral presentation. Few professional scholars let a year go by without presenting a paper at a conference, or at least attending a conference and listening to other people present their papers. And few students get through a term without having to make an oral presentation in class. Although the oral presentation can seem to students to be a punitive or cruel assignment — arbitrary and nerve-wracking — it is in fact an authentic element of scholarly life.

Most people feel some anxiety at speaking formally in public. If you are among this majority, you should not see your anxiety as a bad sign: totally relaxed people often seem to give the worst presentations, offhand and pointless. Maybe they underestimate the real and undeniable challenges in making themselves interesting for 10 or 20 uninterrupted minutes.

> *yeh um well I haven't really got anything prepared I thought I'd just give you some of my thoughts on this um yeh*

Feeling a little stress on these occasions is probably not only normal but productive: it will make you work harder at getting ready. What follows is some advice on preparing for an oral presentation.

6.9.1 Make your material fit the time available

Few presenters of papers have too little to say; many have too much. If their presentation reports work that is in preparation as a written paper or essay, they are especially likely to have too much to say. And many presenters underestimate how much time it will take to deliver their material.

Although other factors contribute to the success or failure of an oral presentation, I have come to believe that making your material fit the time available is just about the most important task in preparing for a presentation. If you have too much to say, you will rush, and talk too fast — and listeners will have a hard time following. Or you will have to stop before you have made your most important points. Or you will edit as you speak —

OK um well I'll have to skip this there isn't time um let's see OK so another point is that um

— and risk leaving out parts of your reasoning that are necessary to making the whole comprehensible and meaningful.

. Some long-winded presenters get mad when their time is up. Maybe they are overcome by the stress of the situation. Maybe they have mistaken the oral presentation for some other genre, like the article or essay. Maybe they feel that their thinking is so important that it should not be subjected to limitation. But the typical 20-minute allotment for a conference paper is fair enough both socially and cognitively: it shares time among more speakers than longer allotments would do; it pretty nearly matches a listening audience's capacity for attending to a complex argument. Equally, if you are assigned a 5- or 10-minute presentation in class, this allotment will neither impose on your listeners nor confound them. Take comfort in time restrictions and work within them.

As a general rule, eight double-spaced typed pages becomes a twenty-minute presentation.

6.9.2 Keep in mind that written and spoken English differ

The eight-page rule assumes that presenters write out their materials and then read their writing to their listeners. In the first edition of this book, I argued against this practice for several reasons, all developing from the inescapable fact that writing and talking are not the same, and neither are reading and listening. While people have many strategies for understanding the spoken genres (conversations, for example, or class discussions, or consultations with doctors or loans officers), they have few strategies for understanding written genres read out loud (legal contracts, to take an extreme example, or, closer to our concerns, university essays). The different situations in which speaking and writing come about produce different styles.

We could say that, at the most basic level, written and spoken genres separate from each other along the lines of differences between **planned** and **unplanned** discourse (a distinction made by Ochs [1979] more than 20 years ago, and still cited widely as having large implications). Situations served by writing include time for planning and revising; situations served by spoken genres — although they will be informed by habit and established routines — do not include time for planning and revising. The presence or absence of planning results in different styles.

The oral presentation lies between writing and speaking. While it is spoken, it is certainly not unplanned. As *listeners*, people are used to the styles that arise in unplanned discourse. But, hearing an oral presentation, they are faced with a planned text. To accommodate their listeners' predicament, presenters can take certain steps. They can

- Repeat main points frequently (maybe more often than they think they should) to help their listeners keep important material in mind. We know that articles and essays use repetition, too, to confirm readers' interpretation of detail. But readers have further means of confirming their understanding of the material that is being presented: they can *slow* the pace of their reading, dwelling on important points to get them firmly positioned on their mental desktop. Listeners can't do this. So oral presentations should be more repetitive than articles and essays.
- Introduce frequent messages about the argument. Unlike readers, listeners don't know where they are in the discussion — near the end, or a long way from it; at a division between one section and another or in the middle of something; in the middle or at the end of a series of examples. Presenters can orient their listeners by frequently signalling their position in the argument and forecasting its progress: "I will begin by giving some background ...," "Later I will ...," "To show you what this means, I will describe ...," "To conclude, I am going to ...."
- Shift their emphasis from the abstract and general to the concrete and specific. By concentrating on examples, presenters can leave a more enduring impression, replicating the tendency of conversation to turn to the interesting anecdote, the particular case that attracted attention.
- Unload some of the heavy nominal expressions typical of scholarly writing. Although listeners may be used to coping with heavy nominal expressions in their reading, they will be less used to hearing them. Noun phrases are much lighter in speech: whereas writers have time to plan heavy nominal expressions, speakers are more likely to scatter attributes and agents across several clauses. So, while the long noun phrase in —

  > **Extensive longitudinal and cross-cultural research including interviews with and observations of hundreds of children** led Kohlberg to conclude that moral development moves through three levels.

— is characteristic of written scholarly expression, these unpacked, lighter versions more closely resemble the noun phrases typical of speaking:

> **Extensive research** led Kohlberg to conclude that moral development moves through three levels. **This research** was both longitudinal and cross-cultural. **It** included interviews with hundreds of children, and observations of them, too.

- Use visual aids, like handouts or overhead projections. Lists of figures, important quotations, or key terms and phrases can turn listeners temporarily into readers, and support their efforts to understand.

In the first edition of this book, I also recommended that presenters compose their material in note form: words and phrases. By using note form instead of sentences and paragraphs, presenters activate their own natural competence as speakers, using language in ways characteristic of speaking rather than writing. I still think this can be a good idea, but I now also have reservations.

For one thing, note-form materials can balloon and drift over time boundaries. As we expand and explain, we can risk longwindedness, saying more than needs to be said. And, for another thing, many of the very best papers I have heard at scholarly conferences have been read from prepared pages of prose — not notes. If reading a paper out loud works so well at conferences, it may also offer some benefits to classroom presenters, too.

If your classroom situation is informal and colloquial, you might be better off with note-form materials. If, on the other hand, your classroom is a more formal setting, a brief and well-prepared paper read out loud can be very successful. And if you are in fact preparing a presentation for a conference or other public, scholarly occasion, it is probably best to have your eight pages of prose right in front of you. Just remember that the oral presentation is *not* an essay or article. And even if the essay or article is already written and ready to submit to a teacher or a journal, don't be tempted to just read it out loud. Make a new, reduced, and simplified version for presentation (offering your audience copies of the essay version if they are particularly interested in your work). Essays and presentations are different genres.

Assignment

Prepare a 10-minute oral presentation on the research you
described in your proposal (Section 6.8) or on research you are
doing for another assignment. Include in your plans time for discussion: ask your audience to respond to your work with questions, advice, insights, criticisms.

 Position yourself as a researcher reporting on work-in-progress
and offering a scholarly community a contribution to knowledge.
Attend to the voices of the scholarly community.

Works Cited

Clark, Romy, and Roz Ivanic. 1997. *The Politics of Writing*. London: Routledge.
Culhane, Dara. 1998. *The Pleasure of the Crown: Anthropology, Law and First
    Nations*. Burnaby, BC: Talon.
Dempsey, Corinne G. 1998. "Rivalry, reliance, and resemblance: Siblings as
    metaphor for Hindu-Christian relations in Kerala State." *Asian Folklore
    Studies* 57: 51-70.
Fahnestock, Jeanne, and Marie Secor. 1991. "The rhetoric of literary criticism."
    In *Textual Dynamics of the Professions: Historical and Contemporary Studies of
    Writing in the Professional Communities*, eds. C. Bazerman and J. Paradis.
    Madison: U of Wisconsin P.
Giltrow, Janet. 1998. "Modernizing authority: The grammaticalization of con-
    trolling interests in management studies." *Journal of Technical Writing & Com-
    munication* 28(3): 265-86.
Heath, Shirley Brice. 1983. *Ways with Words: Language, Life, and Work in Com-
    munities and Classrooms*. New York: Cambridge UP.
Ivanic, Roz. 1997. *Writing and Identity: The Discoursal Construction of Identity in
    Academic Writing*. Amsterdam: Benjamins.
Latour, Bruno. 2000. "When things strike back: A possible contribution of 'sci-
    ence studies' to the social sciences." *British Journal of Sociology* 51(1): 107-23.
Latour, Bruno, and Steve Woolgar. 1986 (1979). *Laboratory Life: The Construction
    of Scientific Facts*. Princeton, NJ: Princeton UP.
Lu, Min Zhan. 1992. "Conflict and struggle: The enemies or preconditions of
    basic writing." *College English* (December): 891-913.
Miller, Carolyn. 1984. "Genre as social action." *Quarterly Journal of Speech* 70: 151-67.
Myers, Greg. 1989. "The pragmatics of politeness in scientific articles." *Applied
    Linguistics* 10: 1-15.
Ochs, Elinor. 1979. "Planned and unplanned discourse." In *Discourse and Syntax*,
    ed. T. Givòn. New York: Academic Press.
Wenzel, George W. 1999. "Traditional ecological knowledge and Inuit: Reflec-
    tions on TEK research and ethics." *Arctic* 52(2): 113-24.

Appendix A
Techniques for definition

These techniques focus first on the thing-to-be-defined, using the syntactic structure of a particular kind of sentence to accomplish this focus. Taking the thing-to-be-defined as its subject, the **formal sentence definition** isolates the phenomenon for scrutiny. The **expanded definition** relocates the phenomenon amongst other, related phenomena in the world. We could say that the focus of the formal sentence definition is *ideal*. Consider the following:

> PASSAGE 1
> Daycare is the institutional provision of caretaking services to young children, including feeding, supervision, shelter, and instruction.

In this passage, I am ignoring cases where it is hard to distinguish between babysitting and daycare, where children are not exactly fed but feed themselves (or refuse to eat, or bring their own snacks), where care is provided on so informal a basis it might not be called "institutional" at all. I am providing an ideal, formal definition of *daycare*, offering a statement of equivalence: on one side is the phenomenon, *daycare*, and on the other side is the definition:

> ... *the institutional provision of caretaking services to young children, including feeding, supervision, shelter, and instruction.*

The defining side of the statement first enlarges our view by identifying the larger class to which *daycare* belongs —

> ... *the institutional provision of caretaking services* ...

— and then narrows our view again by identifying the features which differentiate *daycare* from other members of its class (from, for example, *health care, corrections, education*):

... to young children, including feeding, supervision, shelter, and instruction.

The following definition shows the same pattern of **enlarging to classify** and **reducing to differentiate**. This is the classical pattern of formal sentence definition. Passage 2 shows this pattern again and also shows one of the development options open to the writer: following formal definition, the writer can "double" the definition by saying what the phenomenon *does*.

PASSAGE 2
Broadcasting is a system of social control which, through the transmission of electronic signals, normalizes the diverse experiences of individuals. Broadcasting interprets events and life conditions in ways which confirm society's ideological centre.

In Passage 2, the definition first expands our focus by identifying the **class** to which broadcasting belongs (systems of social control), and then **differentiates** it from other members of the class (laws or customs, for example). Moreover, Passage 2 shows that formal definition can be in itself a step in an argument. Someone else could have defined *broadcasting* differently — as a result of having interpreted data differently, or having different data to interpret, or having a different disciplinary perspective.

PASSAGE 3
Broadcasting is a system of communication which, through the transmission of electronic signals, illuminates public and private life alike. By linking widespread communities through a shared network of information, broadcasting ensures that citizens in democratic societies recognize common and crucial features of their experience, and enables them to respond to those features as issues.

The definitions in Passages 2 and 3 would serve different arguments. This disparity won't surprise you if you think of definition as the presentation of a high-level, interpretive abstraction which the writer assigns to lower-level observations or data. So the definition is bound to be an expression of the reasoning and insight which have led the writer to assign the name in the first place.

For example, if I interpret the conditions of Brian's experience as *therapeutic supervision*, and I go on to define that phenomenon, my definition will reflect the reasoning which detected in Brian's case the features of constraint, surveillance, and correction of deviance.

PASSAGE 4
Therapeutic supervision is a form of social restraint which targets an individual as deviant and then, through management and monitoring of the individual's daily experience, seeks to adjust his behaviour to conform to a recognized norm.

The formal definition, with its characteristic classification and differentiation, has an authoritative, even "scientific" sound. But, when these definitions are non-technical, they are only proposals. From another point of view, or later on, when more evidence is in, broadcasting and Brian's routine could be defined differently.

Formal definitions can be developed or expanded by:

- *directing readers to pay attention to the word itself*

  Earlier uses of the term **broadcasting** referred to sowing by scattering seeds over a broad area. Modern, electronic broadcasting suggests the same wide scattering: broadcasting focusses not on unique, individual receptors, but on large expanses of population.

  As the term suggests, a **transnational community** transcends the political and geographical borders of the state.

- *comparing the phenomenon to near neighbours*

  Like broadcasting, on-line media disseminate information to a wide audience. And on-line consumers of information, like viewers or listeners, always have the option of calling a halt to the process: the on-line user can log off, the viewer can turn off the TV, and the listener can turn off the radio. But broadcasting differs from on-line transmission of information in the degree of control it exercises over the individual's reception of information. While on-line users can select from a multitude the sites they will visit, and the amount of time they will spend at each one, and choose to follow or ignore links, viewers have less control once they begin to watch. They receive information in the order and at the pace the broadcaster has determined.

  Like transnational communities, immigrant communities form as a result of dislocations: people leave one area and settle elsewhere. Transnational communities differ from immigrant communities in that, while the locus of the immigrant community is in the new place, the locus of the transnational community remains at once in the original location and in the new one.

- *observing the phenomenon in time, tracing its antecedents in history*

Informal care of children by adults other than their parents has a long history which ranges from provisions made by agricultural workers for the supervision of infants while their mothers were employed in harvest or planting to the hiring of tutors and governesses by genteel families in early modern and industrial Europe. Institutional care of children has taken various forms in different historical periods: the foundling hospital, for example, or the orphanage. The phenomenon named by *daycare*, however, is relatively recent and combines historical features of both informal and institutional caregiving: while the family maintains responsibility for the child, non-kin care-providers manage the material and social resources dedicated to the child's daytime welfare. All these practices, historical and contemporary, have in common their responsiveness to socio-economic conditions: child care, and the names for it, change as families' means of livelihood change.

Appendix B

Arranging for speakers to enter into conversation

Exercise

(1) The passages below each describe *change* in the late nineteenth and early twentieth centuries, exposing origins of what we experience today as "normal" or "natural" aspects of the marketplaces of our material cultures. The writers are working in the same discipline and publishing in the same journal. At the same time, however, their emphases are not identical, and they are not in direct dialogue with one another.

Summarize these passages to bring the writers into conversation with one another. In doing so, you will probably need to develop higher-level abstractions — *labour* and *skill*, *social change*, for example — to construct the common ground on which these speakers can meet. Having brought these voices into conversation, you might also consider what questions arise from these studies — possibly questions about changes in the marketplaces and households of our own era.

PASSAGE A

In the late nineteenth century, the emergence of processed food altered the daily consumption habits of millions of U.S. households. Bottled horseradish, canned coffee, packaged meat, boxed cereal, and other mass-produced foodstuffs began to appear on urban grocery store shelves in the decades after the Civil War. Some of these products, such as cold breakfast cereals, graham crackers, and canned soup were new. Others were familiar to retailers and consumers. Shopkeepers, for example, had stocked bulk coffee beans since the colonial period. In certain ethnic communities, women often made their own horseradish. The majority of city and rural households had access to fresh meat. But neither consumers nor tradespeople had previously encountered packaged foods that they could not see, smell, or touch. Most were initially suspicious of the quality and value of such products.

In spite of early skepticism on the part of households and retailers, the food processing industry developed very fast. Between 1859 and 1899, total output expanded 1,500 percent.[1] After about 1880, a relatively small number of rapidly growing companies generated much of this increase. National Biscuit, Swift, Armour, Heinz, Quaker Oats, Campbell Soup, Borden, Pillsbury Flour, Libby, and other businesses produced and marketed a wide range of products for national distribution. By 1900, manufactured food comprised almost a third of the value of all finished commodities produced in the United States.[2]

The rapid development of food processing touched most American consumers. By 1920, virtually all households purchased some other form of value-added foodstuffs.[3] Many of these goods, like Borden's condensed milk or Heinz's mango chutney, introduced novel tastes into American homes. The new food products also shaped domestic working rhythms. Packaged, canned, and bottled meats replaced those once butchered, salted, and pickled at home. Prepared foods introduced convenient substitutes for dishes previously cooked from scratch, altering women's established cooking responsibilities. Campbell's Chicken Noodle soup, for example, could be ready in minutes. By contrast, boiling meat, making stock, chopping vegetables, and adding seasoning for homemade soup took hours. Shopping habits shifted in tandem. At almost all income levels, women bought more processed foods — canned hams, bottled corned beef, packaged cookies — and fewer raw ingredients — flour, baking soda, certain spices — than their grandmothers had.[4]

1   By comparison, general manufacturing rose sixfold over the same period. Donna R. Gabaccia, *We Are What We Eat: Ethnic Food and the Making of Americans* [....]
2   Department of Commerce, *Historical Statistics of the United States* [....]
3   Margaret F. Byington, *Homestead: The Households of a Mill Town* [....]
4   On flour consumption in the late nineteenth and early twentieth centuries, see [....]

Nancy F. Koehn 1999 "Henry Heinz and brand creation in the late nineteenth century: Making markets for processed food." *Business History Review* 73, Autumn, 349-93, 349-51.

PASSAGE B

The American paint industry in 1910 was undergoing profound transformations, including tremendous growth, the degree of concentration of ownership, and in the very definition of their product. The value of paints and varnishes produced in the United States rose by 80 percent between 1899 and 1909, while the value of goods and services in the paint industry increased by almost fifty percent.[9] This growing paint industry underwent qualitative changes as well. The tendency toward concentration of ownership persisted, although the technical and improvisatory nature of the industry permitted a steady accretion of new businesses, maintaining both competition and a plurality of interests. Both the growth and the increasing concentration of ownership in the paint industry at the beginning of the century can be seen in Table 1. The number of manufacturers increased by 30 percent from 1904 to 1919, while the value produced by these firms grew by 400 percent. By 1919, corporate-owned companies accounted for 76 percent of manufacturers, and made 94 percent of the nation's paint and varnishes.[10]

While it is true that many large paint companies consolidated their power by driving out or buying out smaller ones, it oversimplifies the situation in the paint industry to characterize the early twentieth century merely as a time of shrinking competition. From 1899 to 1919 the number of establishments involved in paint manufacture increased by almost 40 percent. Figure 1 shows that the domination by larger firms in the paint industry did not take place until the late Progressive Era. Prior to 1914, the percentage of products manufactured by smaller and medium-sized paint firms remained fairly stable. Alongside reports of mergers and buyouts, paint trade magazines from the period are filled with advertisements from new companies boasting improved products.[11]

Complicating matters, technological developments and changing consumer demands were transforming not only the way paints were marketed, but the very definition of paint. Traditionally, paints were mixed by the user at the time of application, from raw ingredients mixed in local paint stores or chemical supply houses. Skilled painters could custom-blend oils, thinners, and pigments for a particular job. The fast-growing housing market encouraged the development of paints that required less skill to use. From 1899 to 1919, the market share for "ready-mixed" paints rose from 21 to 31 percent of the total value of all paints and varnishes produced in the United States.[12] And since there never had been one standard formula for paints, paint makers had broad latitude for tinkering, prompting one hardware dealer to complain in 1908: "paint (the name covers sometimes more than the article itself will) the word is very much abused."[13]

9 Value of paint and varnish produced in 1899 was about $69,560,000. By 1909 America produced [....]
10 U.S. Commerce Department, U.S. Bureau of the Census. *Historical Statistics of the United States, Colonial Times to 1970* [....]
11 The Commerce Department reported 600 establishments manufacturing paint and varnish in 1899 [....]
12 The value of the ready mixed paints rose from $14,864,126 in 1899 [....]
13 L.D. Howe to Representative Charles Fuller, April 25, 1908 [....]

(Warren 1999: 709–12)

(2) Early in Chapter Three you read a brief excerpt from "The Janet Smith Bill," describing "controversy in the 1920s surrounding the unsolved murder of a young Scottish nanny working for a well-to-do family on the west coast of Canada, a case in which the racist press and political figures accused the family's Asian "butler." Here is another passage from that article, explaining political and legislative context for reaction to that crime. Bring this passage into conversation with Deborah Cameron on *moral panic*, also in Chapter Three.

MARY ELLEN SMITH AND THE POLITICS OF POPULATION
The "hearty and motherly" Mary Ellen Smith was the United Council of Scottish societies' logical choice as the person to introduce its proposed legislation.[26] ... Like other "maternal feminists" of that generation, Smith's politics focused on the production of "clean" children, targeting the bodies of young White women as the "mothers of the race."[27] The numerous reforms that Mary Ellen navigated through the House during these years included new laws regarding

infancy, mothers' pensions, adoption, venereal diseases, and minimum wages for women and children.[28] Mary Ellen Smith also shared concerns with many White nationalists about the link between the sexual activities of individual British Columbians and the "health" of the province. Heavily influenced by then dominant eugenic ideas about heredity and geopolitics, Mary Ellen saw the scientific management of child-rearing as a cure to the social ills of the world and as a key link to the survival of "white British Columbia." She was an early supporter of a sexual sterilization law in British Columbia, which would eventually be passed in 1933.

Mary Ellen Smith was concerned not only about the quality of the children that were being born in British Columbia, but with the quantity of children as well. Smith shared the dominant nationalist belief that British Columbia was an "empty land" that would eventually be filled with Asian immigrants if the White population did not increase. Such questions about the racial identity of British Columbia had preoccupied the White settlers of the province for decades. However, a perceived "fertility crisis" in the 1920s — created by statistics showing that British Columbia's fertility rate had gone from being one of the highest in Canada to the lowest by 1921 — heightened these concerns about the demographics of the province.[31] ... Mary Ellen Smith, influenced by her ideas about "race motherhood," also identified natural increase as a solution to this population crisis .... These concerns about race, nationalism, and gender converged in legislation, introduced by Smith, that aimed at prohibiting the employment of White women in Oriental businesses. In a 1919 amendment to the *Municipal Act*, the BC Legislature made it an offense for businesses "owned, kept, or managed by any Chinese person" to employ "any white woman or girl."[36] Four years later, the BC Legislature repealed this provision (which was harshly criticized by the Chinese consul in Vancouver) and replaced it with the *Women's and Girls' Protection Act*.[37] In its original form, this statute barred laundries and restaurants owned by Orientals from hiring White and "Indian" women.[38] The language of the bill led to a strong protest by the Chinese communities of the province, who called it an "insult to national pride and character defamation." The text was amended before passing into law to delete the references to "Orientals," a legislative move that infuriated women's groups and Victor Odlum.[39]

One perceived threat to White women posed by Orientals that these statutes sought to alleviate was the passing of the drug habit through casual contact (such as that brought about by employment). Popular culture in British Columbia and throughout the Western world had created stereotypical images of Chinese men as opium fiends who lure White women into lives of debauchery through drugs and sex. Contemporary fears about "white slavery" reinforced these concerns about the close association of White girls and Asian men. In 1908, the *Saturday Sunset* reported that "a regular traffic of women is conducted by the Chinese in Vancouver. The Chinese are the most persistent criminals against the person of any woman of any class in this country."[40] In the early 1920s, leading Canadian feminist Emily F. Murphy reproduced these images in her widely read expose of the drug trade in the Dominion, entitled *The Black Candle*.[41] The use of drugs like opium, according to Judge Murphy, led to sterility, which, "in [the] face of persistently falling birthrates," was nothing short of alarming. If these "fallen" White women did become mothers, they produced wretched "half-caste infants" whom they often "farm[ed] out" and then went back to the opium den. These supposed consequences of drug use by White women made Judge Murphy "fearful for the future of the [White] race" in Canada.[42] Such fears were at the root of the *Women's and Girls' Protection Act* in British Columbia and similar legislative initiatives in other provinces. Keeping young White women and Asian men apart was part of a larger nationalist project to protect the White race. Young White women needed to become "mothers of the race," not opium addicts in Chinatown producing Eurasian children. Strict gender roles, corresponding with bourgeois ideas of respectable motherhood, needed to be enforced to achieve these goals.[43] Mary Ellen Smith, while defending the *Women's and Girls' Protection Act* in November 1923, stressed the "common sense" nature of these ideas by declaring: "surely we have the right to protect our own race."[44]

26 Elsie Gregory MacGill, *My Mother the Judge: A Biography of Justice Helen Gregory MacGill* (Toronto: Ryerson, 1955), 151. Although Victor Odlum was an MLA, he was not an obvious candidate to introduce this "women's bill." Also Odlum was preoccupied with piloting the *United Church of Canada Act* (S.B.C. 1924, c. 50) through the House.

27 On the powerful ideology of motherhood at this time, see Anna Davin's brilliant essay "Imperialism and Motherhood," *History Workshop* 5, Spring 1978, 13. For Mary Ellen Smith's ideas, see Mrs. Ralph Smith, "Women and Economics," *Vancouver Sun*, 6 October 1918, 4. Numerous organizations devoted to the question of children and child-rearing became influential during this time. David Brankin, the first president of the Children's Welfare Association of British Columbia, advocated declaring "war on any custom, practises [*sic*], tradition, or false modesty that interferes in any way with the production of clean, healthy children ... [such] conditions will have a far-reaching effect upon our future race unless something is done." See David Brankin, "Please Mind Your Own Business," *Western Women's Weekly*, 18 October 1919, 3, 18.

28 On Mary Ellen Smith's career, see Elizabeth Norcross, "Mary Ellen Smith: The Right Woman at the Right Place at the Right Time," in *Not Just Pin Money*, edited by Barbara Latham and Roberta J. Pazdra (Victoria: Camosun College, 1984), 360-3; Diane Crossley, "The BC Liberal Party and Women's Reforms, 1916-1928," in *Her Own Right: Selected Essays on Women's History in BC*, edited by Barbara Latham and Cathy Kess (Victoria: Camosun College, 1980), 234-5, 242-4. On Ralph Smith's racial views, see Patricia E. Roy, *A White Man's Province: British Columbia Politicians and Chinese and Japanese Immigrants, 1858-1914* (Vancouver: UBC Press, 1989), 96-7, 112; *Hansard*, 16 December 1907, 702.

31 McLaren, *Our own Master Race*, 43; Jean Barman, *The West Beyond the West: A History of British Columbia* (Toronto: University of Toronto, 1991), 229-30.

36 *Municipal Amendment Act*, S.B.C. 1919, c.36, s.13. The provision also made it an offense for an employer to permit a White woman or girl to reside or lodge in such places except as a bona fide customer. On a similar law in Saskatchewan, see James W. St G. Walker, "*Race*," *Rights and the Law in the Supreme Court of Canada* (Toronto: Osgoode Society for Canadian Legal History and Wilfrid Laurier University Press, 1997), chap. 2.

37 S.B.C. 1923, c.76. Correspondence between Premier John Oliver and MLA George Bell in 1920 reveals [....]

38 Professor Walker notes that [....]

39 The convoluted wording of the statute made it unlawful for White and "Indian" women to work in places of business that the local police, "in the interest of morals," found it "advisable"

that they avoid. The *Women's and Girls' Protection Act* was not repealed by the BC Legislature until [....]

40 See Kay J. Anderson, *Vancouver's Chinatown: Racial Discourse in Canada* [....]

41 Emily F. Murphy, *The Black Candle* [....]

42 \ Murphy, *The Black Candle* [....]

43 As Ann Laura Stoler concluded in reference to the colonial experiences of the British and the Dutch [....]

44 "Chinese Coming Here to Protest New Race 'Slur,'" *Victoria Daily Times* [....]

(Kerwin 1999)

(3) The following excerpts are from Mary-Ellen Kelm (1999) "British Columbia First Nations and the Influenza Pandemic of 1918-19." They contact directly some topics in other passages you have read: they refer to the smallpox epidemic mentioned in "Alert Bay" (Chapter Two); they refer to aspects of the racialist sociopolitics described in the excerpt from "The Janet Smith Bill" (above); they mention the residential schools Mary Englund describes in her memoir (Chapter Two) — and in fact Englund herself is cited (although from another context). These passages can also engage, indirectly, other passages you have read: Mary Douglas on an "anthropological approach" to medical cultures; the textbook passage on "tribal teeth"; even the reorganization of diet and work described in the research on packaged foods (Passage A, above). In a summary of Kelm, below, explore common ground amongst these scholarly discourses, and bring the description of the influenza pandemic into conversation with one or two or more of these other voices.

> That was the time all that bunch of Indians come out here and they figured if they got off up here in the bush that they would get away from the flu. There was 16 of them come out here .... They had a big camp at Spey Creek ... about 3 miles up river here. They camped there and one of them used to come down here to the house to get milk all the time. Dad would question him about what was the matter with him. He'd sit on the steps here and just shake all over. All he's say was "sick, sick" all the time. Well there was no reason for him to tell you he was sick. You could see he was sick. But anyway, in a few days he come for a while, for milk and in a while he didn't come anymore. My dad heard them shooting one night up there. He just

thought they were shooting beaver or moose or something that way. But this Indian didn't show up anymore. So, in 2 or 3 days he went to see what was the matter with them. It turned out they were all dead around the camp there. There were just dead bodies lying everywhere. Just where death had overtaken them.[2]

In many ways, the influenza pandemic of 1918-19 is the "forgotten" epidemic; forgotten, at least, by scholars studying British Columbia's First Nations. Much attention has been paid to the timing and severity of late eighteenth- and early nineteenth-century epidemics for what they tell us about the proto-historic and early contact culture and population change. Scholars have argued the significance of these epidemics in softening up indigenous societies for the onslaught of colonization. Few, however, have examined later disease patterns for what they tell us about the nature of cross-cultural relations in the early twentieth century.[3]

At least in part, this academic amnesia is due to an absence of reliable data. For three years, from 1917 to 1919, the Department of Indian Affairs reported that there were exactly the same number of births and deaths each year on reserves across the province (Figure 1). This is clearly impossible, and other government agencies recount different figures. The Vital Statistics Branch reported 670 flu-related deaths among First Nations between October 1918 and June 1919, but it had begun to report vital events among registered Indians just one year before, and officials knew that under-reporting was likely.[4] Meanwhile, locked away in the offices of Department of Indian Affairs in Ottawa, agents' reports, probably the most reliable population data available (although no doubt imperfect), showed numbers of dead at nearly twice the reported figures. Across the province, agents recorded that 1,139 Aboriginal people had died from the flu in British Columbia. They also noted that, given the number who, like the Carrier (described in the above quotation), had fled into the bush, their figures were probably low.[5] Clearly, the flu had been much more devastating among First Nations than the department's own reporting permitted Canadians to know.[6]

★ ★ ★

[...] by the early twentieth century, the First Nations had already undergone considerable cultural change, and much of this change affected their health. Reserve allocations were constantly subject to alteration according to government, settler, or missionary wants. In 1912-15, the McKenna-McBride Commission toured the province conducting hearings on the subject of reserve lands. Many Aboriginal leaders complained to this commission that the reserves were inadequate to their needs. There was not sufficient room to grow crops or raise cattle, and, even if there had been, few reserves had adequate water supplies either for personal or agricultural uses. The people had, at the urgings of missionaries and Indian agents, adopted European-style housing, which the same spokespeople for European "civilization" frequently decried as being overcrowded, under-ventilated, and unclean. Few reserves had adequate sanitation systems.[12] While much traditional food was still available and still popular among the First Nations, traditional subsistence patterns had been abbreviated and adapted to the changing economy of British Columbia.[13] Coastal groups particularly found themselves more often at the fish canneries (numbering nearly fifty in 1911) in the summer and fall than at lineage-controlled fishing sites.[14] Interior and some coastal groups traveled throughout the summer and fall harvesting berries and hops. Conditions at the canneries and the hop-fields left much to be desired. At the canneries, housing was allocated according to race, with Aboriginal people getting only crude shacks, often without adequate sanitation, in which to set up housekeeping for months at a time.[15] At the hop-fields of the Fraser Valley, torrential rains could flood latrines and deprive families of dry clothing or habitation.[16] Residential schools contributed to a general state of ill-health among First Nations, as they, through underfeeding, overwork, and various forms of abuse, weakened the children for whom they were supposed to care. Early in the century reports of the Department of Indian Affairs decried "the scandalous procession" that led from the schools to the cemeteries.[17]

At the same time, the government attempted to wean First Nations from their own medicine by appointing departmental physicians to each agency and by outlawing, through an 1885 amendment to the Indian Act, much Aboriginal ceremony. Departmental physicians were, however, a mixed bag.

Few saw work among First Nations as a vocation, and most took departmental contracts in order to supplement the meager incomes to be had from private practice in remote locations in the province. Though some of the doctors were industrious, innovative, and caring, too many were practicing medicine on the frontier because no other place would have them. More than one departmental physician would have lost his/her contract with the Department of Indian Affairs for drunkenness, incompetence, or old age had there been another doctor to fill his/her place. Quite often there wasn't, or if there was, the replacement physician was not much better. Few good doctors stayed in these positions, so turnover was high, and long vacancies at posts were common. Even the good doctors, who had a commitment to rural British Columbia, frequently divided their practices with the local non-Native settlement and had a contract with the railroad or church in addition to their work with the Department of Indian Affairs. And, after 1902, when doctors' payment changed from a per-visit basis to a very low fixed salary, there was little incentive to spend more time on reserve when paying non-Native patients beckoned.[18]

★ ★ ★

Along the Fraser Valley and in the Interior, the first Nations were particularly hard hit. At Chilliwack, all the students at Coqualeetza Residential School were affected, and one child, from Skidegate, died. All the children at St. Mary's Residential School also became ill, and there was little that could be done for them. As Lil'wut elder Mary Englund remembers:

> We got it. We just stayed right in bed; every girl that was in the convent was in bed. I was so sick then. I tried to fight it, you know, and the nun kept saying, "you'd better go to bed", she'd say. So finally, I went to bed and she came upstairs and took my temperature. My temperature wasn't too bad, so I went to bed and I just covered up and I stayed right in bed. I'd cover my head and all and just stayed right there. Every once in a while the nun would come by and she'd say, "Are you still alive?"

Here, as well, only one child died. But at nearby Pitt Meadows, forty deaths occurred among an Aboriginal population of 260. Further inland, the Lil'wut were affected especially badly by the disease.

★ ★ ★

Aboriginal people too responded in a number of ways that fit both within their own and adopted systems of healing around them. Many availed themselves of non-Native medicine. Evangeline Pete, a Sto:lo elder, remembers going to hospital with her whole family when they got the flu. They stayed for three months. Her brother died there and her father was so weakened by the disease that he died a year later.[86] Others checked themselves into the segregated barracks designated for "Indians" in Kamloops.[87] Fourteen cannery workers made their way to the Port Essington hospital; five died.[88] Some Carrier men were treated at the Prince George Hospital.[89] But many who wanted to use Euro-Canadian medicine were denied the opportunity. Departmental doctors, their allegiances almost always divided, focused their attention during the epidemic on their non-Native patients. Carrier elder Mary John remembers that the departmental physician did not visit Stoney Creek once during the epidemic.[90] In other cases, the shortage of doctors for these positions meant that doctors taken sick or even killed during the epidemic were not replaced. The 1,400 Lil'wut who were taken ill during the epidemic lost their only doctor when Dr. McPhail died of heart failure and no replacement could be found.[91]

Others used their own medicine; some with good results. Heilstuck people used devil's club, swamp gooseberry, and water hemlock for relief during the Spanish Flu epidemic.[92] The Gitksan also used devil's club.[93] The s★★ of the Spuzzum people were diligent in their attempts to cure their people of the dread disease.[94] Tsil'co'tin people brought in a renowned healer called Abiyan.[95] People also used non-Native products in Aboriginal ways, and Aboriginal products in non-Native ways. Tsil'co'tin elder Eagle Lake Henry, for instance, used Lysol and rum to keep the flu away. The rum was administered like a prescription, and the Lysol was added to a water bath like Epsom salts. Eagle Lake Henry and his wife first cleaned their house with the Lysol but then daubed cloths in the disinfectant and hung them on the interior walls of the house, just as cedar might be hung in a house, to purify it.[96] Okanagan people sweat-bathed to cure themselves of the disease. They made tea from the mentholated sage brush of the region, and one observer later described it as "an infallible remedy for the Flu. Made into a strong tea and drinking it hot, effects a cure within three or four days with no after attack of [pneumonia]. It [was] a vile smelling, nauseating liquid."[97] Finally, people responded to the deaths in traditional ways as well, at least until they were overwhelmed by the number of deaths. At Kitamaat feasts followed the first two deaths, but, after that, the dead were buried unceremoniously and [the people] feasted later.[98] Others found themselves in deep existential crisis, trying to cope with the desire to heal the sick through shamanic power while remaining faithful to Christian teaching.[99]

★ ★ ★

The second most common element of First Nations flu stories attributes the flu to non-Aboriginal causes, primarily contact with Whites. On one hand, we know that this is simply an accurate depiction of a pandemic disease that undoubtedly did spread into Indian reserves from nearby White settlements or by communication along transport lines established by non-Natives. On the other hand, it is also clear that to Aboriginal writers telling about the flu, older indigenous conceptions of disease causation seem apt. In some cases, linking the 1918 flu with the earlier smallpox epidemics, about which stories abound of infected blankets being traded or given to unsuspecting Natives, establishes the connection between pandemic disease and European culpability.[107] In other stories, Europeans, like witches, were seen to shoot disease into people. Such is the case with the Tsil'co'tin narrative, "The Big Flu." Here is what Eugene William says about how one man saw the disease coming:

> After the disease finally quit, Eugene said his father
> Sammy Williams' older brother, named Amed, went to
> Tsuniah where Sammy was staying and told him all
> about the disease that hit Nemiah. Sammy said he
> couldn't believe what happened. Surprised I guess.
> Because Sammy said he dreamt about this disease. He

was dreaming that some soldiers came over to Nemiah and shot this disease with all kinds of colours
through the sky in his dream. That's why Sammy
Williams decided to stay at Tsuniah a little longer.[108]

In this account, Sammy Williams acts as a seer, predicting
disaster and being able to take appropriate action to defend
himself against it. His account fits nicely into indigenous
accepted wisdom concerning witchcraft-related illnesses.
With regard to these, illness can be sent into a person either
through object or spirit intrusion.[109] In order to confirm the
connection between Euro-Canadian culpability and the flu,
Eugene Williams, who reports on his uncle's vision, links the
disease with the one major confrontation between Tsil'co'tin
and Euro-Canadian road-builders, the so-called Chilcotin
War, when he says, "this disease came from the Chilcotin
War." The Chilcotin War itself was sparked, at least in part, by
the smallpox epidemic of 1862 and a Euro-Canadian road
builder's threat that he could make the disease come back.
Williams' statement makes sense only if we place it within
the broader context of Aboriginal understanding of disease
causation and the linkages they see between epidemic
episodes and Euro-Canadian witchcraft and treachery. More
gently, Augusta Tappage connects smallpox and the flu in the
same story, describing the role that Hudson's Bay Company
traders played in the dissemination of the former and returning soldiers in the diffusion of the latter.[110]

The third common element among First Nations flu histories relates to a strong sense of Euro-Canadian betrayal felt by
Aboriginal sufferers of the disease. By 1918, most First
Nations in the province had heard the admonitions of Indian
Agents and missionaries, who insisted that if only they would
live like White people, if only they would confine themselves
to Euro-Canadian allopathic medicine, then they would stop
dying at such alarming rates. What the 1918 flu proved to
them was, first, that "modernization," whatever non-Natives
promised, was no key to health, and, second, that when non-
Aboriginal lives were at stake, the resources of the government and its sanctioned medical personnel would go first, not
to the First Nations, but to Euro-Canadians [....] Eugene
Williams attributes the infection to a Tsil'co'tin man who

traveled to a nearby White community to buy lumber to build a dance hall for a Christmas dance because their own houses had only dirt floors. In this way, the desire for non-Tsil'co'tin material goods is implicated in the spread of disease.[111]

2 Ernie Kaesmodel, "Stone Interview" (unpublished interview), Willow River, British Columbia, 8 June 1997.
3 To a certain extent, this is the result of [....]
4 British Columbia, "Vital Statistics, 1919" [....]
5 National Archives of Canada [....]
6 The reasons for this faulty reporting are unclear. It may be [...]
   ★ ★ ★
12 British Columbia, "Proceedings," *Royal Commission on Indian Affairs for the Province of British Columbia*, 1912-15.
13 James Andrew McDonald, "The Marginalization of the Tsimshan Cultural Ecology: The Seasonal Cycle," in Cox, *Native People Native Lands*, 199-218.
14 McDonald [....]
15 NAC, DIA, Black Series, RG 10 V4045, f351304, various correspondence, 1915, 1916; NAC, DIA Black Series [....]; Tommy Williams to Agent, 30 July 1927; NAC, DIA [....]
16 NAC, DIA, Black Series [....]
17 Mary-Ellen Kelm, *Colonizing bodies: Aboriginal Health and Healing in British Columbia, 1900-50* (Vancouver: UBC Press, 1998), 57-82.
18 NAC, NHW, IHS, RG 29 V2765, f822-1-A901, pt. 1, Paget, memo, 20 January 1915 [....]
   ★ ★ ★
86 Sto:lo Nation, Archives, "Evangeline Pete Story," typescript, n.d.
87 Kamloops *Telegraph*, 5 November 1918.
88 NAC, DIA, Black Series [....]
89 Hall, *The Carrier*, 20.
90 Moran, *Stoney Creek Woman*, 24.
91 Kamloops *Telegraph*, 14 November 1918.
92 Margaret Whitehead, *They Call Me Father*, 53-54.
93 BCARS, Marius Barbeau Papers, Add. MSS 2102, B-F-89.9, Benyon was informant to Marius Barbeau, 1920.
94 Laforet and York, *Spuzzum*, 126.
95 Terry Glavin and the People of Nemiah Valley, *Nemiah: The Unconquered Country* (Vancouver: New Star, 1992), 90.
96 Ibid.
97 Jay Miller, ed[....]
98 "Death Toll," *Missionary Outlook*, 1919.
99 Jay Miller [....]
   ★ ★ ★
107 Speare, *Days of Augusta*, 30.

108 Glavin, *Nemiah*, 91.
109 Kelm, *Colonizing Bodies.*
110 Speare, *Days of Augusta*, 30-31.
111 Miller, *Mourning Dove*, 192.

(Kelm 1999: 23-24)

Primary Documents

Agar, Michael. 1994. "The intercultural frame." *International Journal of Intercultural Relations* 18(2): 221-37.

Alcock, J.E., D.W. Carment, and S.W. Sadava. 1994. *A Textbook of Social Psychology*. 3rd ed. Scarborough, ON: Prentice Hall.

Allen, Ann Taylor. 1999. "Feminism, social science, and the meanings of modernity: The debate on the origin of the family in Europe and the United States, 1860-1914." *The American Historical Review* 104(4): 1085-1113.

Arnold, Bettina. 1999. " 'Drinking the feast': Alcohol and the legitimation of power in Celtic Europe." *Cambridge Archaeological Review* 9(1): 71-93.

Bar-Yosef, Ofer, and Steven L. Kuhn. 1999. "The big deal about blades: Laminar technologies and human evolution." *American Anthropologist* 101(2): 322-38.

Bhabha, Homi K. 1994. "Now newness enters the world." In *The Location of Culture*. London: Routledge.

Bodley, John H. 1997. *Cultural Anthropology: Tribes, States, and the Global System*. 2nd ed. Mountain View, CA: Mayfield.

Bornstein, Brian H. 1994. "David, Goliath, and Reverend Hayes: Prior beliefs about defendants' status in personal injury cases." *Applied Cognitive Psychology* 8: 233-58.

Bruggink, Thomas H., and Kamran Siddiqui. 1995. "An econometric model of alumni giving: A case study for a liberal arts college." *The American Economist* 39(2): 53-60.

Buchanan, Neil H. 1999. "Taxes, saving, and macroeconomics." *Journal of Economic Issues* 33(1): 59-75.

Burgess, Keith. 1994. "British employers and education policy, 1935-45: A decade of 'missed opportunities'?" *Business History* 36(3): 29-61.

Calhoun, Cheshire. 1994. "Separating lesbian theory from feminist theory." *Ethics* 104: 558-82.

Cameron, Deborah. 1990. "Demythologizing sociolinguistics: Why language does not reflect society." In *Ideologies of Language*, ed. John E. Joseph and Talbot J. Taylor. London: Routledge.

Cameron, Deborah. 1995. *Verbal Hygiene*. London: Routledge.

Chavez, Leo R. 1994. "The power of the imagined community: The settlement of undocumented Mexicans and Central Americans in the United States." *American Anthropologist* 96(1): 52-73.

Chorpita, Bruce F., Anne Marie Albano, and David H. Barlow. 1998. "The structure of negative emotions in a clinical sample of children and adolescents." *Journal of Abnormal Psychology* 107(1): 74-85.

Christian-Smith, Linda K. 1991. "Readers, texts, and contexts: Adolescent romance fiction in schools." In *The Politics of the Textbook*, eds. Michael W. Apple and Linda K. Christian-Smith. New York: Routledge.

Clark, Romy, and Roz Ivanic. 1997. "Writing, politics and power." *The Politics of Writing*. London: Routledge.

Clifford, James. 1997. *Routes: Travel and Translation in the Late Twentieth Century*. Cambridge, MA: Harvard UP.

Coates, Jennifer. 1996. *Women Talk: Conversation between Women Friends*. Cambridge, MA: Blackwell.

Counts, Dorothy Ayers, and David R. Counts. 1992. " 'They're my family now': The creation of community among RVers." *Anthropologica* 34: 168-70.

Darlington-Hammond, Linda. 1994. "Performance-based assessment and educational equity." *Harvard Educational Review* 64(1): 5-30.

Dasenbrock, Reed Way. 1987. "Intelligibility and meaningfulness in multicultural literature in English." *PMLA* 102: 10-19.

Datta, Saikat, and Prabal Roy Chowdhury. 1998. "Management union bargaining under minimum wage regulation in less developed countries." *Indian Economic Review* 33(2): 169-84.

Daveri, Francesco, and Ricardo Faini. 1999. "Where do migrants go?" *Oxford Economic Papers* 51: 595-622.

della Paolera, Gerardo, and Alan M. Taylor. 1999. "Economic recovery from the Argentine Great Depression: Institutions, expectations, and the change of macroeconomic regime." *Journal of Economic History* 59(3): 567-98.

Dempsey, Corinne G. 1998. "Rivalry, reliance, and resemblance: Siblings as metaphor for Hindu-Christian relations in Kerala State." *Asian Folklore Studies* 57: 51-70.

Ditz, Toby L. 1994. "Shipwrecked; or, masculinity imperiled: Mercantile representations of failure and the gendered self in eighteenth-century Philadelphia." *The Journal of American History* 81(1): 51-80.

Dixon, John, and Kevin Durrheim. 2000. "Displacing place-identity: A discursive approach to locating self and other." *British Journal of Social Psychology* 39: 27-44.

Douglas, Mary. 1996. "The choice between gross and spiritual: Some medical preferences." In *Thought Styles*. London: Sage.

Eckes, Thomas. 1994. "Features of men, features of women: Assessing stereotypic beliefs about gender subtypes." *British Journal of Social Psychology* 33: 107-23.

Ellis, Mark, and Panikos Panayi. 1994. "German minorities in World War I: A comparative study of Britain and the U.S.A." *Ethnic and Racial Studies* 17(2): 238-59.

Endler, Norman S., and Rachel L. Speer. 1998. "Personality psychology: Research trends for 1993-1995." *Journal of Personality* 66(5): 621-69.

Englund, Mary. 1981. "An Indian remembers." In *Now You Are My Brother*, ed. Margaret Whitehead. Victoria, BC: Provincial Archives.

Evers, D. Elaine, Charles Sasser, James Gosselink, Deborah Fuller, and Jenneke Visser. 1998. "The impact of vertebrate herbivores on wetland vegetation in Atchafayala Bay, Louisiana." *Estuaries* 21(1): 1-13.

Finke, Laurie. 1993. "Knowledge as bait: Feminism, voice, and the pedagogical unconscious." *College English* 55(1): 7-27.

Foot, David K., and Daniel Stoffman. 1996. *Boom, Bust and Echo: How to Profit from the Coming Demographic Shift*. Toronto: Macfarlane Walter & Ross.

Gamoran, Adam. 1993. "Alternative uses of ability grouping in secondary schools: Can we bring high-quality instruction to low-ability classes?" *American Journal of Education* 102: 1-22.

Geschwender, James A. 1992. "Ethgender, women's waged labor, and economic mobility." *Social Problems* 39(1): 1-16.

Giddens, Anthony. 1990. *The Consequences of Modernity*. Stanford UP.

Glenberg, Arthur M., Jennifer L. Schroeder, and David A. Robertson. 1998. "Averting the gaze disengages the environment and facilitates remembering." *Memory and Cognition* 26(4): 651-58.

Greening, Daniel W., and Barbara Gray. 1994. "Testing a model of organizational response to social and political issues." *Academy of Management Journal* 37(3): 467-98.

Grimm Brothers. 1969. "The Goose-Girl." In *The Blue Fairy Book*, ed. Andrew Lang. New York: Airmont.

Grossman, Herschel I. 1999. "Kleptocracy and revolutions." *Oxford Economic Papers* 51: 267-83.

Hagedorn, John M. 1994. "Neighborhoods, markets, and gang drug organizations." *Journal of Research in Crime and Delinquency* 31(3): 264-94.

Heath, Shirley Brice. 1983. *Ways with Words: Language, Life, and Work in Communities and Classrooms*. Cambridge UP.

Heyes, C.M. 1998. "Theory of mind in nonhuman primates." *Behavioral and Brain Sciences* 21: 101-48.

Higgs, Robert. 1999. "From central planning to the market: The American transition, 1945-1947." *The Journal of Economic History* 59: 600-23.

Hobbs, Peter V., and Arthur L. Rangno. 1998. "Microstructures of low and middle-level clouds over the Beaufort Sea." *Quarterly Journal of the Royal Meteorological Society* 124: 2035-71.

Hom, Alice Y., and Ming-Yuen S. Ma. 1993. "Premature gestures: A speculative dialogue on Asian Pacific lesbian and gay writing." *Journal of Homosexuality* 26(2/3): 21-31.

Huntington, Henry, and the Communities of Buckland, Elim, Koyuk, Point Lay, and Shaktoolik. 1999. "Traditional knowledge of the ecology of beluga whales (*Delphinapterus leucas*) in the Eastern Chukchi and Northern Bering Seas, Alaska." *Arctic* 52(1): 49-61.

Husbands, Christopher T. 1994. "Crisis of national identity as the 'new moral panics': Political agenda-setting about definitions of nationhood." *New Community* 20(2): 191-206.

Hyland, Ken. 1999. "Academic attribution: Citation and the construction of disciplinary knowledge." *Applied Linguistics* 20(3): 341.

Kabeer, Naila. 1994. "The structure of 'revealed' preference: Race, community and female labour supply in the London clothing industry." *Development and Change* 25: 307-31.

Keller-Cohen, Deborah. 1987. "Literate practices in a modern credit union." *Language in Society* 15: 7-24.

Kelm, Mary-Ellen. 1999. "British Columbia First Nations and the influenza pandemic of 1918-19." *BC Studies* 122 (Summer): 23-47.

Kerwin, Scott. 1999. "The Janet Smith Bill of 1924 and the Language of Race and Nation in British Columbia." *BC Studies* 121: 83-114.

Khalid, Adeeb. 1994. "Printing, publishing, and reform in Tsarist Central Asia." *International Journal of Middle East Studies* 26: 187-200.

Killingray, David. 1994. "The 'rod of empire': The debate over corporal punishment in the British African colonial forces, 1888-1946." *Journal of African History* 35: 210-16.

Koehn, Nancy F. 1999. "Henry Heinz and brand creation in the late nineteenth century: Making markets for processed food." *Business History Review* 73 (Autumn): 349-93.

Kolodny, Annette. 1994. "Inventing a feminist discourse: Rhetoric and resistance in Margaret Fuller's *Woman in the Nineteenth Century*." *New Literary History* 25(2): 355-82.

Laber, Emily. 2000. "Designer drugs: Tailoring medicines to fit the patient." *The Sciences* (July-August): 8-9.

LaFollette, Hugh. 2000. "Gun control." *Ethics* 110: 263-81.

Lane, D.E., and R.L. Stephenson. 1998. "A framework for risk analysis in fisheries decision-making." *ICES Journal of Marine Science* 55: 1-13.

Lee, Thomas W., and Terence R. Mitchell. 1994. "An alternative approach: The unfolding model of voluntary employee turnover." *Academy of Management Journal* 19(1): 51–89.

Lesure, Richard. 1999. "Figurines as representations and products at Paso de la Amada, Mexico." *Cambridge Archaeological Journal* 9(2): 209-20.

Levine, Paul L., and Joseph G. Pearlman. 1994. "Credibility, ambiguity and asymmetric information with wage stickiness." *The Manchester School* 62(1): 21–39.

Lin, Chia-Chin. 2000. "Applying the American Pain Society's QA standards to evaluate the quality of pain management among surgical, oncology, and hospice inpatients in Taiwan." *Pain* 87: 43-49.

Livingstone, Sonia. 1994. "Watching talk: Gender and engagement in the viewing of audience discussion programmes." *Media, Culture and Society* 16: 429-47.

Lu, Min-Zhan. 1992. "Conflict and struggle: The enemies or preconditions of basic writing?" *College English* (December): 891-913.

Lupton, Deborah, and John Tulloch. 1999. "Theorizing fear of crime: Beyond the rational/irrational oppositions." *British Journal of Sociology* 50(3): 507–23.

Masson, Michael E.J., and Mary Anne Waldron. 1994. "Comprehension of legal contracts by non-experts: Effectiveness of plain language redrafting." *Applied Cognitive Psychology* 8: 67-85.

Mayes, Patricia. 1990. "Quotation in spoken English." *Studies in Language* 14(2): 325-63.

McGuire, John. 1998. "Judicial violence and the 'civilizing process': Race and transition from public to private executions in Colonial Australia." *Australian Historical Studies* 111: 187-209.

Milroy, James, and Lesley Milroy. 1991 [1985]. *Authority in Language: Investigating Language Prescription and Standardisation.* 2nd ed. London: Routledge.

Nash, June. 1994. "Global integration and subsistence insecurity." *American Anthropologist* 96(1): 7-30.

Neiman, Paul J., et al. 1998. "An observational study of fronts and frontal mergers over the Continental United States." *Monthly Weather Review* 126: 2521-52.

Nemutanzhela, Thiathu J. 1993. "Cultural forms and literacy as resources for political mobilisation: A.M. Malivha and the Zoutpansberg Balemi Association." *African Studies* 52(1): 89-102.

O'Connor, Denis. 1987. "Glue sniffers with special needs." *British Journal of Education* 14(3): 94-97.

Olick, Jeffrey K. 1999. "Genre memories and memory genres: A dialogical analysis of May 8, 1945 commemorations in the Federal Republic of Germany." *American Sociological Review* 64: 381-402.

Oliver, Pamela E., and Daniel J. Myers. 1999. "How events enter the public sphere." *American Journal of Sociology* 105(1): 38-67.

O'Toole, Alice, Kenneth A. Deffenbacher, Dominique Valentin, and Hervé Abdi. 1994. "Structural aspects of face recognition and the other-race effect." *Memory and Cognition* 22(2): 208-24.

Pearson, G. 1999. "Early occupations and cultural sequence at Moose Creek: A Late Pleistocene site in Central Alaska." *Arctic* 52(4): 332-45.

Pratt, John. 1999. "Norbert Elias and the civilized prison." *British Journal of Sociology* 50(2): 271-96.

Prestwich, Patricia E. 1994. "Family strategies and medical power: 'Voluntary' committal in a Parisian asylum, 1876-1914." *Journal of Social History* 27(4): 799-818.

Quillian, Lincoln. 1999. "Migration patterns and the growth of high-poverty neighborhoods, 1970-1990." *American Journal of Sociology* 105(1): 1-37.

Quintero, Gilbert A., and Antonio L. Estrada. 1998. "Cultural models of masculinity and drug use: 'Machismo,' heroin, and street survival on the U.S.-Mexican border." *Contemporary Drug Problems* 25: 147-65.

Raasch. S., and D. Etling. 1998. "Modeling deep ocean convection: Large eddy simulation in comparison with laboratory experiments." *American Meteorological Society* 21: 1786-1802.

Rauch-Elnekave, Helen. 1994. "Teenage motherhood: Its relationship to undetected learning problems." *Adolescence* 29: 91-103.

Reiger, Kerreen M. 1989. " 'Clean and comfortable and respectable': Working-class aspirations and the Australian 1920 Royal Commission on the Basic Wage." *History Workshop* 27: 86-105.

Salager-Meyer, Françoise. 1994. "Hedges and textual communicative function in medical English written discourse." *English for Scientific Purposes* 13(2): 149-70.

Salomone, Ann Masters. 1994. "French behind bars: A qualitative and quantitative examination of college French training in prison." *The Modern Language Journal* 78(1): 76-84.

Scott, Rebecca J. 1994. "Defining the boundaries of freedom in the word of cane: Cuba, Brazil, and Louisiana after emancipation." *American Historical Review* (February): 70-102.

Seymour, Susanne. 1994. "Gender, church and people in rural areas." *Area* 26(1): 45-56.

Sheldon, Amy. 1990. "Pickle fights: Gendered talk in preschool disputes." *Discourse Processes* 13: 5-31.

Shieffelin, Bambi B., and Rachelle Charlier Doucet. 1994. "The 'real' Haitian creole: ideology, metalinguistics, and orthographic choice." *American Ethnologist* 21(1): 176-200.

Shoenberger, E. 1994. "Corporate strategy and corporate strategists:

Power, identity, and knowledge within the firm." *Environment and Planning* 26(3): 443-51.

Smith, Edward L., Jr. 1985. "Text type and discourse framework." *Text* 5(3): 229-47.

Smith, Sidonie. 1993. *Subjectivity, Identity and the Body: Women's Autobiographical Practices in the Twentieth Century.* Bloomington: Indiana UP.

Smith, Thomas S., and Gregory T. Stevens. 1999. "The architecture of small networks: Strong interaction and dynamic organization in small social systems." *American Sociological Review* 64: 403-20.

South, Scott J., and Kyle D. Crowder. 1999. "Neighborhood effects on family formation: Concentrated poverty and beyond." *American Sociological Review* 64: 113-32.

Speck, Dara Culhane. 1987. *An Error in Judgement: The Politics of Medical Care in an Indian/White Community.* Vancouver, B.C.: Talonbooks

Stratman, James F. 1994. "Investigating persuasive processes in legal discourse in real time: Cognitive biases and rhetorical strategy in appeal court briefs." *Discourse Processes* 17: 1-57.

Sull, Donald N. 1999. "The dynamics of standing still: Firestone Tire & Rubber and the radial revolution." *Business History Review* 73: 430-64.

Tannen, Deborah. 1990. *You Just Don't Understand: Women and Men in Conversation.* New York: Ballantine Books.

Tiratsoo, Nick, and Jim Tomlinson. 1994. "Restrictive practices on the shopfloor in Britain, 1946-60: Myth and reality." *Business History* 36(2): 65-84.

Todaro, Michael P. 1997. *Economic Development.* New York: Longman.

Tuffin, Keith, and Jo Danks. 1999. "Community care and mental disorder: An analysis of discursive resources." *British Journal of Social Psychology* 38: 289-302.

Verkuyten, Maykel, Wiebe de Jong, and Kees Masson. 1994. "Similarities in anti-racist and racist discourse: Dutch local residents talking about ethnic minorities." *New Community* 20(2): 253-67.

The Voyages of Jacques Cartier, 1534. Trans. H.P. Biggar. In *Literature in Canada, Vol. I,* eds. Douglas Daymond and Leslie Monkman. Toronto: Gage.

Waern, Yvonne. 1988. "Thoughts on texts in context: Applying the think-aloud method to text processing." *Text* 8(4): 317-50.

Warren, Christopher. 1999. "Toxic purity: The professive era origins of America's lead paint poisoning epidemic." *Business History Review* 73: 705-35.

Wassink, Alicia Beckford. 1999. "Historic low prestige and seeds of change: Attitudes toward Jamaican Creole." *Language in Society* 28: 57-92.

Wearne, Phillip. 1996. *Return of the Indian: Conquest and Revival in the Americas*. London: Cassell.

Weinberger, Daniel A. 1998. "Defenses, personality structure and development: Integrating psychodynamic theory into a typological approach to personality." *Journal of Personality* 66(6): 1061-77.

Wenzel, George W. 1999. "Traditional ecological knowledge and Inuit: Reflections on TEK research and ethics." *Arctic* 52(2): 113-24.

West, Cornel. 1990. "The new cultural politics of difference." In *Out There: Marginalization and Contemporary Cultures*, eds. Russell Ferguson, Martha Gever, Trinh T. Minh-ha, and Cornel West. Cambridge, MA: MIT Press.

Willott, Sara, and Chris Giffin. 1999. "Building your own lifeboat: Working-class male offenders talk about economic class." *British Journal of Social Psychology* 38: 445-60.

Wong, Siu Kwong. 1999. "Acculturation, peer relations, and delinquent behavior of Chinese-Canadian youth." *Adolescence* 34(133): 107-19.

Zelizer, Viviana A. 1994 [1985]. *Pricing the Priceless Child: The Changing Social Value of Children*. Princeton, NJ: Princeton UP.

Zervakis, Jennifer, and David C. Rubin. 1998. "Memory and learning for a novel written style." *Memory and Cognition* 26(4): 754-67.

Index

passive voice, 237
Plain Language, 344
position, 14, 52–53, 56, 103, 106, 330
  of readers, 104
  subject, 324
post-colonialism, 325, 337
post-modernism, 322–23
present tense, 303
  present perfect, 300
  present progressive, 299
  simple present, 298–99, 303–04
presupposing vs. asserting, 305–09
proposals, 321, 381–84

qualitative vs. quantitative research, 271, 334–36

readability, 15, 321–22, 340, 344
reading, 176
  as social process, 310
  comprehension, 167
  episodes, 187–207
  structures of, 181
  theories of, 180
relevance, 183–85, 190, 225
reported speech, 76, 247–50, 252, 262–65, 272, 285, 330, 353. *See also* citation
  and indeterminacy, 281
  double reporting, 69
research questions, 89, 269, 375–76, 383
research review and permission ethnography, 373

research sites, 371–73, 382–84
  criteria, 372

scholarly language, 209–11, 214
  complications of, 212
  exclusion, 213
school-room essay, 26–27, 246
sentence style, 224–29
student writing, 164, 177, 180, 354
  commentary, 163–66, 169, 176
  complaint tradition, 158–59, 163–64, 166, 177
subjectivity, 14, 296, 323–24, 330
summary, 29, 43–57, 68–69, 73, 76, 79–81, 127, 227, 248, 265
  of narratives, 85–100
symbolic domination, 158, 160
syntactic density, 214

talking back, 343, 345, 347
taxonomy, 122, 225
text-diacritical statements, 297–98
textbooks, 147–48
  composition, 163
  speakers, 148
think-aloud protocol, 167–73, 176–81
topics. See research questions

undergraduate writing. See student writing

written vs. spoken English, 57, 59, 386, 388

Using 0,9835 tons of Rolland Enviro100 Print instead
of virgin fibres paper reduces your ecological footprint of:

 17 trees
1 tennis court

 61,601 L of water
176 days of water consumption

 933 kg of waste
19 waste containers

 2,425 kg CO2
16,224 km driven

 27 GJ
126,819 60W light bulbs for one
hour

 7 kg NOx
emissions of one truck during 22
days